LUTHERAN HIGHER  EDUCATION in North America

Richard W. Solberg

AUGSBURG Publishing House • Minneapolis

LUTHERAN HIGHER EDUCATION IN NORTH AMERICA

Copyright © 1985 Lutheran Educational Conference of North America

All rights reserved. Except for brief quotations in critical articles or reviews, no part of this book may be reproduced in any manner without prior written permission from the publisher. Write to: Permissions, Augsburg Publishing House, 426 S. 5th St., Box 1209, Minneapolis MN 55440.

Scripture quotations unless otherwise noted are from the Revised Standard Version of the Bible, copyright 1946, 1952, and 1971 by the Division of Christian Education of the National Council of Churches.

Library of Congress Cataloging-in-publication Data

Solberg, Richard W., 1917–
LUTHERAN HIGHER EDUCATION IN NORTH AMERICA.

Bibliography: p.
Includes index.
1. Lutheran Church—Education (Higher)—United States—History.   I. Title.
LC621.S65   1985   377'.841   85-28757
ISBN 0-8066-2187-7

Manufactured in the U.S.A.   APH 10-4168

1   2   3   4   5   6   7   8   9   0   1   2   3   4   5   6   7   8   9

CONTENTS

FOREWORD

For 75 years the Lutheran Educational Conference of North America (LECNA) has provided an important forum and arena for the leadership of Lutheran higher education. Here they have shared ideas to forge, enhance, and, in times of change, create those values and characteristics which have been the hallmark of Lutheran higher education since its early days in North America.

In providing major resources to research, publish, and distribute the history of *Lutheran Higher Education in North America*, Aid Association for Lutherans (AAL) pays tribute to LECNA's 75 years of service contributing to the unique role of Lutheran higher education on this continent.

AAL is proud to be a part of this milestone achievement. It has afforded our organization another opportunity to be of service to Lutheran colleges and universities.

HENRY F. SCHEIG
Chairman of the Board and Chief Executive Officer
Aid Association for Lutherans
Appleton, WI 54919

PREFACE

The Lutheran Educational Conference of North America is pleased to present this volume to the reader. Its purpose is to tell the Lutheran story in higher education and to identify the contribution of Lutheran colleges and universities to the church, to society, and to higher education in North America. While there are several histories of individual Lutheran colleges and church bodies, none has provided an overview of the history and mission of Lutheran higher education.

The genesis of this project dates from 1978 when the Task Force on LECNA Objectives recommended provision for "occasional research and studies of topics of particular interest to Lutheran colleges and universities." In 1980 a study committee was appointed and in 1981 the history project was launched. Encouraging and supporting the formative phase of the study were program sessions at the LECNA annual meetings of 1979, 1980, and 1981 which explored various dimensions of the Lutheran heritage in higher education.

The History Project Committee acknowledges with appreciation those who contributed to the study. Financial support was extended to the project by the Division for College and University Services of The American Lutheran Church, the Board for Professional Education Services of the Lutheran Church–Missouri Synod, the Division for Mission in North America of the Lutheran Church in America, and LECNA itself. Major funding for the project was provided by the Aid Association for Lutherans. We are extraordinarily grateful to the board and staff of AAL for their generous financial support and their personal interest and encouragement. We also note with gratitude the stra-

7

tegic contributions of LECNA secretaries, J. Victor Hahn, who was with us as the project began, and Arthur Puotinen, who saw the project completed. Their support for the project was more a matter of personal enthusiasm than of administrative duty.

In the final analysis, responsibility for the project rested in the hands of author Richard W. Solberg. Dr. Solberg brought to the project his professional credentials as a historian, a deep fund of personal experience in the church and its colleges, a remarkable capacity for work, and a good spirit. More than any other person, idea, or event, this project is Richard Solberg's.

In the book of Joshua we read about the placing of 12 stones in Gilgal to serve as a reminder of God's deliverance. By analogy, may this stone—this history—reflect the nature of God at work, exhibiting the creative instincts of generations of people in Lutheran higher education; reflecting the fruits of God's Spirit, especially forbearance, patience, generosity, and unity; and revealing a gracious God at work among God's people, forgiving and renewing them, their colleges, and the church.

PAUL J. DOVRE
Chairman, History Project Committee
Lutheran Educational Conference of North America

ACKNOWLEDGMENTS

During the research and writing of the story of Lutheran higher education generous assistance and encouragement came from many sources. An editorial committee appointed by the Lutheran Educational Conference of North America provided leadership and direction for the entire project and reviewed successive chapter drafts. Its membership included Paul Dovre, Louis T. Almen, Morris A. Anderson, Harold R. Dunkelberger, S. Philip Froiland, Gerhardt Hyatt, Ronald Matthias, Arthur L. Olsen, Walter Rosin, Ralph Schultz, Joseph M. Shaw, Michael Stelmachowicz, August R. Suelflow, and James M. Unglaube. LECNA secretaries, J. Victor Hahn and Arthur Puotinen, provided executive services for the committee and faithfully administered the project.

At every Lutheran college and seminary in North America the institutional president designated a representative resource and contact person for the project. These persons made available materials dealing with their institutions and served as facilitators for campus visits by the author on nearly every Lutheran campus. Librarians and archivists at colleges, universities, seminaries, and synods, as well as those of major Lutheran church bodies, historical societies, and the Lutheran Council in the U.S.A. were generous in their assistance.

Members of the project committee and campus contact persons contributed written responses to inquiries and in some instances prepared substantive resource papers. I am especially indebted to several persons who prepared research papers in specialized areas: Robert Bloom, James Hamre, Anna Mae Hayden, Gerhard Ottersberg, Milton Sernett, Robert Parsonage, Kent Weeks, and Ruth Wick.

Personal interviews were granted by Arthur Ahlschwede, H. George Anderson, Conrad Bergendoff, Edgar Carlson, Orville Dahl, Donald Heiges, Albert Huegli, Edward Lindell, Dale Lund, Robert Marshall, and Sidney Rand. The transcript of a recorded interview with J. C. K. Preus was provided by Ronald Matthias.

In addition to members of the editorial committee who read the entire text, portions of the manuscript were read by James Albers, H. George Anderson, Charles Glatfelter, Albert Huegli, C. Arild Olsen, Carl T. Solberg, and Mary M. Solberg.

June N. Solberg served as project secretary, handling correspondence and organizing resource files. She also offered indispensable encouragement and critiques, entered innumerable textual revisions on the word processor, and prepared the final manuscript, including bibliography and index, for publication.

Maps and charts were designed by James Unglaube.

To these contributors and to all others who have provided encouragement and support in the completion of this book, I extend sincere appreciation.

RICHARD W. SOLBERG

1 REFORMATION ROOTS

Almost exactly 300 years separated the death of Dr. Martin Luther, professor in the Saxon University of Wittenberg in 1546, and the founding of a Lutheran college in the state of Ohio bearing the same name. The educational tradition established by the Wittenberg professor had evolved through three tumultuous centuries of European history, crossed the Atlantic, and been reaffirmed by his spiritual heirs in an institution of higher learning in a different language and a different culture.

Wittenberg College in Ohio was neither the first nor the last of such institutions to be established in North America by the followers of Luther. The Lutheran commitment to the alliance of faith and learning has been attested time and again over the span of two centuries, during which millions of German and Scandinavian immigrants spread across the North America continent. A concern for an educated clergy and an informed laity equipped for productive citizenship motivated the establishment of hundreds of educational institutions to meet particular needs in special times and places. Nevertheless, it is by no means self-evident that because Martin Luther was a university professor and a university provided a platform for the launching of the Lutheran Reformation, the Lutheran church should be operating colleges and universities in late 20th-century North America. The passage of four centuries of modern history has been attended by massive changes in culture, religion, politics, and education. Neither the church, the state, nor the university of today is comparable in structure, stature, or mode of operation with its 16th-century counterpart.

Martin Luther operated in an essentially medieval society, and Wittenberg itself was located on Europe's eastern cultural frontier. Feudal relationships still dominated Germany, and the antiquated Holy Roman Empire provided the political backdrop for the events of the Reformation. The medieval concept of the universal church was still very real to Luther when he entered the University of Erfurt, only nine years after Columbus's historic voyage of discovery. The theories of Copernicus would not be published until three years before Luther's death, and neither Kepler nor Galileo would be born for another quarter of a century.

The German University

The medieval university, however, had been flourishing in several places in Europe for well over 300 years before Luther's time.[1] The earliest universities at Bologna, Paris, and Oxford had been in operation since the 11th and 12th centuries, and Germany had several of its own by the 14th century. Luther himself was a product of the standard medieval Latin school system, which culminated for him at the University of Erfurt, with its traditional four faculties of Arts, Law, Medicine, and Theology.

Within this academic structure and under the credentials it provided, Luther was able to undertake the biblical study that produced his historic theological insights. His recognized position within this establishment also assured him of a platform from which to speak and of a serious hearing among the ecclesiastical and political powers of his time. The Saxon Elector Frederick the Wise had founded the University of Wittenberg in 1502, only 15 years before Luther posted The 95 Theses. Frederick's pride in the prominence Luther brought to his young university and a sense of obligation to protect his professor from papal and imperial redress strengthened the important support this powerful imperial elector gave to the cause of the Reformation.[2]

Although Luther himself was exceedingly critical of the universities, expending some of his earthy rhetoric upon them as "asses' stalls and devil's training centers,"[3] it was their curricula, methodology, and personnel that he assailed. Neither he nor his later disciples made any serious attempts to modify their structure in Reformation territories. The basic four-faculty pattern remained substantially unchanged into modern times.[4]

The university at the time of Luther was the apex of a complex educational system which, although far from universal in scope, offered rudimentary learning opportunities to a considerable number of people. The basic units of this system were the monastery school, which not only attended to the preparation of future members of the monastic orders, but also, through so-called external schools, offered instruction to children of the parish. They were supplemented by a pattern of cathedral schools, chantry schools, and guild schools, all conducted by monks or priests under ecclesiastical direction. As urban society and municipal government developed in the later Middle Ages, some of the guild schools and parish schools became "burger schools," supported and controlled by secular authorities.

Young boys who were destined for the priesthood, however, or for one of the learned professions of theology, law, or medicine, undertook an extended course of study, the essence of which was the mastery of Latin grammar, rhetoric, and logic. Luther himself pursued this course in Mansfeld, Magdeburg and Eisenach over a period of 10 years from the age of 8 to 18. Only then, in 1501, was he qualified to matriculate in the arts faculty of the University of Erfurt.

As distinguished from the graduate faculties of theology, law, and medicine, the arts faculty was the undergraduate division of the university with studies leading to both the baccalaureate and master's degrees. On the basis of his sound preparation in the *Trivialschulen* Luther was able to complete the baccalaureate in 18 months and the master's degree in two and one-half years. His studies included the classic Latin authors such as Cicero, Vergil, and Livy. The philosophy taught at Erfurt was dominated by scholasticism, though humanism was beginning to make some inroads. Aristotle's physics, metaphysics, and ethics were standard curricular subjects. Upon the completion of this undergraduate work, Luther entered the graduate faculty of law in 1505, but shortly thereafter left the university for the monastic life of the Augustinian Order.

His doctorate in theology was awarded by the University of Wittenberg in 1512 only after he had completed his monastic novitiate, been ordained a priest, and engaged in extended postgraduate studies while also lecturing in the arts faculty at Wittenberg.

All of this occurred before Luther, on the authority of his appointment as doctor of theology, undertook his historic lectures on the Epistle to the Romans. With the aid of his developing knowledge of Greek, which he had begun to study seriously only in 1514, he made the revolutionary discovery of the true meaning of God's righteousness, through which he saves sinners by grace alone.

From this time forward the drama of the Reformation unfolded as Luther translated the implications of his discovery into action. He gained the support of his faculty colleagues, opposed the indulgence traffic, responded to critics, engaged in debate, challenged the authority of Rome on the basis of Scripture, was ordered to retract his errors, and after an imperial confrontation was banned by the Holy Roman Empire and excommunicated by the pope.[5]

The Need for School Reform

Meanwhile, the University of Wittenberg became the nerve center for the movement, and Luther and his colleagues the recognized ecclesiastical advisers. As the teachings of the Reformation gained support among both clergy and laity, it became clear that substantial changes would have to be made in educational programs to insure that children would be taught the basic elements of the gospel.

At first Luther was convinced that children should and could be taught by parents in the home. With this in mind he developed a series of manuals for family use, including sermons on the Ten Commandments, an explanation of the Lord's Prayer, and a "little Prayer Book" with instructions on how to teach children to pray. Finally, in 1529 came the Small Catechism, "in the plain form in which it is to be taught by the Head of the family."

But events during the years 1521–1525 were not encouraging to Luther's hopes for an orderly system of family religious education. By no means everyone in Wittenberg had renounced allegiance to Rome and adopted the new theology. Luther himself was in temporary exile following his confrontation with the emperor at Worms and his excommunication by the pope. In his absence Andreas Carlstadt and Thomas Münzer were leading an extremist movement in Wittenberg which belittled all education as unnecessary for the liberated Christian. An uprising of German knights led by Franz von Sickingen and Ulrich von Hutten and the revolt of the peasants added to the climate of instability.

In the face of these upsetting events that seemed to call for the exercise of some external authority to prevent chaos, Luther and his colleagues turned to the civil authorities and laid on them the responsibility for education, "so that young people may be raised to be peaceful and decent." This significant shift in Luther's views on educational responsibility is reflected in his "Address to the Councilmen of All Cities in Germany that They Establish and Maintain Christian Schools," prepared and published in 1524.[6]

"First of all," he declared, "we are today experiencing in all the German lands how schools everywhere are being left to go to wrack and ruin. . .." No one, he said, is any longer willing to have his children attend them. While the present sad state of the schools might understandably bring parents to such a conclusion, Luther complained that the parents were neither willing nor able to undertake the educational task themselves.

If the cities are to be saved from the ruin of Sodom and Gomorrah, the council and the authorities would have to assume the responsibilities upon which the parents have defaulted. "Since the property, honor, and life of the whole city have been committed to their faithful keeping," the councilors "would be remiss in their duty before God and man if they did not seek its welfare and improvement day and night with all the means at their command."[7]

A visitation of the parishes in Electoral Saxony led by Luther himself in 1528–1529 only served to reconfirm the disastrous state of the schools. Aroused by these reports and by Luther's sharp admonitions, civil authorities began the process of school reform, drafting school ordinances, often with the advice and counsel of Reformation leaders. A system of public education emerged in which religious instruction was included as an integral part of the curriculum.

The patterns of the schools varied widely, depending on the size and location of the municipalities and the dates of the reforms. Elementary schools using only the German language were developed for those who had no intention of pursuing a learned profession but needed only the basic skills of reading and writing the vernacular.[8]

Luther's Educational Philosophy

By 1530 Luther had concluded that the complete success of the Reformation could be achieved only with the second generation of Lutherans trained from childhood in the new evangelical tradition. His sermon of 1530 "On Keeping Children in School" contains his rationale for the establishment of higher schools to supply pastors and teachers to lead a new generation and the civic leadership that would assure good and orderly government.[9]

Schools of this kind would follow the humanistic approach to learning as exemplified in the Wittenberg Latin School, founded in 1533 under the special direction of Luther and Melanchthon.[10] This conviction, that a thorough intellectual preparation of professional leadership for church and community is fundamental to the broad intentions of the Reformation, has provided the driving impulse for higher education within the Lutheran tradition.

While Luther himself was not primarily an educational reformer, his writings and sermons left no doubt of the close interrelationship between his theology and experience and the purpose and content of the new educational programs. In the wake of his experiences in Wittenberg following his return from the Wartburg, he showed no reluctance in enlisting civil authority in support of Christian schools.

The Lutheran Reformation harbored no intent to break the mutually supportive relationship between the medieval church and state. It was, after all, the prince of Saxony who was Luther's protector; and the Augsburg Confession received official status through the signatures of German princes and municipalities. Many of the ordinances assuring instruction in the Catechism and establishing administrative control of the schools by the city councils were written by Wittenberg clergy and enacted by the civil authorities.

Luther's doctrine of the orders of creation gave full support to such an alliance. In a world under God's authority, governments were ordained to restrain evil and maintain a peaceful and orderly society. This included assuring safety for the teaching and preaching of the gospel. It is not difficult to understand Luther's readiness to enlist the support of the state when social unrest and confusion threatened the teaching of the young.

Furthermore, his doctrine of vocation, rooted in the concept of the priesthood of all believers, opened the way for the promotion of all kinds of education as preparation for service to God and to society. The professions, as Luther saw them, were not merely means for earning a living but rather the areas in which each person contributed to the welfare of his brothers and sisters.[11]

The breadth of Luther's educational philosophy is illustrated in the three social spheres within which appropriate curricula could be developed. The *Lehrstand*, or teaching order, included persons in the scholastic professions, notably the pastors and teachers, responsible for the ministry of the gospel. They must be learned and well trained in the humanistic disciplines, especially in the languages that are essential in interpreting the Word of God. The *Wehrstand* comprised persons learned in the law, equipped for public service for the ordering of public affairs and the maintenance of a just society. The *Nährstand*, the "nurturing" group, included girls and women, who carried a particular responsibility for the education of children.[12] To assure its well-being the temporal community must have both capable and well-educated men and women. For this reason Luther urged "the establishment everywhere of the very best schools for both boys and girls."[13]

Within this inclusive concept of education for life and service, no area of serious preparation was excluded. Luther, however, was especially concerned for the preparation of the *Lehrstand* and the *Wehrstand*, and his sermon "On Keeping Children in School" provides some lively descriptions of both the need for and the necessary components of training for the ministry and for public service.

In his plea for more candidates for the ministry he sounds very much like a modern American Lutheran bishop concerned over an inordinate number of pastoral vacancies in his synod or district. For the 1800 parishes in Saxony alone, he said, there were only 800 pastors, and in half of all the schools in Germany, probably only about 4000 pupils. "If we do nothing about this," he complained, "and if the princes especially do not try to see that the boys' schools and the universities are properly maintained, there will be such a scarcity of men that we shall have to give three or four cities to one pastor and ten villages to one chaplain, if indeed we can get that many men."[14]

Of almost equal concern to Luther was the provision of qualified teachers and schoolmasters. "Next to that of preaching," he declared, "this is the best, greatest, and most useful office there is. Indeed, I scarcely know which of the two is better."[15] Yet there was an appalling shortage of teachers in Germany, without whom the Reformation could not prosper.

As for public servants, Luther reminded the civil administrators of the large numbers of kings, princes, counts, lords, cities, and villages in Germany. To fill all those positions, he asked, "Where shall we be getting the educated men three years from now, when here and there the shortage is already beginning to be felt?. . . Those who study in these times will become so highly prized that two princes and three cities will yet compete for one scholar."[16]

Beyond these groups, Luther stressed the need for physicians, educated merchants and businessmen, people "who can do more than simply add, subtract, and read German."[17]

Luther and the Liberal Arts

Schools that could supply this wide range of needs required a curriculum solidly grounded in the study of languages. Latin was to be the basic tool, but Greek would also be included in the upper levels, and for those intending to become theologians, Hebrew as well. Greek and Hebrew grammar was especially important for future pastors as an aid in interpreting the Holy Scriptures. The world of secular literature would also be opened to them through a mastery of these languages.

"I am persuaded," wrote Luther, "that without knowledge of literature pure theology cannot at all endure, just as heretofore, when letters have declined and lain prostrate, theology, too, has wretchedly fallen and lain prostrate; nay, I see that there has never been a great revelation of the Word of God unless he has first prepared the way by the rise and prosperity of languages and letters, as though they were John the Baptists. . .."[18]

Beyond languages Luther emphasized the liberal arts and extolled their beneficial effects in broadening the intellectual horizons and cultural sensitivities of students. Through the teaching of history children "would hear of the doings and sayings of the entire world, and how things went with various cities, kingdoms, princes, men, and women. Thus they could in a short time set before themselves as in a mirror the character, life, counsels and purposes, successful and unsuccessful, of the whole world from the beginning; on the basis of which they could then draw the proper inferences and in the fear of God take their own place in the stream of human events. In addition they could gain from history the knowledge and understanding of what to seek and what to avoid in this outward life and be able to advise and direct others accordingly."[19]

Poetry and rhetoric were also essential elements in the curriculum. "It is my desire," wrote Luther, "that there shall be as many poets and rhetoricians as possible, because I see that by these studies, as by no other means, people are wonderfully fitted for the grasping of sacred truth and for handling it skillfully and happily. . .. Therefore I beg of you that at my request (if that has any weight) you will urge your young people to be diligent in the study of poetry and rhetoric."[20]

Though often criticized for his medieval views of science, Luther sounds surprisingly modern in his advocacy of direct investigation as the best way of learning about nature. "We are at the dawn of a new era," he declared, "for we are beginning to recover the knowledge of the external world which we had lost through the fall of Adam. We now observe creatures properly, and not as formerly." He could not resist a jibe at Erasmus, the sophisticated humanist, who "does not care to know how fruit is developed from the germ," but "passes all that by. . .and looks upon external objects as cows look upon a new gate."[21]

Luther's enthusiasm for a broad liberal curriculum reached its height when he spoke of music. "If I had children and could manage it," he wrote, "I would have them study not only languages and history, but also singing and music. For what is all this but mere child's play? The ancient Greeks trained their children in these disciplines; and they grew up to be people of wondrous ability, subsequently fit for everything."[22] Together with music, which "drives away all care and melancholy from the heart," Luther recommended gymnastics, which "produces elasticity of the body and preserves the health."[23]

In view of the kaleidoscopic turn of events on the Wittenberg stage in the 1520s and 1530s, it is not strange that Luther was more involved in coping with real situations than in developing educational theories and constructing systems to implement them. Under more favorable circumstances he might well have laid greater stress upon the elementary school as an extension of the primary educational responsibility of the family. As it was, the limited knowledge and competence of parents and the scarcity of well-equipped teachers and pastors made it necessary first of all to develop leaders for both church and community.

The Reformation in Germany shifted the responsibility for rudimentary education from the monks and priests to the secular authorities. The religious dimension of instruction was provided by Luther's Catechism, which according to the new school ordinances became a regular part of the curriculum. These so-called vernacular schools, inexpensive to operate and limited in educational goals, became so popular both among the town councils and the general citizenry that Luther and his colleagues actually feared they were luring potential leadership away from the more rigorous Latin schools.

It was, therefore, the Latin schools to which the Reformers directed their major attention. Instruments of reform were the municipal and provincial school ordinances regulating class organization, curriculum, lesson plans, and reading lists. Latin schools normally operated four or five classes. First graders learned their ABC's from primers and by year's end were expected to read simple Latin texts and to write legibly. Latin grammar came in second grade and some beginnings might even be made in Greek. Both Greek and Latin readings, on increasing levels of difficulty, continued through fifth grade. The major reforms in these schools, in addition to the more stringent standards of administration, were the introduction of evangelical instruction through the Catechism, and the humanistic emphasis, achieved through the study of Greek language and literature.[24]

This trend was developed even more extensively by Philip Melanchthon through the later establishment of the classical secondary school or gymnasium, which prepared the Latin school graduate for university entrance. Together with Luther, Melanchthon was also responsible for reorganizing the curriculum of Wittenberg University.[25] Lectures on the Bible, Augustine, and the ancient church fathers replaced the scholastic treatment of Aristotle and Peter Lombard. Wittenberg became the first university in Germany to teach both Greek and Hebrew in addition to Latin. Melanchthon also took the lead in reorganizing other German universities along the lines of Christian humanism and helped to establish new universities at Marburg, Jena, and Königsberg.[26]

The Broadening Stream

In the years following the Reformation these institutions were the transmitters of the Lutheran tradition in higher education. Fed by a stream of young men well-schooled in the humanistic Latin schools and gymnasia, the German universities became the creators and interpreters of the theological and intellectual currents which flowed through Europe for the next three centuries. Basic to Luther's own principles and experience was the freedom of investigation. Each discipline, whether theology, philosophy, or science, had an integrity of its own, and was not subject to any other. Such a stance, rooted in the conviction that God is Creator and Lord of the earthly as well as the heavenly kingdom, paved the way for the modern concept of academic freedom for which the German university would later become almost a synonym.

Sydney Ahlstrom has described the flow of the Lutheran tradition through the religious and intellectual life of post-Reformation Europe in three major currents: the scholastic, the pietistic, and the critical.[27] These currents flowed mainly through the universities and the churches, but they also affected life and thought at every level of society in every Lutheran country in Europe. Their influence extended beyond Europe into other parts of the world, not least into North America, depending upon which current was dominant when particular groups of emigrants left Germany or Scandinavia.

The Lutheran scholastic tradition arose in the midst of fierce religious debates and wars of the 16th and 17th centuries over confessional and doctrinal differences. This was an age of coercion, and even Luther's theology, with its affirmation of Christian freedom, was imposed on all subjects living within the borders of a territory whose ruler professed to be Lutheran.

According to the scholastic tradition Lutheran doctrine was embodied in formalized statements, notably the Formula of Concord of 1580. Efforts to maintain Lutheran orthodoxy against both Roman Catholic and Reformed assaults resulted in finely drawn expositions of Lutheran theology that tended to become intellectual exercises rather than professions of a living faith.

Among the earliest to resist such formalism and to seek a balance between theological orthodoxy and personal piety was a Saxon pastor, Johann Arndt. His devotional books, dealing with *True Christianity*, written in the early years of the 17th century, influenced the personal lives of Lutheran pastors and laypersons during his own time and for nearly four centuries thereafter. Later in the 17th and early 18th centuries Philipp Jakob Spener and August Hermann Francke continued such efforts at the University of Halle to redress the balance of overintellectualism in Lutheran theology and religious life.[28] During this period, shortly after 1700, the early migrations of German Lutherans to America took place. It was from Halle that Gotthilf August Francke, son of the older Francke, impelled by the evangelical outreach characteristic of pietism, sent young Henry Melchior Muhlenberg as a missionary pastor to gather together the scattered German Lutherans and to plant the Lutheran church in America.

As the 17th century was marked by a scholastic orthodoxy followed by a pietistic reaction in the early 18th, the latter part of the 18th century was characterized by the rise of rationalism. New discoveries and new human achievements enhanced the image of man and his ability to probe the secrets of the natural world. This new impulse reached its climax in the ideas of the French Revolution, which elevated the human to full supremacy.

In Germany the age of rationalism signaled a deemphasis upon traditional confessional distinctions. In 1817 the king of Prussia even decreed the union of the Lutheran and Reformed churches within his realm. Against this violation of Lutheran confessional integrity a new orthodoxy asserted itself. Klaus Harms, archdeacon at Kiel, reissued Luther's 95 Theses and added his own 95 theses against rationalism and the Prussian Union. Inspired in part by the 300th anniversary of the Augsburg Confession, a movement for Lutheran renewal began in the University of Erlangen. Governmental pressures for a unified Prussian Church were nevertheless stringent enough to force many loyal Lutherans, both in Prussia and neighboring Saxony, to forsake the land of the Reformation to establish a new Zion in North America.

2 FOOTHOLD
IN AMERICA

The exploration and colonization of the New World virtually coincided with the Reformation and even shared some of its root causes. Well within the lifetime of Martin Luther and John Calvin the great Spanish empire was founded in Mexico and South America. When Luther was debating John Eck at Leipzig in 1519, the Spanish conquistador Hernán Cortéz was completing the conquest of the Aztec empire in Mexico. Only a few years later, in 1530, while Lutherans were consolidating their ranks after the Diet of Augsburg, Jacques Cartier was exploring the St. Lawrence River in North America for the French king, Francis I. By the time the Lutherans adopted the Formula of Concord in 1580, John Hawkins and Francis Drake were plundering the Spanish Main in the name of Queen Elizabeth and the rising power of English nationalism.

Meanwhile, the Reformation had come to England under auspices much more political than religious. Having failed in his effort to secure papal approval for his divorce from Catherine of Aragon, Henry VIII renounced the authority of the pope and in 1534 declared himself to be head of the English church. At the king's behest the English bishops, and scholars at Cambridge and Oxford, were obliged to develop a theological rationale for the newly emerging church, and in the process sought the counsel of both Lutheran and Reformed theologians on the Continent. Early Lutheran influences were strong, but Calvinist theology became increasingly evident in the revised prayer books. The 42 Articles of Religion issued in 1553 clearly demonstrated that the English Reformation would favor Geneva rather than Wittenberg.

It was less clear, however, just what form of Calvinism would prevail. During the subsequent stormy interlude from 1553 to 1558, when Catholic

21

Mary Tudor occupied the English throne, it was uncertain whether Protestant-ism in any form would survive. Efforts by James I, the first of the Stuart kings, to compel conformity to the rites of High Church Anglicanism after 1603 brought into the open a full spectrum of dissent, loosely defined as ''Puritan,'' but ranging from the moderates who wished only to excise the remnants of Ro-man Catholicism and ''purify'' the church, to those who wished to withdraw completely and organize themselves in ''separate'' congregations.

Merchants who formed the backbone of England's rising middle class, many of whom were already active in overseas trading and colonizing ven-tures, were strongly represented within these dissenting groups. As the politi-cal pressures increased, one enterprising group of businessmen secured a new charter for the Massachusetts Bay Company with authority to remove the entire operation of the company to New England. With this authorization and the grant of land described in their charter, they solicited a substantial number of fellow adventurers and prepared to launch an overseas colony. Under the lead-ership of John Winthrop they sailed for New England on March 29, 1630, with a fleet of four ships and 400 persons. By the end of the year 600 more joined them. The years immediately following have been described as ''the swarming of the Puritans'' in New England. By 1643 more than 20,000 people had made their way to Massachusetts. A trading company had been transformed into a commonwealth.

The leadership of this colony was well salted with graduates of the Uni-versity of Cambridge, the intellectual and theological capital of English Puri-tanism. From the outset these men saw their venture as a covenant among themselves and with God. Both civil and church order should therefore be es-tablished in accordance with God's will and Word as directed in the Holy Scriptures. Church membership was reserved for those who could give person-al testimony to a saving religious experience. Laws were based on Scripture, especially on the Old Testament, with stress upon Sabbath observance and aus-tere personal conduct. Virtues of piety, thrift, and self-control were especially honored, in the expectation that such exercises might give evidence of God's favor and assurances of eternal election. Congregational church government found its counterpart in the town meeting and in representative assemblies, which came to be the characteristic New England legislative pattern.

While the ''swarming of the Puritans'' resulted in the founding of a clus-ter of colonies in New England, the continuing instability of the political and religious climate in England opened the way for the establishment of other col-onies of differing patterns and purposes. But the spirit of Puritanism, with its moral legalism and its ''gospel'' of work, and even much of its institutional form, entered into the colonial foundations of British America with such vitali-ty that it remained a dominant force throughout the histories of both the United

States and Canada. Other traditions have made rich contributions to American and Canadian cultural and religious life, but they have done so in the context of a social and political ethos initially shaped by Puritan values and institutions.

The English College in America

One of the most influential elements in the transmission of these values has been the important role the Puritans accorded education, particularly higher education. The leadership of the New England colonies included the best of the English university tradition from both Oxford and Cambridge. William Brewster of Plymouth Colony, John Winthrop and John Cotton of Massachusetts Bay, and John Davenport of New Haven were representative of a host of other highly educated leaders, both clergy and laity. Their Puritan religion was quite literally a "religion of the book," depending heavily upon biblical precept and pattern for life in both church and state.

Fully in keeping with the character of the Puritan enterprise, in 1636, only six years after the arrival of the first colonists, the General Court of Massachusetts voted to give 400 pounds towards the founding of "a schoole or colledge." The rationale for such attention to higher learning, even in a frontier outpost, was almost self-evident.

> After God had carried us safe to New England, and wee had builded our houses, provided necessaries for our livelihood, reared convenient places for God's worship, and settled the Civill Government; One of the next things we longed for, and looked after was to advance Learning and perpetuate it to Posterity; dreading to leave an illiterate Ministry to the Churches, when our present Ministers shall lie in the Dust.[1]

Harvard College, so named to honor the young minister who died in 1638 and left his property and library to the infant institution, became the first of a long succession of colleges established in the English pattern on American soil. Characteristic of this pattern was the independence and autonomy of the individual English colleges. The "fellows" or teachers of the colleges constituted the governing corporation, and provided both housing and instruction to the students while assigning to the university the routine function of granting degrees. The so-called "higher faculties" of theology, law, and medicine, which became central to the German universities, did not develop at Oxford and Cambridge. Instead, the English university functioned as a community of residential undergraduate colleges dedicated to the single aim of the "virtuous education of youth."[2]

This pattern quite naturally came to dominate higher education throughout the colonial period in America. Indeed, it persisted until well past the middle of the 19th century, when the modern American university emerged in response to the impact of the German universities and the demands of a developing scientific and technical society.

During the hundred years following the establishment of Harvard in 1636, only two additional colleges were founded, William and Mary in 1696 and Yale in 1701. A succession of six more were established in the 30 years before the American Revolution. Four of them, Princeton (1746), Brown (1765), Rutgers (1766), and Dartmouth (1769), were products of the evangelical fervor following the first Great Awakening, which created a new demand for an indigenous ministry. Both King's College (Columbia) (1754) and the College of Philadelphia (1755) had Anglican roots, but in the process of their development into degree-granting institutions, manifested less religious consciousness than the others.[3]

All the colonial colleges were independent foundations responsible to local boards of control, operating under a charter or other authorization from the civil government. Like the English colleges, they were small baccalaureate institutions, limited largely to a liberal arts curriculum heavily weighted toward classical languages. Though neither owned nor governed by any formal ecclesiastical structures, their identification with a particular religious tradition was unmistakably reflected in the membership of their boards and in the person of the president and the professor of divinity, both of whom were likely to be leading members of the clergy.

The number of students in attendance at the colonial colleges was never large, and the number of graduates was even smaller. Nevertheless, those institutions, augmented by a continuing influx of persons trained in both English and continental universities, provided colonial America with a highly literate intellectual leadership fully conversant with European political and religious thought.

Lutheran Migration to America

The only non-English colonies to be established on the Atlantic seaboard between Spanish Florida and French Canada were the Dutch colony of New Amsterdam and a Swedish settlement on the Delaware River. In these two colonies the earliest Lutheran settlers appeared. In 1638 Sweden, at that time one of the leading powers of Europe, entered the colonial field with the establishment of a settlement where the city of Wilmington now stands. The colony prospered, spreading north and south along the Delaware. But in 1644 it was conquered by the Dutch of New Amsterdam, and the Dutch in turn capitulated to a British force in 1664.

Nevertheless, beginning in 1639 with the Reverend Reorus Torkillus, the first regular Lutheran minister in America, a succession of Swedish pastors sent by the Archbishop of Uppsala served these congregations, made up of both Swedes and Finns, for nearly 200 years. As late as 1768 there were 3000 members in the Lutheran congregations on the Delaware. A close personal relationship developed between Henry Melchior Muhlenberg, the senior German Lutheran pastor in Philadelphia, and the Swedish provost, Charles M. Wrangel. But after Wrangel's recall to Sweden in 1768, relationships between the German and the Swedish Lutherans virtually ceased. After 1787, when their constitutions were altered to permit either Lutheran or Episcopalian clergy, the Swedish congregations were gradually absorbed into the Protestant Episcopal Church.[4]

A few Lutherans were among the first settlers when the Dutch West India Company established its trading posts and settlements at Albany in 1623 and Manhattan Island in 1625. Because of the company's restrictive religious policy Lutherans were compelled to participate in Dutch Reformed services. By 1649, however, they organized their own congregation and appealed to the Lutheran Consistory in Amsterdam to intercede for them with the directors of the company. On two occasions, Lutheran pastors arrived, only to be deported by the company. Not until the conquest of New Amsterdam by the English in 1664 did the Lutherans receive permission to call their own pastor, and even then they encountered disappointing delays.

Finally, in 1671, almost 50 years after the founding of the colony, the Amsterdam Consistory sent Bernhard Arnzius, "a gentle personage and of very agreeable behavior," who served the New York and Albany congregations faithfully for 20 years. After Arnzius died in 1691, the congregations there were left to fend for themselves. Indeed, for a six-year period from 1691 to 1697 there was not a single Lutheran minister in all of continental North America. In 1701, with the help of a new Swedish pastor in Philadelphia, Andrew Rudman, the New York congregation called Justus Falckner, a German pietist who had studied at Halle. In accord with the approved practices of the Amsterdam Consistory, Pastor Rudman and two Swedish pastors ordained him in Gloria Dei, the "Old Swedes' Church" in Philadelphia.[5] For more than 20 years Falckner ministered, largely in the Dutch language, to the Lutherans of New York and the Hudson Valley.

During virtually the entire period of German immigration to North America, beginning about 1680, Germany itself was divided into a patchwork of independent principalities, kingdoms, and cities. A single unified German state did not come into being until 1870. Partly as a consequence of this lack of unity, the origin and character of German emigration varied widely. The "swarming" of the English Puritans had no counterpart for the Germans. Groups of Germans continued to arrive in North America from a variety of places, for a variety of reasons, over the course of 250 years. Their religious backgrounds were as varied as the political map of Germany, including Roman

Catholics, Lutherans, Reformed, Moravians, Mennonites, Amish, Dunkers, Schwenkfelders, and, especially in the mid-19th century, many who were professedly antireligious.

In the colonial years the religious needs of German immigrants were served only sporadically, and often ill-served, by a variety of itinerant immigrant clergy, or in the latter part of the 18th century, by a relatively small number of missionary pastors from Germany. In contrast to the English Puritans of the previous century, whose leaders were learned and prosperous members of the middle class and whose entire migration was a well-organized religious crusade, the German immigrants of the 18th century were poor and dispossessed, dependent upon the patronage of others even for their passage to America.

The first group of significant size were the so-called Palatines who came in the first decades of the 18th century. They were mostly farmers, refugees from southwestern Germany along the upper Rhine and near the French border. Victimized first by the depredations of the invading French armies of Louis XIV and in 1708 by the worst winter in many generations, thousands of farmers fled down the Rhine Valley into Holland and across the channel to England. Some remained in England or Ireland, but most were transported at the expense of the British government to New York and up into the Hudson Valley where they were contracted to produce tar, hemp, and shipmasts for the British navy. When the plans of the British government for this project failed, most of the Palatines stayed in the Hudson Valley or moved into the Mohawk and Schoharie valleys of New York as farmers. Even after the initial influx of 1709 others continued to come, settling as "redemptioners" in North Carolina, Virginia, and South Carolina, where they were committed to work out the cost of their passage after arrival.

One of the most dramatic Lutheran migrations reached a successful conclusion in the newly established English colony of Georgia in 1734. For nearly 200 years Lutherans in Salzburg, Austria, had maintained their faith in the face of religious wars and Catholic persecution. In 1731 they were expelled from Austria, and finally, after a pilgrimage across Europe, 91 of them found their way, with British government assistance, to General Oglethorpe's colony of refuge. Others followed, and by 1741 the colony numbered 1200 persons. Through the mediation of Gotthilf Francke at the University of Halle, they were supplied with two young missionary pastors, John Boltzius and Israel Gronau.

By far the largest German immigration to the American colonies was directed to Pennsylvania. Because of disappointment over the treatment accorded earlier immigrants in New York, and in response to the favorable publicity circulated by William Penn for his colony, the mainstream of German immigration shifted to Philadelphia. Between 1735 and 1745 the high tide was reached, and by 1750 there were at least 40,000 Lutherans in Pennsylvania.

The Lutherans who entered Pennsylvania were preceded by representatives of dissenting sects driven from their homes in Lutheran, Reformed, or Roman Catholic territories in Germany. First to accept the invitation of William Penn when he opened his colony in 1682 was a group of Mennonites. They were followed by the Dunkers, the Amish, and the Moravians.

The Moravians traced their origin to the pre-Reformation Hussite movement in Bohemia and Moravia in the 15th century. A few of its survivors fled in 1722 to Saxony, where they found refuge at Herrnhut on the estates of Count Nicolas von Zinzendorf. As the settlement grew, Zinzendorf himself became more deeply involved in their community life and was later consecrated as their bishop. Missionary zeal kindled by the pietism that had been part of Zinzendorf's own early training led a group of Moravians to undertake a missionary venture in 1735 to the Creek and Cherokee Indians in the colony of Georgia. On their voyage to America their leader, Augustus Spangenberg, met John Wesley, the founder of English Methodism. Wesley later attributed his notable "conversion" experience in 1738 to the influence of Spangenberg and to the reading of Luther's Preface to the Epistle to the Romans.

Meanwhile, another great English evangelist, George Whitefield, invited Spangenberg and his group to join him in Pennsylvania where Whitefield planned to establish a mission school for Negroes. Theological differences, however, led to a separation, and the Moravians established their own settlement at Bethlehem, Pennsylvania. They were joined there by Zinzendorf himself, who had come to America in 1741 in response to persistent reports concerning the spiritual destitution of the German immigrants. He had hopes of drawing together all the Germans in America into a single ecumenical communion. In pursuit of that mission, he visited many congregations that were without pastors, including several Lutheran parishes.

In 1733, several years before Zinzendorf's arrival, John Christian Schultze, a Lutheran pastor near Philadelphia, accompanied by two laymen, visited Dr. Frederick Ziegenhagen, the Hanoverian court chaplain in London, asking for help in establishing churches and schools for the German Lutherans in Pennsylvania. "We are not able to accomplish this work by our means," an open letter declared. Indeed,

we live in a country where money is scarce, and where every man has enough to do to support himself, under Divine assistance, by the labor of his hands. If this work, which is good in itself and so well calculated to promote the Glory of God and the true Religion of Christ, should be neglected, then would all our fond hopes be blasted, and our children and descendants would finally slide back into the condition of the heathen.[6]

Ziegenhagen relayed the call for help to Gotthilf Francke at the University of Halle in Germany, but reports from Philadelphia of dishonest handling of funds collected in Europe by Schulze and his associates caused Francke to postpone any positive response. Moreover, before recommending any pastor to the congregations in Philadelphia, Francke insisted that they guarantee a cash salary and give assurance that they would pay for the pastor's expenses if "for weighty reasons" he felt it necessary to return to Germany.[7] Only after a lapse of eight years, when Francke learned of the arrival in America of Count Zinzendorf, representing himself as a Lutheran, did he take the historic action which led to the permanent establishment of a Lutheran church in the American colonies.[8]

Planting the Lutheran Church in America

That action was the commissioning at Halle in 1741 of a young pastor named Henry Melchior Muhlenberg as a missionary to the scattered German Lutherans in America, to rescue them from sectarian incursion and revive their Lutheran loyalty. In fulfilling these tasks Muhlenberg carried to the New World the reforming force of 18th-century German Lutheran pietism. This movement, centered at the University of Halle, laid stress upon commitment in daily Christian life, devotional piety, and zeal for Christian missions rather than emphasis upon the precise doctrinal formulations that characterized much of 17th-century Lutheran orthodoxy.

Philipp Spener and August Hermann Francke were early leaders of German pietism. Francke himself was one of the founders of the University of Halle in 1694, as well as a number of charitable institutions for orphans and other needy persons. The impulse for Lutheran missions in India also originated with Francke. Men from Halle would supply more pastors and teachers for Lutheran settlements and congregations in America during the 18th century than any other single source. Even before Muhlenberg, the Falckners in New York and New Jersey and Boltzius and Gronau in Georgia had provided pastoral leadership for German Lutherans in America. In the half-century following 1742, 24 ministers were sent from Halle to serve German congregations in America.

Indeed, the mid-18th century climate in both Protestant Europe and America was dominated by a strongly evangelical spirit. Pietism in Europe was matched by the Evangelical Revival in Great Britain and by the Great Awakening in colonial America. George Whitefield, John Wesley, Nicholas von Zinzendorf, Gilbert Tennent, and Jonathan Edwards were all contemporaries of Henry Melchior Muhlenberg.[9] It would be strange indeed if the Lutheran tradition, which first became securely anchored in America in such times, did not carry into its formative years a distinctly evangelical character. At the same time Halle pietism left no doubt of its strong commitment to the Lutheran confessions. Throughout the often chaotic conditions of migration and settlement, Lutheran pastors and congregations consistently contended for their Lutheran confessional identity against the assaults of both sectarianism and rationalism.

Justus Falckner, for example, who ministered in New York and had been trained at Halle, titled his church register in 1703 "The Church Book of the Christian Apostolic Protestant Lutheran Congregation Adhering to the Unaltered Confession of Augsburg." William C. Berkenmeyer, who was sent to New York by the Consistories of Hamburg and Amsterdam in 1725 following Falckner's death and who ministered in the Hudson Valley for 25 years, was even more strongly confessional. Henry Melchior Muhlenberg himself always insisted upon formal subscription to the Augsburg Confession as he went about his task of reviving faltering Lutheran congregations and organizing new ones.

When Muhlenberg embarked for America, he had a missionary commission from the authorities at Halle, but the congregations in Philadelphia had never agreed to the stringent conditions Francke had laid down at the time of their original request in 1734. Only after initial visits with Halle clergy in South Carolina and Georgia did Muhlenberg travel northward to Philadelphia, from whence had come the plea for help eight years earlier. The situation he encountered there in November 1742 was a classic example of the problem he had been sent to deal with. The Moravian Bishop Zinzendorf was actually preaching in one Lutheran congregation, and the presence of two unlicensed itinerants was causing division and dissension in several others in and near Philadelphia. Within four weeks Muhlenberg was able to resolve the tensions and, as an officially authorized and ordained pastor, to assure them of a Lutheran ministry.

Three congregations extended him a call, and he was installed as pastor of the "United Congregations" of Philadelphia on December 27, 1742. Through his ministry the congregations prospered and grew, built new church structures and established parish schools. Inquiries and requests for help began to flow in from far and wide. Muhlenberg traveled extensively in his missionary role, preaching and administering the sacraments, confirming, encouraging, settling disputes, and organizing congregations.

When additional help arrived from Halle, Muhlenberg was able to visit more distant outposts in Pennsylvania and Maryland and southward into the Carolinas, where Lutherans had begun to settle in large numbers after 1730. His meticulously kept journal relates his hazardous travels in graphic detail.

> Often the roads, the streams, wind, frost, snow and storms are such that one would not drive a dog out into them; yet the pastor must make his rounds. The gracious God has rescued me many a time from imminent peril of death

and preserved my poor bones, though occasionally both horse and rider fell.[10]

Muhlenberg further described his effort to counteract the proselytizing activities of the Moravians, and the confusion produced by "pretenders" or unauthorized "vagabond preachers," but also of his satisfaction in sharing the gospel with devout hearers in isolated places.[11] In carrying out these tasks Muhlenberg never saw himself as a church superintendent fulfilling a commission to "plant the church," but rather as a missionary pastor participating in the *ecclesia plantanda*, a church in the process of being planted.[12]

There followed what has been called the most important single event in American Lutheran history. On August 26, 1748, the day after St. Michael's Church in Philadelphia was dedicated, 6 clergy and 24 lay delegates met to establish the Pennsylvania Ministerium, the first Lutheran synod in North America.[13] This fundamental ecclesiastical structure, together with the written constitution for St. Michael's Church, adopted in 1762, provided models for the Lutheran churches of America during the crucial years when vast population influxes multiplied their numbers far beyond Muhlenberg's imagination.

The years between 1748 and the American Revolution were years of significant growth for organized Lutheranism in America. New congregations were organized. Standards for both congregations and pastors were established. The stream of German immigration continued. In 1749, the year after the first meeting of the Ministerium, 12,000 Germans landed in Philadelphia alone. Redemptioners who completed their terms of service were eager to occupy their own land, and many of them moved up the river valleys of eastern Pennsylvania, across the Susquehanna, down the Shenandoah Valley into Maryland, Virginia, and North Carolina. In 1747 Muhlenberg reported to the fathers at Halle:

> I have noticed that within the five years I have been here hardly half of the original members of my country congregations have remained. Some of those who left departed this life, but most of them have moved a great distance. . .to the frontier of Pennsylvania and to Maryland and Virginia. Meanwhile, the congregations have not become smaller, but instead have grown, because every year more and more Germans are coming in.[14]

The number of Lutherans who settled in the southern colonies never equaled the concentration in Pennsylvania. On the eve of the American Revolution there were only 20 Lutheran churches in Maryland and 18 in Virginia. The first Germans settled in western North Carolina in 1747, but only in 1772 did the first Lutheran pastor arrive, sent by the Lutheran Consistory in Hanover, Germany. By 1776 there were about 15 congregations or preaching places in North Carolina and an equal number in South Carolina, most of the latter having been established by immigrants entering the colony from the Atlantic seaboard. Far to the north in Nova Scotia even smaller numbers of German Lutherans, resisting the pressures to become Anglicans, established congregations in Halifax and Lunenburg in 1745 and 1750.

While it is difficult to establish precise statistics, it seems likely that as the American Revolution began, there may have been a total of 120,000 nominal Lutherans scattered through the English colonies from Georgia to Nova Scotia. Most were Germans and only a small portion of them were active members of congregations.

Muhlenberg's great achievement in the 45 years of his ministry in America was undoubtedly the establishment of the structural identity, polity, and liturgy of the Lutheran church in America. He was also aware of the importance of an indigenous ministry to meet the needs of an emerging church, but he saw his primary task as that of a missionary called to gather the scattered Germans into Lutheran congregations. The designing and building of educational institutions to develop future leadership would be the responsibility of the succeeding generation.

A Tradition in Transit

Within a scant 100 years the impulses of the Lutheran Reformation moved from Germany into England, Holland, and Scandinavia, and from each of these new bases crossed the Atlantic to place its indelible mark on the settlement of North America. As their inheritance from Wittenberg, the English Puritans brought a deep concern for an educated clergy and a laity literate in the Scriptures. Even under primitive conditions they lost no time in founding Harvard College to care for that concern. The New England college became a part of the American heritage and later provided the structural model for much of Lutheran higher education in North America.

As Lutheran populations began to move from Germany to America, missionaries from the University of Halle, a German university in the tradition of Luther's Wittenberg, first reached out to supply their pastoral needs. Led by Henry Melchior Muhlenberg, they established a Lutheran foothold in America and a channel for the transit of the Lutheran educational tradition to the new world.

3 EARLY VENTURES IN LUTHERAN HIGHER EDUCATION

Plans and Postponements

Even before Muhlenberg brought order and structure to the Lutheran church in America, the ideal of an educated ministry received full support among Lutheran congregations. Whether in the Dutch settlements of New Amsterdam and Albany, New Sweden on the Delaware, or among the Salzburgers in Georgia, persistent—if not always successful—efforts were expended to secure devout and qualified pastors. In the period of colonization this always meant looking to Europe, to the mother churches of Lutheranism and the universities from which those churches drew their clergy. Uppsala, Göttingen, Leipzig, Tübingen, Erfurt, and especially Halle were important names for Lutheran congregations in colonial America.

In spite of valiant efforts, relatively small numbers of pastors were recruited, and the sad spiritual plight of the immigrant was rehearsed in a constant flow of letters calling for help. It was such a plea that finally brought Henry Melchior Muhlenberg to Pennsylvania, where the harsh realities were everywhere apparent.

He, too, repeated the call to Halle for more help, especially in view of the rapidly increasing flow of German immigrants into Pennsylvania. But it became clear to him that even with the added support, which now began to come, there was no way that an adequate supply of pastors from Germany could match the flood of new settlers. Only a long-range effort to develop a native ministry would suffice.

As a first step in this direction in 1749, the year following the organization of the Ministerium, Muhlenberg purchased a 49-acre tract of land in

Philadelphia on which to build a school, a seminary, and a home for the aged. It appears to have been his intention to follow the example of his mentors in Halle where a complex of church-related institutions had been established in close connection with the university.

The construction of new churches, however, took precedence, and the project was not pursued. In 1765 a gift of money to establish a "higher school" or seminary was invested in Philadelphia real estate and in loans that promised to yield an income of 70 pounds annually. Muhlenberg saw this as a "splendid beginning of the desired endowment," but insufficient to maintain a seminary. Still later, in 1771, when the fathers in Halle and London sent money to pay a long-standing debt on Lutheran church property near Philadelphia, Muhlenberg deeded the property, including buildings and grounds, to the donors for the purpose of establishing an orphanage and a school.[1]

Muhlenberg continued to place heavy reliance upon the financial and theological resources at Halle. He was not ready, he stated in his report in 1773, "at least not for some time," to dispense with the flow of thoroughly trained ministerial supply from Germany. Even for the support of a catechetical seminary, he explained, neither the overburdened pastors nor the heavily indebted congregations were able to take the initiative. He might also have added that his own heavy pastoral responsibilities in Philadelphia, and the added burden of counseling pastors and congregations from Nova Scotia to Georgia had taxed his own strength almost beyond its limits.[2]

Kunze's Seminarium

The man who deserves to be recognized as the pioneer in Lutheran higher education in North America is John Christopher Kunze. Recently ordained in Germany, he arrived in Philadelphia in 1770 to serve as assistant to Muhlenberg and Christopher Emanuel Schulz, the two pastors of St. Michael's and Zion congregations.

Kunze was born near Mansfeld in Saxony in 1744. He took the preparatory course in the Halle schools, and studied theology for three years at the University of Leipzig. For three additional years he taught in the celebrated classical school at Kloster Bergen near Magdeburg, where, according to his own statement, he developed a special liking for the teacher's calling, particularly the teaching of languages and other advanced studies. At the age of 26 he was ordained and sent to America by the Halle mission fathers. He was accompanied on his journey by two of Muhlenberg's sons, who had been studying theology at the University of Halle and upon arrival was welcomed into the Muhlenberg home. In 1771 he married Muhlenberg's daughter, Margaretta.[3]

As early as January 1773, less than three years after his arrival, he had determined to establish a school for languages and sciences. In a report written to Halle in May, he acknowledged that the Palatinate and Swabian farmers, who constituted the largest part of the German Lutheran constituency in Pennsylvania, might not provide an immediate clientele for such a school. He felt, nevertheless, that a beginning must be made. With the aid of a young Dane, newly arrived in America with a law degree from the University of Halle, Kunze announced the opening of his "Seminarium" on February 15, 1773. From the announcement of its curriculum it was clear that his intention was to operate a thoroughgoing Latin school, modeled after the preparatory school at Halle for boys who had already completed the elementary levels. Greek and Latin were to be taught, but also English and German, geography and history, philosophy, mathematics, and "other sciences." Thirteen students enrolled the first year.[4]

In order to maintain the school Kunze organized "The Society for the Propagation of Christianity and Useful Knowledge among the Germans in America." Foreign patrons, societies or synods, and individuals might hold memberships. Each member was required to contribute 10 pounds to the treasury, and received the right to free tuition. The Pennsylvania Ministerium agreed to become a member, recommended the society to its congregations, and appointed a "procurator" to receive and transmit gifts from pastors or congregations.[5]

The support system designed by Kunze may well have been suggested by the variety of privately endowed institutes, mission and charity schools which prospered in the Halle area and with which he had personal experience. In any event Kunze anticipated by many years the most common pattern for the founding and initial support of Lutheran church-related colleges in America. Individuals or associations of Lutheran pastors and laypersons have characteristically taken the initiative for the establishment of such schools, soliciting private contributions, and only subsequently calling upon synods for endorsement and continuing support.

Muhlenberg himself seems to have had some misgivings about his son-in-law's ambitious plans. He therefore withheld his active support from the Seminarium, even refusing to announce the project at the public services of the congregation. His major concern was that contributions to Kunze's school might jeopardize support for the parochial school at St. Michael's and Zion. Furthermore, he feared that too strong an emphasis on scholarly preparation for ministry would delay the training of missionary pastors which he regarded as of immediate and crucial importance.[6]

A seminary "for learned school-teachers and preachers," he wrote just after Kunze's school opened, would require spacious buildings costing several thousand pounds. Furnishings would cost several more thousands, and wood and food several hundred. At least three professors would have to be maintained at 300 hundred pounds each in order "to maintain and instruct twenty to fifty pupils free of charge and manufacture them into German theoretical school teachers and pastors."

> We have here in America large English institutions of that sort, academies, colleges, and universities. In these institutions every year large crowds of young gentlemen are created bachelors, masters, licentiates, doctors of law and doctors of medicine, and they are let loose on the world. Then the poor suckers wander to and fro. They have used up their small resources and have no way of making a living. They cannot dig, to beg they are ashamed, and so they sometimes become public charges.[7]

More useful for the growth of the church, Muhlenberg wrote in his journal, would be a practical seminary,

> in which with divine help catechists could be trained and made competent and willing to teach school during the week and preach a sermon on Sundays and festival days! It would not be necessary to torment such candidates with foreign languages over a period of many years; it would be sufficient if they possess native intelligence, a compendious knowledge and experience of the marrow and sap of theology, the ability to write a tolerable hand, an understanding of the mother tongue and English, and possibly also the declensions and conjugations of the Latin language, a robust constitution able to endure every kind of food and weather, and preeminently, a heart that loves the Savior of the world and His sheep and lambs.[8]

In spite of Muhlenberg's lack of enthusiasm for Kunze's enterprise, the Seminarium continued to prosper with the support of its sponsoring society. By 1775 it had an enrollment between 20 and 25 students, but during the course of the year several students withdrew to join military organizations. The Second Continental Congress began its sessions in Philadelphia in May 1775, and warfare broke out in New England. But even through 1776, when the 13 colonies declared their independence in the old colonial statehouse nearby, the school remained in operation.

Then in September 1777, British forces under General Howe occupied the city of Philadelphia. They commandeered both St. Michael's and Zion churches and the nearby school building which had housed the Seminarium and, as Dr. Kunze's minutes book tersely states, "made an end of this institution." A courageous and forward-looking educational venture thus became a casualty of war. Had the Seminarium survived, it might well have become the first Lutheran college or, possibly, the first theological school in America. It was, in any event, the first successful attempt to transfer in institutional form the Lutheran tradition in higher education to the North American continent.

The Quest for University Chairs of Theology

After wintering in relative comfort in Philadelphia while Washington and his troops were enduring the rigors of Valley Forge only a few miles away, the British withdrew from the city in the spring of 1778. The revolutionary legislature of Pennsylvania immediately resumed authority. One of its early actions, in response to alleged Anglican and pro-British tendencies on the part of the provost and board of the College of Philadelphia, was to suspend its charter and establish in its place a new institution with the somewhat inflated title of the University of the State of Pennsylvania.[9]

By decision of the legislative assembly in 1779, the new university's board of directors included, along with various public officials, the senior ministers of the six principal religious groups in Philadelphia: Episcopal, Presbyterian, Lutheran, Reformed, Baptist, and Roman Catholic. Since Muhlenberg, during the British occupation, had moved from Philadelphia to a residence in a rural parish outside Philadelphia, Kunze, as the senior Lutheran minister remaining, became the Lutheran member of the board. His fellow members also named him to the committee to draft a plan for the university structure. Although his initial suggestion for the establishment of a professorship of divinity was tabled, the board agreed to a professorship of philology and appointed Kunze himself to this chair, with the title Professor of German and Oriental Languages. The appointment necessitated his resigning his board membership, but he was replaced by Henry Helmuth, another scholarly Halle-trained pastor who had joined Kunze in Philadelphia after a 10-year pastorate in Lancaster.

It seems clear that Kunze had in mind a university-based course of study for the preparation of Lutheran pastors. Unable to achieve this, he settled for the basic language studies he regarded as essential for a pastor, but would also provide sound preparation for law, medicine, or other learned professions. The German Society of Philadelphia, the counterpart of the earlier association that had sponsored the Seminarium, supported the new *Institut*, even underwriting the expenses of the first two students of German.[10]

But the candidates for such a course were few, and Kunze doubted whether even among the few any would go on to study theology. Apparently the situation had not changed greatly from that which Kunze had described six years earlier in a letter to the Halle fathers. "In general the Germans here are not very much interested in the sciences, for they see little opportunity for enjoying an advantage of them. Accordingly they have little idea of more extended education."[11]

A few years later Kunze was invited to New York to assist in reorganizing two congregations which had suffered greatly during the war. During his visit he happened to see the new charter of Columbia College, in which he read the following sentence: "If any congregation or individuals of whatever form of religion, will assure the University [i.e., Columbia College] an annual salary of at least two hundred bushels of wheat, a professorship of theology shall be established in that form of religion to which the donors belong, and they shall name the incumbent."[12] This was the opportunity Kunze had hoped would develop at the University of Pennsylvania, but which had failed to materialize, probably because of the prevailing unstable political climate. Although the University of Pennsylvania subsequently honored him with a doctorate of divinity (at a ceremony in which George Washington also received an honorary doctorate of laws), Kunze was deeply disappointed. When the Lutheran congregations in New York extended him a call in 1784, he accepted.

Upon his arrival in New York as pastor of the United German Lutheran Churches, Columbia College immediately recognized his scholarly standing by appointing him both as a member of its board of regents and as Professor of Oriental Languages. But his hopes for a professorship of theology fared no better than in Philadelphia. Almost a year after his arrival, he wrote to Halle, "As yet, not a student has presented himself. Meanwhile, I am using the time to improve myself in Hebrew and Arabic. But I soon hope to have some students."[13]

Two years later the situation had still not improved and he resigned his professorship. In 1792 he was reelected to the same chair, but after three more lean years, he resigned again, acknowledging that his efforts to associate the teaching of Lutheran theology with other scholarly and professional disciplines in a university framework had failed.

His successors at the University of Pennsylvania were also obliged to accept this reality. Both Helmuth and his pastoral colleague, John Frederick Schmidt, who also taught in the University's German *Institut*, were unable to offer formal theological studies. Though by 1785 more than 70 students were enrolled in German and Classical Studies, several interested in studying theology, Schmidt wrote to Halle that he and Helmuth would have to provide this opportunity privately, within the limits of their own pastoral responsibilities.[14]

The Revolutionary Climate in Education

The war for independence brought about significant social changes in the life of the American colonies. Not only were the political ties with Great Britain severed, but for many colonials independence also meant the end of aristocratic rule within the colonies themselves. Many more citizens won voting rights. New and revolutionary state governments took office. Former colonies, all asserting their independence, wrote new constitutions, adopted bills of rights, and forbade the establishment of the church.

Education, too, suddenly became important, to assure the new government of competent popular leadership. Although the colonies had a long history of collegiate education reaching back to the founding of Harvard College in 1636, neither Harvard nor any of the other eight colleges established in the colonial period were popularly oriented. At the outbreak of the Revolution, it has been estimated, only about one of every 1000 colonials had ever attended college. Even fewer had graduated.[15]

Several of the legislatures of the newly independent states took action to establish colleges, either granting charters to groups of individuals or, as in Georgia, North Carolina, and Vermont, actually authorizing state universities. While there was no effort on the part of the revolutionary state governments to exclude private initiative in the establishment of colleges, it was assumed that educational institutions serving a public function would be subject to some degree of popular control. Efforts were made in six states to bring existing colleges under state influence. Harvard and Yale were pressed to increase public membership in their corporations. King's College changed its name to Columbia, and for a time became part of a new State University of New York. The new charter creating the University of the State of Pennsylvania provided for broad public representation on its board of directors, even stipulating certain officials of the government.[16]

But the Supreme Court stepped in, handing down a decision that placed limits on government's role in higher education. The famous Dartmouth College case, argued by Daniel Webster and finally settled in 1819, was the outgrowth of continuing attempts of the State of New Hampshire to control the selection of the Dartmouth College board. Chief Justice John Marshall ruled that the college charter, granted by King George III in 1769, was a legal contract, the obligations of which could not be impaired without violating the Constitution of the United States. Attempts of the New Hampshire legislature to modify the Dartmouth charter were therefore illegal. Marshall's decision established the right of private educational institutions to elect their own trustees and to conduct their affairs without state interference. The Dartmouth case has since been cited as the legal cornerstone of private higher education in the United States and the catalyst for the founding of hundreds of denominational colleges during the 19th century.[17]

The First Lutheran College

In Pennsylvania one of the most ardent promoters of college education was the famous physician Benjamin Rush. He was by no means a radical, but he was sensitive to the political and cultural significance of the masses of German and Scotch-Irish immigrants who were at last beginning to exert their influence in elections. To provide educational opportunity for them he sought to establish a second college in the interior of Pennsylvania, removed from the dominant influence of the capital city of Philadelphia. In 1783 he was successful in securing a charter from the state legislature for Dickinson College at Carlisle.

Although it was to be a Presbyterian school, especially for Scotch-Irish youth, Rush was eager to secure the participation of the Germans as well. To achieve this, he secured the appointment of several prominent Lutheran and Reformed laypersons and clergy as trustees, including the president and secretary of the Pennsylvania Ministerium. A resolution of the Dickinson board addressed to the Ministerium reflected a mixture of patriotic and ecclesiastical concern on the part of the Presbyterian leadership. "As fellow citizens of the state," they declared, "you are equally interested with us in the success of our undertaking. Your sons, we expect, will associate with ours in Dickinson College. Your churches, we hope, will be supplied in common with ours with ministers of the gospel educated in this college, and the learned men of your body we hope will compose part of our faculty of professors."[18]

The Ministerium responded by authorizing three Lutheran trustees and promising "assistance and support, through contributions and recommendations." There is, however, no indication that these promises were ever fulfilled, or that any more positive response was made by the leadership of the German Reformed church.[19]

Disappointed but not discouraged by his failure to enlist German support for Dickinson, Rush redirected his efforts and began to urge the Germans to establish a college of their own. Identifying himself as "a Friend to Equal Liberty and Learning in Pennsylvania," he published "An Address to the Citizens of Pennsylvania of German Birth and Extraction" in the *Pennsylvania Gazette* for August 31, 1785. Noting that Germans constituted nearly one-third of the population of the state, he remarked, "They fill the treasury with their taxes, and their blood was shed liberally in the establishment of the independence of the State." Yet few of their sons "fill the learned professions or possess office in the State."[20]

Answering criticisms often directed against the Germans for clinging so doggedly to their language, Rush declared that a German college would "prepare the way for the Germans to unite more intimately with their British and Irish fellow-citizens, and thus to form, with them, one homogeneous mass of people."[21]

A positive response to Rush's letter came from several German pastors, especially Henry Helmuth and Henry Ernst Muhlenberg of the Lutheran church, and Caspar Dietrich Weiberg and Johann Wilhelm Hendel of the German Reformed church. Helmuth was already instructing a considerable number of students in the German *Institut* in Philadelphia, but he was nevertheless convinced that there should be a German institution separate from the university. The younger Henry Muhlenberg and his brother Peter, who was a member of the Supreme Executive Council of Pennsylvania, found further support among such prominent non-Lutheran leaders as Robert Morris, Thomas Mifflin, and, of course, Benjamin Rush. On December 11, 1786, the leaders petitioned for the establishment of a college at Lancaster with such "powers and privileges as are usually given to colleges," and the granting of public lands to supplement private support. The charter was granted on March 10, 1787, to Franklin College, named in honor of Benjamin Franklin, Chief Executive of the Supreme Council of Pennsylvania.

The stated purpose of the college was to diffuse knowledge so as "to preserve our present republican system of government, as well as to promote those improvements in the arts and sciences, which alone render nations respectable, great and happy." Beyond this, the college would "promote an accurate knowledge of the German and English languages, also the learned languages of mathematics, moral and natural philosophy, divinity, and all other such branches of literature as will tend to make good men and useful citizens."[22]

The founders of Franklin College thus gave initial expression to one of the distinctive motives for the founding of Lutheran colleges in North America throughout the next 100 years, namely, the equipping of ethnic immigrant groups to become full participants in the community life of their adopted land. The further claim that education for responsible and useful citizenship was best attainable through a curriculum based on the liberal arts sounded yet another theme which would characterize much of future Lutheran higher education in North America.

The governance plan for Franklin College provided for 45 trustees, of whom 15 should be Lutheran, 15 Reformed, and 15 from "any other society of Christians." Seven Lutherans and seven Reformed clergy were named as charter members of the board. Non-Lutheran members included several prominent political leaders of the Commonwealth: Benjamin Rush, Thomas Mifflin, Thomas McKean, Robert Morris, George Clymer, and William Bingham.[23]

On June 6, 1787, while the federal Constitutional Convention was in session in Philadelphia, Franklin College opened in Lancaster. Members of the Pennsylvania Ministerium and the German Reformed Synod, both of which were meeting in Lancaster at the time, marched together in solemn procession to Trinity Lutheran Church, where Henry Ernst Muhlenberg, son of Henry Melchior Muhlenberg, was inaugurated as first president of the first college chartered in North America in which Lutheran leadership was exercised.[24]

However, in spite of its impressive roster of sponsors, generous initial gifts by Benjamin Franklin and others, and a grant of 10,000 acres of public land in northern Pennsylvania, Franklin College did not prosper. Very few German youth from the rural parishes were able or willing to enroll in college-level study, especially in the English language. The sponsoring church organizations provided little or no practical support, and no funds were allocated by the state legislature. Under these conditions competent faculty could not be retained and the high scholastic standards which had been projected had to be abandoned. Although the college maintained a corporate existence until 1850, it never granted a baccalaureate degree.[25]

The Beginnings of Hartwick

While Franklin College was struggling through its first discouraging years, a most unusual sequence of events was moving toward an historic meeting in the Albany Coffee House in New York City, a meeting that would result in the founding of the first Lutheran theological seminary in North America. Participating in this meeting on September 15, 1797, were three distinguished personalities, Jeremiah van Rensselaer of Albany, scion of the great Dutch landholding family of the Hudson Valley; Frederick Augustus Conrad Muhlenberg of Philadelphia, son of the Lutheran patriarch and the first elected Speaker of the United States House of Representatives; and John Christopher Kunze, pastor of Trinity Lutheran Church, Manhattan, erstwhile professor of Oriental Languages at Columbia College and president of the recently founded New York Ministerium.

Van Rensselaer and Muhlenberg were the appointed executors of the estate of John Christopher Hartwick, an eccentric Lutheran pastor who had died the previous year. In his will Hartwick had bequeathed his extensive landed estate in the Cooperstown area in upstate New York to Jesus Christ as chief heir. Specifically, he had directed that an educational institution be established for the preparation of ministers and missionaries and for the instruction of Indians.[26]

Hartwick was a theological graduate of the University of Halle who had crossed the Atlantic in 1746 in response to a call from the German Lutheran congregations in the Hudson Valley town of Rhinebeck. He served there only briefly and in fact had difficulty in remaining long in any of the succession of parishes he served, because of his frequent absences, prickly personality, untidy personal habits, and poorly delivered sermons. But he got on well with the neighboring Indians. Chiefs of the Mohawk nation sold him a 36-square-mile tract of land on the edge of the Catskill Mountains, title to which was confirmed by royal patent in 1761.

On this land he intended to establish his training institutions and also to develop colonies of settlers who would pledge to live as Christians and loyal members of the church. However, since he moved so frequently, he was unable to administer his estate personally. He therefore appointed a man named William Cooper as his agent. Over the course of 30 years Cooper, the father of James Fenimore Cooper, managed by shrewd dealings to gain title for himself to most of Hartwick's land. At the age of 82, while visiting at Clermont-on-the-Hudson, the home of Robert Livingston, who would later negotiate the Louisiana Purchase, Hartwick died.[27] His will, which he carried in his saddlebags, was placed in the hands of Jeremiah van Rensselaer, whom he had designated as one of his executors.[28]

It was to carry out the terms of this document that the historic meeting took place in the Albany Coffee House in New York City. Hartwick had directed that the land remaining in his patent should be formed into a regular town, but since most of the land had already been sold or leased, the executors decided that this would not be practicable. Instead they agreed that the remaining resources should be applied immediately to the establishment of a theological and missionary institute.

The location of the school was not immediately determined, but a faculty of three was appointed so that instruction might begin without delay. Dr. Kunze was appointed Director and Professor of Theology at a salary of $500 per year. It was agreed that he would remain with his congregation in New York and teach in his home. In charge of the preparatory course was the Reverend Anthony Braun, pastor of Ebenezer Lutheran Church in Albany, a former Roman Catholic missionary to the Indians. Given the title of Professor, Braun undertook to give collegiate-level instruction in the languages and sciences and also Christian instruction to any Indians who might present themselves. He, too, was to teach in his home. The third faculty member, the Reverend John Frederick Ernst, pastor at Athens, New York, was to settle on the Hartwick tract as pastor and teacher on the more elementary levels. Two other men were named as potential professors of mathematics, natural and moral philosophy, and learned languages, but their appointments were held in abeyance until a seminary building could be erected.

Kunze began theological instruction immediately in his Manhattan parsonage and thus formally launched Hartwick Seminary as a Lutheran theological school. Until Kunze's death in 1807, instruction continued, though very few students were enrolled. One reason for the small numbers undoubtedly was that the seminary had no permanent location. Unsuccessful efforts were made to establish it in New York City, in Albany, in Schoharie, and in Cooperstown.

Finally, all efforts having foundered and the original executors of the Hartwick will having died, the new executor conferred with the officers of the New York Ministerium and decided in 1811 to establish the seminary where Hartwick had originally intended—on his own land. There, in a rural valley in Otsego County, about four miles from Cooperstown, a building was erected for the seminary and a new brick house of 13 rooms for the professor. In 1815, in this isolated community with only a scattered few Lutheran residents

Hartwick Seminary finally found a home, bringing together at last under a single roof its academic, collegiate, and theological departments. Eight years later, in 1823, it retrieved Hartwick's personal library of 400 volumes that had been placed in the care of Union College in Schenectady at the time of Hartwick's death.[29]

Rationalism in America

The limited success of these efforts at Lutheran institution building in the closing years of the 18th century must not be judged too harshly. Even in the best of times the founding of colleges and seminaries has demanded unusual levels of courage and persistence on the part of committed leaders. But the final two decades of the 18th century witnessed the lowest ebb of spiritual vitality in the entire history of the American people.[30] War seldom builds spirituality either among its participants or its victims, and the American Revolution was no exception. Parish life was disrupted as men were called away for military service. Many church buildings suffered damage. Political divisions between Tories and Patriots split congregations.

Even more significant was the religious chill which settled over the churches, both in Europe and America, as the age of pietism gave way to the age of rationalism. In its less aggressive form rationalism simply undertook to affirm the validity of the Christian faith on the grounds of its reasonableness. In its more aggressive manifestations rationalist theology subjected the basic Christian doctrines to the test of reason, discarding those which failed to meet the test, and often emerged with a bloodless residue of moralistic admonitions. Its most advanced exponents acknowledged only a distant and impersonal God, who handled the management of the universe through a set of natural laws that could be discovered and understood by reasonable human beings and employed by them to build a peaceful and orderly society. This was essentially the "gospel" embodied in the Declaration of Independence and otherwise eloquently proclaimed by such American deists as Thomas Jefferson, Ethan Allen, and Thomas Paine.

In Europe the roots of rationalism lay deep within the scientific revolution introduced by Copernicus, Galileo, and Newton and interpreted in philosophical and political terms by John Locke and his contemporaries in the late 17th and early 18th centuries. By the end of the 18th century it found its most radical political expression in the French Revolution. Its theological impact in Europe was demonstrated in the erosion of the evangelical fervor fomented earlier in England through the revivals of John Wesley and in Germany through the work of Spener and the Franckes. By an ironic turn of events, the University of Halle, which had been the wellspring of pietism and missionary outreach—not least for American Lutheranism—had become by 1780 the fountainhead of rationalistic theology in Germany.

One of the cultural effects of the War for Independence was the wave of popularity for all things French which swept the country. Victory had been secured with French assistance. Lafayette became a national hero. And, shortly after American independence had been won, France had a revolution of its own, modeled at least philosophically on the same premises as the American Revolution.

The teaching of French began as early as 1779 and spread quickly through American collegiate curricula, often as a substitute for Greek. French philosophy was heady fare for students. Students at Harvard in the 1790s boasted of being atheists. At Princeton undergraduate deists held a Bible burning. Open indifference—if not open opposition—to religion was in vogue.

This was true not only on college campuses. Churches, too, felt the impact of religious indifference. The Anglican Church, already stigmatized by the Toryism of virtually its entire clergy, was most severely infiltrated by rationalism, and was regenerated by a few loyal and devout leaders only with great difficulty.

Lutherans also felt the impact of European rationalism. By the time Kunze and Helmuth came to Pennsylvania, the younger Francke was dead (1769) and the university at Halle had already moved away from its earlier pietism. Although both men were loyal to the Lutheran confessions, Kunze's differences with Muhlenberg on the essentials of ministerial education suggest that the fires of Halle pietism had measurably subsided since Muhlenberg began his missionary career 25 years earlier.

Rationalist influence among Lutheran clergy manifested itself not in any flagrant embrace of deism or denial of divine revelation, but in a general toning down of Lutheran convictions and the modification of certain traditional Lutheran practices. Such tendencies were evident, for example, in the liturgy and hymnal published by the New York Ministerium in 1817. The liturgy published the following year by the Pennsylvania Ministerium virtually eliminated congregational responses and the traditional observances of the church year.[31]

The most learned, controversial, and easily identifiable Lutheran rationalist in America was Frederick Henry Quitman. A student of John S. Semler, the "father of rationalism" at Halle, Quitman arrived in New York in 1795, after several years as a missionary in the Dutch West Indies. He served various congregations in New York for 30 years. After Dr. Kunze's death in 1807 Quitman was elected president of the New York Ministerium and held that office for 21 years.

His catechism of 1814, intended to replace that of Luther, was based on the assumption that "the grounds of rational belief are natural perception, the authority of competent witnesses, and the unquestionable arguments of reason."[32] His zeal for rationalism, however, apparently failed to reach deeply into the congregations, for in 1824 he expressed disappointment at the large number of copies which still remained unsold. The short life of the like-minded *Helmstedt Catechism* in North Carolina in the 1780s also suggests that Lutheran doctrinal loyalties were not easily undermined, even in the heyday of popular rationalist ideology.

More of a hazard to a vigorous Lutheranism was the tendency to minimize denominational identities which accompanied the general religious apathy. The New York Ministerium declared in 1797 that it would not acknowledge a new Lutheran church in places where Episcopal services were available and actually initiated negotiations for merger with the Episcopal Church.[33] In Pennsylvania and Delaware the entire Swedish Lutheran Church went over to the Episcopalians. In Pennsylvania the German language had always provided a particular bond between Lutherans and Reformed; in many instances they had shared church buildings. Even after the failure of their common venture in Franklin College, the two churches tried, again without success, to establish a joint theological seminary. As late as 1817 both Lutheran and Reformed synods endorsed a "Common Hymnal" to replace the Muhlenberg Hymnal. In the new unionistic climate their common roots drew Moravians and Lutheran pietists closer together. The first secretary of the Lutheran synod of North Carolina, Gottlieb Shober, was a Moravian, and Ernest Hazelius, who became professor of theology at Hartwick Seminary in 1815, received his early training as a Moravian, though he was later ordained as a Lutheran.

During these years of revolution, war, and political readjustment, the supply of Lutheran clergy from Europe virtually dried up. The last Halle missionary came in 1786, and after the Revolution began no further help could be expected from the Lutheran court chaplains in London.

The churches were therefore almost entirely dependent upon an indigenous supply of new clergy. Even before the Revolution, when immigration outran the missionary zeal of the mother church, the system of private apprenticeships had been introduced. Well-trained pastors, specially designated by the Ministerium for the task of teaching, guided promising young men in language and theological studies. In 1792 the constitution of the Pennsylvania Ministerium formalized a procedure whereby candidates were carefully examined by experienced pastors and given initial approval as catechists. After a probationary period, the synod granted them a limited license to preach. Only upon final approval and receipt of a call from a congregation or from the synod could a candidate qualify for ordination. This system became the standard transitional stage in the ministerial training program for the Lutheran church in

America between its period of European dependency and its ecclesiastical maturity.

The delay in this transitional process was not caused by a lack of competent and motivated Lutheran scholars and teachers. Both Columbia and the University of Pennsylvania had eagerly sought the scholarly services of men like Kunze, Helmuth, and Schmidt. But these men and the dozens of others who trained several generations of Lutheran clergy in their homes and studies were also full-time pastors, often serving several congregations, and undertaking missionary journeys to preaching places in frontier communities. Largely university trained themselves, they maintained the Lutheran tradition of a well-educated and confessionally conscious clergy. In so doing they prepared the way for the formal system of higher education that would develop as the Lutheran church in America gained in strength and maturity.[34]

4 THE ROAD
TO GETTYSBURG

Colleges for a New Nation

As in most other aspects of this nation's history, the American Revolution forms a great watershed in the history of American higher education. The colonial period is by definition the period of dependency on Europe in virtually every respect, including college education. Over the course of 150 years nine collegiate institutions were founded in the American colonies, all of them modeled on the English pattern.

But from the independence of the new nation to the Civil War, a period half as long as the colonial era, more than 700 institutions of higher learning were established in North America. While all bore some structural resemblance to the English residential colleges, their style and character were so strongly reflective of a new age, a new nation, and new impulses that it is only fitting to describe their founding and growth as part of a clearly identifiable and distinctive American college movement.

Only about 25% of these colleges survived, but even their high mortality rate is dramatically descriptive of a new age in America that placed a high value on all freedoms—even the freedom to fail! But lest this be understood only as an age of many failures, it must be noted that 182 colleges founded in these same years have survived to the present day as permanent parts of an American system of higher education unique in the world.[1]

Of course, many of the same educational and cultural developments in America would eventually have taken place even if the Revolution had not occurred when it did. Most American historians agree that the political separation finalized in the treaty of 1783 only ratified the social and cultural split be-

tween England and the colonies that had been widening for many years. Three thousand miles of ocean and the impact of the American wilderness in shaping values, institutions, and attitudes could hardly be expected to produce any other result. Indeed, the process of estrangement may even have begun as early as 1630, when the colonists of Massachusetts Bay first formed themselves into a self-governing commonwealth.

That the trend toward self-reliance was under way in higher education well before the Revolution is demonstrated by the founding of six new colleges in the 30 years between 1746 and 1776, each one in response to a set of special American circumstances. Following the Declaration of Independence came a stronger demand for popular legislative control of all educational institutions—a new departure in American higher education that from its beginning had been conducted almost entirely under religious auspices.

One of the most dramatic expressions of the new sense of public concern for education was the passage of the Land Ordinance of 1785 by the United States Congress even before the Federal Constitution came into being. It provided for the survey and sale of public lands in the western territories that became a part of the new nation in 1783 and set aside one section of land in each township for the support of public schools. Since its principle was adopted as standard practice as the nation moved westward, the Ordinance of 1785 has been properly recognized as one of the important landmarks in the history of American public education. Not so well known is the fact that Congress also applied this principle to the support of public universities when it made subsequent land grants and sales, long before the passage of the famed Morrill Act of 1862. This benevolent stance toward higher education resulted in the founding of eight state universities before 1816, all of which are still in operation.[2] But the major task of promoting higher education in the United States from the

Revolution to the Civil War was not to be borne either by the states or the federal government. The American college movement was carried forward by private individuals and associations, operating for the most part as agents of religious denominations.

The Religious Impulse

It is ironic that a series of religious developments which occurred during a period of low spiritual vitality, and which were themselves expressions of religious apathy, should have created the setting for a resurgence of churchly activity in America. In states where religious conformity had been enforced by law since colonial times, freedom to profess any religion, or no religion at all, now was assured. Particularly in states where the Anglican church had been a privileged institution, church and state were effectively separated. European ties which had served as lifelines of support for several churches were severed, and these orphaned groups were forced to organize into "denominations" and to depend upon the voluntary support of the laity.

Such developments would have been unthinkable in the highly charged religious climate in which most of the colonies had been founded, or even 50 years before the War of Independence began. But a revolution which expressed its rationale in the philosophy of the Enlightenment and many of whose leaders were Deists could view disestablishment and the dissolution of links with Old World churches as welcome signs of liberation from religious restraints. Because these old patterns of privilege and dependency were destroyed, the way was opened for new religious leadership to break through the pall of religious apathy and to launch their mission of evangelism on the opening frontiers of the great West.[3]

The instrument through which the churches were rejuvenated and empowered to bring in the "golden day of democratic evangelicalism"[4] was the Second Great Awakening. It is not easy to identify the precise point at which this phenomenon began nor fully to isolate or evaluate its effects. It appeared almost simultaneously in widely separated areas of the country and expressed itself in a variety of external patterns. Its earliest manifestations in the parishes of Connecticut were followed in 1801 by a college-wide revival at Yale. Under the earnest preaching of President Timothy Dwight, one-third of the entire student body was converted. The New England visitations were not accompanied by the emotional excesses that characterized the wave of revivals that began at Gasper River and Cane Ridge in Kentucky in the summer of 1800 under the preaching of James McGready and Barton Stone. These tumultuous, frequently hysterical camp meetings gathered thousands of people in the forest clearings and built to a climax of individual and mass intensity through six or seven days and nights of unremitting exhortation. Great numbers of the "slain" rose up as "new creatures" to swell the membership especially of the Methodist and Baptist churches of the western frontier.[5]

The impulses from the New England Awakening also flowed into the West, where land-hungry easterners and European immigrants were rapidly populating new states and territories. Of particular significance in the story of the American college movement is the fact that eastern institutions of higher learning were intimately involved in the effort to evangelize the West. Not only were Yale and Williams and Princeton centers in which the Awakening itself found expression. These colleges also provided leadership for the network of voluntary associations which served as instruments for promoting the evangelization of the West and eventually the spiritual and cultural enrichment of the entire nation. Graduates of Yale had a hand in founding at least 16 colleges before the Civil War, and a Presbyterian historian claims that Princeton sponsored 25.[6]

Although there is little question that the overwhelming initiative in the founding of virtually all American colleges before 1860 was religious in origin, ecclesiastical organizations played only a minor role in the process. In most cases the organized, voluntaristic structures known in America as "denominations" came into being only after the American Revolution had severed the ties of religious dependency on Europe. Episcopalians, Methodists, and Roman Catholics all founded their American organizations in the immediate postwar years. Congregationalists and Baptists were by definition locally oriented. Presbyterians and Lutherans had only begun to develop their synodical structures in prerevolutionary years.

Before 1830 most colleges were founded by individuals, societies, or groups of individuals who professed to be Baptists or Presbyterians or Congregationalists, but the college founders were not agents of an ecclesiastical authority. Nor was the number of institutions founded before 1830 especially large. Presbyterians and Congregationalists were most active, but together they founded only 10 permanent colleges between 1800 and 1830.[7]

The American College Movement

During the three decades preceding the Civil War, however, the college movement virtually exploded across the frontier, still remaining in private, largely religious hands. Of the 182 permanent collegiate institutions founded before the Civil War 133 were established between 1830 and 1860. Presbyterians and Congregationalists continued their earlier activity, often jointly. Methodists and Baptists entered the field with great vigor, especially after 1830, founding 21 and 30 permanent colleges respectively before the Civil War. The Methodists even stepped in to rejuvenate faltering Presbyterian institutions such as Dickinson and Allegheny Colleges. And for every successful venture in college founding, according to Donald Tewksbury's research, there were four failures.[8]

The reasons for this rapid proliferation of colleges are varied. For the denominations which placed strong emphasis upon an educated ministry, Presbyterians, Reformed, Congregationalists, Episcopalians, and Lutherans, colleges were first established to provide such leadership. Methodists and Baptists, who generally opposed the ideal of a highly educated ministry, especially in their early history, entered the field later. Beyond the missionary concern of all denominations for the evangelization of the frontier, there was an increasing popular, even patriotic conviction that learning was essential to progress, economic success, and upward mobility. Eager to share corporately in such blessings, communities vied to have colleges established in their midst because of the prestige the very presence of such institutions would bring.[9]

It was actually this proliferation of colleges, independently founded but professing some denominational identity, that brought church organizations into direct and responsible relationship with the colleges. The financial panic of 1837 took a heavy toll among the struggling frontier colleges, and sent many of them to eastern sources seeking relief from accumulated indebtedness. Unable to meet all these requests individually, rescuers in New England in 1843 proposed a cooperative plan for aiding the western colleges. They formed the Society for the Promotion of Collegiate and Theological Education at the West, to assist colleges and seminaries, but also to establish conditions on which aid should be given.[10]

This organization, established largely under Congregational auspices, became the first denominational agency to affirm any corporate responsibility toward colleges claiming religious identity. In keeping with Congregational polity it was a private society rather than an ecclesiastical agency but it established the basis upon which other denominations would eventually establish responsible relationships with colleges desiring to be church-related. As the denominations became stronger and more assertive of their identity, they sought ways of bringing their related institutions under supervision and control. The Presbyterian Church USA established a Board of Education as early as 1819 for the limited purpose of aiding needy students, but in 1848 extended its responsibilities to include institutions. The United Presbyterians followed in 1859, the Baptists in 1888, and the Methodists in 1892. The General Synod of the Evangelical Lutheran Church was the first of the Lutheran bodies to establish a Board of Education in 1885.[11]

The prevailing trend in the relationship between churches and colleges of virtually all denominations after the middle of the 19th century, and even into the 20th century, was toward greater church involvement and control. Eligibility standards for recognition and for financial assistance established by church boards required that the president of the college and certain percentages of its trustees be members of the sponsoring denomination and, in some cases, that they be elected by a denominational convention or synod. In several instances denominational pressure was exerted to induce a college to move to a location more strategic for the denomination. New institutions founded without denominational sanction could not expect financial support. While it is true that a strong trend toward secularism was invading all of American society as the end of the 19th century approached, and that all colleges and universities felt its impact, the relationships between denominational colleges and their sponsoring churches were being strengthened rather than weakened during these same years.[12]

Lutherans Enter the College Movement

The involvement of Lutherans in the main currents of religious life in 19th-century America has received scant attention from general church historians. Nor have Lutheran historians made serious attempts to relate developments within their church to the wider religious history of this country. The explanation lies at least partially in the fact that from its beginnings in America the Lutheran church was a foreign-language church, and that its growth, even throughout the 19th century, has come about largely through the immigration of non-English-speaking people and the productivity of their families. In addition to these linguistic and ethnic singularities, a strong sense of historic Lutheran identity was reinforced during the latter half of the 19th century by new currents of confessional Lutheran theology from Germany and Scandinavia. Debate among Lutherans has tended to revolve around questions of doctrinal faithfulness rather than the social and political issues which more frequently exercised other American denominations.

Virtually all other denominations, with the exception of smaller German groups and some Roman Catholics, were English-speaking and therefore able to exercise a broader popular appeal, largely through revivalistic methods. Methodists, Baptists, and Presbyterians thus grew rapidly in frontier America to become the largest of Protestant denominations. English-speaking settlers who moved from the eastern seaboard states also assumed political and cultural leadership in the newer western communities, while German and Scandinavian immigrants were being torn between safeguarding their European heritage and finding their place in a new and strange environment.

Nevertheless, Lutherans did become significantly involved in the college movement common to nearly all American denominations. More than 20 colleges, 10 of which are still flourishing, were established under Lutheran auspices before the Civil War. Motives for their founding were similar to those of other denominations which placed high value on an educated clergy, and they also reflected common concerns for patriotism, Americanization, vocational and professional training, and community building.

In their initial permanent institutional venture Lutherans demonstrated the centrality of their historic concern for a theologically well-grounded ministry by founding a seminary first. Gettysburg Seminary, founded in 1826, was the parent of Pennsylvania College, chartered six years later, in 1832. Although the curriculum of the college offered a variety of opportunities, its primary purpose was to provide the linguistic and literary foundation for the study of theology.

Credit for this pioneering achievement belongs to a brilliant young Lutheran pastor, Samuel Simon Schmucker. Following graduation from the University of Pennsylvania he served a theological tutorial under his own father. Before becoming a candidate for ordination himself, Schmucker also studied for 19 months at the recently established Princeton Theological Seminary. This exposure left some Puritan imprint on his theology and confirmed some of the pietistic tendencies inherent in his own heritage, but also focused his attention on the need for specifically Lutheran institutions of higher learning. When he left Princeton at the age of 20, he confided to his journal that his three "earnest desires" for the welfare of the Lutheran church in America were to translate "one eminent system of Lutheran Dogmatics," to establish a seminary, and to found a college.[13] By the time he reached age 33 he had fulfilled all three of these desires.

The Seminary at Gettysburg

About the time of Schmucker's ordination into the ministry, developments within the church were in process that would provide both the setting and the opportunity for his historic role as the founder of Lutheran institutions. As the new nation had expanded, so also had the church. Two additional Lutheran synods had come into being outside the boundaries of the original Pennsylvania Ministerium: New York in 1792 and North Carolina in 1803. The Ministerium itself had established outlying "conferences" in Ohio, and in Maryland and Virginia, that by 1820 had constituted themselves as independent synods. In 1820 four of these synods met to organize a General Synod, a federative structure which sought to provide some sense of unity among all American Lutherans. Although its constitution acknowledged virtually complete local synodical autonomy, the Ohio and Tennessee Synods remained cautiously aloof. Within two years the New York and Pennsylvania Ministeriums had also withdrawn, responding to fears of members who saw the General Synod as "an aristocratic spiritual congress" threatening to impose on them the horrors of ecclesiastical despotism.[14]

The General Synod might easily have succumbed to these exaggerated fears of centralized authority had not Samuel Schmucker urged the remaining synods, including his own Synod of Maryland and Virginia, to persevere and to hold conventions in 1823 and 1825. One of the basic objectives of the General Synod expressed in the constituting convention of 1820 was the establishment of "seminaries of education," and it was Schmucker's deep interest in the founding of a Lutheran theological seminary that spurred his efforts to keep the organization alive. Both aims received further encouragement in 1825 when pastors and congregations west of the Susquehanna River broke away from the Pennsylvania Ministerium, formed the West Pennsylvania Synod, and joined the General Synod.[15]

In 1824 Schmucker gathered a group of six young men in his parsonage at New Market, Virginia, and for 10 months directed their study of theology. When in a sermon delivered before the Synod of Maryland and Virginia he described his work and urged that his students become the nucleus of a general church institution, several young pastors determined to bring the matter before the next synod convention in 1825. Among these pastors were Charles Philip Krauth and Benjamin Kurtz, who, together with Schmucker, were subsequently appointed by the synod "to report a plan for the immediate organization of a theological seminary."[16] When their plan, authored by Schmucker, was presented to the convention of the General Synod two weeks later, it was also adopted by that body.

The initiative for the establishment of Gettysburg Seminary thus came from the Synod of Maryland and Virginia, with the added support of the new West Pennsylvania Synod, on whose territory the seminary would eventually be located. The General Synod responded to the challenge and appointed agents, even promising to pay their expenses, to travel throughout the United States to solicit contributions for the seminary. Appointments were not limited to constituent synods of the General Synod, but individuals were invited from all synods. Benjamin Kurtz was even commissioned to travel in Europe to solicit funds and books for the proposed seminary. The enthusiasm and persistence of Samuel Schmucker had at last catalyzed the long-simmering Lutheran yearning for a seminary for the entire Lutheran church in America. It seemed only proper that this dynamic young pastor should be named by the newly elected board of directors as the first professor of the new seminary.[17]

Much remained to be done before instruction could begin. While the quest for money and books went on, a location had to be determined for the school. This crucial decision was reached through a process already well established among American colleges and seminaries and destined to become virtually standard for future Lutheran institutions as well. Several communities were invited to enter bids, involving pledges of cash, land, and buildings. Accessibility, health factors, and promise of future community growth were also given careful consideration. After study, hearings, and site visits an authorized committee made its decision, accepting the bid of Gettysburg over those of Hagerstown, Maryland, and Carlisle, Pennsylvania. The offer of $7000 and use of vacant Gettysburg Academy facilities until permanent quarters could be built promised opportunity for an early opening of the new seminary. Instruction began on September 5, 1826.[18]

The Founding of Pennsylvania College

When the first students assembled, Schmucker discovered that most had little foundation in either classical or scientific studies. In vain he tried to make up deficiencies through private tutoring. By the year's end the trustees decided to establish a classical school in the same building as the seminary.

Two years later, when the Academy building was put up for sheriff's sale, Schmucker personally bought the property for $1,160, thus assuring its continued use by the seminary as well as the preparatory school. To enlist wider church involvement he asked 20 of his Lutheran clerical colleagues to give $50 each for the support and enlargement of the classical school and the repurchase of the Academy building. In return they could elect the trustees of the school and enroll their children without paying tuition.

A new prospectus, circulated from Philadelphia to Charleston, announced the expansion of the course of study to five years and the addition of a scientific department with its own instructor. The school was renamed the Gettysburg Gymnasium, its five-year curriculum resembling the German pattern for a university preparatory school, roughly equivalent to a classical preparatory school and two or three years of college work. Courses taught included five years of Greek and Latin, four years of mathematics through calculus, ancient and modern geography, philosophy, political economy, moral philosophy, English grammar, and rhetoric.[19]

Not only did these improvements upgrade the quality of preseminary preparation, but they also attracted enough nontheological students that the new institution was obliged to expand. After two years, Schmucker called together a group of leading citizens of Gettysburg and Adams County and secured their support of a plan to turn the Gymnasium into a full-fledged college and to seek a charter from the Pennsylvania legislature. He described his intention to establish a college on the American model, with a broad appeal, aimed to meet the needs of any qualified person, ''unsectarian in its instructions, but at the same time. . .prevailingly under Lutheran influence and control.''[20]

With the backing of this local committee Schmucker journeyed to Harrisburg to seek a charter for the college. Upon arrival he discovered that it was customary for the state to issue charters as acts of the legislature and not as separate documents. Consequently, he was obliged to spend several days reviewing available charters, especially those of Lafayette and Dickinson Colleges. These charters provided the models, both in substance and in language, for the legislation which Schmucker drafted for Pennsylvania College. In keeping with the common practice in all Pennsylvania college charters since 1780, no reference was made to a denominational affiliation. His proposed charter provided that in the selection of teachers, trustees, and students, no person should be rejected because of "conscientious persuasion in matters of religion."[21] However, since most of the "patrons" of the college who would choose the trustees were the Lutheran pastors who had advanced the money to establish the Gettysburg Gymnasium, there was little danger of the college's being controlled by other than Lutherans.

Considerable opposition was voiced in the legislature by those who feared that approval of the charter would constitute an invitation to the college to seek state funding as well. Since it was already an established policy of the state to help finance institutions of higher learning, the fear was well founded. Still other legislators frowned on all institutions of higher learning on the grounds that only the sons of the wealthy could attend and that such exclusiveness was "contrary to the spirit of the Constitution and the genius of our government."[22]

Schmucker countered the opposition by distributing formally signed petitions among pastors and friends who forwarded them with signatures to members of the legislature. He also delivered an address before the legislators in support of the charter. According to his own account he based his plea on "the claims of the Germans in Pennsylvania to legislative sanctions in the establishment of a college for their Anglicised descendants."[23] Beyond this the charter promised that the college would train teachers competent in both German and English, for service in the emerging Pennsylvania public school system. Schmucker's appeal to the German vote, together with the support he received from Governor George Wolf, himself a German Lutheran, carried the day. The charter of Pennsylvania College at Gettysburg won final approval on April 7, 1832.[24]

According to the charter, the college corporation consisted of the "patrons" who had been subscribers for the Gettysburg Gymnasium, and the Gettysburg citizens who had assisted Schmucker in his efforts to secure a college charter. Five of these men became "patrons" by subscribing $25 each to the new institution, and thereby also became qualified to participate in the election of the 21 members of the original college board of trustees.

The organization meeting of the board was held on July 4, 1832, and was preceded by a gala public event that featured a procession directed by military marshals and led by the Gettysburg Guards. The published order of march listed "Strangers and Citizens," "Invited Strangers," students of the gymnasium and the seminary, teachers, professors, clergy, patrons, and finally "The Orator of the Day, accompanied by the Officiating Clergymen." The procession began at the Academy building and terminated in the Presbyterian Church where the Honorable Calvin Blythe, Harrisburg judge and one of the college's distinguished supporters, delivered the oration.[25]

The college opened officially on November 7, 1832, with an enrollment of 65 students, including 23 in the college and 40 in the preparatory department. The first faculty consisted of the two teachers of the gymnasium, Michael Jacobs and Henry L. Baugher, and the two seminary professors, Samuel Schmucker and Ernest Hazelius, both of whom contributed their services without compensation. The local Episcopal clergyman, Rev. J. H. Marsden, was invited to teach botany and mineralogy. Until Charles Philip Krauth was chosen as president in 1834,[26] one of the professors served as chairman of the faculty.

Principles and Programs

Since this institution was the first permanent college established by Lutherans in North America,[27] its founding marking the point at which Lutherans formally became participants in the American stream of collegiate education, it may be well to take special note of its character and the factors which brought it into being.

Pennsylvania College[28] was first and foremost the product of the historic concern of Lutherans for a well-educated and carefully trained ministry. The college grew directly out of the experience of the founders of Gettysburg Seminary, who found in their first students serious deficiencies in academic preparation. Schmucker's call for a classical academy, and subsequently for a gymnasium and a college, echoed Martin Luther's insistence upon the reform of the 16th-century Latin schools to assure substantial preparation of candidates for theological study in the German universities. Luther's emphasis has become an integral part of the Lutheran tradition in higher education, expressed in the subsequent founding of nearly every Lutheran college in North America.

If the curriculum reflected the traditions of the Old World, the sponsorship of the college conformed to the ways of the New. Although founded by Lutherans and controlled by Lutherans, Gettysburg College was independent of any formal ecclesiastical control. In this respect it reflected the prevailing pattern among religiously oriented colleges founded in the United States at this particular time. The pattern was partly rooted in economic practicalities and partly in the religious climate of the time. The synodical structures of Lutheranism were in no position to undertake the financial support of a college; even the seminary had to depend almost entirely upon the solicited gifts of individuals. The same was to a great extent true of institutions related to other denominations as well.

Schmucker's expressed intent that the college should be "unsectarian in instruction," though under Lutheran auspices, reflected not only his personal conviction, but also the common emphasis in the founding of collegiate institutions by Presbyterians, Baptists, Congregationalists, Reformed, and others. Only in the 1840s and 1850s did the "era of good feelings" among American denominations begin to break down into competitive and often destructive rivalries. Part of the later rivalry was expressed in denominational efforts to assert control over existing colleges and to found new institutions in order to "capture" territories and converts.[29]

In many respects Gettysburg College was an integral part of the American college movement that embraced colleges of all denominations. Its founder was a graduate of Princeton Seminary whence had emerged a strong impulse for college founding. Lutherans had already been involved in two previous collegiate ventures, Dickinson and Franklin, though neither of them had met with marked success. Lutheran clergy involved in the Gettysburg schools were graduates of Jefferson and Dickinson Colleges and of the University of Pennsylvania.[30] An invitation to Daniel Webster, legal counsel in the famous Dartmouth College case, to address the public event celebrating the charter of Gettysburg College, though not accepted, further reflected Schmucker's sensitivity to the American college scene.

Much of the rhetoric heard from speakers' rostrums as colleges were being founded during the youthful years of the Republic sounded the optimistic notes of progress and national pride. Education was extolled as the key to a prosperous future for state and nation, and, if allied with religion, the promoter of both individual and public virtue and morality. The oration delivered by Judge Calvin Blythe of Harrisburg at the charter celebration on the Fourth of July gave clear witness that in this respect also Gettysburg College was a child of its times.[31]

One of the factors infrequently recognized in the establishment of the college, and indeed in the life of the Lutheran church of that time and place, was the intensely political climate characteristic of the Commonwealth of Pennsylvania, within which the German element had only begun to wield influence commensurate with its size.

Schmucker was fully aware of this political dimension when he went to Harrisburg to seek a charter for Gettysburg College from the state legislature. The charter provision that there should always be a professor of German at the college confirms the distinctive ethnic dimension in the character of the college. Gettysburg College thus established one of the hallmarks of Lutheran higher education in America, namely, the special character of almost all the colleges in the Lutheran tradition as conservators of a European ethnic heritage. At Gettysburg College it was a German tradition; later Lutheran colleges would channel the traditions of Norway, Sweden, Denmark, and Finland into the cultural life of America.

Finally, the role of both seminary and college at Gettysburg must be understood in the theological and intellectual context of the 1820s and 1830s. Samuel Schmucker and his associates represented in part what has been described as the "countervailing" character of Lutheran theology and practice in relation to the patriotic Puritanism and revivalism which emerged in America after the Second Great Awakening.[32] But they also absorbed some of the characteristics of the popular theology. Schmucker had studied at Princeton, where the presence of John Witherspoon—who had brought the philosophy of Scottish Realism to America—was still very much alive. This philosophy had softened the sharp edges of radical rationalism but had left a residue of indifference toward confessional standards that seriously weakened the sense of identity among the mainline churches. There is no doubt that some of these tendencies were prevalent in Schmucker's emphasis on "unsectarianism" and his inclusion in the curriculum of both the gymnasium and the college such currently standard college courses as Moral Philosophy, Natural Theology, and the Evidences of Christianity. Nevertheless, the curriculum of the college clearly reflected the intention of providing the basic biblical languages for pretheological students. It also incorporated philosophy, mathematics through calculus, English grammar, rhetoric, and natural philosophy. Well in advance of later popular trends, several individual electives were offered in German, French, Hebrew, Mineralogy, Botany, and Navigation.

A strong emphasis on science was also evident in the curriculum. The chemistry course introduced experimental methods to supplement lectures and demonstrations. Professor Michael Jacobs' course on Meteorology, introduced in 1841, was among the earliest offerings in the field among all American colleges.

One of the early student organizations on the campus was the Linnaean Association, a scientific society created in 1844 by Professors Jacobs and John G. Morris. From this society came the initiative to erect a building to house the scientific collections of the college. Enthusiastic students assisted in fund-raising and in actual construction, and in 1847 Linnaean Hall was completed as the second building on the campus. The dedication speaker noted this occasion as "an interesting event in the history of American colleges. . ., the first time that an edifice devoted to Natural History, conceived, designed, erected, and completed through the agency of students has been dedicated in this country."[33]

Evidence that the college trustees also shared an interest in science was apparent as early as 1839 when, at the request of a group of physicians, they approved the establishment of a medical school in Philadelphia under the authority of the college charter. Over the course of 22 years it attained a very respectable reputation in training more than 150 medical doctors.[34]

Enrollments in these early years were never large, and without the income from the tuition of students in the preparatory department the college department might not have survived. Before the Civil War the college enrollment averaged about 75 students, and at no time did it reach 100. Enrollments in the preparatory department averaged about 80 per year. College graduates before 1860 totaled 303, an average of 11 per year.[35]

Financial resources for the college were extremely limited, especially since possible contributions from congregations were already being solicited for the support of the newly completed seminary building and for its operating costs. Consequently, at the second meeting of the college board a committee was appointed to apply to the state legislature for an appropriation.

The Commonwealth had been subsidizing colleges since revolutionary days, and since 1810 annual grants to colleges had frequently been made by the state legislature. At the session convened in December 1833, a bill was introduced in Harrisburg by Thaddeus Stevens, staunch supporter of universal education and later one of Pennsylvania's most famous congressmen, granting $18,000 to Gettysburg College for the erection of a new building.[36] The college was also included in annual appropriations of $1000 awarded to several colleges from 1838 to 1845, after which financial stringency caused the state to discontinue the practice.[37] Thereafter, stronger appeals were made to Lutheran congregations and individuals through the columns of the popular English language Lutheran Observer, edited by Benjamin Kurtz, trustee and friend of the college and later the founder of Susquehanna University. Some additional help was secured through the sale of scholarships, the interest from which would provide tuition for a student designated by the purchaser. These efforts, together with student tuitions and fees of $30 a year that brought in about $4000 annually, enabled the college at least to maintain solvency in its crucial early years.

Outreach and Influence

Since Gettysburg College was established for the express purpose of providing an appropriate preparation for the study of theology and thus for a soundly educated Lutheran clergy, it is fair to inquire how well it fulfilled this intent. Even after the founding of the seminary and the college, private tutoring of theological candidates still continued. Only gradually was it possible for the seminary to insist on a college degree as an entrance requirement and to establish a full three-year theological course. Nevertheless, of the 303 students who received bachelor's degrees from the college before 1860, 165, or 54%, became pastors. Over the college's first century, 1200 of its 4,322 alumni entered the ministry.[38]

That the college also served in its early years as a contributor to community leadership in the nation is demonstrated by the professional distribution of its alumni from 1832 to 1860. Forty-seven of the 303 graduates studied law, and 22 medicine; 29 became teachers or college professors, and 10 undertook business ventures. In its first 100 years the college contributed 258 lawyers, 241 medical doctors, 1,106 teachers and 637 business executives.

In one vital respect Gettysburg College earned a place among Lutheran colleges similar to that of Yale for the Congregational Church and Princeton for the Presbyterians. As Lutheran colleges were established in ensuing years, Gettysburg College furnished the founders or first presidents for at least 12 institutions, 8 of which are still in existence: Wittenberg, Roanoke, Capital, Newberry, Thiel, Muhlenberg, Susquehanna, Carthage, and Midland. Of the eight members of its second graduating class in 1835, three became founders or presidents of Lutheran colleges; one member of the class who left college before graduation also became a college president. From 1832 to 1932 a total of 52 of its alumni became college presidents, most of them in Lutheran colleges. In addition to this signal service of providing younger Lutheran colleges with top leadership, Gettysburg sent them 386 alumni to teach as professors in this same formative period.

While the college was making these key contributions to the extension of Lutheran higher education, it was also deeply involved in the life and growth of the church. Although structurally separate, the college and the theological seminary were closely related, sharing as they did in the complete preparation of ministers for the church. Faculty members frequently taught in both college and seminary; trustees were interchanged. Charles Philip Krauth, elected in 1834 as the first president of the college, had come to Gettysburg the preceding year on a call to teach in both institutions. Twelve of the 17 men appointed to the college faculty before 1860 were Lutheran clergymen. Most of these men and many of the members of the college board were also leaders in the several Lutheran synods which were served by Gettysburg institutions.

When the state discontinued its subsidy in 1845, a special financial appeal was made to Lutheran pastors, noting that the college had no endowment but depended largely upon tuition and fees from Lutheran students.[39] The appeal was not very successful. But in 1850 help came from an unusual source and had the additional effect of establishing the first formal relationship between the college and an official entity of the Lutheran church.

In that year a merger was proposed between Franklin College in Lancaster, Pennsylvania, and Marshall College, an institution of the Reformed

Church, in Mercersburg, Pennsylvania. Rather than participate in the merger the Lutheran trustees of Franklin College, who had held a one-third interest in the school since it was founded in 1787, were persuaded to convey that interest to Gettysburg College. Funds thus received totaled $17,169.61, and these were placed in an endowment to support a Franklin Professorship of Ancient Languages at Gettysburg College. Under the terms of the merger the Lutheran trustees of Franklin College joined the Gettysburg College board, and the board was empowered to elect the first incumbent of the new Franklin Professorship.

Thereafter, holders of the professorship were to be nominated by the Ministerium of Pennsylvania, the original sponsor of Franklin College. In addition, the Ministerium agreed to raise additional funds to establish a joint professorship in German to be shared by the seminary and the college. Through its power to nominate the Franklin and the German professors and to control the funds for the German professor, the Ministerium of Pennsylvania became officially involved in the support and governance of Gettysburg College. The distinguished first incumbent of the Franklin chair was Frederick Augustus Muhlenberg, great-grandson of the Lutheran patriarch, grandson of the first president of Franklin College, and himself a trustee and professor of that institution.[40]

For 17 years Dr. Muhlenberg taught at Gettysburg College and worked to develop a closer relationship between the college and the strongly German-oriented mother synod of American Lutheranism. Part of his time was devoted to the solicitation of funds to support the Ministerium's joint professorship of German. His distinguished career of service to Lutheran higher education later included the presidencies of two Lutheran colleges, Muhlenberg and Thiel.[41]

The Context of Theological Conflict

The decade before the Civil War was also the period during which the theological crisis in Pennsylvania Lutheranism reached its climax, involving both the seminary and the college. Since the founding of Gettysburg Seminary the theological climate of American Lutheranism had been gradually shifting toward a more conservative confessionalism. The conditional affirmation of the Augsburg Confession which Samuel Schmucker had professed in his inaugural pledge in 1826 had seemed conservative enough in contrast to the waning rationalism of the early 19th century. But by 1850 the faculties of both seminary and college, and indeed much of Lutheranism, had become divided between the liberalism of the so-called "American Lutherans" and the conservatism of the so-called "Old Lutherans" who took their stand on the historic unaltered Augsburg Confession. The latter group also rallied to the German language as a bulwark for the preservation of the pure doctrine. Samuel Schmucker and his long-time colleague Benjamin Kurtz made a final attempt in 1855 to redefine Lutheran doctrine in "American" terms, but their Definite Synodical Platform was soundly rejected by virtually every synod. The controversies which ensued resulted in a synodical cleavage in the Lutheran church which would persist for more than 50 years, and would lead directly to the formation of both a new seminary and a new college.[42]

The "crisis in American Lutheran theology"[43] was to affect the church on a far wider front than Pennsylvania. It would reach into the South as well with the added complications of the Civil War. It would affect the newer areas of the West into which the new waves of German and Scandinavian immigration were already flooding. Doctrinal division would add to the inevitable ethnic divisions among Lutherans, who brought at least five different European languages with them into the great Midwest. And in every case the desire to prepare pastors to preach the Word with understanding would produce new schools of theology and colleges to supply them with well-prepared candidates. The Gettysburg story is therefore only a beginning.

5 THE OHIO STORY

On August 17, 1830, a shy and troubled 18-year old farm boy from rural Maryland named Ezra Keller slipped hesitatingly into his seat in the Gettysburg Gymnasium. As the result of a conversion experience the previous year he had determined to prepare himself for the ministry, and over his father's strenuous objection had begun his studies with a neighboring pastor. Five months later, still unreconciled to his father, Ezra Keller trudged the 40 miles on foot to enter the newly established Gettysburg Gymnasium.

Across the table was his teacher, another 18-year old, older than Keller by two months. His name was William Morton Reynolds, already a graduate of Gettysburg Seminary and a budding student of classical languages. There is no record of any special personal relationship between these two young men except that Reynolds is the only teacher that Keller mentions in his diary.[1]

The careers of Keller and Reynolds did not directly cross again, but in traveling different paths each performed an important role in the progress of Lutheran higher education toward the West. Ezra Keller became the founder of Wittenberg College and William Reynolds the first president of Capital University.

These two Ohio schools, less than 50 miles apart, founded within five years of one another, exemplified much of the character of the Lutheran church in the West and the particular problems it faced during the years before the Civil War. They reflected the strong ethnic flavor of the Lutheran church, enhanced by the arrival of thousands of new German immigrants. They both demonstrated the strong theological orientation of the Lutheran church and its traditional concern for an educated clergy. They also exemplified the Lutheran tendency to establish synods, colleges, and seminaries to support particular theological positions. The two schools further exemplified two divergent educational philosophies, both of which claimed validity as Lutheran but pursued their goals through differing educational structures and curricula.

The Search for Lutheran Identity

The Ohio scene, especially after the War of 1812, was bursting with the vitality of the expanding frontier. People flocked in by the thousands from all parts of the eastern states and from Europe. Between 1810 and 1820 the population of the state more than doubled, reaching 581,434 in 1820 and almost a million 10 years later. Because there were natural routes of access from the northeastern, middle, and southern states, the political, cultural, and religious variety of the whole eastern seaboard converged on Ohio. During the 1830s the freshly built National Road crossed the state and an extensive network of canals linked Lake Erie and the Ohio River. All the major political issues and viewpoints of the nation were represented and debated in Ohio, with only a rare consensus on any one of them. Religious patterns likewise varied, from New England Congregationalism in the Western Reserve to camp-meeting revivalism imported across the Ohio River from its home range in Kentucky.

Very much a part of this cultural variety were the thousands of German newcomers. All the German religious groups were represented, Lutherans and Reformed, Roman Catholics, sectarians, and, after 1848, even atheists. The Lutheran spectrum, too, was present, including pietists, revivalists, unionists, and confessionalists.

As the population of the state grew, so did the Lutheran church. The Pennsylvania pattern of the previous century was repeated, as the need for pastors far outran the supply. At its first convention in 1818 the newly organized

Ohio Synod resolved to "make all possible provision to train young preachers and to instruct them in the Latin and Greek languages as well as other sciences and learning which are necessary for this important pastoral office."[2] A pastor in Tarlton, Ohio, even opened a preparatory academy for a few months in 1819, but lack of both funds and qualified personnel delayed the beginning of formal theological instruction for another decade.[3]

More help in meeting the clergy shortage might have been provided had the newly formed synod been willing to work more closely with its eastern counterparts. The Ohio Synod refused to participate in the formation of the General Synod in 1820, fearing possible usurpation of local autonomy by a centralized ecclesiastical authority.

Even more deeply rooted was the desire among most of the Ohio Synod pastors to preserve the use of the German language. German was predominant among both clergy and laity in Ohio, and it was well known that—except in the rural heartland of the Pennsylvania Ministerium—English was making rapid advances in the eastern states and would therefore predominate in the General Synod. Too close an association with the eastern synods could eventually promote the erosion of the mother tongue in the congregations of the Ohio Synod.

However, the activities of aggressive and rapidly growing American denominations in Ohio constituted a far more powerful threat than association with eastern Lutherans. Revivalism was the standard mode of evangelism among Methodists, Baptists, and Presbyterians. While the emotional excesses of the Kentucky camp meeting held little attraction for most Lutherans, many English-speaking pastors encouraged "seasons of refreshing" in their congregations. Prayer meetings, Sunday schools, and temperance crusades, too, were among the "new measures" employed by revivalist groups that found advocates among so-called "American Lutherans."[4] Pastors who watched their young people forsaking the church of their parents in favor of English-speaking denominations pressed the Ohio Synod for more extensive use of English. In 1840 the first of a series of secessions by English-minded groups of congregations took place, resulting in the formation of a separate English Synod of Ohio.[5]

The Language Issue and Theology

When the language question became involved with issues of theology, the scene was set for the major conflicts that produced two rival seminaries and two colleges in Ohio. The first organized theological instruction in Ohio was given by Wilhelm Schmidt, a young pastor in Canton, in 1830. Schmidt had recently arrived from Germany, having received a full theological education at the University of Halle-Wittenberg.[6] Within a year he took over a parish in Columbus and continued to serve there without compensation as the sole professor of the German Evangelical Lutheran Seminary. In addition to serving his four-congregation parish and instructing as many as nine seminary students, Schmidt took on a further assignment by the Synod to raise funds for the school. The strain proved to be too great. His health broke, compelling him to take a leave of absence in 1837–1838. He contracted typhoid fever and died in 1839 at the age of 36.[7]

After 1840 and the secession of the English Synod the theological dimension gained greater prominence in the developing conflict. The English Synod not only affirmed the English language and the "new measures," but also took issue with the "Old Lutheran" view of the Confessions, a view which it attributed to the Ohio Synod. The "Old Lutherans" not only regarded the unaltered Augsburg Confession and Luther's Catechism as definitive expositions of Lutheran doctrine, but also ascribed normative authority to the entire *Book of Concord* of 1580. The English Synod saw such meticulous adherence "to every minutia and shade of doctrine of the Augsburg Confession" as a violation of the Lutheran principle of liberty of conscience.[8] It embraced instead the position of Samuel S. Schmucker of Gettysburg Seminary who acknowledged the Holy Scriptures as the inspired Word of God and a faithful guide for faith and conduct, but regarded the Augsburg Confession as only a "substantially correct" interpretation of fundamental scriptural doctrine.[9]

The "Old Lutheran" view was strongly reinforced after 1830 by the arrival of immigrant pastors from Germany, who brought with them both a renewed appreciation of the confessional heritage of the Lutheran church and an emphasis on the German language as the bulwark of pure doctrine.[10]

The conflict which ensued dominated the Lutheran church in North America for half a century and created divisions that reached far beyond the borders of Ohio. One of its immediate effects was to generate the impulse for the establishment of both Wittenberg College and Capital University.

After the death of Wilhelm Schmidt in November 1839, the Joint Ohio Synod, as it was known after 1833, took immediate steps to replace him as professor of theology in the Columbus seminary. An invitation went out to Rev. Charles F. Schaeffer of Hagerstown, Maryland, who arrived in Columbus in May 1840. The selection of a bilingual professor who actually preferred English indicates an effort on the part of the Joint Ohio Synod to conciliate the English District pastors, and if possible to prevent their secession. Not only did the effort fail, but the appointment two years later of a second professor, Friedrich Winkler, of Newark, New Jersey, who had a marked preference for German, touched off an open conflict in the seminary and the synod.

Tensions between the two professors developed to such a degree that the board of directors called for the resignation of both men. Schaeffer complied, but Winkler refused and continued to conduct classes. The synod met in special session in June 1844, at Zanesville, to examine the issue raised in the dispute, namely, whether theological instruction should be given exclusively in the German language. By a vote of 38 to 10 the synod supported the Germans.

The victory of the German party aroused immediate indignation, and the controversy continued into the regular meeting of the synod a year later. By this time the climate had changed. Professor Winkler was dismissed, and the synod adopted a modified resolution permitting lectures in both languages. Once again indignation flared, this time from the German pastors. Even the synod's reaffirmation of the primarily German character of the seminary failed to prevent the most ardent advocates of exclusivity from entering a formal protest and eventually withdrawing entirely from the synod.[11]

The Founding of Wittenberg College

Present as a visitor at the Zanesville Convention was Ezra Keller, recently appointed first professor in the new Literary and Theological Institute of the English Synod that had begun operation in Wooster, Ohio, only a month earlier. He had come to the convention in the hope that agreement could be reached to open an English department at the Columbus seminary as a step toward the establishment of a single educational institution for the West in which all Lutherans could unite. But Keller left the convention convinced that the mission of the Columbus seminary was primarily directed to the preparation of German-speaking pastors for German Lutheran congregations. The English language, he concluded, "can never obtain prominence in that institution without disturbing its peace and the peace of the Church."[12]

The only alternative, if the Lutheran church were to fulfill its mission and ministry in the West, would be to establish an institution "of an American character and spirit—such a one as the college and seminary at Gettysburg combined would constitute."[13] Keller was convinced that there was both a need and a readiness for a school "in which parents can give their sons a good business or classical education, and where candidates for the ministry can obtain their preparatory and theological course."[14]

Keller was not satisfied that Wooster was a good location for such a school. With the English Synod's approval he therefore explored several alternate sites west of Columbus, in Springfield, Xenia, and Dayton, in the direction of population movement.[15] During his investigation he even visited Fort Wayne, Indiana, to invite participation by the newly formed Lutheran Synod of the West.[16]

The final decision regarding the location of the college followed a pattern that had already become standard procedure for American colleges. In the growing West, towns and cities vied with one another as centers for trade, commerce, and culture. An educational institution of any kind was a prize worth bargaining for, and most forward-looking towns were eager to enter competition to secure a college. In the case of Wittenberg, two bids were offered. Xenia offered $4,281 in cash. Springfield pledged $4,667, plus building materials and a choice of five sites. Springfield's location on the National Road, the highway to the West, finally tipped the scales in its favor.[17]

On March 11, 1845, the legislature of the state of Ohio granted a charter to the Board of Directors of Wittenberg College. At its first meeting thereafter, the board appointed a building committee, directed the opening of the preparatory school, and elected William M. Reynolds of Gettysburg College as its first president. Reynolds, however, declined, and the board turned to Ezra Keller, asking him to assume administrative responsibilities in addition to his duties as professor of theology and pastor of two local congregations.[18]

Keller's American Model

Although Ezra Keller's term as president of Wittenberg was cut short by his untimely death at the age of 36, after only two years in office, his character and educational philosophy clearly marked the direction of the institution he had founded. He was deeply aware of his debt to the Gettysburg institutions where he had been so cordially received as a young lad and had received both his college and seminary training. He had studied under Samuel S. Schmucker, and continued to be his disciple in theology and practice. A third generation German-American, he preached in both languages, but preferred English. His first pastoral assignment in 1836 was an extended missionary journey into Kentucky, Illinois, and Missouri, where he experienced at first hand the physical rigors and spiritual desolation of the frontier. Before accepting the call to the English Synod seminary in Ohio at the age of 32, he had served as a parish pastor in Taneytown and Hagerstown, Maryland.[19]

Early in 1845 Keller wrote a series of articles for the *Lutheran Observer*, describing the need for a college and seminary in the Miami Valley of Ohio and setting forth his own educational philosophy. He felt strongly that Lutheran responsibility in higher education should not be limited to the preparation of ministers but extended to the education of responsible leadership for the entire community.

"It is a shame and a curse to any people not to patronize learning and possess intelligence," he wrote, and a special reproach to Lutherans, "who. . .came from the land of science, of colleges, of universities, and who are called after a man who was the ornament and chief supporter of the most distinguished university of the sixteenth century, and who was among the first in the revival of learning in that age."[20]

If the Lutheran church is to exert any significant influence for good in the nation, it must provide thorough and careful education.

> Those denominations who carefully and thoroughly educate their children, generally occupy the important stations in the nation. . . . Their sons become physicians, jurists, legislators, and other important functionaries in the state, by which offices they acquire a mighty influence, as members of the church. . . . And this ought to be the case. Civil government is a decisive institution, and wicked men are not fitted for its administration. . . . It is therefore the duty of the church to educate her sons to take the reins of government into their hands—to administer the important "ordinance of God"—to be our judges, jurists, governors, legislators, to be our statesmen, and in this capacity the more useful as Christians.[21]

Keller left no doubt as to the origin of his ideas on education. It was from "the parent branch of the Protestant family that these excellent political principles came, which gave existence to our free institutions. The world did not know that 'all men are created equal' until Luther brought the hidden Bible out of the dust and had the boldness to proclaim its truth to the world."[22]

The thread of historical tradition which Keller saw so clearly leading from Luther's Wittenberg to his Wittenberg might well have been broken except for the missionary zeal of 18th-century pietists. From the University of Halle the westward outreach of Gotthilf Francke sent Muhlenberg and Kunze across the Atlantic to Pennsylvania. Reaffirmed by Samuel S. Schmucker in the Pennsylvania institutions at Gettysburg, the Lutheran educational tradition was carried yet another step westward into Ohio by Ezra Keller. Appropriately, Keller again invoked the creative power of this tradition, "What but the zeal and the faith of Francke, and the liberality of those who aided him, are needed to bring it to a speedy and glorious accomplishment?"[23]

More than any Lutheran educator of his generation, Ezra Keller represented the effort to establish a Lutheran educational institution according to an American model. While he stood firmly within the Lutheran tradition in his concern for a well-educated clergy, his plan for Wittenberg called for a combining of a college and a divinity school within a single institution, under the same board and faculty. Previous Lutheran ventures had followed the German model, drawing a clear distinction between the theological faculty or seminary and the classical preparatory school or gymnasium. The basic purpose of the classical school was to equip students with the necessary linguistic tools for the study of theology. Other students might enroll, but no attempts were made to offer courses to meet their special needs.

Keller consciously chose instead to model Wittenberg College after the New England pattern and cited Harvard, Yale, and such Ohio Schools as Kenyon, Oberlin, and Denison as distinguished examples. "Such an arrangement," he wrote, "will save both means and men—and will make the two departments a common interest—will give unity of council, aim and effort in the Faculty—and will make the two mutually beneficial to each other."[24]

His efforts were encouraged in 1847 by a grant of $600 from the New England-based Society for the Promotion of Collegiate and Theological Education at the West. This was the first of a series of grants to Wittenberg College in recognition of its emphasis on liberal education and its declared readiness to serve students in the English language on a nonsectarian basis.[25]

The adoption of this new pattern of organization made a distinctive contribution to the enhancement of liberal arts education among Lutheran colleges in North America. While only a few other Lutheran institutions have actually incorporated collegiate and theological education under a single board and faculty, collegiate liberal arts education rather than limited pretheological education has become the major focus for a large segment of the Lutheran church in North America.

The Dream of a German University

As Wittenberg College came to represent the forces at work in Ohio to Americanize the Lutheran church in language, liturgy, and theology, Capital University and its parent institution, the Evangelical Lutheran Seminary in Columbus, came to represent the effort to preserve traditional Old World Lutheran patterns and practices, and especially the German language. From its organization in 1818 the Ohio Synod had emphasized its character as a German synod, and defined its theological seminary in 1830 as a "German Institution." Also founded in the tradition of "the faithful Francke in Germany," the seminary was committed by the synod "to educate young men for the Ministry in the German Lutheran Church" and to promulgate the doctrines of the Augsburg Confession "literally, purely, and unadulterately."[26] The seminary constitution of 1833 did permit "other citizens" to enroll, but only as long as their presence did not hinder the main purpose of the institution.[27]

In 1839 the synod authorized a collegiate department, but no action followed until 1842—just as the language controversy was about to break. At that time the synod empowered a committee to establish a college separate from the seminary to offer instruction in science and literature. A charter was secured from the Ohio legislature in 1843 for an institution to be called Germania College. The venture, however, failed to survive the synodical tensions that even forced the temporary closing of the seminary in 1846–1847.[28] A later effort on the part of the English District of the synod in 1848 resulted in the chartering of Muhlenberg College (not to be confused with the Pennsylvania institution), but it, too, closed at the end of its first year.[29]

During the tension-filled years from 1842 to 1847, concerns for the welfare and even the survival of the seminary dominated the attention of the synod leadership. Education at the college level, as the failure of both the Germania and Muhlenberg College ventures attests, commanded only sporadic interest or support. But with the appointment of William F. Lehmann as theology professor and the reopening of the seminary in the fall of 1847, the seminary board again began to consider the college question.

After consultation with several leading citizens of Columbus, the board applied to the state legislature in November 1849, for a charter for Capital University. Granted in March 1850, the charter reflected the board's intention to launch this ambitious venture as a cooperative project between church and community. The name selected for the university proclaimed its identification with Ohio's chief city and the seat of its state government. Ten of the 24 seats on the new board were reserved for prominent citizens of Columbus, 10 for the seminary board, and 4 for district representatives of the Joint Synod.[30]

The title *university* was new and significant. For the first time in America, Lutherans attempted to transplant the classical structure of the German university, with its four faculties of Letters, Law, Medicine, and Theology. It was hoped that the Starling Medical College of Columbus would become the medical faculty of the university; a law faculty could surely be assembled in Ohio's capital city; the seminary itself would continue as the theological faculty; and the faculty of letters would be the undergraduate college.[31]

Unfortunately, the medical college was not interested in becoming part of the university, and support for a law school failed to materialize. When the university opened in the fall of 1850 in newly purchased quarters, only the seminary, the college, and the "grammar school" were functioning. The initial student body numbered 136, of whom 12 were college students, 13 seminarians, and 111 enrolled in the "grammar school."[32]

To direct the fortunes of their grandly conceived venture the trustees turned to Dr. William Morton Reynolds of Gettysburg, Pennsylvania. Reynolds was well known as a writer and educator, currently principal of the preparatory academy and Professor of Latin in Gettysburg College.[33] As editor of the *Evangelical Review*, he was favorably known to the conservative Joint Synod as an outspoken critic of Samuel Schmucker's "American Lutheranism," which he had assailed as unhistorical and confessionless.[34]

The new president was inaugurated on May 21, 1850, in the First Presbyterian Church, selected because it was one of the largest places of assembly in the city of Columbus. His inaugural address, emphasizing the character-building role of education, was well received by the assembly that included a representation from the Constitutional Convention in session at the time in Columbus for the revision of the Ohio State Constitution.[35]

Although begun auspiciously and with great expectations, the presidency of William Reynolds was not destined for success. Several circumstances contributed to the steady erosion of his effectiveness and, after a tenure of only four years, brought about his resignation in 1854.

Capital Sets Its Course

The concept of an institution modeled after the medieval German university and governed cooperatively by church and community was probably too ambitious for the realities of the Ohio frontier. Moreover, it seemed to embrace educational goals and methods that were not in accord with established policies and practices of the Joint Synod.

As it became clear that their ambitious plans were not attainable, the synod and the seminary board declared more limited goals. The intent of the "university innovation," according to the catalog of 1850, was simply to organize an institution of general education in order "to give young men preparing for the ministry of the Gospel, and others resorting to the literary department of that Institution more thorough instruction than they had hitherto enjoyed."[36] Their central intent, even in a program of general education was to prepare young men for the Lutheran ministry. To assure this, the seminary remained "under the government of its original Board of Trustees, and has undergone no change by becoming the Theological Department of the University."[37]

As thus described, the university was simply the theological seminary, governed by its own board, plus a collegiate department and grammar school governed by a board comprised of the seminary board supplemented by representatives of the Columbus community.

Such a narrowing of the scope of the university was no doubt disappointing to community leaders, although many families continued to send their children to the grammar school. President Reynolds seems not to have understood nor accepted the narrowed intent of the synod leaders, for he came under severe criticism for giving disproportionate attention to community associations and neglecting synodical responsibilities.

The resignation of William Reynolds as president of Capital University in 1854 came about as the result of a combination of circumstances. He was clearly unable to find a proper balance in the tenuous alliance between the leaders of the Columbus community and the leaders of the Joint Synod. In addition, the language problem of the 1840s had by no means disappeared. Fed by a steady influx of immigrants, German continued to be the preferred language of the Joint Synod and its congregations. President Reynolds, though fluent in German and several other languages as well, was most comfortable in English. His frequent associations with the English-speaking community in Columbus, which provided most of the students for the college and the grammar school, seemed to threaten the German character of the school. His two appointments to the college faculty were both English-speaking, which meant that with the exception of Dr. William F. Lehmann, the seminary professor, the university faculty gave little encouragement to the use of German.[38]

However, it was the issue of confessional Lutheranism that catalyzed the final break between Reynolds and the Joint Synod. Reynolds had been a student of Samuel Schmucker at Gettysburg and, as most of his other contemporaries, had responded favorably to Schmucker's denominational tolerance and to the so-called "new measures" of "American Lutheranism." But during his later years as a faculty member at Gettysburg College his views had changed, and he had become a strong proponent of the Lutheran confessions. His own experience was a reflection of a growing conservative trend in eastern Lutheranism. By 1850 a younger generation of theologians led by men such as Charles Porterfield Krauth, son of the first president of Gettysburg College, Beale Schmucker, son of Samuel S. Schmucker, and Reynolds himself, were assuming leadership.

A further indication of this trend was the decision of the conservative Pennsylvania Ministerium to rejoin the General Synod in 1853. Although it had been one of the initiators of the General Synod in 1820, the Ministerium had withdrawn almost immediately and had remained aloof for 30 years. As a one-time member of the Ministerium, Reynolds was understandably pleased when the Ministerium decided to reestablish its ties with the General Synod.

When he suggested that the Joint Ohio Synod follow suit, however, the conservative majority soundly defeated the proposal, asserting pointedly that in their judgment, the Ministerium and the General Synod did not "stand on Lutheran ground." By association, Reynolds' own orthodoxy also fell under serious suspicion. Although by Pennsylvania standards he was a conservative, he seems not to have understood the degree to which the "Old Lutheranism" of the Joint Synod had been influenced by the influx of German immigrant pastors. Their confessional conservatism exceeded that of the most conservative of the new generation at Gettysburg.[39]

Reynolds' resignation, followed by those of the two faculty members he had appointed, precipitated a crisis that threatened the life of the university and led to another schism in the synod. A significant segment of the Joint Synod, represented by the English District, supported Reynolds and saw his resignation and that of his faculty appointees as a blow to the academic prestige of the university and an unfair judgment on the orthodoxy, piety, and learning of President Reynolds and his colleagues. In 1855 the English District withdrew from the Joint Synod, thus becoming the second English-language group to take such an action.

The precarious state of the university after Reynolds' departure called for extensive reorganization. Enrollments had declined in the latter part of Reynolds' administration. Seventy-five students were enrolled in 1855, of whom only four were in the collegiate department and 16 in the seminary. One friend of the college described the gloomy prospects. "Matters were in bad shape in every way. Not only had enemies endeavored to excite prejudice against us in the city as narrow-minded and bigoted Lutherans, but our finances were in almost inextricable confusion.''[40]

The brief two-year administration of Rev. Christian Spielman served mainly as an opportunity to assess damages and to establish new direction for Capital University. With community support virtually gone, the broadly-based university board served no good purpose, and the synod decided to effect a reorganization that would bring the university under direct church control.

Periodic secessions of English-oriented congregations and steady accessions of pastors and other immigrants from Germany greatly strengthened both the German character of the Joint Synod and its allegiance to the strong confessionalism of the ''Old Lutherans.'' The emerging leader in the Joint Synod was Matthias Loy, pastor in Delaware, Ohio. Encouraged by his local pastor to enroll in the Columbus seminary, he had entered in 1847 and become one of William Lehmann's first students. Lehmann and Spielman introduced him to ''Old Lutheranism'' through the Missouri Synod paper, Der Lutheraner. Through reading C. F. W. Walther's writings, Loy was changed from an ''American Lutheran'' to an ''Old Lutheran.'' As later president of the Joint Synod, he was instrumental in establishing ties with the Missouri Synod which nearly resulted in the merging of their seminaries.

Loy took the lead in a reorganization of the board which removed all ambiguity concerning the control of Capital University. It was under this board that William F. Lehmann, professor of theology in the seminary, became president of Capital University in 1857, an office he held for 23 years, until his death in 1880. To Professor Lehmann the historian of Capital University has applied the descriptive words of Emerson, ''An institution is the lengthened shadow of one man.''[41]

A Case of Creative Diversity

Before the Civil War burst upon the United States in 1861 Wittenberg College and Capital University had emerged from the controversies of language and theology attending their births and were well along on their respective educational journeys. Both were loyal institutions of the church, firmly committed to their Lutheran heritage. But their stated goals, their patterns of governance, their institutional structures, and their curricula were markedly different. Both provided for the preparation of Lutheran pastors. Capital structured its governance and curriculum primarily to serve this purpose. Its collegiate department, modeled to a large extent after the German gymnasium, served primarily as a preparatory school for the seminary. The board of directors of the seminary also governed the college and established its policies.

Wittenberg, following instead the pattern of the New England colleges, incorporated its theological department within the college. Even with the generous endowments for the theology department from Dr. and Mrs. Michael Hamma that led to the establishment of a separate administration for the Hamma School of Theology in 1900, theological study was regarded as an integral part of the educational program of Wittenberg College.[42] The collegiate curriculum continued to offer to all students, including theological candidates, a broader spectrum of courses emphasizing cultural and intellectual development and leading to service in a variety of professions. Its governing board was broadly representative of church and community, yet strongly church-oriented.

Variations of these two patterns, both rooted in a Lutheran understanding of vocation and committed to the preparation of an educated ministry, have continued to characterize the stream of Lutheran collegiate education in North America to the present day.

6 PARTICULARISM IN PENNSYLVANIA

Most of the leading spokesmen on both sides of the controversies which divided American Lutheranism between 1845 and 1867 were products of the Gettysburg institutions. In Ohio, Ezra Keller and Samuel Sprecher at Wittenberg and William Reynolds at Capital headed institutions representing conflicting educational and theological views. In Pennsylvania, Benjamin Kurtz and Frederick A. Muhlenberg, also both Gettysburg men, represented even wider differences. They not only disagreed with each other, but both of them were strongly opposed to the educational and theological stance of the Gettysburg of the 1850s. Kurtz regarded Gettysburg as too formal and confessionally bound. Muhlenberg thought Gettysburg too ''Americanized'' and not ''confessional'' enough. Each became president of a new institution in Pennsylvania that reflected his particular convictions.

The Dream of Benjamin Kurtz

Benjamin Kurtz, ''the stormy petrel of American Lutheranism,'' founded the Missionary Institute, later to be known as Susquehanna University in Selinsgrove, Pennsylvania. Kurtz was one of the most profiled American pietists since Henry Melchior Muhlenberg. His grandfather, John Nicolas Kurtz, had come from Halle in 1745 to assist Muhlenberg as a catechist and was the first man to be ordained by the Pennsylvania Ministerium. Benjamin Kurtz was born in 1795, studied theology privately under Rev. George Lochman of Lebanon, Pennsylvania, and was licensed to preach by the Maryland Synod in 1815. He was one of the founders of the General Synod and a close associate of Samuel Schmucker in the founding of Gettysburg Seminary. At the age of 32

he undertook a 20-month mission to Europe to collect money and books for the projected seminary.[1] For 30 years he edited *The Lutheran Observer* in Baltimore, the most influential Lutheran church paper in America in the English language.[2]

An articulate and often bombastic proponent of "American Lutheranism," Kurtz did much to shape the course of Lutheran church life for three decades. Among the causes he advocated were revivalism, temperance, and denominational tolerance. One biographical critic labeled him "Puritan in theology and Methodist in practice."[3] He was bilingual, but his ardent Americanism even led him to admit some sympathy toward the antiforeign movements of the 1850s. One of his more earnest concerns was the lack of an adequate supply of ministers and consequent loss of church members. He was willing to send out "pious and sensible laymen" as missionaries after a brief course of preparatory reading. "We need plain and moderately educated, as well as showy and profoundly learned men," he said, "and there are neighborhoods and churches to which the former are better adapted and in which they can do more good than the latter. . .."[4]

With rising anxiety he watched the conservative trend developing at Gettysburg Seminary where even his old friend Samuel Schmucker seemed unable to stem the tide. After Schmucker's younger colleagues turned against their former mentor, Kurtz attacked Gettysburg Seminary for dispensing a theology of the head rather than of the heart. Kurtz never conceded that the kind of 16th-century Lutheran confessionalism that seemed to be gaining ascendancy among Lutherans in America would survive. In 50 years, he predicted, the tide would turn and "American Lutheranism" would again reclaim its leadership role in the broader "evangelic-protestant" culture of America.[5]

As the controversy increased in intensity, Kurtz determined to move beyond the printed page and the spoken word. "Action, *action*, prompt and judicious ACTION, is what we want," he wrote in *The Lutheran Observer*, May 18, 1855; "let us *act*, not *intend*."

The Defeat of "American Lutheranism"

The action he called for in May began with an explosion in September 1855. A group of "American Lutherans" meeting informally had pressed Dr. Schmucker to prepare a formal statement for the guidance of those who opposed the trend toward confessionalism in the church. This statement, written by Schmucker in consultation with Kurtz and Samuel Sprecher, president of Wittenberg College, bore the title, "A Definite Synodical Platform." Although it was distributed anonymously, there was little doubt of its authorship.

The platform was essentially a revision of the Augsburg Confession, and synods were urged to adopt it as their confessional basis. Among the "errors" in the Augsburg Confession that it proposed to eliminate were approval of the mass, private confession and absolution, baptismal regeneration, and the real presence of Christ's body and blood in the Lord's Supper. Since the Platform claimed that it did not omit any "fundamental doctrine of Scripture," its authors contended that it was in accord with the position of the General Synod.[6]

Except in three small synods in Ohio the Platform was roundly rejected by the constituency of the General Synod. The deluge of books, essays, and sermons which virtually inundated the church, expressing unqualified disapproval of such tampering with the historic document of Lutheran identity, made it clear that "American Lutheranism" had become obsolete.[7] But the supporters of the Platform were not ready to concede. Schmucker continued to defend his position, both on the lecture platform and in the columns of *The Lutheran Observer*. Benjamin Kurtz responded to critics with notably less emotional restraint than Schmucker and was answered in kind by the editors and contributors to conservative journals such as the *Evangelical Review*.

Founding the Missionary Institute

Kurtz's response—he had said, "let us *act*, not intend"—was to found the Missionary Institute, through which he hoped to bolster the crumbling structure of "American Lutheranism." In a career filled with controversy this was probably the most controversial and possibly the least understood venture of his 70 stormy years.

As chairman of a Maryland Synod committee in October 1856 he introduced a resolution recommending the establishment of the Institute. There was enough agreement on the need for a mission seminary in the church to approve Kurtz's resolution by a vote of 21 to 9. The synod-elected Board of Managers met in Kurtz's editorial offices in Baltimore in December and approved his plan for structure and curriculum. The purpose of the Institute was to be ". . .the education of pious and soul-minded men for the office of the holy ministry and for the mission field at home or abroad."[8] Its direction was placed in the office of a superintendent who would also serve as chairman of the faculty. The list of subjects to be taught included the usual courses for a theological seminary except for the classical languages. An academic and scientific course was also included that, although distinctly secondary in Kurtz's plan, years later would become the main focus of the school. A subsequent meeting of the board elected Kurtz as superintendent and professor of theology.

The nature of the school suggested a frontier location, but Kurtz was aware that the strength of conservatism among Lutherans in the West would assure the Institute an unfriendly reception. A resolution to locate the Institute in Baltimore County won temporary approval, but when Kurtz offered to sell a piece of his own property for the location of the school, the board declined. When it then opened the process to competitive bidding, towns and cities in states as far west as Illinois and Iowa deluged the board with offers. Eventually the field was narrowed to several communities in central Pennsylvania where Kurtz's views still enjoyed strong support.[9]

When it became clear that the Institute would most likely have to locate outside the boundaries of the Maryland Synod, the board requested that for legal reasons the synod declare it a self-perpetuating board and dissolve all synodical connections with the Missionary Institute. Immediately after this request was approved, Kurtz resigned from the Maryland Synod and, together with nine other dissidents, organized the Melanchthon Synod.[10] This gave Kurtz the second of the two instruments through which he intended to continue the battle for "American Lutheranism."

By May 1858, the contest over the location of the Institute had been settled in favor of Selinsgrove in central Pennsylvania. Competition among four communities had been spirited and occasionally marred by charges of favoritism and misrepresentation. The pastor in Bloomfield, one of the contenders, claimed his community to be more Lutheran than its rival, Loysville, since it had four churches while Loysville had "only one-half of one, and this is in dispute."

While admitting that Loysville might offer greater financial inducements than Bloomfield, he suggested that Kurtz "ought to see the clay road between here and Loysville for half the year. The stage upset twice within a few weeks," he wrote. "Now are we to drag our students over such a road—mud road—for fifteen miles? If Bloomfield is not more suitable than Loysville, then let it [the Institute] go to Loysville. Let it go where no one can find it, or, if found, can get away from it."[11]

In this competition, however, cash subscriptions counted for more than either Lutheran statistics or road conditions. Enterprising town leaders of Selinsgrove, headed by Samuel Domer, pastor of the local congregations, conducted a campaign that netted subscriptions of $22,000. This pledge, together with the assurance of at least 50 students and the free temporary use of one of the buildings of Trinity Lutheran Church, won the approval of the Institute's board. A disgruntled Loysville booster observed, as its final plea, that the board could not have located "a more sickly place. . .along the Susquehanna" than Selinsgrove.[12] Local citizens, however, provided Kurtz with a "Certificate of Healthfulness," refuting the Loysville claim that Selinsgrove was a haven for malarial fever.

One of the conditions placed on their offer by the citizens of Selinsgrove was that a female college and a classical school be established in conjunction with the proposed Missionary Institute. Kurtz accepted this condition as long as the Institute remained the "chief establishment, the *sun* around which all other establishm'ts must revolve. . .."[13] To ensure that their demands for lay education would be honored, the townspeople insisted that financial subscriptions be divided equally between the Institute and the Female College.

Kurtz was the only member of the original Board of Managers to survive the move from Baltimore to Selinsgrove. At its first meeting in May he was elected president of the board, superintendent of the Institute, and first theological professor. The board also laid plans for the first building and applied to the Court of Common Pleas of Snyder County for a charter for the Missionary Institute of the Evangelical Lutheran Church. Full degree-granting powers were authorized, though no baccalaureate programs were undertaken until 1894. A separate board was established for the Selinsgrove Female College.[14]

Two thousand people watched the laying of the cornerstone of the first building on September 1, 1858. As significant as the number present, however, was the notable absence of any representative from Gettysburg Seminary. Professor Henry L. Baugher, who had been invited to deliver an address, refused, stating he was opposed to the project and felt similar aims could be attained at one of the existing schools.[15]

By October 7 the Institute was in full operation. Seven teachers took turns meeting with 119 students in the single lecture room of Trinity Lutheran Church. Thirty-four of the students were women, who would transfer to the Female College when separate facilities became available. The faculty Kurtz had assembled was carefully selected to advance the goals of "American Lutheranism." Henry Ziegler, second theological professor and Kurtz's assistant, played an especially important role. Since Kurtz continued to reside in Baltimore and visited Selinsgrove only occasionally, Ziegler was, in fact, in charge of the Institute.

An early graduate of Gettysburg College and Seminary in the days when Samuel Schmucker's influence was dominant, Henry Ziegler had come to Selinsgrove in 1843 as co-pastor of Trinity Lutheran Church.[16] His community relationships were well established through his marriage to the daughter of John App, a local builder, influential in bringing the Institute to Selinsgrove. Ziegler was a trusted friend of Kurtz and, during his previous pastorate in Williamsport, Pennsylvania, had assisted Kurtz in soliciting support for the Institute. Peter Born, pastor in nearby Sunbury, headed the classical department. Christopher C. Baughman, former principal of the Virginia Collegiate Institute and the Hagerstown Female Seminary, became principal of the Female College. All three men were dependable supporters of the "new measures" and revivalism.

Kurtz and Ziegler were officially installed in their respective offices on November 14, 1858. In his inaugural address Kurtz proclaimed the design, necessity, and special character of his new "school of the prophets." He laid primary stress upon the need for more pastors. The Missionary Institute, he said, was precisely adapted to meet such "exigencies of the church." It would offer a practical course of two years or less, directed to the special needs of pious and talented men who at the age of 25 or 30 felt called to the gospel ministry. Pointing to St. Paul and the other apostles as examples, Kurtz observed that God does not limit his call to "unmarried young men."[17]

To the objections that such a shortened practical course would lower the standards of theological education, Kurtz replied that, on the contrary, the Institute would raise them. Many synods, he pointed out, were still admitting men to the preaching ministry on the basis of private instruction and a small amount of practical work.

Without specific references to the continuing controversy in the church between the American and the Confessional parties, Kurtz skillfully described the kind of institution that supported his point of view. He saw the Institute as the instrument for resisting the rising wave of conservatism which had already enveloped Gettysburg Seminary and the Ministerium of Pennsylvania and made his own Maryland Synod for him an inhospitable spiritual home.

But his hopes for the "dawning of a new day" in the Lutheran church were ill-founded.[18] Kurtz continued the fight on the lecture platform and through the columns of The Lutheran Observer. But the Missionary Institute never fulfilled its stated purpose. From its beginning it included other, ultimately stronger elements: a two-year classical department and a female academy. In these lay the future of the institution.

Moreover, the educational program had scarcely begun when the Civil War broke upon the nation and the very life of the Institute itself was endangered. Enrollments declined and initially generous financial support decreased. In the face of the critical need for funds, the board even undertook a disappointing venture in oil drilling in western Pennsylvania, hoping to profit from the great "oil boom" that followed Colonel Edwin L. Drake's discovery in 1859.[19]

Most of the responsibility for the Institute during these years devolved upon Henry Ziegler, especially in view of the declining health of Kurtz, whose role in the affairs of the Institute decreased steadily until his death in 1865. It was Ziegler who had to keep things going during these years. He was at the same time administrator, sole professor of theology, pastor of two congregations, and chief fund-raiser for the Institute. The emotional strain of the wartime climate and the continuing barrage of criticism descending on the Institute as a result of Kurtz's unrelenting attacks on "sectarian symbolism" added to burdens which nearly broke Ziegler's health—if not his spirit.

The Institute in Perspective

After the Civil War the theological controversy continued, with conservatives gaining steadily. The Institute, too, came under increasing attack, during which the "American Lutheran" cause sorely missed its chief protagonist, Benjamin Kurtz. From the outset the theological department of the Institute had depended heavily upon tuition income from students in the classical department, where enrollments were several times greater. Moreover, as the theological department drew its enrollment from students who trained in the Institute's own classical department, the distinctions between ministerial training at the Missionary Institute and Gettysburg Seminary tended to become differences in degree rather than in kind. In 1867 there was even an effort to terminate the rivalry and merge the theological department of the Institute with Gettysburg Seminary. The effort was vigorously opposed, as were several subsequent suggestions to discontinue the theological program at Selinsgrove.[20] Not until 1933 did Kurtz's theological experiment come to a close. By that time the Missionary Institute itself had long since been transformed into a modern liberal arts institution called Susquehanna University.

In its relation to the internal theological controversies of mid-19th-century Lutheranism, the Missionary Institute occupied a position analogous to that of Wittenberg College. Kurtz and Ziegler in Pennsylvania had their counterparts in Keller and Sprecher in Ohio. All four were disciples of Samuel Schmucker, and all four opposed the rising tide of confessionalism and Lutheran particularity after 1840. In each case their opposition crystallized into institutions embodying and promoting their viewpoints and those of their supporters. Kurtz's actions in founding the Missionary Institute were colored by an anti-establishment bias that characterized the radical wing of "American Lutheranism." Opposed to formalism, whether in liturgy or polity, he harbored a distrust of church organization, a distrust that was reflected in his secession from the Maryland Synod and his insistence that the Board of the Institute be self-perpetuating and free from any synodical control. Although the Institute received some support from members of the Melanchthon Synod and the Central Pennsylvania Synod, on whose territory the Institute was located, neither the board of the Institute nor of the later Susquehanna University has ever relinquished its independent character.[21]

While Kurtz and Ziegler maintained the centrality of the Institute's theological program, the two adjunct institutions established at the insistence of the citizens of Selinsgrove eventually determined the permanent educational character of the Institute. The original Board of Managers described the classical department as an integral part of the Institute, "designed to afford to Students the necessary facilities for acquiring a respectable business education and also to prepare themselves for the Junior and Senior Classes of College."[22] The first published curriculum of the "Collegiate Department" in 1859 outlined a two-year program embracing the studies of the freshman and sophomore years. The Missionary Institute may thus lay convincing claim to operating the earliest intentionally defined junior college curriculum in the United States.[23]

The Female College, separately administered under the experienced hand of Christopher C. Baughman, had begun with 34 students in 1858; by 1865 it had an enrollment of 129. But increasing costs, shortage of capital, and the rise of public education with new educational emphases eventually forced the school to close. Its facilities were taken over in 1873 by a normal school for teachers. At the same time, however, the Missionary Institute opened its doors to women, thus becoming one of the early coeducational colleges in the East.[24]

Crisis in the General Synod

Muhlenberg College in Allentown was the second of the Pennsylvania colleges to emerge as the result of theological controversies of the mid-19th century. Although it was not actually chartered until 1867, the events which brought Muhlenberg College into being are rooted in the same conflicts that resulted in the establishment of two Lutheran colleges—instead of one—in Ohio. The issues of language and confessional loyalty were especially intense in the heavily German areas of eastern Pennsylvania served by the Pennsylvania Ministerium. The earliest and the largest of the Lutheran synods in America, the Ministerium had resisted the inroads of both the English language and the influence of American denominationalism. It had even remained aloof from association with other Lutheran synods that formed the General Synod in 1820. When it finally joined the General Synod in 1853, it made clear its intention to reserve control of its internal affairs, and instructed its delegates to protest and withdraw if the General Synod ever took any action conflicting with the "old and long-established faith of the Evangelical Lutheran Church."[25]

Conservative leaders of the Ministerium were understandably disquieted by the appearance of the Definite Synodical Platform in 1855. Although the General Synod overwhelmingly rejected the Platform, the fears of Ministerium delegates were reinforced when in 1859 the General Synod voted to admit Benjamin Kurtz's schismatic Melanchthon Synod to membership. The crisis came in 1864 when the Franckean Synod applied for membership in the General Synod. This small synod, located largely in western New York, had never officially subscribed to the Augsburg Confession. Its application was at first rejected, but when Franckean delegates explained that in adopting the Constitution of the General Synod, they had also accepted the Augsburg Confession, the Franckeans were granted conditional admission.

The delegates from the Pennsylvania Ministerium objected. Recalling the conditions on which the Ministerium had entered the General Synod in 1853, the delegation withdrew from the sessions "in order to report to the Synod of Pennsylvania at its approaching convention."[26] Although the delegates of the Ministerium did not intend their action as a full withdrawal from the General Synod, it was so interpreted.

In the months immediately following, a long-smoldering desire among conservative members of the Ministerium for a separate theological seminary came to a head. This desire was based partly on doctrinal issues and partly on the need for more German-speaking pastors, a need which Gettysburg was not able to supply.

Early in 1864 Samuel Schmucker resigned from Gettysburg Seminary, concluding a career of 38 years as professor of theology. Convinced that the seminary board would not select a successor who would fulfill its expectations, the Ministerium of Pennsylvania proceeded in its convention in July 1864 to establish a seminary of its own in Philadelphia. It elected Charles Porterfield Krauth, editor of the conservative *Lutheran and Missionary*, as professor of systematic theology. Dr. Charles F. Schaeffer, German professor at both Gettysburg College and Seminary, and Dr. W. J. Mann, a German-born Philadelphia pastor, became the other professors. Since the German Professorship at Gettysburg was supported by an endowment controlled by the Pennsylvania Ministerium, Schaeffer carried the endowment, as well as most of the German theological students at Gettysburg, with him to Philadelphia.[27]

These events heightened the tensions between the General Synod and the Pennsylvania Ministerium. When the General Synod met in Ft. Wayne, Indiana, in May 1866, its presiding chairman, Dr. Samuel Sprecher, president of Wittenberg College, refused to seat the delegates of the Pennsylvania Ministerium, claiming that their withdrawal during the 1864 convention disqualified them. The Ministerium thereupon formally withdrew from the General Synod and shortly thereafter invited all Lutheran synods that acknowledged the unaltered Augsburg Confession to join in organizing a new general body "on a truly Lutheran basis."[28] Thirteen synods sent delegates to a preliminary convention in December 1866. In November 1867, the first regular session of the "General Council of the Evangelical Lutheran Church of North America" was held in Fort Wayne, Indiana.

The Ministerium Founds a College

Sentiment for the establishment of a separate college for the Pennsylvania Ministerium had existed for many years before the crisis of the 1860s. Much of it reflected the desire for a greater emphasis on the German language than was being offered at Gettysburg College. The endowment of the German professorship at the college in 1850 was regarded by many in the Ministerium as only a temporary and largely inadequate solution.

Theological tensions after 1855 heightened interest, and in 1860 the Ministerium appointed a committee to explore the possibilities of establishing a separate college. The chairman of this committee was Rev. Samuel K. Brobst, for nearly 20 years an advocate of higher education for German youth in Allentown.[29]

An editor of a German-language monthly for Lutheran youth, Brobst had been instrumental in bringing Rev. Christian R. Kessler, a pastor of the Reformed church, to Allentown in 1848 to establish the Allentown Seminary for the preparation of teachers. When classical studies were added, the enrollment rose to more than 200 students and the school was obliged to enlarge its facilities. Under Kessler and later under Dr. William M. Reynolds, formerly president of Capital University, the Seminary continued to serve students from the Allentown area from 1848 to 1864.[30]

The first recommendation of the synod's college committee in 1861 was to transfer Dr. Charles F. Schaeffer, the synod-supported German professor, from Gettysburg College to the Allentown Seminary. The synod did not accept this proposal, but the following year adopted a resolution commending the Allentown Seminary as a preparatory school for its prospective ministerial candidates. It also authorized a visiting committee to arrange study programs for these students and to oversee examinations on behalf of the synod.

When in 1863 the synod expressed interest in expanding the seminary to include a normal department and courses in Lutheran doctrine, the proprietors of the school, two prominent Lutheran laymen, decided to apply to the state for a full collegiate charter. The prompt approval of the request was no doubt facilitated by the readiness of the proprietors to offer military training for recruits to the Union army. Under its charter of 1864 the reorganized Allentown Collegiate Institute and Military Academy was authorized to grant baccalaureate degrees in both arts and sciences.

By 1866 the synod committee was ready to recommend that the property of the Allentown Collegiate Institute be purchased outright. "General satisfaction," declared the committee, "can only be given by placing this institution under the direct supervision of Synod."[31] Moreover, the proprietors were eager that the synod should have the property and were prepared to sell it on favorable terms.

The synod therefore empowered a committee of seven clergy and three lay members headed by Rev. Samuel Brobst "to secure the collegiate buildings at Allentown. . .for the use of our Synod, but in such a way as not to place the Synod under any pecuniary responsibilities."[32] Fulfilling such an assignment called for both ingenuity and imagination. The proposed solution of the problem was to form a joint stock company and to meet the purchase price of $30,000 by selling 300 shares of stock at $100 each. When the sale of stock had been assured, a new charter was secured, and the Allentown Collegiate and Military Institute formally closed in June 1867.

A new charter authorized a board of 18 trustees, 12 of whom were to be elected by the stockholders and 6 by the synod from among the stockholders.[33] The rechartered institution was named Muhlenberg College, in honor of Henry Melchior Muhlenberg, father of Lutheranism in America and founder of the Ministerium of Pennsylvania.

Muhlenberg College in Perspective

One of the first actions of the new board on February 2, 1867, was to elect the Rev. Dr. Frederick A. Muhlenberg, great-grandson of the Lutheran patriarch, as the first president of the college. A graduate of Jefferson College, a Presbyterian school in western Pennsylvania, the new president had served as professor in Franklin College from 1839 to 1850. When the separation of Lutheran and Reformed interests in that college occurred in 1850, Dr. Muhlenberg became the first incumbent of the Franklin Professorship of Ancient Languages at Gettysburg College, a position he held for 17 years, until his election to the presidency of Muhlenberg College.

The inauguration of the president and the official opening of the college took place on September 3, 1867. As the ceremonial procession from St. John's Lutheran Church reached the court house, the Allentown Cornet Band played special arrangements of "Old Hundredth" and "A Mighty Fortress." The chairman of the board of trustees delivered a personal charge to each of the seven faculty members and called upon Dr. Muhlenberg for his inaugural address.[34]

The college, Muhlenberg declared, had been founded to meet the special needs of the large German Lutheran population of eastern Pennsylvania. Other institutions were indeed available in the Lehigh Valley, but they were neither German nor Lutheran. Gettysburg College had been tried and found wanting. There had been, in fact, "doubts of its appropriateness from the very beginning," he said, "but necessity urged us to assent to the arrangement" in the hope that the school might eventually be moved closer to the center of Lutheranism.[35] Only 25 students from the territory of the Ministerium were currently attending Gettysburg College, a number entirely disproportionate to the 50,000 members of the synod. If the future leadership of the church and appropriate nurture of German culture were to be assured, eastern Pennsylvania needed its own college.

There was no question concerning the kind of educational program such an institution would offer. There would be no irresponsible venturing into specialized or utilitarian training. The curriculum would be firmly based upon the classical languages and mathematics, "the grand staple in all the curricula of studies in the institutions of the Old and New Worlds—in Oxford and Cambridge, in Berlin and Göttingen, in Athens and Edinburg, in Harvard and Yale."[36]

Not only should the students of Muhlenberg College be imbued with an appreciation of their cultural heritage, but they should be "as eminent for Christian attainments as for their sound scholarship." For the achievement of the ideal of a Christian education Muhlenberg invoked the example of "the great and good men who were raised up by God to carry forward the blessed Reformation—the Elector of Saxony, Luther, and Melanchthon"—who established the University of Wittenberg. From that university young men from many countries went forth to spread the truth. Muhlenberg College was founded to "go forward in the same career of usefulness and fame."[37]

Finally, the new president sought to place his college within the historic stream of confessional Lutheran theology. Its stance would be courageously and strongly denominational. Muhlenberg faculty and students, he declared, will "rejoice that they are permitted to live in a locality where it is not an odious thing to be a good and consistent Lutheran."[38]

On the morning after the inaugural ceremonies, the college officially opened, with a total of 161 students in attendance. College students numbered 25; the remainder were in the so-called academic or preparatory department. Teaching responsibilities were divided among the seven faculty members and the president who, in addition, bore the burden of administration and fund-raising.[39]

The most serious problem confronting the college in its first decade was financial. Although the synod had mandated the founding of the college, it assumed no financial or governing responsibilities. Entirely dependent on private donations and laboring under heavy indebtedness from its beginning, the college was scarcely able to survive the financial collapse of 1873 which virtually paralyzed the economy of the entire nation. At the urgent request of the trustees, the synod finally agreed to adopt the college as a synodical institution and to provide the necessary moral and material support. This was accomplished through a charter amendment in 1876 that assigned the responsibility to the synod for electing all 30 members of the board of trustees. Having thus secured a firm commitment of synodical support for the college, Dr. Muhlenberg resigned in 1876 to accept a professorship in Greek in the University of Pennsylvania.[40]

As Muhlenberg College concluded its first decade, it had added further clarity to an emerging pattern of Lutheran collegiate education in America. The primary motive for its establishment, as for each of its Lutheran predecessors, was to assure a supply of well-educated pastors for the Lutheran church. The conservation of an ethnic heritage, so explicit in Muhlenberg's beginnings, continued to characterize the founding of Lutheran colleges for the next half-century. The study of classical languages and the liberal arts, commended by Luther and Melanchthon, was central in Muhlenberg's curriculum—as it would be in the curricula of Lutheran colleges yet to be established. Nor could there be any question of the commitment of Muhlenberg College to the mission of the Lutheran church or the synod which had called the college into being.

A College for Western Pennsylvania

During the same decade in which Muhlenberg College was established in eastern Pennsylvania, another Lutheran institution, Thiel College, was emerging in the western part of the state. Not only were these two colleges founded contemporaneously, but also their leaders shared similar theological positions. One of Thiel's distinguished early teachers, Henry Eyster Jacobs, looking back on these years, referred to Thiel as the "twin sister of Muhlenberg College."[41] It was no doubt the intimacy of such early common ties that moved Dr. Frederick A. Muhlenberg, Muhlenberg's first president, in his later years to accept the invitation to serve as third president of Thiel College (from 1891 to 1893).

The man who called Thiel College into being in 1866 was Dr. William A. Passavant, one of the most dynamic and imaginative personalities in the history of North American Lutheranism. A graduate of Jefferson College in Canonsburg, Pennsylvania, he studied theology at Gettysburg Seminary. From his pastorate in Pittsburgh his influence extended into almost every aspect of the life of the Lutheran church in his generation. As founder, president, and later mission superintendent of the Pittsburgh Synod, he was instrumental in organizing more than 60 new congregations and made the initial contacts which resulted in the organization of the Nova Scotia Conference of the Pittsburgh Synod. For many years he edited the influential church periodicals, *The Missionary* and *The Workman*.

More than any other churchman of his time, Passavant embodied the characteristic Lutheran emphasis on institutional ministries, a part of the church's rich heritage from the Franckes at Halle. Inspired by a visit to Theodor Fliedner's great institutional center in Kaiserswerth, Germany, in 1848, Passavant introduced deaconess work in the Lutheran church in America and founded several hospitals, orphanages, and homes for the aged and for epileptics. His contributions to Lutheran higher education included the founding of the Chicago Lutheran Theological Seminary as well as Thiel College.[42]

The setting in which Thiel was founded was quite different from the closely knit German-Lutheran enclave in which Muhlenberg was located. Populated far more by Scotch-Irish Presbyterians than by German Lutherans, western Pennsylvania was frontier territory for Lutherans. Until Passavant led the organization of the Pittsburgh Synod in 1845, the scattered pastors and congregations were obliged to seek fraternal support from the distant Pennsylvania synods east of the mountains or from the synods in Ohio.

Only after the organization of the Pittsburgh Synod was any serious effort made to provide preparatory training for pastors in western Pennsylvania. Until then, several future Lutheran leaders had attended Jefferson College, a Presbyterian school in Canonsburg, for pretheological study. David and Michael Jacobs, both of whom later taught at Gettysburg; William Reynolds, president of Capital University; Samuel Brobst, one of the founders of Muhlenberg College; Frederick Muhlenberg, its first president; and William Passavant—all were Jefferson alumni.[43]

After 1845 several academies had emerged in western Pennsylvania to offer basic classical training for prospective ministers. Some were private ventures, others under the auspices of the Pittsburgh Synod. Most of them, however, had closed either because of financial problems or loss of enrollment as the result of the Civil War.[44]

It was the providential meeting of William A. Passavant, a churchman with vision, and A. Louis Thiel, a generous benefactor, that made possible a Lutheran college for western Pennsylvania. Thiel was a German immigrant who had used funds salvaged from a failing dry-goods business in Pittsburgh to purchase stock in one of the many oil companies organized in western Pennsylvania following the great oil boom of 1859. More fortunate than most, the company struck oil and Thiel's investment was multiplied.

Eager to share his good fortune the pious Mr. Thiel confided to his pastor, William Berkemeier, that in gratitude to God he wanted to give one-tenth of the profits "to the interests of His Holy Kingdom." Remembering the many benevolent ventures that Dr. Passavant had inspired, Pastor Berkemeier introduced Louis and Barbara Thiel to him. On January 1, 1865, they placed in Passavant's hands the sum of $4000 to be used wherever he felt it might best glorify God.

As a former synod president and home mission superintendent, Passavant was keenly aware of the shortage of pastors for the growing number of congregations in western Pennsylvania. The oil boom of 1859 and the industrial explosion in coal, iron, and railroads during the Civil War had brought massive population increases that rendered the pastoral shortage even more acute. His suggestion that the gift be used to establish an institution for the education of the youth of the church and for young men studying for the ministry was warmly received by Mr. and Mrs. Thiel.[45]

Passavant also had in mind a location for the school, in Phillipsburg on the Ohio River, 25 miles west of Pittsburgh, easily accessible to students from western Pennsylvania, Ohio, and West Virginia. The property of a former resort hotel and an adjoining house were purchased and remodeled. On a Sunday afternoon in October 1866, when the Pittsburgh Synod was meeting in convention in Rochester, Pennsylvania, the entire delegation ferried across the Ohio River to Phillipsburg to attend the dedication of Thiel Hall.[46]

When the school opened, five students, three girls and two boys, enrolled; during the year the number increased to 30. Classwork was largely limited to the classical languages, German, English, and some mathematics. Until a full collegiate program had been established, students desiring to earn a baccalaureate degree completed their work at Muhlenberg College.

The initial faculty reflected the breadth of Passavant's acquaintance among the newer groups of Lutherans in the West. His selections represent the first instance of any eastern Lutheran college drawing upon these new resources for faculty members. Rev. E. F. Giese, pastor in Milwaukee, was appointed principal and first professor. Giese had received university training in Germany and had been sent by the Berlin Mission Society to serve a parish in the Wisconsin Synod. As the second year opened with increased enrollment, Rev. William Kopp, a graduate of Augustana College and Seminary at Paxton, Illinois, was called as the second professor. When Giese left after two years to accept a parish in New York, Passavant invited as his successor young Henry Eyster Jacobs, later to become professor of systematic theology at Philadelphia Seminary and one of the most distinguished Lutheran theologians in America.[47]

At the meeting of the Pittsburgh Synod in 1869 Dr. Passavant presented a resolution offering Thiel Hall to the synod as a gift from Mr. and Mrs. Thiel and suggested at the same time that the synod seek a charter for a full four-year synodical college.[48] The synod approved Passavant's resolution and accepted the gift with deep appreciation. Before adjourning, it elected a board of trustees and instructed them to request the legislature of Pennsylvania to grant a charter to Thiel College of the Evangelical Lutheran Church.[49]

When the charter was approved in April 1870, it was not yet certain where the college would be permanently located. The hazardous Ohio River crossing had raised serious questions about the Phillipsburg site. Relocation offers from several communities in western Pennsylvania were received by the board. A pledge of $20,000 and a choice of building sites by the borough of Greenville was finally accepted.

The college opened on September 1, 1870, with 23 students and 3 professors. The president and first professor was Henry Warren Roth, a native of western Pennsylvania and a graduate of Gettysburg College. He had been pastor of a congregation in Pittsburgh and was a member of the first elected board of trustees of Thiel College. He served as president of the college from 1870 to 1888.[50]

With the founding of Thiel the roster of Lutheran colleges in Pennsylvania was complete. Established over a 35-year period, these colleges reflected the growth of the Lutheran church in Pennsylvania and also the theological controversies that marked those turbulent years. All of them shared in the broad educational mission described by William A. Passavant at the laying of the cornerstone of the first permanent building at Thiel in 1872.

> We can conceive of nothing more praiseworthy in the service which men can perform for their fellow men, than to send back to his home, at the end of his college course, the young man in the dew of youth, healthful in body, ingenuous in heart, pure in life, cultivated in intellect and established in the faith of Christ. The world needs such men and the Church needs them. They are wanted at the bar, in the ministry, in the healing art, in the editorial chair, in the school room, in every department of business, commerce, trade, in agriculture and the mechanical arts, everywhere, men of piety, of a positive faith, of a true manhood, who know in whom and in what they believe, and stand up in their place as God's witnesses among their fellows! No want of society is greater than the want of such men![51]

Yet there was also great variety among the Pennsylvania colleges in the circumstances of their founding and their patterns of governance. Gettysburg and Muhlenberg Colleges were founded by joint stock companies, from which members of governing boards were elected. The Missionary Institute was governed by a self-perpetuating board. Thiel was established by an individual person and originally financed by a gift from a single benefactor. Only after it had been in operation for several years was the school given to the Pittsburgh Synod, to be governed by a synod-elected board.

Each of the four colleges in Pennsylvania made some distinctive contribution to the life of the church and of Lutheran higher education. Gettysburg College, as the earliest of them all, became the major source of presidential leaders for other Lutheran colleges. The Missionary Institute reminded the church of a dimension of ministry which speaks from the heart as well as from the book. Muhlenberg College raised the standard of Lutheran confessional faithfulness. Thiel, reflecting the benevolent and inclusive spirit of its founder, became the first Lutheran college to open as a coeducational institution and to maintain itself as such throughout its history.

7 Lutheran Higher Education in the South

The story of the Lutheran church in the South is the story of a church in diaspora. Most of the early German settlers entered the southern colonies by way of Pennsylvania either as new immigrants or as transplants from eastern Pennsylvania. Especially after 1750, as the more desirable lands were taken up, settlers moved west and south, following the Shenandoah Valley along the foothills of the Blue Ridge Mountains, into Virginia and the Carolinas. Others, earlier and in smaller numbers, entered the southern colonies directly along the Atlantic seaboard from rural Virginia to Charleston and Savannah.

At first their numbers were not great enough for them to establish communities and congregations strong enough to secure or support their own pastors. In most instances they were dependent upon itinerant ministers until they could secure help either from Europe or from older settlements to the north. Since the southern colonies were under direct rule of the British crown, permission to make such appeals to Europe had to be received from royal governors in Virginia and the Carolinas. Until the American Revolution, Lutheran court chaplains of the Hanoverian kings of England were helpful in mediating several such requests to Lutheran consistories in Germany on behalf of settlements in Virginia, North Carolina, and Georgia. As late as 1793, when the "Special Virginia Conference" was organized as a geographical subunit of the Pennsylvania Ministerium, there were only four Lutheran pastors regularly serving congregations in Virginia.[1] Not until 1803, when the North Carolina Synod came into being, was there any separate Lutheran synod in the South. At the time of its organization it, too, had only four pastors, two of whom had been trained in Germany.[2]

94

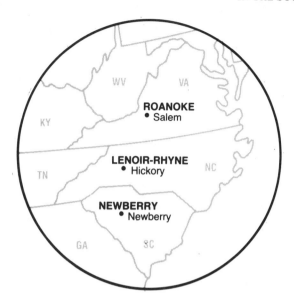

External Pressures and Internal Tensions

The impulse for the establishment of Lutheran institutions of higher learning developed slowly in the South. The prevailing rural character of southern society and the lack of internal transportation discouraged the development of all educational institutions, both public and private, until well into the 19th century. Southern Lutherans were particularly disadvantaged by their small numbers and by the scattered character of their settlements. They were thoroughly mixed with English-speaking neighbors and had none of the opportunities or incentives to establish schools for the preservation of German culture which were at hand in the compact and populous German settlements of eastern Pennsylvania.

Even maintaining a Lutheran identity under these circumstances was difficult in communities dominated by Presbyterians, Methodists, and Baptists. The use of the English language by these groups and the general popularity of religious revivals after 1800 made significant inroads, especially among younger German Lutherans. The success of revival preaching even suggested to many that formal education inhibited rather than enhanced the ministry of the gospel.

A final deterrent to the development of organized education among southern Lutherans was the persistence of intersynodical rivalries and doctrinal disputes. The origin of these tensions was an internal dispute within the North Carolina Synod between 1815 and 1819 over the authority of the synod to license and ordain clergy. At that time the North Carolina Synod was the only synod in the South, and its affiliated pastors and congregations were spread across North and South Carolina, Virginia, and eastern Tennessee. When a conflict arose over the renewal of the license of a young theological candidate, David Henkel, he and three other pastors, including his father and his brother, withdrew from the North Carolina Synod and in 1820 formed the Tennessee Synod.[3]

The Henkels were also critical of the liberal Lutheranism of the North Carolina Synod and its close fraternal relations with other denominations. Encouraged by the Henkels several congregations and pastors who shared their ecclesiastical and doctrinal views joined the new synod. Within a few years the Tennessee Synod included members in North and South Carolina and especially in the Shenandoah Valley of Virginia. Following a later schism in the synod itself, it lost all of its congregations in Tennessee. Its name thus came to represent a point of view rather than a geographical territory. The Tennessee Synod also remained aloof from the General Synod when it organized in 1820, both beause it was suspicious of centralization and because in its judgment the General Synod did not give sufficient acknowledgment to the Bible and the Augsburg Confession.

The controversy engendered by the formation of the Tennessee Synod not only brought schism and bitterness to the North Carolina Synod but also disunity and weakness to Lutheranism in Virginia. Hopes for a single Lutheran synod in Virginia were frustrated for a full century. The need for pastors in all parts of the South continued critical, but neither North Carolina nor the two small Virginia synods that finally came into being in 1829 and 1842 were able to undertake any organized effort to meet the need. Nor did the Tennessee Synod manifest interest in higher education, stressing instead church extension and religious publication through the Henkel family press in New Market, Virginia. Throughout the period before the Civil War most southern pastors continued to be trained, often inadequately, under the tutorship of ordained clergy.[4]

Initiative in the Southeast

The pioneer in promoting formal theological education for Lutherans in the South was Dr. John Bachman, a pastor in Charleston, South Carolina. A native of New York, Bachman was called in 1815 to St. John's Lutheran Church in Charleston and served as its pastor for 55 years. In addition to providing leadership for the Lutheran church for more than half a century, Bachman was widely recognized as a naturalist, with publications in the fields of botany, ornithology, and zoology. He was an associate of John J. Audubon, collaborating in two of Audubon's most significant works, *Birds of North America* and *Quadrupeds of North America*.

His interest in establishing a Lutheran seminary in the South dated from the decade before 1820, when similar concerns were being expressed in New York, Pennsylvania, and Ohio. When Bachman learned in 1818 that North Carolina Lutherans were planning a seminary, he sent an encouraging letter to the synod offering financial assistance. A year later he sent gifts of $221.75 from St. John's and $25.00 from other South Carolina congregations. The schism that resulted in the formation of the Tennessee Synod in 1820 ended the North Carolina efforts. A portion of the funds, however, was returned to St. John's and placed in a synod fund for future establishment of a seminary in the South.

Meanwhile, Bachman tutored several young ministerial candidates and encouraged others to attend Hartwick Seminary and, after 1826, Gettysburg. One of his first suggestions after becoming president of the newly established South Carolina Synod in 1828 was to establish a seminary "in our Southern country." Bachman's proposal, however, did not meet with unanimous approval among members of the synod. In early 1827, 40 up-country Lutherans had petitioned the synod for a general discussion of the seminary issue in each congregation before making any decision. In their judgment neither the gospel, the Word of God, nor human experience supported the need or the desirability of a seminary.

Bachman responded with an address to the 1830 synod convention on the importance of sound ministerial education. He undertook to answer the objections southern Lutherans had gleaned from revivalist preachers who viewed education of the clergy as a barrier to the free working of the Holy Spirit. Bachman noted that in Old Testament times Samuel and others were teachers in the "schools of the prophets." The apostle Paul had attended Gamaliel's school. Luther had taught in a university. Both Hartwick Seminary and Gettysburg Seminary had already proven their value to the church. Moreover, he concluded, with only one professor to begin with, the cost would not be great and books would be donated.

When a committee report indicated that by January 1831 $3000 had accumulated in the seminary fund, the synod voted to create The Classical Academy and Theological Institute of the South Carolina Synod and authorized the election of a professor and a board of directors. The Classical Academy was essential for the preparatory training of theological students and also for defraying the cost of the theological department. The Academy was therefore opened to male students over 10 years of age. A 23-year-old professor of ancient languages at the College of Charleston, the Rev. John G. Schwartz, who had studied under Dr. Bachman, was elected as first professor of theology. Five young men began their studies in February at the residence of Colonel John Eichelberger in Pomaria, South Carolina, only to have their work interrupted eight months later by the untimely death of their young professor.[5]

Again it was Bachman who took the initiative. Following a decision to relocate the seminary in Lexington, South Carolina, he invited Dr. Ernest L. Hazelius from Gettysburg Seminary, one of the most colorful figures of early American Lutheranism, to succeed Schwartz. Born in Silesia in Germany in 1777, Hazelius, at the age of five, had been brought by his parents to the aged Moravian bishop at Herrnhut, Polycarp Mueller, who solemnly dedicated the young boy to the work of the ministry. Had it not been for this incident, his life would have been quite different, for Catherine the Great, empress of Russia, had sought to adopt him as her own son. During their younger days Catherine and Ernest's mother had been schoolmates in Germany and their friendship had continued even after Christiana Brahtz married a local watchmaker and Sophia Augusta Frederica, princess of Anhalt-Zerbst, married Peter III of Russia.

At the age of 10 young Ernest was asked to make his own decision about his future. Remembering the blessing of the saintly old bishop, he chose the ministry rather than the Russian imperial court. He attended Moravian schools, studied theology, and in 1800 came to America to teach classics in Moravian schools in Nazareth, Pennsylvania. Ordained by the Lutheran Ministerium of New York in 1809, he served congregations in New Jersey until called to Hartwick Seminary in 1815 as professor of theology and principal of the classical department. During his 15 years at Hartwick he also traveled widely as a missionary pastor in northern New York and Canada.

In 1830 he was called to Gettysburg as Professor of Biblical and Oriental Literature and German Language, in order to give greater emphasis to German in the seminary. Three years later, at Bachman's invitation, he succeeded John Schwartz at the newly established southern seminary in Lexington, South Carolina. The man who turned his back on the Imperial Russian Court thus earned the distinction of serving in three of the first four theological seminaries established by Lutherans in America. He remained at the Lexington seminary for 20 years until his death in 1853.[6]

Newberry College and the Civil War

Since none of the eight students who began their theological study under Hazelius in January 1834 had received any college training, it was necessary from the beginning to offer basic preparatory work in English and the classics. With the assistance of an additional instructor, Hazelius undertook this task. Indeed, for several years thereafter the primary, preparatory, and classical departments of the Lexington Institute not only provided preliminary training for theological studies, but also offered one of the few opportunities available in the state at that time for organized primary and secondary education.

By 1854 the preparatory and classical departments had grown sufficiently for the synod to initiate steps to raise the Academy to the level of a degree-granting institution. Two years later, in 1856, under the leadership of Dr. John Bachman, a charter was secured for Newberry College, to be located together with the seminary in Newberry, South Carolina. Bachman became the first chairman of the board of trustees. Rev. Theophilus Stork, a Philadelphia pastor and graduate of both the college and seminary at Gettysburg, was chosen as first president.

By the end of the first year, 1858–1859, the new institution drew more than 100 students, although only six enrolled in the collegiate department and only two in the seminary. A leap in enrollment to 174 in 1859–1860 was the last encouraging sign before the disasters attendant upon the Civil War descended upon the infant college.[7]

President Stork resigned after only a year in office. His successor's term was even briefer. Dr. James A. Brown, another Gettysburg man, had come to Newberry the previous year as professor of theology. He had made no secret of his political views and when war broke out he announced to a special meeting of the faculty and students that he had been born in the Union, reared in the Union, and hoped to die in the Union. He therefore proposed to return to his native Pennsylvania and join the ranks in defense of the Union. The escort which accompanied him to the railroad station shortly thereafter may well have been more than a gesture of southern courtesy.[8]

For its third president in three years Newberry turned to a southerner, Josiah P. Smeltzer, a pastor from Salem, Virginia. Military enlistments and a smallpox epidemic reduced enrollment at the college to 64 men in 1862–1863 and 30 in 1864. The only gifts for the support of the college in 1862, according to the president's report to the synod, were "some German books, photographs of some leading clergymen, a bust of Luther, and two full-sized portraits—one of Luther and one of John C. Calhoun."[9] In 1864, with a greater display of patriotism than wisdom, the Board invested the college's $46,000 endowment in Confederate bonds rather than cotton, as recommended by President Smeltzer.

Early in 1865 the college closed. For a few weeks part of the college building became a military hospital for wounded Confederate soldiers. When news of the northward advance of General Sherman's army from Savannah reached Newberry, local citizens broke into the building and raided the stores of food, clothing, and medical supplies, rather than leaving them to the mercy of the troops. From July to September Union forces occupied the city and established headquarters at the college. To supply themselves with water for bathing the troops stopped the gutters and collected rain water on the roof of the building. Water seeped through the walls, undermined the foundations, and completely destroyed what had been one of the finest college structures in the entire South.[10]

The destruction of Newberry College was only a small example of the carnage visited on great areas of the South. Armies foraged and fought in practically every southern state. General Sherman's legendary march through Georgia ''from Atlanta to the sea'' in late 1864 had an equally savage counterpart in his advance northward into South Carolina, the state which most northerners held responsible for starting the war. Six months after the war, Carl Schurz, the German-American journalist, reported that the countryside along Sherman's march ''looked for many miles like a broad streak of ruin and desolation—the fences all gone; lonesome smokestacks, surrounded by dark heaps of ashes and cinders, marking the spots where human habitation had stood. . ..'' Charleston was ''a vast graveyard with broken walls and tall blackened chimneys for monuments.''[11] Railway tracks around Columbia were torn up for 30 miles in every direction. The surviving Confederate soldiers who received General Grant's generous terms of surrender at Appomattox had little but disaster to greet them as they returned to their homes.

That Newberry College was able to recover at all from such a catastrophe is a tribute to its doughty president, Josiah Smeltzer, and to the hospitality of a congregation in the mountain resort town of Walhalla, South Carolina. St. John's Lutheran Church offered the use of its buildings to the stricken institution in 1868. With the college bell, the remnant of a library, and a few blackboards and benches as its total assets, Newberry College resumed operation, and granted its first baccalaureate degree in 1869.[12]

Educational Pioneering in Virginia

The second attempt to meet the continuing dearth of qualified clergy in the South resulted in the founding of Roanoke College. This time, initiative came from a young graduate of Gettysburg Seminary who was induced by the urgent personal plea of a layman to accept the call as pastor of St. John's Lutheran Church of Middlebrook in the Shenandoah Valley of Virginia. As a young man, David Frederick Bittle had been directed in 1830 to Gettysburg Gymnasium by the Reverend Abraham Reck, the same missionary pastor who had encouraged Ezra Keller, later president of Wittenberg College, to study theology. Bittle, Keller, and Theophilus Stork, later president of Newberry College, all were members of the second class to graduate from Gettysburg College, in 1835.[13]

Bittle's association with leaders of Lutheran higher education at Gettysburg had prepared him for his role as a pioneer educator for southern Lutheranism. He had married Louise Krauth, the sister of Charles Philip Krauth, president of Gettysburg College. His own studies had been aided by a grant of funds through the American Education Society, mediated by Samuel Schmucker. The urgency of the call personally delivered to him as he completed his theological study impressed him with the great need for pastors in the church.

Bittle's interest in education found expression almost immediately upon his entry into the Virginia Synod. He was elected secretary and the following year president of the synod's Education Society, an organization that raised funds to assist ministerial students. In 1842 he entered enthusiastically into the first churchwide Lutheran fund appeal in America on behalf of higher education. In commemoration of the 100th anniversary of Henry Melchior Muhlenberg's arrival in America, the General Synod sponsored a Centenary Appeal for $150,000 to endow five Lutheran institutions: Gettysburg College and Hartwick, Gettysburg, Columbus, and Lexington Seminaries. Bittle secured more than $1000 in pledges from his own congregation.

Also in 1842 he was instrumental in bringing the Reverend Christopher C. Baughman to nearby Staunton to establish a missionary congregation and to serve as principal of a classical school Bittle had already begun in his own home. Both his own Virginia Synod and the newly formed Synod of Western Virginia endorsed the new venture and on August 6, 1843, 18 students began their studies in the log buildings of the Virginia Institute.

According to the 1840 census only 16% of the white population of Virginia between the ages of 5 and 20 were in attendance at any school. The Institute, therefore, gave the church an opportunity not only to assist young men preparing for the ministry, but also to offer a general education for others in the community.

Instruction at the Institute began at the high school level and advanced with the progress of the students until two years of college work were given. The faculty encouraged graduates to go on to Gettysburg College to complete their baccalaureate degrees. When a charter was granted in 1844, the school became known as Virginia Collegiate Institute. Its board of trustees was a self-perpetuating body with 6 members elected from the Synod of Western Virginia, 12 from the Virginia Synod, and 5 non-Lutherans.

In 1845 David Bittle accepted a call from his home parish in Middletown, Maryland. Thereafter Christopher Baughman guided the Institute through its most difficult years, including the move in 1847 to its permanent location in Salem, Virginia. Salem was chosen because of its location midway between the two sponsoring synods. There was none of the usual bidding for the college by rival towns, nor was there even a Lutheran congregation in Salem. Land had to be purchased and temporary quarters rented in an abandoned Baptist church until a college building could be erected.

To supplement the modest tuition income, funds for the land, building, and operation were solicited by Jacob Scherer, financial agent of the college. He advertised in *The Lutheran Observer*, sought donations from congregations, borrowed from individuals and from the Centenary Fund of the Western Virginia Synod, and sold scholarships at $100 each, good for the tuition of one student for five years.

Enrollment gradually increased. Of the 38 students in 1849–1850, 14 were candidates for the ministry. In 1851–1852, 20 of an enrollment of 60 indicated the same intent. Such numbers of pretheological students eager to complete their college degrees led the Synod of Virginia to encourage the trustees to seek a four-year college charter. Professor Baughman, however, felt there were already enough colleges in Virginia, and it would be a greater service to church and community to maintain a high quality preparatory school. When a student delegation threatened to leave the college, Baughman reluctantly yielded. After the trustees had requested and received a charter for Roanoke College in 1853, Baughman reaffirmed his convictions by resigning to become principal of the Hagerstown Female Seminary in Maryland.

When the board of trustees met to elect a president for the newly chartered college, they turned again to the founder of the original Virginia Institute, David F. Bittle. Since his return to Maryland in 1845, Bittle had given continued evidence of a deep commitment to Lutheran higher education. He had brought the issue of higher education for women before the Maryland Synod in 1849 and even resigned his pastorate the following year to raise funds to establish the Hagerstown Female Seminary. His 111-page "Plea for Female Education," issued in 1851 to awaken the church "to her true position and responsibility in the great educational movements of the age,"[14] was doubtless a factor in stimulating the remarkable wave of Lutheran seminaries for women which appeared in the decades preceding and immediately following the Civil War.

His inaugural address as the first president of Roanoke College gave further evidence of the breadth of his educational interests. "The most momentous duty of one generation to another," he declared, "is its education." How this obligation is honored will determine whether the next generation will be "better men than we are, better qualified to incur the responsibilities of life, to possess superior wisdom and a more refined humanity." Using terminology characteristic of liberal arts colleges he declared the objective of a collegiate education to be the development and discipline of the whole man, intellectually and morally. Students at Roanoke College were to learn what to study, how to study, and how to evaluate what they learned. This was to be accomplished through a curriculum emphasizing languages, mathematics, science, philosophy, and religion, not patterned after either German or English models, but "a thoroughgoing American system adapted to the precise needs of the democracy in which we live."[15]

It seems to have been clear to the president from the beginning that if the college were to survive in an area where there were few Lutherans, it would have to make its appeal as broad as possible. A brochure entitled ''An Appeal to the German Population of Virginia and Adjacent States'' in the summer of 1853 was a plea for more ministerial students, but also for more college-trained leaders in lower schools and for a better-educated laity. Roanoke College, it stated, was not a theological school but a ''purely literary'' institution offering instruction in ''a regular collegiate course.''[16]

Roanoke College Survives the War

A combination of courage, vision, and daring characterized the leadership of the college in the years immediately preceding the Civil War. Energetic appeals to congregations, pastors, and the local community brought increased enrollments and financial contributions. As the college opened in September 1854, 80 students responded, and in the spring of 1855 the first four graduates received their baccalaureate degrees. By 1860 enrollment reached 118, including 46 students of college grade.

With a growing college department it was necessary to enlarge the faculty and expand the curriculum. A chair in modern languages was established in 1855; Italian and Spanish were offered as optional languages. English grammar, composition, and declamation became requirements for all students. A chair of natural sciences was created in 1856, emphasizing chemistry as applied to agricultural needs. Lectures were also given in anatomy and physiology. The president had a special hobby of buying worthwhile books at bargain prices, and by 1861 the college library numbered 4000 volumes, with a strong emphasis in the natural sciences.

As enrollments increased, additional facilities were also needed. An enlarged dining hall was erected, a new wing added to the Administration Building and two small buildings constructed adjacent to the main building. Only after the contracts of $4000 were let for the two small buildings did Dr. Bittle inform the Synod of Western Virginia of his actions. ''It is true that the state of our treasury hardly admits of such extensive building operations,'' he admitted, ''but it is impossible for the institution to succeed in the prosecution of its future course unless we have the accommodations which these buildings will afford.''[17]

To raise the funds necessary for these projects and to pay the indebtedness the college had incurred in moving to Salem without any financial aid from community or church, President Bittle and a full-time financial agent spent much of their time in private solicitations. Traveling both in their home territory and throughout the northern states, they established a pattern of financial support that was to characterize Roanoke College throughout its entire history. Although their efforts never brought the college into affluence, they were able, both before and after the Civil War, to enhance its reputation far beyond the borders of Virginia.

In addition to his duties as president, professor, and fund-raiser, David Bittle also served as pastor of three congregations, including the college church, which he and his brother Daniel helped to organize. Nor did he neglect the spiritual care of students. In his 1860 report to the synods he noted that 15 of the 30 graduates of the college since 1855 were either in the ministry or were preparing for it. Reflecting something of his own evangelical orientation, he added, "Every year we have had a number of hopeful conversions among the students, and we endeavor to make religion the main characteristic of the college."[18]

A combination of good fortune and imaginative policy-making enabled Roanoke College to avoid the catastrophic effects of the Civil War experienced by many other colleges in the South. When the war broke out in April 1861, all but 17 of the 118 students left the college, and the faculty canceled commencement exercises. But rather than close the school the trustees agreed to offer instruction to boys not yet old enough for military service and, until the number of boys increased, also to admit girls. Confederate authorities gave full support to this effort. The Surgeon General of the Confederacy even vetoed a proposal to use the college buildings as a hospital. "If we succeed in establishing the Confederacy," he wrote, "we want intelligent men to control it, and if there is any locality in which a college can exist in these times, it must be protected."[19]

Fortunately for the college there were no major military operations in its vicinity during the war. In December 1863 a federal unit appeared in Salem, burned some military supplies, and held a student militia company overnight as prisoners, but did no damage to the campus.

Almost unbelievably, the enrollment figures during the war years rose progressively from 70 to 130, as parents throughout Virginia sent their boys to the comparative safety of the Roanoke campus. Older students, too, returned, largely disabled veterans with honorable discharges.

During the same period the steady tuition income and the continued diligence of David Bittle in soliciting gifts also improved the financial condition of the college. Food supplies became increasingly difficult to secure as the war drew to its close. On one occasion, Dr. Bittle purchased a herd of 14 beef cattle and personally drove them 70 miles across country from the neighboring county, successfully avoiding foraging parties of both Union and Confederate troops.

In other wartime activities, Dr. Bittle often preached to Confederate troops, and on one occasion Roanoke students organized and presented a benefit program which netted $1300 for Confederate hospitals. As the war ended, Confederate currency deteriorated in value to the point that creditors refused to accept it. Caught thus with $1000 of Confederate money on hand, President Bittle hurried off to Richmond where he had heard he could buy books for the college library very cheaply. Just as he was about to board the train, he was advised of the surrender of General Robert E. Lee. In his later accounting to the trustees on the disposition of college funds Dr. Bittle reported, "The remaining sum perished in my hands."[20]

President Dreher's Quest

The remarkable story of Roanoke College during the Civil War has an equally astonishing sequel in the postwar decades. David Bittle continued as president for 11 more years, though his rather unorthodox financial operations were somewhat curtailed after 1868 by the appointment of a full-time fiscal manager. The finance committee of the board determined that no contract for any new building could be let without a major vote of the entire board. But the library continued to grow, reaching 14,000 volumes by the purchase of a part of S. S. Schmucker's library with private gifts.

In 1869 a young Confederate veteran named Julius Daniel Dreher entered the junior class at Roanoke and immediately demonstrated special abilities in the field of public relations. During his summer vacation in 1870 he toured the cotton states on behalf of the college and after graduation in 1871 he was appointed to the faculty and placed in charge of college correspondence. As a result of his visits and correspondence, students began to arrive from Mississippi, Louisiana, Texas, and Tennessee. He started a college newspaper through which he reported on his visits through the South. In 1874 the total enrollment reached 160 students, 56 of whom came from 16 states outside Virginia. Following his additional appointment as financial secretary of the college in 1875, Dreher visited cities as far north as Philadelphia and Boston. In spite of the persisting influence of the financial panic of 1873, he brought back cash and pledges of more than $12,000 toward the construction of a library building.

After the death of David Bittle in 1876 and a brief two-year transitional administration, 32-year-old Julius Daniel Dreher succeeded to the presidency of Roanoke College and gave it distinguished leadership for 25 years.

The patterns of student recruitment that he introduced while field representative of the college continued to attract students from beyond the borders of Virginia. At no time between 1870 and 1900 were fewer than 13 different states represented among the Roanoke students, and on two occasions there were as many as 22. The response of President Bittle to a request for a college catalog in 1870 led to the enrollment of the first Choctaw Indians from the Indian Territory of Oklahoma. Before 1900, 36 others followed, several of whom later became civic and church leaders in the Choctaw nation.

Several foreign countries were also represented in the student body of Roanoke College, largely through international contacts established by President Dreher. The first of eight Mexican students came in 1876. The Japanese who first enrolled in 1888 aroused an interest which led to a missionary program in Japan by the United Synod of the South. Among the numerous Koreans at Roanoke were the first young men of that nation to earn a baccalaureate degree anywhere in the world. One of the students was the son of the Emperor.

President Dreher continued to employ the same patterns of fund-raising he had used so effectively as financial secretary of the college. Looking back upon his presidency, Dreher described himself as "a peripatetic college president in perennial search of a deficit extinguisher." His routine, as described by the college historian, began each year in September when he presided at the opening exercises.

> In October or November, he would begin to make his round of northern cities, usually returning south for the Christmas vacation. In January he would go north once more, where he would remain until April or May, until it was time to prepare for commencement and the annual meeting of the Board. And part of the summer vacation would be spent in participating in some conference, or in canvassing for students. . . .[21]

His visits in the North were productive of substantial income for the college, most of which unfortunately had to be channeled into the operating fund rather than the endowment. Dreher did not ignore the two Virginia synods to which the college was related, but their limited financial resources would not have been able to keep the college alive. The economic condition of the entire South after the Civil War was a disaster, and as President Dreher once observed, support for higher education in the South was never enthusiastic. Most of the church support that reached Roanoke College came from individuals rather than synods. According to one account the college "was beneficiary to oceans of ecclesiastical good will and to an infrequent trickle of ecclesiastical money."[22]

Yet both the board and the administration consistently affirmed the Lutheran character of the college, reported regularly to the synods, maintained a strong religious dimension in the curriculum, and contributed substantially to the preparation of Lutheran clergy. Of the 520 alumni of the college at its 50th anniversary in 1903, 173 had entered the ministry. Beyond this very specific contribution to the church in the South, one that fulfilled the traditional mission of Lutheran higher education, Roanoke also carried a witness on the church's behalf into both social and cultural spheres that the church itself would enter only after many years. It was a pioneer in its outreach to native Americans and to international students. During a time of national crisis it identified itself with its community in a way no other college in the state of Virginia was able to do, adjusting its academic program to meet the needs of the young people of the state. Through its presidents it represented in all parts of the nation a high regard for positive spiritual and cultural values as exemplified in liberal arts education.

The Flowering of Southern Collegiate Education

The decade of the 1850s, immediately preceding the Civil War, witnessed a remarkable flowering of Lutheran interest in higher education in the South. Traditional concerns for pretheological training were never absent during these years, but they were subordinated to a surge of interest and support in the church for general secondary and collegiate education and a strong emphasis on education for women.

At least partially responsible for this new enthusiasm was the wave of economic prosperity experienced by the entire region. Economic conditions in the southern states were better than at any time in the nation's history. Tobacco production doubled between 1849 and 1859. Cotton prices were at an all-time high level and all southerners proudly agreed with planters and cotton jobbers that "Cotton is King!" On the political scene southern politicians of the Democratic party controlled the nation's tariff and land policies. A strong sense of "southern nationalism" found expression in the desire to develop leadership and maintain the standards of the "southern way of life." Education of both men and women would contribute to the achievement of these goals.

Sharing in both the prosperity and the optimism of the times, Lutherans in the South responded to the challenge. By 1861 five new colleges and female seminaries had been established under Lutheran auspices. At the urging of its president, the Reverend Joseph Linn, the North Carolina Synod amended its constitution in 1852 to permit the sponsoring of an educational project.[23] After experimenting with a high school for boys, the synod applied in 1859 for a charter for North Carolina College, a degree-granting institution "for the instruction of youths in the various branches of science, literature and art."[24] Neither charter nor constitution gave any indication of intent to train theologians. Yet the president, Daniel Bittle, brother of the Roanoke president, was required to subscribe to the same doctrinal oath to which Samuel S. Schmucker had subscribed when he became first professor at Gettysburg Seminary 33 years earlier.

The careful efforts of President Linn to assure the new college of regular funding constitute one of the first serious efforts on the part of an eastern synod to undertake the responsibilities of institutional support for college education. The synod earmarked its "Centenary Fund," originally created to help ministerial students, for enlarging the college endowment to assure the regular payment of faculty salaries. The "Seminary Fund," for the support of the South

Carolina seminary, was likewise transferred to the college. A women's group came into existence to raise funds for scientific equipment. A ministerial candidate was commissioned to travel through the synod, soliciting funds and preaching on behalf of the college at Sunday services. A realistic pastor reminded the synod that college support had long-term implications. "The expenditures at the first will necessarily be large," he warned, and with prophetic foresight added, "and must continue to increase."[25]

At the same time that North Carolina College was chartered as a synodical enterprise, Susan Bigelow Bittle, wife of the president, established the Mount Pleasant Female Seminary, later known as Mont Amoena Seminary, as a private venture. Her school survived the war, won synod adoption in 1869, and even received a state charter authorizing the granting of academic degrees. For 63 years it maintained an unbroken existence in Mount Pleasant, closing only in 1922.[26] Three other female seminaries opened under Lutheran auspices in the South during the 1850s. Following his eloquent plea for women's education in 1851, David Bittle helped establish the Hagerstown Female Seminary in Maryland in 1852. In 1853 John G. Morris and Benjamin Kurtz founded the Lutherville Seminary, also in Maryland. Both schools operated collegiate departments and in later years awarded baccalaureate degrees.[27]

In Virginia a female seminary opened at Wytheville in 1859, survived the war, but closed in 1870. Its immediate successor in 1871 was Marion College for Women, the last of the Lutheran colleges for women. Marion College ceased operation in 1967.[28]

The two men's colleges described earlier in this chapter also received their charters as degree-granting institutions in the 1850s, Roanoke in 1853 and Newberry in 1856. In both instances the college charters affirmed broad educational objectives, placing primary stress upon general education for leadership rather than pretheological education.

Postwar Efforts at Recovery

The tragedy of the Civil War drew the curtain on southern enterprise of every kind. The momentum for Lutheran higher education generated in the South during the 1850s was never fully regained. The hopeful ventures at Newberry and North Carolina Colleges were forced to close. Financial resources melted away, and in Newberry's case even its buildings were destroyed. An entire generation of young men of college age was virtually wiped out. The president of the Synod of South Carolina reported in 1865, "All our Theological students proper, as well as those preparing for the ministry have either fallen upon the battlefield, or died from disease; not one has escaped."[29] The only remaining college for men, Roanoke, owed its survival to a fortunate location and unusually resourceful leadership in funding and recruitment.

The seminaries and colleges for women that were established in the 1850s fared better than the men's colleges. Even in the face of the hardship conditions that prevailed throughout the South, female colleges struggled to remain in operation or, if forced to close temporarily, to reopen. The Maryland schools had the advantage of location in a border state that remained under Union occupation during most of the war. After the war was over, between 1865 and 1890, at least 20 additional female seminaries and colleges were established by Lutherans in Virginia, Tennessee, and the Carolinas.[30] Most were short-lived, because of insufficient financial resources. The new schools generally offered only academy-level work, although several, such as the Staunton Female Seminary and Marion College in Virginia, also offered one or two years of collegiate work. These schools were established, conducted, and even owned by Lutheran pastors, many of whom sought by teaching to supplement their meager parish salaries. In several instances the schools were officially endorsed by synods, but in no case did they receive direct synodical financial support. Their popularity among the Lutheran congregations reflected the prevailing concern of middle-class southerners that their children, especially their daughters, not be obliged to associate with blacks and lower-class white children in the emerging public schools.

In the face of almost overwhelming odds the three Lutheran colleges for men also resumed baccalaureate instruction after the war. Thanks to the 109 students enrolled in its academy department, Roanoke was also able to provide instruction to 36 college students in the fall of 1865.[31]

The North Carolina Synod reopened its college at Mt. Pleasant in 1867 under the presidency of Louis A. Bikle. For more than 30 years the synod and the college struggled together to maintain North Carolina College as a degree-granting institution. But in the face of declining enrollment and depressing financial conditions the school was obliged to close in 1902.[32] Limited collegiate work was continued in the college facilities through the Mount Pleasant Collegiate Institute under the direction of Professor G. F. McAllister.[33]

After a nine-year exile in its mountain retreat in Walhalla, South Carolina, Newberry College returned to its prewar location in 1877 with a new president, George W. Holland, and began the arduous task of reconstruction and renewal. Creditors agreed to cancel remaining claims against the college property, and the city pledged $15,870 for the construction of a new building on the site of the original structure. During a 15-year period beginning in 1884, the college shared its new building with the synod's theological seminary. The seminary had salvaged its modest endowment at the end of the Civil War but had no permanent facilities. The annual endowment income of $1000 a year helped to support both seminary and college programs. Under the depressed economic conditions of the postwar decades in the South enrollments grew slowly, reaching 200 when the college celebrated its 50th anniversary in 1906. In 1913 the South Carolina Synod was persuaded to accept sponsorship of a newly established college for women. Chartered as a degree-granting institution, Summerland College awarded 143 bachelor's degrees before 1926, when it was merged with Newberry. Strengthened by the added enrollment Newberry was able to withstand the depression of the 1930s and to achieve full regional accreditation in 1936.[34]

The Story of Lenoir-Rhyne

During the 1850s the Tennessee Synod also shared the impulses for educational expansion that had energized the leaders of other Lutheran synods in the South. A proposal for the founding of a college came before the synod convention of 1852, but progress was halted by the secession of the Holston Synod in 1860. During Civil War and Reconstruction simple survival constituted the major agenda, but by 1874 the synod was ready at last to establish its own college.[35]

Three small communities in western North Carolina, Conover, Newton, and Hickory, pledged funds and offered land as a site for the college. Conover's pledge of $2500 prevailed over the offer of a 23-acre tract of land from the estate of Colonel Walter Lenoir, wealthy retired judge in Hickory. In 1877 Concordia College came into being, and by 1889 was enrolling more students than its facilities could comfortably handle.[36]

Since opportunities for expansion in Conover were limited, a group of four pastors proposed relocating the college in Hickory. The group included the president, Robert A. Yoder; the professor of theology, Andrew L. Crouse; the financial agent, William P. Cline; and a trustee and former president, Jason C. Moser. These men secured a formal renewal of the Lenoir offer with the added assurance of the facilities of an academy building on the Lenoir estate. Neither the college board nor the synod, however, found the proposal acceptable.

Yoder then resigned as president of Concordia and the Hickory group organized an association to accept the Lenoir offer and establish a new college in Hickory. As the school year opened in September 1891, two Lutheran colleges, Concordia and Lenoir, located in small towns only eight miles apart, awaited the arrival of their students and some indication from the Tennessee Synod as to which school would receive its official blessing.[37]

The test came when the president of the board at Concordia nominated a Conover man to succeed Professor Crouse as professor of theology at Concordia. Not only did the convention of the Tennessee Synod refuse to elect the Conover man but it instructed its ministerial students who were receiving financial assistance from the synod to enroll in Lenoir College rather than Concordia.

Interpreting the synod's action as a vote of no confidence in Concordia College, the board of trustees invited the Missouri Synod to provide both a president and a professor of theology for the school. To the chagrin of the Lenoir supporters the Missouri Synod promptly responded by sending the needed replacement. On May 29, 1892, the Reverend W. H. T. Dau, a pastor of the Missouri Synod, was installed as president. At its fall convention the Tennessee Synod withdrew its "fostering care" and Concordia College passed under the sponsorship of the Missouri Synod until it closed in 1935.[38]

The college in Hickory opened in September 1891, with 63 students under the personal direction of the four ministers who had accepted the Lenoir grant. During the year they secured a charter from the Superior Court in Catawba County, according to which the college, named in honor of its benefactor, was authorized to grant "such literary and honorary degrees as are usually conferred in colleges."[39]

Although Lenoir College was entirely under private control, the trustees had every intention that it should eventually belong to the Tennessee Synod. A statement of "Fundamental Principles," announced when the cornerstone of the new building was laid, left no doubt of these intentions. The school was to teach "Christianity in its purest form." The Bible and Luther's Catechism were to be standard textbooks and no one was to be elected to the board or the faculty who was not in "full communion with some strict and faithful Lutheran congregation known to the electors." The school was never to pass under control of any synod which did not accept and acknowledge all the confessions of the Lutheran church.[40]

By 1893, 14 students of theology were attending the college, and both synod and college were eager to establish a formal relationship. Action, however, was delayed by an effort to assuage the animosities aroused by the establishment of Lenoir College. At the invitation of Professor Crouse, the synod's professor of theology, a series of "free conferences" was held, attended by representatives of the Tennessee Synod, the Missouri Synod, and the Ohio Synod, which in the meantime had also established a school in Hickory.

Instead of promoting unity among Lutherans in Catawba County, the conferences widened the separation. Theological differences between Missouri and Tennessee, especially on the doctrine of predestination, were sharpened by emotional charges that the Missouri Synod had intruded into North Carolina and "taken over" both congregations and college. The Missourians responded that Concordia trustees had invited the Missouri Synod to appoint a president at a time when the Tennessee Synod had manifested no interest in the school. The presence of the Ohio Synod in the debates completed a sorry scenario in which

Lutheran synods of Tennessee, Missouri, and Ohio contended over territorial rights in a single county in North Carolina![41]

For a time it seemed that the well-intentioned efforts of Lenoir College to promote Lutheran unity in Catawba County might even jeopardize its ties with the Tennessee Synod. But by 1895 the Tennessee Synod was ready to move beyond the "fostering care" which it had pledged to Concordia, and accord Lenoir College its "hearty moral and financial support." In return the college agreed to increase its board membership from 6 to 13 and to permit the synod to nominate 7 new members and to fill all future vacancies occurring on the board. In 1899 the deed to the school property was transferred to the Tennessee Synod and the college came under its full control.[42]

During the early years of the 20th century there were further efforts to unify the complicated Lutheran educational ventures within the state of North Carolina. In 1902, with financial pressures weighing heavily upon North Carolina College, the North Carolina Synod responded to an invitation from the Tennessee Synod to discuss consolidation. At that time the Tennessee Synod owned Lenoir College and also recognized Gaston College, an institution privately operated by a pastor of the synod.[43] The North Carolina Synod owned North Carolina College for men and Mont Amoena Seminary for women and also recognized Elizabeth College, a women's college privately operated by a Lutheran pastor in Charlotte.[44]

The quest for cooperation lasted nearly a decade but local loyalties and uncertainty of purpose prevented any decisive action. The final effort in 1910 foundered on the issue of coeducation. Lenoir College had admitted both men and women from its beginning while the North Carolina Synod insisted upon separate schools for men and women. Both Mont Amoena Seminary and the Mount Pleasant Collegiate Institute therefore continued to operate, though neither was able to maintain full collegiate status or financial stability. Mont Amoena closed in 1922 and the Collegiate Institute in 1935. Only through the merger of the North Carolina and Tennessee Synods in 1921 were the resources of the two bodies finally united in support of a single four-year college. A year later the fiscal stability of Lenoir College was assured by a $300,000 gift from Daniel Rhyne, a wealthy cotton-mill owner. In grateful recognition of his generosity, the name of the college was changed to Lenoir-Rhyne, thus joining the names of the two great benefactors of the institution.[45]

8 THE SECOND GERMAN MIGRATION

One of the pioneer historians of American immigration has reminded us that a significant part of all human history deals with mankind in motion.[1] Examples abound, beginning with the scattering of the nations at the ill-fated tower of Babel. Until the vast displacements in the 20th century, however, no movement of population had displayed such massive proportions as the European migrations of the 19th century. Between 1814 and 1914, 50 million emigrants set out from their homes in Europe to all parts of the world. Almost as awesome is the fact that 35 million of them came to the United States and Canada.

For Americans the year 1814 marked the end of the War of 1812 with England, sometimes called the Second War for American Independence. Peace had also come to Europe after the Napoleonic Wars, and the youthful United States entered a period of commercial overseas expansion, internal growth and national self-affirmation which found its classic expression in the Monroe Doctrine of 1823. The first use of the word *immigrant* dates from 1817.[2] The process of immigration had been going on for 200 years, but during the 17th and 18th centuries settlers were known as "emigrants." They migrated "out" of something; by 1817 they were migrating "into" something, namely, the new nation which had come into being. Before the Civil War five million immigrants entered the United States, largely from Germany and the British Isles. During each decade the numbers increased, until 2.5 million entered between 1850 and 1860. By 1860, 1,276,000 persons of German birth lived in the United States.

The migration of the Germans during these years was by no means confined to the United States. Nor was this country always the first choice of the

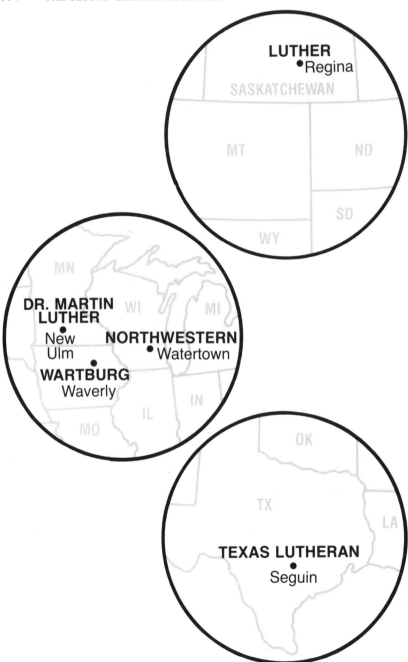

emigrant. Financial crises in the United States in 1819, 1837, and 1857 cooled enthusiasm for America for a year or two following each depression. From 1818 to 1828, when fewer than 1000 Germans were entering the United States each year, an average of 25,000 a year established themselves in the new kingdom of Poland. Newly independent South America, especially Brazil, also attracted many during the 1820s.

Political and Economic Motives for Emigration

By 1825, however, the effects of the depression of 1819 in America had worn off and the call for laborers in the warehouses and mills, on canals and turnpikes, had been spread throughout Europe by ship captains and recruiting agents. Prevailing economic and political conditions in Germany were especially favorable for emigration. The Congress of Vienna in 1815 sought to restore the old monarchies which Napoleon had overthrown. But the ideals of political liberalism, inspired by the American and French Revolutions, pressed toward the surface in every European country, producing general restlessness and erupting into open revolutions in 1830 and 1848. In the wake of each uprising many of the most able and independent citizens were forced to seek refuge abroad.

Economic changes also undermined the stability of the old order. The Industrial Revolution, powered by steam, announced the end of the medieval craft guilds. Steamboats initiated a new era in transportation; power looms threatened to replace the domestic textile weaver; and changes in agricultural machinery and methods made farming uncertain. Artisans, small farmers, and craftsmen, with readily marketable competencies, were attracted by the beckoning opportunities in a new land.

A large part of the German emigration of this period was drawn from the energetic and productive middle class which possessed both skills and resources to finance their venture. Stimulated by reports such as Gottfried Duden's widely read *Report on a Journey* (1829) and by letters from emigrants, a variety of well-financed group migrations was organized. The Giessen Society sent several shiploads by way of Baltimore and New Orleans to establish a colony at St. Charles, Missouri. A later venture, by the *Mainzer Adelsverein*, under Baron von Solms-Braunfels brought over 700 settlers to Texas in 1844. This "second German migration" was quite different from that of peasant refugees driven from their Palatine farms by hunger and deprivation in the early 1700s and forced to sell their own services to pay for their passage. The new emigrants were not hopeless victims of circumstance but enterprising persons unwilling to become victims of changes in their homeland.[3]

German immigrants entered the United States and Canada through all the major seaports, from Quebec to New York and Baltimore. Some remained in the East, but most, utilizing the old and new highways, traveled by canal and riverboat or by turnpike into the western states of Ohio, Indiana, Michigan, and Missouri. Large numbers entered the United States at New Orleans or Galveston, having traveled from Bremen or LeHavre on American ships which had unloaded southern cotton at these European ports. From New Orleans they moved up the Mississippi River to St. Louis or Cincinnati and turned these cities and the surrounding areas into centers of German language and influence.

The Religious Factor

Among the German emigrants, although by no means the largest number, were persons responsive to the religious conditions which prevailed after the Congress of Vienna. In the spirit of the new Prussian nationalism, King Frederick William III proclaimed for his kingdom a national church organization combining Lutheran and Reformed churches. Announced as it was on the 300th anniversary of the Reformation in 1817, many hailed the creation of the Prussian Union as a hopeful sign of renewal in the church that had languished under the deadening influence of rationalism.

But the Union came under severe attack, especially from Lutheran pietists who were supportive of a spiritual awakening (*Erweckung*) in Germany and who identified their emphasis on "spirituality" with loyalty to the Scriptures and the Lutheran confessions. At the same time a new interest in Luther and Lutheran theology was rising in Germany, also occasioned by the Reformation anniversaries in 1817 and 1830. Klaus Harms, archdeacon at Kiel, reissued Luther's 95 Theses and added 95 of his own against the Prussian Union and rationalism. A new edition of the Augsburg Confession appeared in 1819, and the Erlangen edition of Luther's Works in 1826. These events ushered in a confessional revival which stimulated theological studies in the universities of Germany and profoundly affected Lutheran churches throughout Europe and America.

As the power of the state was employed to force conformity to the new liturgy of the Prussian Union, Lutheran resistance mounted. Especially after 1830 many pastors were arrested or suspended from office. Some fled to neighboring Saxony or Pomerania. Others migrated to Australia or America, taking groups of dissenters with them. One group of 700 Silesians followed their pastor to Australia in 1838. A large group went to America in 1839 under the leadership of Johannes Grabau, a pastor in Magdeburg, who had been twice imprisoned for his refusal to use the Union liturgy. Following his release he and a Prussian army captain, Heinrich von Rohr, led 1000 immigrants from Magdeburg to Hamburg and Liverpool and thence by five ships to New York. Some remained in New York and Albany; von Rohr accompanied a larger group to Milwaukee, Wisconsin. The majority, however, settled with their pastor in Buffalo, New York.

Shortly after his arrival, Grabau established Martin Luther College and Seminary in Buffalo, one of the earliest Lutheran educational ventures in the West. In an effort to draw together other Lutheran immigrants who had also fled Germany in protest against the Prussian Union, he issued a pastoral letter (*Hirtenbrief*), seeking to establish a unified ministry, and suggesting the establishment of a school for the preparation of teachers.[4] The letter went to pastors of the Saxon colony in Missouri, whose members had left Germany about the same time as Grabau's group. The Missourians, however, deeply involved in their own internal problems at this time, delayed their response. In 1843 they rejected Grabau's proposal, finding his authoritarian view of the ministry unacceptable. So did other Lutheran pastors in Wisconsin and Michigan. Those who agreed with Grabau organized the Buffalo Synod in 1845, and adopted the college and seminary in Buffalo for the preparation of synodical clergy. The synod itself maintained a separate existence until 1930, when it became one of the constituent synods in the formation of the American Lutheran Church.

The Saxon Migration

The Saxons in Missouri to whom Grabau addressed his pastoral letter in 1840 exerted the greatest influence of any single European emigrant group in the 19th century on the development of Lutheranism in America. Their leader, and the organizer of their migration, was Martin Stephan, pastor of St. John's Church in Dresden. A popular preacher and strong advocate of pietism and confessionalism, he vigorously opposed both rationalism and the Prussian Union. The devotional and discussion groups he organized and conducted as part of his ministry extended his influence far beyond the limits of his parish. Criticism of the manner in which these informal group meetings were conducted brought Stephan into conflict with civil and religious authorities and led in the fall of 1837 to his arrest and suspension from office.[5]

Apparently Stephan had long considered founding a colony of emigrants. Ten years earlier he had sought the advice of a visiting American pastor, Benjamin Kurtz, regarding possible sites in the United States. The events of 1837 moved him to action. During the following winter he secretly enrolled a company of prosperous farmers, artisans, and professional men from Dresden and Leipzig, and created a common fund to defray the costs of transportation and settlement. Included in the group were several young pastors and theological candidates who looked to him as their spiritual father and confidant.

In July 1838, Stephan publicly announced the intention of his group to seek refuge in America. Released at the last minute from detention by the authorities, Stephan joined his party of 700 at Bremen. Five ships departed in November for New Orleans; one was lost at sea. A riverboat voyage up the Mississippi River brought the pilgrims to St. Louis in January 1839, and ultimately to Perry County, about 100 miles south of St. Louis. There they purchased 4500 acres of land and prepared to build their "new Zion."

During the voyage Stephan was elected "bishop," but after arrival serious questions arose concerning his conduct, both personal and financial. Just as the move was to be made from temporary quarters in St. Louis to the Perry County tract, a painful investigation by the bishop's subordinates substantiated charges of immorality, and Stephan was deposed and expelled from the colony. At the same time it became clear that under the bishop's oversight, the business and financial affairs of the emigration association had been grossly mismanaged. The common treasury was found to be badly depleted and in a state of confusion. Inadequate preparation had been made for housing and feeding the settlers now ready to occupy their new homes in Perry County.

The hot and humid summer of 1839 during which this transition was made was marked by spiritual disillusionment, bitterness, and physical deprivation. Five different settlements were laid out, each named for a Saxon city which, at this point, most of the colonists regretted ever having left. While cabins were being built, the people lived in tents, open sheds, or shelters made of branches and foliage. Church services were held in the open "camps" of the settlers, led by clergy who were members of the colony.

College in the Wilderness

In the midst of the traumatic autumn of 1839 a surprising notice appeared in one of the two German newspapers in St. Louis, the *Anzeiger des Westens*, over the signature of four of the Lutheran clergy of Perry County: Theodore Brohm, Johannes Buenger, Ottomar Fuerbringer, and C. F. W. Walther. These pastors announced their intent "to establish an institution of instruction and education," offering "all branches of a Gymnasium, which are requisite for a genuinely Christian and scientific education, such as: Religion, the Latin, Greek, and Hebrew, German, French and English languages, History, Geography, Mathematics, Physics, Natural History, fundamentals of Philosophy, Music, Drawing."[6] The completion of the course would prepare a student for "university studies."

Lacking any formal parish call at this time and having only the virtually bankrupt emigration treasury as a source of financial support, these pastors not only made their considerable educational resources available as teachers but actually constructed the school building itself. Buenger personally dug the well, while the other three erected a 16-by-21-foot log cabin with the help of women and children who carried clay to fill the chinks between the logs.

A donation of $35.50 from the congregation in St. Louis enabled them to apply the finishing touches, so the school could open on December 9, 1839. On that day a neighboring pastor wrote in his diary, *"Initium Gymnasii nostri, quod Angli vocant College"* (The opening of our Gymnasium, which the English call a College).[7] In all probability it was neither gymnasium nor college except in the future hope of its founders. Its first pupils included 6 boys, ages 7 to 15, 4 girls, ages 5 to 12, and one boy named Columbus Price, age unknown.

Pastor G. H. Loeber, who later became one of the teachers, commented in retrospect upon the purpose of the school and the motivation of its founders, "There was no immediate need for more ministerial candidates," he wrote, "since we had a considerable number of them, but there was need. . .to unite and retain the gifts and services of those candidates [theological graduates, not yet ordained] for a school project of this kind. It was for this reason that a few of these candidates voluntarily resolved to establish in this country a so-called college, largely at their own expense, and instruct a few gifted boys in Christianity and the common school branches. . .."[8] When Loeber made his observation in 1845, three of the four founders had already moved on to other, more promising fields of activity.

By this time also, the dreams of a university had yielded to the realities of a wilderness church. By 1843, German congregations both in St. Louis and Perry County were calling for teachers for their parochial schools, and with the assurance of financial support from these congregations, the log college in Perry County turned its major attention to fulfilling this need.

Among the hundreds of thousands of German immigrants who came to America between 1830 and 1860, such closely knit and religiously motivated colonies as those led by Grabau and Stephan were not typical. Organized in Germany on religious grounds, such colonies were well supplied with pastors within their own groups. Most other immigrants who came as individuals or families found themselves in cities or rural communities in which churches were few and German-speaking clergy were rare. Efforts of the older eastern synods in America to supply pastors for the growing West were valiant but inadequate.

Missionaries for America

The appeal to Europe for pastoral help which had been sounded 100 years earlier to meet the needs of the first German migration to America was now repeated on behalf of the second, even larger exodus. The appeal was heard in many parts of Germany and resulted in a stream of missionary pastors to North America which compares favorably with European missionary efforts being directed during the same period of time to the continents of Asia and Africa. This missionary impulse came from private societies similar to those which charac-

terized the revitalized spiritual climate in England and America in the early
19th century. Such societies recruited talented young men, provided them with
basic theological and practical training and sent them as pastors or teachers to
be assigned by Lutheran synods in America or to open new fields of work.

As early as 1833 the Basel Mission Society responded to the call of Swabian settlers in Michigan and sent Friedrich Schmid as pastor.[9] The
Langenberg Society of Barmen sent Johannes Muehlhaeuser, who later founded
the Wisconsin Synod, to New York as a missionary teacher in 1837. Beginning
in 1851 the St. Chrischona Society in Switzerland supplied the Texas Synod
with pastors for 45 years.[10] Societies in Berlin, Dresden, Bremen, and Hamburg also heard the call for help and included America, as well as Asia and
Africa, in their missionary outreach.

The society that exerted the greatest influence on the development of the
Lutheran church in America was established by Johann Konrad Wilhelm
Loehe (1808–1872) in Neuendettelsau in Bavaria. His interest in America was
kindled by the earnest appeal of an immigrant pastor, Friedrich Conrad
Dietrich Wyneken (1810–1876), who was revisiting his homeland after
serving for three years as a pastor in Indiana. Wyneken's plea for help, which
was widely circulated in the German church press and in pamphlet form in
1840 and 1841, caught Loehe's attention. Fired by the idea of sending young
men to America as church workers, Loehe began to solicit support for such a
program through the spoken word and through the columns of a newspaper
edited by a neighbor pastor.

Loehe himself never traveled to America, but he was indefatigable in
getting others to do so. By 1842 he had trained and sent his first two workers,
Adam Ernst, a journeyman shoemaker, and Georg Burger, a coat weaver, to
the Ohio Synod in Columbus. In the next 10 years he prepared and sent 100
young men as students and candidates of theology to America, most of whom
eventually became pastors or teachers in the Ohio, Michigan, and Missouri
Synods. From 1854 until the time of his death, Loehe sent 81 additional men to
serve as pastors and teachers in the Iowa Synod.

One of the ablest men Loehe sent to America was Dr. Wilhelm Sihler
(1801–1885), highly educated in philosophy and philology at Berlin and Jena.
While engaged in tutorial work in Riga, Latvia, he read Wyneken's appeal and
under Loehe's tutelage crossed to America in 1843. A settlement of Bavarians
in Pomeroy, Ohio, invited him to be their pastor, and the Ohio Synod ordained
him in 1844 just as the controversy broke out over the exclusive use of German
in the synod's Columbus seminary. Strongly supportive of the German language and critical of unionistic tendencies in its communion practices, Sihler
and several others withdrew from the Ohio Synod in 1845. At the same time
Wyneken, following his return from Germany in 1843, had become increas-

ingly critical of what he perceived as Methodistic practices in American Lutheranism, especially in the Ohio Synod and in his own Synod of the West. In the interest of establishing a strictly confessional, German-speaking synod, Sihler, Wyneken, and several others who left the Ohio and Michigan Synods initiated conversations with C. F. W. Walther in St. Louis. After a series of preparatory meetings in 1845 and 1846 in Cleveland and Fort Wayne, a convention in Chicago in April 1847 organized the "German Evangelical Lutheran Synod of Missouri, Ohio, and Other States."[11]

The Seminary at Fort Wayne

From 1842 to 1845 most of the men sent by Loehe affiliated with the Ohio Synod and studied at the Columbus seminary. After Sihler's withdrawal, however, Loehe's interest in the Ohio Synod cooled. In order to provide a more dependable confessional environment for his students, he asked Sihler to establish a separate seminary in Fort Wayne, Indiana, and supplied 11 students for its initial class in October 1846. Since no building was ready to house the students, members of Sihler's congregation took them in until a four-room house near the parsonage could be rented. When the Missouri Synod was organized in 1847, Sihler asked Loehe to transfer control of the Fort Wayne seminary to the Synod. Loehe not only agreed, but for several years thereafter sent money, books, and a steady stream of students. Between 1847 and 1861, 106 pastors, most of them recruited in Germany by Loehe, were trained at Fort Wayne and entered the service of the Missouri Synod. The demand for their services was so great that they were often deployed as missionary pastors or teachers after only a brief theological orientation. The first formal graduation did not occur until 1859, when a class of 17 completed the prescribed course of study. Even after Concordia Seminary at St. Louis was able to offer a full theoretical course in theology, the Fort Wayne seminary remained as the synod's major source of clergy supply.

When the Saxon congregations in Perry County and St. Louis emerged from their disillusioning experience with Martin Stephan's version of the episcopacy, they adopted, under Walther's leadership, a doctrine of the ministry which vested the authority of that office in the congregation. This doctrine became a source of tension between Loehe and the Missouri Synod. Loehe believed the Scriptures attributed special apostolic authority to the office of the ministry and regarded the Missouri position as dangerously democratic and unbiblical. In an effort to reach an understanding with Loehe, Walther and Wyneken made a special trip to Germany in 1851. Their differences could not be bridged. Within two years relations between Loehe and the Missouri Synod came to an end.

The final separation between Loehe and the Missouri Synod was not so much a matter of disagreement on a single doctrinal position on the nature of the ministry or the nature of the church; rather, it was the contention of Walther and Wyneken that without full doctrinal agreement there can be no fellowship. This principle has continued to guide the Missouri Synod in its relations with other Lutherans.

In the history of Lutheranism in America the Missouri Synod served the second German migration in much the same way as the Pennsylvania Ministerium served the earlier German migration of the colonial period. The leaders of the Ministerium in the 18th century were instrumental in gathering their widely scattered German countrymen into congregations, affirming their Lutheran identity in the pluralistic religious climate of a new land. So also, the Missouri Synod in the 19th century became the major instrument in rallying the new German Lutheran immigrants in a reaffirmation of loyalty to the historic confessions of the church and to the language and culture of their homeland.

The educational program of the Missouri Synod has been anchored in the conviction of its leaders that the teaching of the true doctrines to its children and its youth is a primary responsibility of the church. From the time of its organization in 1847 the synod has expressed this concern through the establishment of parochial schools and schools for the preparation of pastors and teachers to serve its parishes. The development of its comprehensive system of higher education is the subject of a later chapter.

The Beginnings of the Iowa Synod

Wilhelm Loehe's missionary zeal for America, like that of several other German societies of his time, was directed toward the conversion of the "heathen" as well as the redemption of the Germans. To this end he developed plans for selected groups of emigrants, accompanied by a pastor, to establish missionary communities in the vicinity of Indian settlements. As the site for his first venture, Loehe chose Saginaw, Michigan, where some Lutheran mission work was already under way among the Chippewa tribes. His settlers arrived in June 1845, and established a community called Frankenmuth. Loehe's rather elaborate plans contemplated additional colonies, and included a hospice, or *Pilgerhaus*, providing shelter and health care for new settlers, and a seminary to prepare Christian teachers for the new colonies.

During their visit to Germany in 1851, Walther and Wyneken had indicated that the Missouri Synod badly needed a teacher-training institute as a supplement to the work of the practical seminary for pastors at Fort Wayne. Loehe agreed and took steps to provide such a school at Saginaw, complete with a director and students. In April 1852, Georg Martin Grossmann, a theological candidate from Erlangen, arrived in the Michigan colony with five prospective teachers. Since the projected hospice was not yet built, Grossmann rented a vacant store and began a course of instruction on July 1, 1852. Both he and his students also assisted in the construction of the school facilities.[12]

Thus began the school that after multiple relocations and internal reorganizations would eventually emerge as Wartburg College of the American Lutheran Church. Its first class completed its course after one year, and four of the graduates immediately found places in congregations of the Missouri Synod. Loehe was about to send a second group of students when doctrinal dissension arose between Grossmann and the Missouri Synod pastors in the Saginaw area over the same issues which had divided Loehe and Walther. Grossmann and Johannes Deindoerfer, a neighboring pastor who also supported Loehe's views, resisted the efforts of the local Missouri pastors and congregations to induce them to accept the Missouri position. When Grossmann was confronted with the option to turn over the seminary to the Missouri Synod or to leave, he and Deindoerfer chose, with Loehe's blessing, to leave and to take the school with them.[13]

In 1853, after an exploratory visit in quest of a new location, the two pastors, accompanied by a group of their supporters from the congregations in Saginaw and Frankenhilf, set out for Dubuque, Iowa. Loehe sent word to the members of the second class of students who were already en route to Saginaw, redirecting them to Dubuque, where they met Grossmann and Deindoerfer. Dubuque was intended simply as an assembly point, pending the permanent establishment of the colony. While Deindoerfer led a part of the group out to establish a foothold on a tract of land in Clayton County, 50 miles northwest of Dubuque, Grossmann remained in Dubuque with his family and the six students. With funds forwarded by Loehe, he rented a house, built some rough furniture, and began instructing his students on November 10, 1853.

In July 1854, another group of settlers arrived from Germany and joined Deindoerfer at the new colony, which he had named St. Sebald, in honor of the patron saint of Nürnberg. Together with two new pastors who arrived from Neuendettelsau at the same time, Grossmann and Deindoerfer organized the Iowa Synod. In accord with suggestions sent by Loehe, the new synod took immediate steps to reconstitute the school which had been transferred from Saginaw to Dubuque.

The Search for Educational Goals

In a situation where no congregations yet existed the primary need was for missionary pastors rather than teachers. Accordingly, Grossmann agreed to give additional instruction to the two graduates of the teachers' seminary, thereby launching the first program of theological education for the Iowa Synod. Loehe had also urged Sigmund Fritschel, one of the newly arrived pastors, to establish a Latin school to provide a classical foundation for the study of theology. This marked the emergence of a second new educational enterprise. Teacher education, which had been the original purpose of the school in Saginaw was reluctantly "suspended" in deference to the immediate need for pastors. The hope of restoring it, however, persisted, and was probably one of the factors which retarded the development of a strong classical gymnasium and later of a liberal arts college. The initial enrollment in the "Latin school" numbered three students. In succeeding years the congregations of the synod supplied very few applicants and the recruits which Loehe sent from Germany either entered parishes directly or completed their theological studies in the seminary.

Having begun with only two small congregations in St. Sebald and Dubuque, the Iowa Synod had to depend entirely upon its home mission outreach for survival and growth. Pastors and students from the seminary visited German settlements in northeastern Iowa and southern Wisconsin, often beginning their ministry by opening a school. Where congregations were established, these schools became parochial schools and the pastor generally served as both teacher and preacher. Under this double burden in multiple parishes synod pastors became strong advocates for the reinstatement of teacher training programs.

In their advocacy the pastors found general support among their parishioners. The German immigrants who came to America after the Civil War were of a different character from those who came between 1830 and 1860. The earlier groups tended to be middle-class farmers, artisans, craftsmen, and professionals, generally well-educated people. Later German immigrants came largely from peasant stock, lured by the availability of abundant and cheap land. They were hardy, hard-working people, but they did not share the higher education interests of middle- and upper-class Germans. They were supportive of elementary education for their children, such as could be supplied in a parish school, but saw little reason to send either their dollars or their sons to a church-related gymnasium or college.[14]

These factors relating to the origin and early constituency of the Iowa Synod probably exerted a determining influence on the development of its higher education program. The movement to establish higher schools in most other Lutheran groups in America was based on the expressed need of a local constituency, usually for pastors and teachers. Several Lutheran colleges grew out of community demands for general education beyond the common school as an aid to a cultural transition to a new land and language. The Iowa Synod originated when a school that had been founded in Michigan to meet the need for teachers for an established constituency was moved, with its director and its students, to an entirely new setting in which its original purpose did not meet local needs.

The transformation to a theological seminary was well understood and accepted in the Iowa Synod. But there was never full agreement on the nature of the preparatory program. Although Loehe had urged the establishment of a Latin school as the core of a classical preparation for theological study, most of the pastors and leaders of the synod were themselves products of the practical schools in Germany which Loehe had developed. They had not come up through the rigorous classical program of the German gymnasium and university. Moreover, as new congregations were established, more parochial school teachers were needed. Most pastors felt it would be better to concentrate the limited resources of the synod on the training of teachers, especially since Loehe also continued to send young men from Germany to complete their ministerial preparation at the synod seminary. From 1854 until his death in 1872 Loehe sent 81 pastors or teachers to the Iowa Synod, and an additional 45 came from his schools in Neuendettelsau in subsequent years. [15]

In such a situation, developments in the early program of higher education in the Iowa Synod took place largely in response to pressures of the moment, usually economic, rather than in accord with any clear educational goals. The seminary underwent three relocations before it returned to its original site in Dubuque in 1890. The preparatory division that ultimately became Wartburg College moved 5 times in the first 40 years of Iowa Synod history. In three of these locations it shared facilities and faculty with the seminary. In another it was merged with a newly created teacher-training school. Still later it was separated and removed to another location that also proved to be temporary.

A College on the Move

At its beginning in Dubuque the Iowa Synod school actually had no other financial support than that which came from Germany. As mission congregations were established, some small income began to trickle in for the support of the pastors who served them. But even the modest amounts needed to provide sustenance for the faculty and the students were simply not available.

Instruction had begun in 1853 in rented quarters, but during the second year, with Loehe's help, the school was able to move into a two-story brick residence. This building provided accommodations for the Grossmann family and both dormitory and classroom facilities for the students. During 1856 the costs of maintaining the building and supplying the basic needs of faculty and students became so burdensome that the school was compelled to close for six weeks.

In an effort to provide an adequate economic base for operating the school, the synod decided to buy a farm in the St. Sebald parish to supply food and firewood and thereby reduce operational expenses. It was expected that the purchase of the farm and the cost of a new building could be financed by the sale of the Dubuque property purchased and donated to the synod by Loehe.

But the panic of 1857 intervened. Values dropped and the property was rendered unsalable for several years. When the substantial construction loan for the new building at St. Sebald fell due two years later, the synod was unable even to pay the interest. Even Loehe's resources fell short and only a fund-raising visit to Germany and the Baltic provinces of Russia by Sigmund Fritschel saved the school.

After the Civil War enrollment in the preparatory department increased, reflecting the slow but steady growth of the synod's membership. By 1868 the 30 students in attendance, 15 in each division, placed the housing facilities under severe strain. Even larger enrollments in the immediate future were expected to accompany cooperative agreements bringing students from the Wisconsin Synod and the newly formed German Synod of Illinois.[16]

When an energetic Iowa Synod pastor serving a flourishing congregation in Galena, Illinois, reported in 1868 that an attractive brick building could be bought there at a bargain price, the synod resolved to move the preparatory department to Galena, thus giving the "college" an independent existence for the first time. The seminary remained in St. Sebald, retaining the name *Wartburg*, chosen when the first building had been constructed on the highest point in the vicinity.

John Klindworth, the local pastor and promoter of the move to Galena, was named rector of the college and Pastor Friedrich Lutz, a graduate of St. Sebald, became teacher and house father. Ten students from St. Sebald were joined by 11 others when the college opened on November 1, 1868. The synod intended to operate a six-year gymnasium at Galena, but the low enrollments could not support an enlarged curriculum. Cooperative arrangements with the Illinois and Wisconsin synods failed to develop. Attempts to attract students from the local community were likewise unsuccessful. Language difficulties caused the five recruits from Galena to drop out before completing their first year.

Although the synod itself continued to grow during the seven years of the college's sojourn in Galena, it was not strong enough to support two institutions. Deficits mounted, adding to the already existing indebtedness on the buildings in Galena. Congregations complained that special appeals were becoming an intolerable burden likely to alienate support altogether. The synod convention seriously considered closing the college in 1871.

The synod's decision two years later to move the seminary from St. Sebald to Mendota, Illinois, brought into the open a strain between the college and the seminary that had been developing since 1868. The tensions grew naturally out of the fact that the two institutions were competing for support from very limited resources. The move to Mendota involved the purchase of buildings that formerly housed a college for women sponsored by the Northern Illinois Synod, which had closed in 1870. It also involved the expense of relocating the seminary faculty and the loss of the operating resources supplied by the farm economy at St. Sebald. Moreover, the timing could scarcely have been less propitious since immediately after the move was made, the nation was enveloped in the financial panic of 1873.

Two years later the synod again sought to solve a financial crisis by moving an institution. This time the college was moved to the Mendota campus of the seminary. The sale of the Galena property, together with economies made possible by the sharing of faculty and some facilities at Mendota, relieved the immediate financial pressure on the synod but gave little evidence of clear educational direction.[17]

During the 1880s the synod and the seminary shared to some degree in the return of national prosperity. As long as the synod's pastoral needs were being supplied from Germany, the college received scant attention. Only a few of its students entered the seminary each year. The college continued to function at Mendota during the 80s, but according to the college historian, "that is about all that can be said."[18]

New Beginnings in Waverly

Meanwhile, steps were being taken to restore the original educational focus of the Iowa Synod on teacher preparation. Attempts during the 1860s to reestablish a normal school foundered for lack of financial resources. But in the late 1870s, as the financial depression subsided, Synod President Grossmann personally launched a new program of teacher training.

His school began in the fall of 1878 in the buildings of an orphanage in Andrew, Iowa, with six students. The following year it was moved to Waverly where a citizens' committee pledged $4000 toward the construction of a new building. As usual, costs exceeded estimates and pledges were only partially fulfilled. Not until 1885 was the $2000 debt paid, a substantial balance having been assumed by Grossmann himself. Only then did the synod accept the school as its own.

To save money the synod decided at the same time to move its peripatetic college from Mendota to Waverly. The new building provided accommodations for 50 students, adequate for the combined enrollments of the two schools in 1885, but leaving little room for expansion. Further economies were achieved by combining the first two years of both schools. The teachers course would be completed in one additional year, while three additional years were required to complete a five-year gymnasium course with strong emphasis on Greek, Latin, and German. The combined faculties served both programs.

For the first time the school was officially designated *Wartburg College* and began to take on an increasingly collegiate character, with student literary societies, an expanded library, and laboratory equipment for new courses in the natural sciences. Several professors who would later constitute the core of the Wartburg College faculty were members of the Waverly staff. By the early 1890s college enrollments had substantially increased, while the teacher-training program had begun to decline.

The decline was caused by the maturation of the American public school system. By 1890 elementary public schools were available almost everywhere in Iowa and neighboring states. Even those in small towns offered a better general education than the parochial schools in small congregations. More and more congregations were therefore providing religious education during the summer and sending their children to public schools during the regular school year.

Many pastors, however, felt that the college at Waverly was crippling the teachers' seminary and that the synod should make stronger efforts to preserve the parish school system. Consequently, when a seemingly attractive offer was made in 1893 to provide a campus and a building for the college in Clinton, Iowa, the proposal to separate the institutions and move the college to Clinton received general support.

Signs of Impending Change

A local real estate agent in Clinton offered the synod a 97-acre farm on the outskirts of the city, valued at $75,000, at a bargain price of $25,000. After setting aside 17 acres for the college campus, the remainder was to be subdivided into 384 residential lots. At $300 each the sale of the lots would provide ample funds to pay for the farm and to erect a college building with classrooms, offices, and housing for 100 students. The synod and local agents in Clinton would promote the sale of lots.

The synod resolved to accept the proposal and moved immediately to let contracts for the construction of a new building for Wartburg College in Clinton. About 200 lots were sold, largely to synodical investors, but the yield fell far short of covering building costs. The panic of 1893 intervened to halt residential movement toward the subdivision and left disgruntled purchasers with unsaleable lots. When the college moved to Clinton in 1894, it possessed a spacious campus capable of attractive development and by far the finest structure it had ever owned. But it was also saddled with a debt of $30,000 and a legacy of ill will among its constituents, both of which would require more than a decade to overcome.[19]

The unhappy plight of the college was matched by the gloomy prospects facing the teachers seminary as the decline of parish schools continued. To bolster its sagging enrollment the school turned to a community-service curriculum, supplementing the teachers program with courses in business and music and special winter term courses for the rural areas. These were called "academy courses" to distinguish them from the regular teachers curriculum. To enable its students to qualify for public school teaching, the school began a long-range reorganization of its so-called academy into a genuine high school, offering courses which would meet state accreditation standards.

This process extended well into the 20th century and eventually developed into a two-year junior college primarily adapted to teacher education. Its beginning marked the first step in the adaptation of Iowa Synod schools to the American educational system. The process was both indirectly and inadvertently set in motion by the lay membership of Iowa Synod congregations who gradually abandoned the German parochial school in favor of community schools in which their children could receive a basic education in the English language.

Part of a further effort to bolster enrollment at Waverly was the introduction of pretheological courses for men seeking admission to the practical division of the theological seminary that had meanwhile returned to Dubuque. This addition responded to an acute need in the synod for the local recruitment of pastors, since the supply of missionary pastors from Germany had virtually dried up by the 1890s. In 1896 the synod officially designated this "short cut" course as a "pro-seminary," and recognized similar "feeder" schools in Eureka, South Dakota; Sterling, Nebraska; and Brenham, Texas. The approval of these courses assured the synod of a continuing emphasis on practical rather than theoretical theological training.

Meanwhile, Wartburg College in Clinton, no longer burdened by its association with the teacher-education program, was free to establish the six-year classical curriculum modeled on the German gymnasium. But its heavily weighted courses in Latin, Greek, and German were not competitive with the practically oriented "proseminar" available at Waverly and at other synod academies, and the college at Clinton delivered very few graduates to the seminary at Dubuque.

The Wartburg College catalog of 1894 announced that besides the classical course for preministerial students, scientific, academic, and music courses would be offered. Students taking the scientific course could substitute work in mathematics, science, and mental philosophy for advanced Latin and Greek. The academic course included only the lower levels of instruction and omitted Latin. Even some business courses were offered in an effort to draw community support. But the persistent use of German as a medium of instruction prevented any general success in attracting local enrollments.[20]

During the early years at Clinton the most vigorous advocate of academic reform was Professor Otto Kraushaar. One of the earliest laypersons to teach in an Iowa Synod college, he had joined the faculty in Mendota and made the transitions to Waverly and to Clinton. He urged changes in curriculum and governance to bring the college into closer conformity with the patterns of modern American higher education, and even proposed the introduction of co-education. His proposals of the 1890s became guidelines for changes which materialized only several decades later. The Iowa Synod entered the 20th century with a program of higher education still modeled after the German gymnasium and directed primarily to the preparation of pastors and parochial school teachers. Only after its final return to Waverly and the formation of the American Lutheran Church in 1930 did Wartburg join the company of Lutheran liberal arts colleges.

German Mission to Texas

The outreach of the German missionary enterprise in the mid-19th century extended across the North American continent from Canada to Texas. German settlers entered Texas in the 1830s and 1840s, but the first response to the need for Lutheran pastors came from the great American home missionary, William A. Passavant of the Pittsburgh Synod.[21] He sent two young men to Texas in 1850, one of whom was a product of the St. Chrischona Mission in Switzerland. Letters to Christian Friedrich Spittler, founder of the mission, brought still others who helped to organize the Texas Synod in 1851. Between 1850 and 1895 St. Chrischona supplied the Texas Synod with 85 pastors.[22]

The Chrischona men were missionaries rather than educators. Not until 1868 was any interest shown in establishing a school. At that time the Texas Synod declined the opportunity to purchase a school called Colorado College, established at Columbus, Texas, in 1857 by John J. Scherer, pioneer Lutheran missionary of the Synod of Western Virginia and later president of Marion College in Virginia.[23] After a brief but unsuccessful attempt in 1874 to establish a school to train pastors and teachers, the Texas Synod opened the Evangelical Lutheran College of Brenham, Texas, in 1891, patterning its structure and curriculum on the German gymnasium. In hopes of securing men and means to meet the home mission challenge, the synod affiliated with the Iowa Synod in 1896 and received some financial assistance for the school in Brenham.

In 1912 the college moved to Seguin, Texas, in response to an offer of $20,000 and 15 acres of land from local businessmen. As the Lutheran College of Seguin it offered general academy work, high school courses, and studies preparatory to the practical theological training in the seminary of the Iowa Synod.[24] Its transition to an American high school was inhibited during World War I by its image as a German school. But following the war concerted efforts to accommodate its curriculum to public school standards brought official recognition by the University of Texas in 1923 as an accredited high school. In 1928 junior college work was authorized, and by 1933 the high school program was discontinued.[24] When Trinity College in Round Rock, a small academy of the Augustana Synod, closed in 1929, part of its faculty was taken over by the college in Seguin.[25]

A year later the Texas and Iowa Synods became a part of the American Lutheran Church and the college in Seguin was retained as one of two junior colleges of the new church. Under a new name, adopted in 1932, Texas Lutheran College moved toward senior college status in 1945. It awarded its first bachelor's degree in 1948 and received regional accreditation in 1953. When Clifton College, a small junior college of Norwegian Lutheran origin, merged with the school in Seguin in 1954, Texas Lutheran College became the carrier of three major ethnic Lutheran traditions in higher education in Texas.[26]

The Wisconsin Synod's University

Like the Iowa Synod, the Wisconsin Synod owes its origin to the work of a German missionary society, the Langenberg Society of Barmen in the Rhineland. The flow of German settlers into Wisconsin began as early as 1832 but it reached major proportions only between 1845 and 1860. The earliest Lutherans were members of the Grabau migration of 1839 who, under the leadership of Captain Heinrich von Rohr, continued west from Buffalo, New York, and founded the community of Freistadt near Milwaukee in 1843. Other Lutherans from Pomerania and Brandenburg followed. Missionaries of the Langenberg Society arrived between 1846 and 1849 and established congregations in the Milwaukee area. In 1850 five Langenberg pastors representing 18 congregations met at Granville, Wisconsin, and organized the German Evangelical Lutheran Synod of Wisconsin. Johannes Muehlhaeuser became its first president.

Although its parent mission society in Germany was sponsored by the Evangelical Church of the Prussian Union, the Wisconsin Synod affirmed its Lutheran character from its beginning. As the synod expanded in Wisconsin and neighboring states, the Langenberg Society and later the Berlin Society continued to send pastors and teachers. Seventeen Langenberg missionaries, several of whom had studied at Hermannsburg under the strong Lutheran influence of Louis Harms, came to Wisconsin between 1851 and 1867.

In spite of this assistance synod leaders realized that European sources could not indefinitely supply their need for pastors. During the 1850s they explored several possibilities for sharing in the seminaries of other Lutheran synods. An increasing conservative trend within the Wisconsin Synod prevented its cooperation with the new seminary at Springfield, Illinois, sponsored by the Illinois synods. At the same time an unwillingness to have its candidates imbued with the "exclusive trends" of the Missouri and Iowa Synods made association with their seminaries unacceptable.[27]

Finally in 1860 the newly elected synod president, Johannes Bading, called upon members to establish a seminary of their own. Two years later he went further and reminded the synod "that the pastors and parishioners have no institution for the advanced schooling of their children. . ... Hence, beside a seminary, a college must be founded at the same time or later. That will then take care of the training of German school teachers."[28]

The response was prompt. Heeding its president's appeal, the synod voted to establish both a seminary and a college and to begin theological instruction immediately. In hope of securing financial assistance in Europe, it commissioned President Bading to solicit funds in Germany, Latvia, and even among the German congregations in Russia. Edward Moldehnke, a traveling missionary of the Langenberg Society, educated at the University of Halle, was invited to occupy President Bading's pulpit in Watertown during his absence and to serve as the synod's first theological professor.[29]

A spirited discussion took place in the synod over the relative merits of Milwaukee and Watertown as sites for the new institution. In keeping with the prevailing wisdom of the times, "rural tranquillity" and "the wholesome atmosphere of the country town" prevailed over "the distracting rush of the commercial metropolis." The decision favored Watertown by a vote of 45 to 19.[30]

Encouraged by a pledge of $2000 from citizens of Watertown, a governing board of six members proceeded with plans for a building, the cost of which should not exceed $10,000. Following the selection of a site the ground-breaking ceremonies took place on August 10, 1864.

Academic planning was placed in the hands of the enthusiastic young president, Adam Martin. Though a native-born German, he was a graduate of Hamilton College and Hartwick Seminary, recently ordained by the New York Ministerium. Recognizing that the synod had already established a theological school, he directed his attention to the organizing of an American-style college that would serve the interest of both the synod and the community.

An announcement in the local newspaper by the board of the college invited "all that were desirous to fit themselves for a higher position in life" to enroll. "It is the aim of the founders," the announcement continued, "to make this institution rank with the best in the land. It rests solely with the citizens of the state whether or not this aim is to be realized soon,. . .for it is in their interest that this enterprise is undertaken."[31] President Bading added his reassurance to the community that although the college would be under the jurisdiction of the Wisconsin Synod, "there is no endeavor of persuasion to this or that confession."[32]

At its first meeting with the new president the synod enthusiastically approved his plan to establish an endowment of $100,000 to be raised through the sale of scholarships. Within a short time Martin himself raised $10,000 in the Watertown community alone and within three years a total of $64,000 had been pledged.

The opening of the college coincided with the completion of a new building, erected at a cost of $22,000, the major part of which had been raised in Europe through the diligent solicitations of synod president Johannes Bading. Only a modest debt of $1,400 remained unpaid. As classes began in September 1865, 65 students enrolled. Except for eight seminarians who had already begun their theological studies under the direction of Professor Moldehnke, the students were mostly of English or Irish extraction, children of local residents who had responded to Martin's campaign for the sale of scholarships. At the outset only classes on the preparatory level were offered. Only in 1867 were the more advanced students able to begin college-level work. Virtually all instruction in the academy was in English.

President Martin also delivered his opening address in English, on "The College and the Man, the College and the State, and the College and the Church." He proposed an institution combining "German thoroughness with American practicalness in all things" and reminded his colleagues that in this country "that denomination will count most and will give direction to the development of national life which has done most in the training of efficient men."[33]

His suggestion that the school be named "Wisconsin University" was approved by the board, but during the charter negotiations in 1867 the name was changed to avoid confusion with the newly founded state university. *Northwestern University* was chosen instead and remained the official name of the school until 1910 when the "university" designation was dropped.

During the first year Martin and Moldehnke constituted the faculty both for the academy and the seminary, though Martin was obliged to handle all the English-language courses. By 1867 there were four members on the faculty, and the enrollment, most of which continued to represent the local English-speaking constituency, had risen to 95. Theological instruction was given in German, but English continued to be the medium of instruction at the preparatory level both in college and academy courses. Preministerial students were obliged to take special instruction in English in order to attend college classes in the ancient languages. Dissatisfaction with the secondary role thus assigned to the German language, combined with theological developments within the synod in 1867, produced an abrupt change in the character of Northwestern University.[34]

From University to Gymnasium

During the 1860s American Lutheranism underwent a hardening process in which groups of doctrinally compatible synods drew together into mutually exclusive associations. The Civil War had drawn a political line of separation between northern and southern Lutherans. The formation of the General Council in 1867 had rallied synods which regarded their confessional position to be more authentic than those adhering to the older General Synod. And a movement was under way, led by the Missouri Synod, to gather synods into a still more conservative association to be constituted in 1872 as the Synodical Conference.

In this shifting scene the Wisconsin Synod was drawn in several directions. Its origin lay with the mission societies of the Old Prussian Union that served both Lutheran and Reformed churches in Germany. Since its organization in 1850 it had received most of its clergy through these societies. But it had developed in a climate of midwestern German Lutheranism heavily influenced by the strong confessionalism of the Missouri Synod. By 1865 real or perceived evidences of laxity in doctrine or practice on the part of Wisconsin Synod pastors received critical notice in the widely circulated publications of the Missouri Synod. When President Bading traveled to Germany to solicit funds for the new seminary, the synod was denounced for representing itself in America as Lutheran while it sought aid from "Union" churches in Germany. On the other hand, the Supreme Council of the Prussian Church criticized the Wisconsin Synod for conducting an "exclusive" ministry among Lutherans in America, and therefore refused to release a fund of $10,215 which had been gathered in Prussia for the seminary project.[35]

Assailed from both sides, Wisconsin finally declared itself confessionally in the synod of 1867, and after a brief affiliation with the General Council established fellowship with the Missouri Synod in 1869. Thereupon the Langenberg Society, parent of the Wisconsin Synod, terminated all further support, either in men or money.

This change was promptly reflected in the developments at the college in Watertown. More cordial relations with Missouri opened the way for educational cooperation. After 1870 Wisconsin students of theology were welcomed at Concordia Seminary in St. Louis while Missouri was invited to use the Watertown school as a preparatory gymnasium. In 1870, 34 of the total of 58 students in the preparatory department were supplied by Missouri. In 1873 they numbered 60 of the 100 students enrolled.

President Martin strenuously opposed this change of policy, claiming it constituted a breach of trust with scholarship holders who had made their contributions to the support of an American college and not a German gymnasium. The synod responded by dismissing Martin, but also by constituting parallel

English and German divisions in the college. The English would be self-supporting through student tuitions and the income from invested scholarship funds. Only the German division, or gymnasium, would receive synodical support and would serve as an exclusive training school for the seminary.[36]

The reorganization proposal was presented to the board by Professor August Ernst, a graduate of Göttingen University, one of three new German professors appointed by the board in 1868. Following the resignation of Lewis O. Thompson, professor of Latin, who had served a two-year term as president following Martin's departure, the board invited Ernst to assume the presidency in March 1871. Under his leadership, extending over a half-century, Northwestern University became a full-fledged German gymnasium.

Some of the marks of its American collegiate origin incorporated in the university charter of 1867 remained at least temporarily visible. In 1872 the first four bachelor of arts degrees were awarded. The board also agreed that completion of a theological course at Concordia in St. Louis and the submission of a Latin or German essay would fulfill requirements for a master of arts degree. The academy continued to draw a substantial number of students seeking "a liberal English and business education."

Other changes occurred before the turn of the century. To meet the needs of synodical parochial schools, the academy offerings were broadened to include normal training for teachers. Within the theological preparatory division, however, both the structure and the language of the German gymnasium persisted. Indeed, German continued to be the language of campus conversation at Northwestern well into the 20th century. Though it has long since abandoned the vocabulary of the gymnasium in favor of American collegiate terminology, Northwestern College has remained solely devoted to the preparation of candidates for the study of theology in the Wisconsin Synod.

The synod's program of teacher preparation was transferred in 1893 to Dr. Martin Luther College, founded in 1884 in New Ulm by the Minnesota Synod as a school for prospective pastors and for young men preparing for college or business. When the three German synods of Wisconsin, Michigan, and Minnesota pooled their educational resources in 1893, Dr. Martin Luther became the official teachers college of the Joint Synod. In 1896 it opened its five-year training course to women. The period of greatest expansion occurred after World War II, and the college awarded its first baccalaureate degree in education in 1954. By 1980, when accreditation was achieved, more than 800 students were enrolled.[37]

The most recent addition to the higher education program of the Wisconsin Synod is Wisconsin Lutheran College in Milwaukee. Established in 1973 as a junior college by the Wisconsin Lutheran College Conference, an independent association of congregations belonging to the Wisconsin Synod, this new venture represented an effort without direct synod support to respond to a growing interest in liberal arts education in the synod.

German Colleges in Western Canada

Most of the missionary efforts to serve German immigrants in Canada originated with synods based in the United States. Colonial settlements in Nova Scotia had been virtually absorbed by Anglicans during and after the American Revolution, by the time the Lutheran roots were rediscovered by William Passavant in 1846.[38] Through his efforts as the home mission secretary of the Pittsburgh Synod, Lutheran congregations were revived and eventually organized as the Nova Scotia Conference in 1876. The Pittsburgh Synod also responded to "Father" Adam Keffer who in 1849 walked 250 miles from the German settlements on the north shore of Lake Ontario to plead for pastoral assistance.[39] By 1861 the Canada Synod, the first Lutheran synod in all of Canada, was organized, with all seven of the pastors supplied by the Pittsburgh Synod.

During the latter decades of the century German immigrants continued to enter Ontario, and especially after 1900 pressed westward along the railroads into the great prairie provinces of Manitoba, Saskatchewan, and Alberta. Congregations were organized by missionary pastors of the Canada and Manitoba Synods and virtually all other German bodies based in the United States in a competitive process that was often more imperialistic than evangelistic. Even with the help of the older German mission societies at Hermannsburg and Berlin, there were never enough pastors to serve the endless flow of immigrants into the United States and Canada between 1880 and 1910.

An appeal to Germany from the German Home Mission Board of the General Council in 1881 inspired a young German pastor, Johannes Paulsen, to open Ebenezer Seminary at Kropp, in Schleswig-Holstein, in 1882. His seminary served the General Council much as the seminaries at Steeden and Breklum served Missouri and the General Synod. More than 200 young men from Kropp became pastors in congregations of the General Council, about 40 of them in Canada, before the seminary closed in 1930.[40]

The first initiative to establish a Canadian seminary came from the western prairies where pastors of the General Council, several of them products of the Kropp Seminary, organized the Manitoba Synod in 1897. Because of the great distance separating western Canada and the General Council Seminary in Philadelphia, the Manitoba Synod determined to establish its own seminary in 1913. A permanent site was secured in Saskatoon in the newly established province of Saskatchewan and a building readied for occupancy in 1915. The first director, Pastor Juergen Goos, and two members of the faculty were graduates of the Kropp Seminary. The two-year curriculum of the Evangelical Lutheran College of the Synod of Manitoba and Other Provinces was offered in English and German and included basic introductions in both Latin and Greek.[41] When theological instruction was added in 1918, the school became known as Lutheran College and Seminary of Saskatoon. After 1932 the college program was integrated with the neighboring University of Saskatchewan. The seminary has subsequently become the nucleus of an inter-Lutheran theological center.

On November 16, 1913, in the same year that pastors of the Manitoba Synod reached the decision to establish their school, dedication services were held for a similar preministerial academy of the Joint Ohio Synod in Melville, Saskatchewan. Since 1905 the Ohio Synod had been actively engaged in mission work in Canada, and by 1915 its Canada District, with more than 100 congregations, was the largest German Lutheran body in western Canada.[42] Although its basic purpose was the preparation of young men for the study of theology, Luther Academy was coeducational, and its curriculum included a variety of basic high school subjects and even shorter courses in agriculture.[43]

In 1925 the Ohio Synod decided to move the school to the city of Regina and to reestablish it as Luther College, offering a four-year high school course and one year of collegiate work. At the same time an affiliate relationship was established with the University of Saskatchewan. Since 1926, under the distinctive Canadian pattern of institutional relationships, Luther College has developed a fully accredited and independently administered baccalaureate program in federation with the University of Regina.

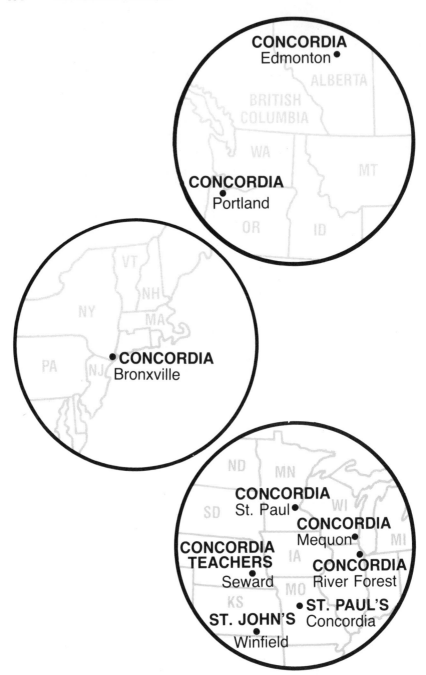

9 THE MISSOURI SYSTEM

One of the most distinctive developments in the history of Lutheran higher education in North America has been the emergence of the educational system of the Lutheran Church–Missouri Synod. In 1984 this system embraced 1,705 elementary and 70 high schools, 13 colleges and 4 theological seminaries. It enrolled nearly 200,000 students and employed nearly 10,000 teachers.[1] Because of its well-defined purpose and structure and its success in preserving its identity for nearly 100 years, its beginnings and rapid growth warrant particular attention.

Several factors in the times and circumstances of the founding of the Missouri Synod contributed to the special character of its educational system. The groups which formed the nucleus of the synod had come to America as organized communities. The Saxons, especially, who came to St. Louis and Perry County in 1839, had been enlisted in Germany as members of an emigration association with an organized structure, a common treasury, and a common purpose: to find a place where they could engage in worship and profess their faith freely without danger of either ecclesiastical or civil interference. They were led by Lutheran clergy who were well-grounded theologically and saw as their mission the preservation of the gospel and the integrity of the Lutheran confessions against rationalism and unionism.

The lay members of the association were largely middle-class persons, craftsmen, prosperous farmers, and professional people, including both lawyers and government officials. As partners in the emigration society they had made substantial contributions to the common treasury. As concerned members of Lutheran parishes they shared the religious convictions of the pastors

139

who were also their partners, and especially those who had taken the initiative in forming the association. As educated persons themselves, they were also concerned for the general and religious education of their children. They made certain that religious instruction was given on shipboard, and they took steps to establish parochial schools in temporary quarters immediately upon their arrival in St. Louis. With the full spectrum of crafts and professions represented among them, it was their intention to establish a self-contained community in the new land. To this end they purchased a large tract in Perry County, about 100 miles south of St. Louis, on which to plant their colony.

The internal misfortunes and resultant public scorn they experienced after their arrival in Missouri may even have strengthened their sense of community. The collapse of Bishop Stephan's leadership made it necessary for the members of the community to reexamine and restore the authority of the association under which their common venture had been undertaken. The same circumstance compelled them to reexamine the basis of their spiritual community and leadership and led them to affirm the primacy of the congregational community as the base of ecclesiastical and spiritual authority. The clergy, though initially reluctant to acknowledge this basic principle, were led by Pastor Walther to accept the congregational principle as the scriptural foundation for the doctrine of the church and the ministry.[2]

When the Missouri Synod itself was organized in 1847, this doctrine of the church had become fully accepted among Walther's followers. The synod was not seen as an association of clergy but as the association of congregations in which their representatives made decisions for the church as a whole. Thus from its outset the Missouri Synod in convention exercised direct control of mission programs, educational enterprises, publications, and the establishment of policies and priorities. In the educational field parochial schools were virtually required of all member congregations. The establishment of schools to prepare pastors and teachers became the responsibility of the synod. Made explicit in the initial constitution of the Missouri Synod, these assignments established the framework for a uniform, clearly defined, and centrally controlled system of education.[3]

Of further importance in the formation of the Missouri system was the strong contingent of clergy who participated in the Saxon immigration. In the original company of colonists who arrived in St. Louis in 1839 were no fewer than six ordained clergy and nine candidates of theology, all of them theological graduates of German universities. These were later augmented by such strong personalities as Friedrich Wyneken and Wilhelm Sihler, who were also university-educated and products of the orthodox confessional movement in midcentury German theology.

It was probably a blessing that the flawed leadership of Martin Stephan was uncovered and dealt with at the very outset of the colony's life in America. Traumatic as it was, it freed Walther and his colleagues to assume positions of authority and leadership based upon a strong congregational mandate. Once the office of the ministry had been tendered to a pastor, his leadership in spiritual and theological matters was accepted and honored by the congregation. Under the leadership of such well-educated and theologically like-minded clergy the synod could become an effective instrument for maintaining orthodox Lutheranism.

A third factor which contributed to the establishment of the Missouri system of education was the firm commitment of the founders to the German language. For a group as large and self-contained as the Missouri Saxons there was a natural tendency to hold to the mother tongue. The presence of 50,000 fellow Germans in St. Louis in 1860, among a population of 160,000, encouraged the continued use of German. Finally, and perhaps most important in the development of the church, was the clergy's conviction that the use of the German language provided a bulwark for the preservation of an orthodox religious faith among both adults and children. When the Perry County college was moved to St. Louis in 1849, one of the stipulations was that German alone be the medium of instruction. This emphasis remained unchallenged for more than 50 years and served as a shield for protecting the developing educational system from the influences of the American system of education.

Missouri's Log College

The Missouri system, however, was not created by a single act of the synod, nor was it projected as such in the minds of synod leaders. It emerged in response to the needs of the synod and grew as the synod grew. There was no suggestion of a "system" of higher education in the college at Dresden and Altenburg in Perry County. There were, to be sure, some dreams of a future university on the part of the four pastors who in 1839 ran the announcement of its opening in the St. Louis German press. This was a private undertaking at the initiative of Lutheran pastors in whom the tradition of higher education was so ingrained that even in the inhospitable wilderness of Perry County they were moved to found a college. In so doing they exemplified the commitment to higher education which was transmitted by Luther and Melanchthon to succeeding generations of Lutheran pastors and scholars and carried to North America by missionary pastors from a variety of European universities. They also displayed the same initiative that motivated John Christopher Kunze, Samuel Schmucker, David Bittle, and other pioneer Lutheran educators who ventured to establish institutions of higher learning, even in the absence of a mandate, or even an assurance of synodical support.

The first suggestion that the Perry County college might serve the needs of the church in a broader context came from an unemployed weaver who had moved to Perry County from St. Louis. In May 1843 he wrote to his former congregation in St. Louis, calling their attention to the need of preparing teachers for the schools of the church. His letter aroused the interest of the St. Louis congregation, and with the encouragement of Pastor Walther the congregation undertook a monthly subsidy of $7 for the college and $5 per month for the teacher's salary. They also requested that the school stress language instruction for the training of future Lutheran teachers and pastors rather than a humanistic curriculum preparatory to university entrance. As it turned out, this effectively changed the character of the college to a preparatory school for church workers.[4]

The following year the St. Louis congregation officially adopted the Perry County school through a resolution declaring it to be *eine Gemeindesache*, a "matter of the congregation."[5] In so doing, it laid the foundation stone for the churchwide system of preparatory schools for church workers which would become one of the distinctive features of the Lutheran Church–Missouri Synod. It also introduced, if only temporarily, a new pattern of institutional relationship and support among Lutheran institutions of higher learning, namely, a congregationally related college and seminary.

While the school remained for six more years in Altenburg, the St. Louis congregation continued to provide support for both teachers and students. The Perry County congregations supplied foodstuffs and wood and contributed the services of their pastors as part-time teachers. By 1845 the older students were receiving theological instruction, while younger boys were studying Latin and Greek and other subjects common to the curriculum of a gymnasium. The first two graduates of the seminary completed their training in 1847 and 1848.

During these years the St. Louis and Altenburg congregations directed the operation of the school to the minutest detail. They bought the books. They supplied clothing for poor students. They hired and paid part-time teachers. By vote, the St. Louis congregation bestowed the title *professor* on Pastor Loeber. They even asked students to send class essays to be read to the congregation.[6]

When in 1847 the Missouri Synod was organized, the congregations were immediately confronted with the request to transfer responsibility for the school to the synod and to move it to St. Louis. After four years of administering the affairs of the school in Altenburg, the supporting congregations had developed a sense of ownership which they would relinquish only if they could be assured of equally careful direction by the synod. Only after protracted discussions extending over a two-year period would the congregations agree to transfer full responsibility to the synod.

To safeguard their school's special character they laid down specific conditions. It must serve the Lutheran church and train pastors and teachers only for the Lutheran church. It must instruct only in the German language. There were to be both a gymnasium and a seminary, and—such was the emphasis upon training for the laity—the gymnasium should also be open to young people not intending to study theology. If the synod so desired, other nontheological faculties might be added, as long as the main function of the institution as a theological seminary was not jeopardized. The congregations concluded their document of transfer with the benediction, "The blessings of the Lord crown this institution forever and ever."[7]

Concordia College in St. Louis

On December 16, 1849, nine students and one teacher, the Reverend J. J. Goenner, boarded a riverboat at Wittenberg Landing in Perry County and pushed their way northward through the ice floes of the Mississippi to their new home in St. Louis. Three weeks later they moved into the first unit of a new building which would house the institution, now formally named Concordia College, for the next 30 years.

The move to St. Louis marks the first specific step in the development of the Missouri System of education for church workers. For the first time the synod had its own preparatory gymnasium and a seminary for the training of a native supply of theologically well-grounded pastors and teachers. The first professor of theology was C. F. W. Walther (1811–1887), who was at the same time pastor of the St. Louis congregation.

The legal transfer of Concordia College from the St. Louis and Altenburg congregations in 1849 marks the first time in the history of Lutheranism in North America that a synod had formally undertaken full ownership and support of a collegiate institution. Some of the principles and procedures for implementing synodical control of institutions had already been anticipated by the convention of 1848 in accepting the Fort Wayne Seminary. But the convention of 1850 first formally adopted a set of "Statutes for the Concordia College of the Evangelical Lutheran Synod of Missouri, Ohio, and Other States." Significantly, these statutes embodied the main conditions set by the congregations for the transfer of the college to St. Louis. The synod in effect accepted a trust from the congregations for the kind of care and direction which they had provided since 1844, when they first assumed responsibility for the school. In establishing an *Aufsichtsbehörde*, an elected board of control, the synod employed the organizational principle on which the congregations themselves were established.[8] Members of the congregation in turn were familiar with this procedure from their past experience with the structure and operation of the Saxon Emigration Society.

The first responsibility of the board was to make certain that the religious instruction in the college was faithful to the Holy Scriptures and the Lutheran confessions. Beyond this the board was to supervise the teaching and personal conduct of the faculty and to oversee the business affairs of the college. Faculty members were to be elected by the synod convention from a slate of three nominees proposed by a nine-man electoral college composed of board members plus five additional persons. The gymnasium was established as a six-year course followed by three years of specialized theological study.

Major financial support continued to come from the prosperous St. Louis congregation, though the synod established a "college support fund" from which college expenditures, including faculty salaries, were paid. This fund was augmented from a variety of sources, including gifts from congregations and individuals, receipts from the sale of the synodical hymnal and the church paper, *Der Lutheraner*. Tuition was charged only to those not preparing for service in the church.

Although the primary concern of the synod was to establish Concordia College as a school for the preparation of pastors and teachers for the church, there was a strong attempt, especially between 1850 and 1855, to maintain a curriculum embodying the essentials of a humanistic German gymnasium. All of the original Saxon pastors were products of such institutions and in the tradition of Luther and Melanchthon regarded classical schooling as the best possible foundation both for a learned ministry and for responsible professional leadership in society. Pastor G. H. Loeber, one of the Perry County pastors who also taught in the college, had already sounded this note in a report to the congregations in 1845, while the school was still in Altenburg. "We are keeping that aim of general education in mind now," he wrote, "and shall let nothing, God willing, divert us from it as long as we live."

Though Loeber died in 1849, just before the college moved to St. Louis, his convictions were affirmed by Walther himself in an address delivered at the laying of the cornerstone of the new Concordia. The church, he declared, must be the patroness of the arts and sciences, learning and culture. Her preservation, expansion, and defense require her to foster the humanities. A few weeks later he wrote in *Der Lutheraner*: "The preparatory college is to be an institution in which, generally speaking, the subjects of the German gymnasium are taught, but with such changes as are indicated by. . .the language, the constitution, and other conditions of our new fatherland. For this reason the following subjects are included in the curriculum: the English language. . . geography and history of this country, chemistry, the sciences, and political economy. Because of this the gymnasium will approach the character of the institutions in this country known as colleges. . .."[9]

Walther stated explicitly that "not only the college department, but in certain respects also the Seminary, is open to boys and young people of other than the Lutheran confession, and to other than German-speaking people."[10] Non-Lutherans might, upon request, be excused from religious instruction and religious exercises. Students of theology from other denominations would be welcome to attend lectures in the seminary.

Walther was clearly eager to establish cultural bridges between the German-speaking community and its American neighbors. In a plea to the congregations to make use of the opportunities offered by Concordia, he wrote, children of German-speaking parents ought to receive an education equal to that of "the best English schools of similar character," but which would not estrange them from their own people. To the "English public" Concordia offered "an opportunity in this country for a thorough German education, for which parents sometimes send their children to Germany, but at the same time a German education that is geared to local [American] conditions."[11]

The appointment of Adolph Biewend as professor of philosophy in 1850 gave further evidence of the serious intent to commend the new institution both to the German and American publics as a collegiate experience. Although born in Germany, Biewend was fluent in English and had previously taught at Columbian College in Washington, D.C. At Concordia he taught in both the gymnasium and the seminary and consistently advocated the use of the English language. His untimely death in 1858 at the age of 42 deprived the synod and the college of one of their most promising agents of German-American understanding.[12]

The response to the appeals on behalf of the college and seminary during its first decade in St. Louis was not enthusiastic. At the end of 1850 only 16 students were enrolled, 6 in the seminary and 10 in the gymnasium. By 1855 a total of 93 students had matriculated, 8 of whom were non-Lutherans and 25 who were nonministerial students. Only 8 graduated.

Focus on Theology

After 1855 the outreach of the Concordia educators toward the English-speaking community took a different direction. The response of only eight *Englische* to the college program in a six-year period may well have had a dampening effect. The opening of the first public high school west of the Mississippi—in St. Louis—in 1853 may have suggested the desirability of a more general secondary education to prepare parochial school graduates for nonprofessional work in an English-speaking society.

In the spring of 1855 Pastor J. Clement Miller came to Concordia College from Pennsylvania, partly to perfect himself in the German language and partly to continue theological study. While in St. Louis he opened an English private school, separate from Concordia College but in close harmony with it. Professor Biewend, in fact, referred to it as the English Department of the college. More than 30 students enrolled. When Miller fell ill in the spring of 1856,

Biewend and Wyneken counseled together and as a replacement for Miller invited Pastor J. William Albach, a graduate of Gettysburg Seminary who had previously taught at the Fort Wayne seminary. The English Academy closed shortly thereafter, but a similar school was opened by Immanuel Lutheran Church in St. Louis in 1857 and Pastor Albach was engaged as teacher until he retired in 1889.[13]

Thus, instead of persisting in its first efforts to diversify its collegiate program to offer English language opportunities for nontheological studies, the Missouri Synod elected to encourage English-language secondary schools under separate, private auspices. In commending the Immanuel Academy to the parents of church members Walther used the same rationale for such a secondary school as for the gymnasium, but applied it instead to a general preparation for nonprofessional services in church and community. In both areas, he wrote, virtually paraphrasing Luther, there is a need for "wise, skillful and cultured people, well-informed and experienced in all matters, who are at the same time Christians, to whom one can entrust an important position, and from whom good advice can be obtained; is it not, therefore, your parental duty to figure on leaving children behind who can be used by state and church, able to serve as officers of the congregation, secretaries, treasurers, justices, postmasters, and representatives of the people in the legislature and the Congress, etc.?"[14]

Clearly, by 1859, when his appeal was published, Walther had concluded that the scope of the gymnasium, as exemplified in Concordia College, St. Louis, should be limited to the preparation of pastors. "If they are not to be pastors," Walther explicitly advised the parents, send your children to the Academy rather than to "our Concordia College, where they are obliged to learn much which is of little use outside the calling of a pastor, whereas in the Academy the chief objective is to prepare the students for secular callings."[15]

Several developments were occurring in the life of the synod during the 1850s which contributed to the decision that Concordia College should concentrate upon a thoroughgoing classical preparation for the study of theology. The synod experienced extraordinary growth, as more than half a million new German immigrants poured into the United States in a single decade. "Visitors" were appointed to scout new settlements and organize them into congregations from Wisconsin to Missouri and from Nebraska to Ohio and Michigan, and even as far west as California. Within five years of its organization, the synod had grown from 12 to more than 100 parishes, subdivided into four geographical districts. Much of this growth was achieved through the missionary activity of the pastors who were trained at the Fort Wayne Seminary.

Pastors trained at Fort Wayne far outnumbered both the nucleus of synod pastors trained in European universities and the small number of early graduates of Concordia Seminary in St. Louis. It was Walther's concern for the maintenance of an orthodox Lutheran theology, however, which finally shaped Concordia College and Seminary, and determined the character of the Missouri system of higher education. The Saxon migration itself was an expression of this concern; the organization of the Missouri Synod in 1847 was in part a reaction against principles and practices among Lutherans in America perceived to be contrary to orthodox Lutheranism.

The appearance of the "Definite Synodical Platform" in 1855, authored by Samuel S. Schmucker, confirmed these convictions and gave further evidence to the conservative Saxons of the need for a theologically well-grounded ministry, faithful to the historic Lutheran confessions. In that same year Walther established a professional journal, *Lehre und Wehre*, to foster Lutheran confessionalism. He also initiated a series of four free theological conferences between 1856 and 1859 to gather the forces of conservative Lutheranism among other synods.

While Walther fully supported the use of missionary pastors to meet the emergency needs for pastors and teachers, he was keenly aware of the meager theological foundation which these pioneers of the frontier received. He was convinced that only through an educational system geared to produce thoroughly grounded pastors fluent in the classical languages and committed to the confessions could the Lutheran church be preserved from the eroding influences of Methodistic revivalism and doctrinal indifference. Especially after 1855 Walther sought to strengthen the theological faculty at St. Louis with university-trained theologians faithful to "Old Lutheran" convictions. By 1857 three new professors, all recently arrived from Germany, had been added to the faculty.[16]

Transition to Fort Wayne

The coming of the Civil War was responsible for the next major step in the shaping of the Missouri system of higher education. There is no indication that the political issues which were agitating the nation in 1860 received any special attention at Concordia College. Walther himself was in Europe during much of that year, for health reasons. In the fall elections Lincoln won a mere 10% of the popular vote in Missouri and the secessionist candidate only 19%. The rest were divided between the two Democratic candidates, Stephen Douglas and John Bell. Missouri was clearly a "border" state, without dominant sentiment on either side of the issue of the Union.

Early in 1861 the United States government stationed a company of troops in St. Louis to safeguard the federal arsenal. The local climate following Lincoln's inauguration was quiet enough so that Walther and two other professors attended the Western District convention of the synod in Perry County, beginning April 11. But on April 15 Fort Sumter was fired on and Lincoln called for 75,000 state militia, including 3100 Missourians. Gov. Claiborne Jackson, a states' rights Democrat, denied Lincoln's requisition as "unconstitutional. . . inhuman, and diabolical."[17]

No word of these developments penetrated to Perry County, but when Walther returned to St. Louis on April 17, he found the city in turmoil, with fears at the college running high that the federal arsenal, located less than a mile from the Concordia campus, might be attacked. On April 26 Walther and his colleagues decided to close the college and send the students home. "The immediate surroundings of our college threaten to become the area of conflict between the power of the administration and our state government," he wrote to a friend on the following day. "For that reason we have closed the institution. We are in grave danger since we do not go along with the Republican mob, this revolutionary party, which has now hoisted the banner of loyalty with unspeakable hypocrisy."[18]

St. Louis' only battle of the war, the Battle of Camp Jackson, was fought on May 10. By September the dangers had passed. The city came down on the side of the Union, and the seminary reopened. Meanwhile, however, decisions had been made that radically altered the pattern of the Missouri system of higher education.

A synodical commission had already undertaken a study at the 1860 synod convention to ascertain the desirability of merging the two seminaries at Fort Wayne and St. Louis. Doctrinal, pedagogical, and economic reasons were cited in support of such a move, but the threat of war brought the issue to a speedy decision. The 78 boys in the gymnasium would be safer in Fort Wayne, whereas exemptions from military service could be more readily secured by seminarians in Missouri.[19] A new building in Fort Wayne would also provide accommodations for a larger number of students.

The combining of the two seminaries at St. Louis and the transfer of the Concordia Gymnasium to Fort Wayne established the theological schools in the Missouri system. After 1861, although it retained its legal designation as Concordia College, the St. Louis institution became Concordia Seminary and its curriculum was restricted to theological studies. The university-trained leadership of the synod realized the necessity of a "practical" program but sought at the same time to emphasize the full classical and theoretical course for pastors. The decision to move the Fort Wayne seminary to St. Louis in 1861 was at least in part an effort to raise the standards of the "practical" course as well. From 1861 to 1875 instruction was given in two divisions, theoretical and practical. In 1875 the "practical" division was moved to Springfield, Illinois, permanently restoring the earlier separate identities of the two seminaries.

With the transfer of the gymnasium department of Concordia College from St. Louis to Fort Wayne, a preparatory institution was for the first time assigned a separate geographical location and a faculty and administration distinct from the theological seminary. For the next 20 years it was the synod's only gymnasium. When in 1881 the state of Indiana amended the charter of the Fort Wayne seminary and officially designated the gymnasium as Concordia College, it confirmed the pattern under which the Missouri Synod would eventually establish or adopt 11 other similar institutions as feeders for its major theological seminary in St. Louis. Five of these were in operation before the turn of the century—in Wisconsin, New York, Missouri, Minnesota, and Kansas. Two others were established shortly after 1900 in Oregon and California.

The Missouri Synod has commonly applied the term *college* to the entire six-year gymnasium course in each of its institutions.[20] In relation to the more familiar American pattern, however, the first four years, *sexta* through *tertia*, offered work of high school level and the final two years, *secunda* and *prima*, were analogous to a junior college. As initially constructed in the Missouri system, the entire sequence was heavily oriented toward the classical languages. Over the course of six years students spent one-third of their classroom time on Latin. During the final two years they gave over half of their 32 class hours each week to Latin and Greek. In the remaining hours they applied themselves to mathematics, German, French, religion, history, and geography. This was the curriculum that with only minor alterations was followed in the preministerial schools of the Missouri system for almost 80 years.[21]

The heavy concentration on classical languages conformed to Luther's prescription that a pastor must be able to move fluently in the original languages of the Scriptures. However, classical Greek rather than the Koine Greek of the New Testament was used in classroom exercises. And in reading Homer and Sophocles, Cicero and Vergil, students were not encouraged to appreciate their literary qualities. These authors were seen simply as practitioners of a language, rather than creators of a broad cultural heritage. One student recalled that his study of languages "never really passed beyond the stage of grammatical concern." "One could get an A in this grind," he wrote, "but there was in all truth, nothing stimulating in it, nothing that might have proved an incentive to wider or more independent reading."[22]

Methodology was as inflexible as the curriculum. Teachers trained in Germany used the methods they knew best and taught their successors accordingly. Obedience was the first law of the classroom; recitation and drill precluded discussion. Until the 1930s, according to one analyst of the Missouri system, "there was virtually no change in the educational system through which the embryonic clergy were funneled. Indeed, any effort to introduce new approaches, more compatible with the American educational pattern, whether in administration, in teaching methods, or in curriculum, was frowned upon as a dangerous innovation."[23]

Meeting the Need for Teachers

During its first 25 years the Missouri Synod experienced remarkable growth. Alert leadership and the training and strategic deployment of several hundred missionaries from Germany made possible a vigorous missionary outreach among the steady influx of German immigrants. An initial clergy membership of 22 in 1847 increased to 415 by 1872. Congregations were planted in 24 states from New York to California, with the largest concentrations in the midwestern states, where most of the German immigrants had settled. Stephanus Keyl, who directed the synod's "Pilgrim House" in New York City, welcomed 27,000 immigrants between 1870 and 1883. In one year alone, 1882, he wrote 3,951 letters, many of which directed newcomers to communities served by synod pastors. A missionary in Iowa in 1859 maintained a circuit of 28 preaching places.

To provide pastors and teachers for such an expanding, constantly changing network of congregations and mission stations, and at the same time to mantain a uniformity of doctrine and practice, was a monumental task. After the supply of recruits sent by Loehe came to an end in 1853, Walther was able to interest another German pastor, Friederich Brunn, at Steeden in Nassau, to open a preparatory school for boys and young men willing to work in America. From 1860 to 1878 Brunn sent more than 200 young men to complete their training in the Missouri Synod schools at Fort Wayne and St. Louis. Still others came from the Hermannsburg Mission Institute and from the Basel Mission Society.[24]

The necessary division of the synod into geographical districts in 1854, although seen by some as a hazard to doctrinal unity, opened the way for the development of an indigenous supply of pastors and teachers for the synod and provided a vehicle for extending the synod's system of regionally oriented preparatory schools.

The earliest instance of such regional initiative was also the harbinger of one of the most important features of Missouri's permanent system of higher education, namely, the professional teachers college. Although the need for teachers as well as pastors had been keenly felt even before the organization of the synod, there were only 27 teachers available for 116 parishes in 1854. Men with abbreviated theological training who might better have served as parish teachers were of necessity called by congregations as pastors, with the added responsibility of teaching in the parish school.

This continuing critical shortage moved three pastors and two teachers in the Milwaukee area to start a private seminary solely for the preparation of teachers. Encouraged by promises of support from their local congregations and from district conventions of the synod, they opened their school in January 1855, with 11 students. Three years later the synod itself undertook sponsorship of the school and over the objections of those who wished to maintain a separate institution, moved it to Fort Wayne in 1858 as a department of the seminary. Pastor Philipp Fleischmann, one of the original sponsors of the Milwaukee venture, was added to the Fort Wayne faculty, with particular responsibility for teacher preparation.[25]

When, acting under wartime stress, the synod moved its gymnasium from St. Louis to Fort Wayne, accommodations there became seriously overtaxed. By that time the teacher preparation department had expanded to 36 students and was compelled to relocate in other, entirely inadequate quarters, first in the attic of a local bookstore and later in an abandoned tavern.

At the time the private school in Milwaukee was moved to Fort Wayne, an offer of sponsorship had been extended by the Zion congregation at Addison, Illinois, near Chicago. This congregation had conducted its own parish school since 1840. By 1849 members of the Zion congregation had organized a local society expressly to foster parish education by operating English and German schools in the Addison area. The physical difficulties experienced by the teachers seminary in its new location in Fort Wayne prompted a renewed invitation from the Illinois group in 1862. During an informal evening in the home of Henry Bartling, teacher in the parish school, members of the congregation individually pledged cash support and 20 acres of land if the teachers seminary could be brought to Addison.[26]

 The synod convention of 1863 unanimously accepted the offer and resolved that facilities should be provided immediately so the school could reopen in Addison in September 1864. While the new building was under construction, calls for teachers continued to flow in from parishes at the rate of 30 per year. In one of the earliest acknowledgments of the increasing impact of the developing American public school system, Professor Christian A. T. Selle sent out special appeals to congregations in 1863 and 1864, emphasizing the need for American boys as teacher candidates for the schools of the church. Evidence of the vitality and professional self-consciousness emerging among church school teachers was the formation, as early as 1856, of teachers' conferences to provide in-service training. The synod in convention, however, was not yet ready to respond positively to a memorial from its Eastern District suggesting a synodical school committee to determine the needs of the schools and actively to promote their improvement.

Pending the completion of its new building, the Addison teachers college opened in September 1864, in rented quarters. A student body of 43 men and boys greeted the newly elected president, J. C. W. Lindemann, a German-born graduate of Fort Wayne seminary, and until his election pastor in Cleveland, Ohio.[27] Students ranged in age from young boys to men of 40 years, including Civil War veterans, some of them amputees. Still others were new recruits from Germany sent by Pastor Brunn of Steeden. Arranging a curriculum for such a varied group presented a real challenge to Professors Lindemann and Selle during the initial year. By 1868 a five-year curriculum had been established, including Luther's Catechism and the Lutheran confessions, Bible history, arithmetic, history and geography, drawing and penmanship, German and English. A distinctive feature was the strong component of vocal and instrumental music required of all parochial school teachers.

The rapid increase in enrollment at Addison after 1864 left no doubt that a separate college for teacher preparation was a necessary addition to the Missouri system. From 55 students at the opening of the first year, the numbers rose to 98 in 1868, 136 by 1875, and 239 in 1885. By the end of President Lindemann's 15-year administration 279 graduates had gone to work in synod congregations. Yet during the decade of the 1880s vacancies still exceeded candidates by 40–50% each year.[28]

Although the great demand for teachers created problems of both admission and performance standards, candidates were carefully evaluated. A program of examinations in 1880 records that six students were advised "to seek a life's calling other than that of a Christian teacher."[29] Teacher preparation was among the first areas in the Missouri synod to acknowledge the necessity of a shift of emphasis from German to English. Even in the face of the great shortage of teachers, the Addison faculty was discouraging the importation of teachers from Germany by the late 1880s. President Eugen Krauss, himself a recent immigrant, concluded an article on the subject in 1889 with the blunt advice, "German teachers, stay in Germany."[30] By the early 1890s, instruction in all branches of the teacher-training curriculum except religion had made the transition from German to English.

With the establishment of the teachers' college at Addison, the distinctive place of teacher education in the Missouri system had been established. This institution became the rallying point for a growing cadre of committed teachers, organized for mutual enrichment and nourished by a professional journal, *Evangelisch-Lutherisches Schulblatt*. Known since 1947 as *Lutheran Education*, this journal has been published continuously since 1865.

The Missouri system of parochial schools was established and reached maturity in the face of growing popular support of the American public school system during the same years and in the same midwestern states. Partial explanation of this phenomenon lies in the synod's determined retention of the German language and in its strong emphasis on doctrinal uniformity. But the quality of its program was achieved through a competent program of professional teacher education, begun at Addison and more fully developed in later years at the River Forest (Illinois) and Seward (Nebraska) Concordias.

Regional Prep Schools

During its first quarter-century of rapid growth the Missouri Synod had been largely dependent upon pastors and missionaries from Germany who had completed their training in the synod's seminaries. Future growth would depend upon developing a native ministry from the synod's own congregations. Young boys desiring to prepare for the ministry, however, would have to leave home at the age of 14 to undertake six years of preparatory study at Fort Wayne, Indiana, in the synod's only gymnasium. Many parents were reluctant to send their boys so far from home at such a tender age.

Responding to a special appeal at the synod convention in 1881 for a long-term solution for the increasing shortage of pastors, congregations in several parts of the country took steps to develop local schools which offered the first two or three years of a gymnasium. After completing these courses in a "pro-gymnasium" a boy would be eligible to enter the third- or fourth-year class in Fort Wayne. Between 1881 and 1893 such schools were opened under the auspices of local congregations and pastors in New Orleans; Milwaukee; New York; Concordia, Missouri; and St. Paul, Minnesota.

The New Orleans school closed after five years,[31] but the others eventually became full-fledged gymnasia, joining Fort Wayne as feeder institutions for Concordia Seminary in St. Louis. Two of the early graduates of the Perry County seminary, Christoph H. Loeber and Henry Wunder, opened a pro-gymnasium in Milwaukee under supervision of the Northwestern and Illinois Districts of the synod. Following the pattern which became standard in the Missouri system, the synod itself assumed control of the school in 1887, and in 1891 gave it full approval as a six-year college, coequal with the gymnasium at Fort Wayne.

In the same way, Pastor J. F. Biltz, another graduate of the Perry County seminary, rallied the congregations in and around Concordia, Missouri, to found St. Paul's College in 1883. When the Western District of the synod assumed control in 1885, the support base for St. Paul's College was broadened, and in 1896 it, too, became a synodical pro-gymnasium, sending its graduates on to Fort Wayne or Milwaukee before beginning their theological studies at St. Louis.

Responding to the same synodical appeal that led to the opening of new schools in Wisconsin and Missouri, the pastoral conference of New York requested St. Matthew congregation in lower Manhattan to establish a pro-gymnasium, using the classrooms of its parish academy. Twelve students began their study on September 5, 1881, under the direction of a faculty headed by

Pastor Karl Bohm and St. Matthew's pastor, J. H. Sieker. The Eastern District of the synod undertook official sponsorship and support in 1883. By 1890, however, enrollments and contributions dropped, and the district began to look for a new location, somewhat removed from the hazards and distractions of metropolitan New York.[32]

Several sites, from Poughkeepsie to Staten Island, were investigated, but some "especially courteous agents" of a realty company convinced the district committee that a wooded hilltop elevation called Buttermilk Hill, at Hawthorne in Westchester County, was an ideal spot for a college. A Pittsburgh donor contributed the $9000 purchase price of the land and, with contributions from other individuals and congregations, including a gift of $12,500 from St. Matthew congregation, an imposing building costing $45,000 was ready for occupancy in September 1894. In 1896 the school at Hawthorne was accepted as an official part of the synod's expanding preparatory system, but not until 1907, following its 25th anniversary, was the New York school authorized to offer the full gymnasium course and to bear the proud title of Concordia College.[33]

While adoption of a school by the synod carried with it significant financial support, notably the payment of faculty salaries and eligibility for special grants, synod colleges have also enjoyed continuing support by their founding congregations and districts. In the case of the New York gymnasium, an association called the Lutheran Education Society was organized in 1907 with 145 members to raise money for special needs of the school that could not be met with synod funds. Within a year of its founding, the society was confronted with a formidable challenge involving the removal of the college to a more favorable site and the construction of three major campus buildings. With the completion of the project in 1909 at a total estimated cost of more than $200,000, Concordia College moved into its permanent home in Bronxville, New York, as one of the most handsomely equipped members of the synod's family of preparatory schools.[34]

The rapid growth of the synod in the upper Mississippi Valley inevitably brought about a movement for the establishment of a regional school in that area for the recruitment of ministerial candidates. The synod's Northern District, formed in 1854, was subdivided in 1875 and again in 1881. By 1891 the new Minnesota-Dakota District had 322 congregations and 131 pastors and teachers serving a membership of 50,000 persons.[35]

Initiative for the founding of a preparatory school in St. Paul, Minnesota, came from two prominent leaders of the Missouri Synod, Dr. Friedrich Pfotenhauer, president of the Minnesota-Dakota District, and Dr. Francis Pieper, president of Concordia Seminary, who brought a strong recommendation directly to the synod convention in 1893. An accompanying memorial from the district cited the missionary character of the district as a reason for requesting direct sponsorship by the synod from the outset.

The convention responded to the two eloquent spokesmen with an affirmative vote and an initial appropriation of $25,000, an especially generous grant in the face of the impending nationwide depression of 1893. Thirty boys enrolled in September under the leadership of Professor Theodore Buenger. President Pfotenhauer's address at the opening ceremonies voiced a prophetic reminder to the synod that "we must train ministers to speak the language that the people understand as well as those languages in which God speaks to us."[36]

Within a year the college was able to occupy a six-acre campus, with four buildings vacated when the state of Minnesota moved its reform school for boys from St. Paul to a smaller community in the state. The complete campus, for which the state had originally paid $100,000, was purchased for $21,865, well within the original synodical appropriation. By 1896 when the first class had completed three years of pro-gymnasium studies and were ready for transfer to the gymnasia at Milwaukee or Fort Wayne, total enrollment had reached 68. The synod convention, however, deferred a request for elevation to full college status for six more years.

The synod convention which authorized the pro-gymnasium in St. Paul in 1893 was also confronted with the perennial issue of teacher shortage. The Addison faculty memorialized the convention with the plea for more "feeder colleges" offering the first three years of secondary training and sending students on to Addison for the two final years of teacher training. Synod leadership strongly supported the memorial submitted by the Nebraska District requesting the establishment of a second teachers seminary on its territory. Before the convention assembled at St. Louis, several offers had already been made by Nebraska communities for the location of the school, including a very attractive one from citizens of Lincoln, the state capital.

The urgency of the teacher shortage apparently again overshadowed the rising economic fears. The synod voted to establish a second college especially for teacher preparation, promising to pay the salary of one professor, but leaving all other financial responsibilities with the Nebraska District. A committee of the synod was assigned the task of weighing the various offers of community support and selecting the most favorable site. Four prominent Lutherans in Seward, a small town 80 miles west of Omaha, offered a 20-acre campus and a guarantee of $8000, to be realized from the sale of 200 city lots. The acceptance of their offer, though somewhat less generous than that of Lincoln, probably reflected apprehension over the moral hazards of a "wide open" western city as well as some effective local lobbying for Seward.

The new college, authorized to offer the first three years of basic preparation for teaching, opened in November 1894, under the enthusiastic leadership of its first professor and president, Pastor J. George Weller. In the face of collapsing farm prices and bank closings, the new college took shape on the 20-acre campus and 13 students assembled to begin their instruction.

During the first few years of the tiny college's existence sheer survival was the measure of its success. Another crop failure in 1895 caused the Nebraska legislature to appropriate $250,000 for famine relief throughout the state. Local congregations shared from their own depleted resources. There was little encouragement from the synod, which itself was under severe financial strain. A limited special appropriation by the 1896 convention was accompanied by the cautious observation that "the Synod desires to await the further development of the school."[37] Enrollments were never large, but by 1900, 21 of 27 graduates had gone on to continue their studies at Addison and 3 of them had graduated and returned to teach in Nebraska. After 1896 economic conditions also continued to improve and the need for teachers persisted. In 1905 the college at Seward was elevated to full status as a five-year seminary for teacher training.[38]

Meanwhile, expansion into the Pacific Northwest had resulted in the organization of the Oregon and Washington Districts of the Missouri Synod in 1899, followed by the inevitable plea to the synod for more ministers and parochial school teachers. The response of synod president Francis Pieper to the 1903 convention of the new district was short and clear: "You must raise your own crop." The older California-Nevada District had received the same message, with the result that within two years two Concordias came into being, in Portland in 1905 and Oakland, California, in 1906. Both began under very modest circumstances as pro-gymnasia but prospered with the growth of synod strength in the Far West, becoming fully developed members of the regional support system for Concordia Seminary.[39] By 1920, as synodical expansion also continued in the Canadian Northwest, the Missouri Synod convention voted to establish its first and only college in Canada. Concordia in Edmonton, Alberta, opened in 1921.[40]

Schools of the English Synod

Two other colleges, although not founded as institutions of the Missouri Synod, were closely related, and eventually became integral parts of its educational system. Both were affiliated with the English Synod of Missouri and Other States, a small association of English-speaking congregations sharing doctrinal but not linguistic kinship with the German Missouri Synod. Concordia College in Conover, North Carolina, founded in 1877, was for several years "under the fostering care" of the Tennessee Synod. When this relationship was terminated in 1891, under circumstances described in an earlier chapter (above, pp. 110-111), the college trustees turned to the Missouri Synod for a professor of theology, and in 1893 offered the college to the convention of the English Synod as a gift.

At the same convention in 1893 the English Synod also accepted St. John's English Lutheran College in Winfield, Kansas, as a gift from its founder and builder, J. P. Baden. Baden was a German immigrant, a member of a Missouri Synod congregation who had achieved notable success as a businessman in Winfield. Convinced of the importance of a Christian higher education in the English language for both young men and women, he determined to build and endow a coeducational college that would prepare young men for the ministry, but would offer a variety of other courses as well.

On Christmas Eve in 1892 he informed his former pastor of his intent to give $50,000 to the English Synod for this purpose. Within three months, without any consultation with the synod, he formed a corporation, secured a charter, commissioned an architect, purchased a site, and even took steps to engage a faculty. On April 10, 1893, ground was broken for the building, and one month later Baden offered the English Synod a deed to the college. Overwhelmed by the munificence of the gift, the convention rose to its feet in gratitude and enthusiastically voted its acceptance, apparently assuming that Baden would also maintain the college indefinitely.

The resources of the English Synod, about a dozen congregations, were probably not adequate to support even one college. Yet in the course of a single convention it had accepted responsibility for two. Moreover, the ground had scarcely been broken for the new building in Winfield than the nation was engulfed in the disastrous economic crisis of 1893. J. P. Baden's financial resources were drastically curtailed, and he was compelled to borrow money to complete and furnish the building and to meet initial operating expenses.

School opened in September 1893, in temporary quarters with 5 boys and 6 girls in attendance, all but 1 from Winfield and only 4 of them Lutherans. With the completion of the new building enrollment rose to 27. Courses of study were arranged to accommodate both an American baccalaureate system and the preministerial curriculum of the Missouri Synod. Business students swelled the enrollment to nearly 100 in 1899, while the number of preministerial students ranged from 10 to 20 during the early years.

Only when J. P. Baden submitted his resignation as college treasurer in 1895 did the synod convention understand that it had accepted full responsibility for maintaining the operation of the college. Baden was willing to continue his support but only as one of many contributors. Inevitably, the English Synod turned to the Missouri Synod, requesting financial support for their adopted institution. When the English Synod joined the Missouri Synod as a nongeographical district in 1911, both St. John's and Concordia in Conover were incorporated into the Missouri educational system. St. John's thus became the first coeducational degree-granting institution of the Missouri Synod.[41]

By the turn of the century the Missouri system of higher education had been firmly established. Further growth and refinement would follow, but the closely integrated network of preparatory colleges and seminaries was already recognizable as a unique contribution to Lutheran higher education in North America. The goal of preparing a well-educated and loyal Lutheran clergy motivated the founding of most Lutheran colleges in the 19th century. The importance of the study of classical languages was also generally recognized, though not always attainable in a frontier situation. Some Lutheran synods, especially those which grew out of the later German immigration, also modeled their preparatory schools after the German gymnasium.

But the Missouri Synod with signal success intentionally shaped its entire system of higher education to a single purpose, the preparation of pastors and teachers for the church. As products themselves of a Lutheran university tradition which honored all professions as avenues of service to God, the early leaders of the synod never rejected preparation for them as of no concern to the church. But from a deep sense of missionary responsibility toward the thousands of their countrymen who were entering America in the mid-19th century, they made a conscious choice to meet what they saw as their primary obligation. Driven by an equally deep conviction that they had been given a special task as bearers and defenders of the true faith, they pursued their goals with zeal and determination. In addition to building a nationwide, church-controlled system unique in the history of Lutheran higher education, the Missouri Synod probably achieved greater success in retaining the loyalty of immigrants from their home country than any other Lutheran group in America.

10 ILLINOIS: THRESHOLD TO THE GREAT PLAINS

On October 2, 1839, two weeks after a group of Lutheran immigrant pastors from Saxony announced their intent to open a college in Perry County, Missouri, another group of Lutheran pastors and laymen assembled just 50 miles away in the tiny village of Hillsboro, Illinois, and resolved to establish the first Lutheran institution of higher education in the state of Illinois. This resolution was a statement of intent by the Evangelical Lutheran Synod of the West, a small synod which had been organized five years earlier to coordinate Lutheran missionary work beyond the borders of organized Lutheran synods.[1] Moreover, it also set in motion an intricate chain of events leading to an extensive network of colleges and seminaries that would eventually serve the ethnically diverse Lutheranism of the upper Midwest. The impulse from Hillsboro found eventual expression in Carthage College in Kenosha, Wisconsin; Midland College in Fremont, Nebraska; Augustana College in Rock Island, Illinois; Augsburg College in Minneapolis; Augustana College in Sioux Falls, South Dakota; and both the Lutheran School of Theology at Chicago and Luther-Northwestern Theological Seminary in St. Paul, Minnesota.

No one realized more clearly than these missionary pastors, ministering in communities scattered over five states, that there was a crying need for more pastors in the West. By their next convention they had raised a sum of $1000, but had also concluded that the task of establishing a seminary was too great for such a small synod to undertake alone. However, a promising alternative developed when the English Synod of Ohio separated itself from the Joint Synod. The Synod of the West promptly dispatched a proposal inviting the new synod's cooperation in establishing a joint theological seminary. Though ex-

159

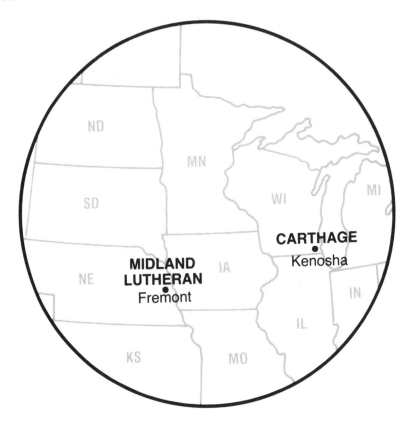

pressing "unfeigned pleasure" at the intentions of the western synod, the English Synod twice declined the invitation, basing its decision upon the imperative need to establish an English-speaking seminary in Ohio.[2]

Roles were reversed two years later, in 1844, when Ezra Keller, professor-elect in the now-established English Seminary in Ohio, visited the convention of the Synod of the West in Fort Wayne, Indiana, and invited its cooperation with the English Synod in supporting their seminary, soon to become Wittenberg College. This counterproposal also failed, partly because of growing tensions between German- and English-speaking pastors in the western synod, but mostly because of geographical distances.[3]

By 1846 it had become clear that both geography and the rapid growth of settlement made it impracticable for a single synod to serve a five-state area. By common consent delegates to the Synod of the West agreed to a territorial subdivision. Three new synods were created. One retained the name of the parent synod but limited its work to the state of Indiana. The new Illinois Synod also included congregations in Missouri. The Synod of the South West served congregations in Kentucky and Tennessee. The same convention that approved this proposal in 1846 resolved that the seminary for these three synods should be located in the state of Illinois. It also named a board of directors and instructed them to secure a charter for The Literary and Theological Institute of the Evangelical Lutheran Church of the Far West.[4]

Beginnings in Hillsboro

During the first session of the newly organized Synod of Illinois in 1846 the board decided to locate the school in Hillsboro, a small community in the southern part of the state, in which the first Lutheran congregation in Illinois had been established in 1832. An academy had been in operation in Hillsboro since 1835, and since 1841 had been under the direction of two Lutheran pastors. The citizens of Hillsboro offered to donate the building and property of the academy to the board of the new college with the understanding that the academy would be retained and kept in operation in those facilities for 20 years. The directors accepted the offer and elected the Reverend Francis Springer, a graduate of Gettysburg Seminary, as president and first professor, and the Reverend A. A. Trimper, principal of the Hillsboro Academy, as the second professor.[5]

When the school opened in January 1847, 79 students were in attendance, no doubt including many of those previously enrolled in the academy. At the outset no theological instruction was offered, but a collegiate department conducted classes in Greek and Latin, mathematics, science, and philosophy, with a few additional courses in natural theology, evidences of Christianity, and mental philosophy. Most of the students were enrolled either in the primary department or in general courses designed to provide an "accurate and substantial English education."

One of the most colorful personalities associated with the Hillsboro college was the first chairman of the board, Pastor John J. Lehmanowsky of Knightstown, Indiana. Lehmanowsky was a Polish citizen of Jewish descent who had turned from the study of medicine to a military career just as Napoleon began his rise to fame and power in France. An excellent swordsman and soldier, he had served as a military aide to Napoleon for 22 years and, during the internment of the great general at Elba, had been directly involved in Paris in the conspiracy for Napoleon's return. Imprisoned and sentenced to be shot, he engineered a storybook escape and made his way to America. For many years he lived in Philadelphia, married, and raised a family of four children, supporting them by teaching fencing and foreign languages. He shortened his name to Lehmann, but in 1824, during the visit of his friend, the Marquis de Lafayette, to the United States, he was persuaded to resume his full name lest he forfeit his claims against the French government in the event the Napoleonic dynasty should be restored. With a gift of money from the Marquis he purchased a tract of land near Knightstown, Indiana, where he practiced medicine and farmed until 1837. In 1836 at the age of 63 he was ordained a Lutheran pastor by the Synod of the West. Until the extended travel became too strenuous for him[6] he served as board chairman and general agent for the college at Hillsboro, traveling as far west as Iowa and Wisconsin, soliciting funds for its support and gifts of books for its library.

Illinois State University

Events in the life of this tiny frontier institution moved quickly to place it in a unique position in the development of American Lutheranism and in the story of Lutheran higher education. Hillsboro was located in southern Illinois where the Lutheran population consisted almost entirely of second- and third-generation German Americans. As early as 1850 there were virtually no persons of foreign birth in the Hillsboro area. English was used both in the churches and as the medium of instruction in the college.

Farther north, however, the waves of new immigrants from Germany and Scandinavia were rapidly moving into the state. If the new Literary and Theological Institute were to serve effectively, some attention would have to be given to the interests of these people. Adding foreign language courses might help, but more basic was the lurking fear that the college was not in a favorable location to serve the new and growing Lutheran constituency. An alarming decline in enrollment in 1850 seemed to confirm these fears and led directly to a decision to move the college.

The prime mover in this decision was the newly appointed Professor of Christian Theology, the Reverend Simeon W. Harkey, until his election a pastor in Frederick, Maryland. In view of the strained financial condition of the college Harkey was asked to devote the first year of his appointment in soliciting funds to endow his own professorship. By the conclusion of the year 1850–1851, during which he met with encouraging success in the East and also in Illinois, especially in the area of Springfield, he became convinced that the college should be moved to a new location.

Harkey was able to win agreement from both the Synod of Illinois and the newly organized Northern Illinois Synod. Their committees chose Springfield, the state capital, as the new location for the college. Eager to enhance its prestige by bringing a college to the community, citizens of Springfield offered 10 acres of land, a building fund of $5000, and the assurance of income from the sale of 100 perpetual $300 scholarships.

The charter of the Hillsboro college was amended by the state legislature in 1852 and the relocated institution was given the pretentious title of Illinois

State University. Apparently carried along by Harkey's optimism and the "boosterism" of a frontier-state capital city, the suggested name of Melanchthon College was dismissed as too modest. The intention, in fact, was to have a university, declared President Springer. Therefore, "Why not at once assume the name of a university?" Indeed, the charter included a provision authorizing the trustees to "establish separate departments besides the usual departments of theology, medicine, and law, a department of mechanical philosophy and also agriculture."[7]

While neither these ambitious projections nor those of Capital University, founded only two years earlier in the state capital of Ohio, ever came to full fruition, they represent the earliest institutional expressions of an unfulfilled dream in the history of Lutheran higher education in North America. The desire to establish a Lutheran university in the European tradition from which so many pioneer Lutheran educators have emerged has been voiced repeatedly but never realized. The divided character of the Lutheran constituency in North America, both in language and theology, has been at least partially responsible. Also the early preoccupation of Lutherans with the preparation of the clergy led them instead to stress undergraduate studies in the classics and the liberal arts.

The new university opened June 2, 1852, with a faculty of 4 and a student enrollment of 82. Temporary facilities were used until an imposing four-story brick building worthy of the name and location of the school could be erected. However, funds for both construction and operation came in very slowly. Not all the promised scholarships were sold, and most of those that were sold exercised an option whereby payment of annual interest of $18 rather than the principal sum of $300 enabled one to "purchase" such a scholarship. Abraham Lincoln used this option to pay the tuition for his son Robert who attended the school for two years.

Both financial problems and internal dissension dogged the university throughout its 16 years in Springfield. Although board memberships were equally distributed between the two synods and the community of Springfield, most support came from persons in the Springfield area. In spite of the presence of such distinguished local citizens as Ninian Edwards and John T. Stewart, Lincoln's law partner, as board members, efforts to tap a $150,000 state fund for colleges and seminaries failed. President Springer attributed the failure to the "vulgar prejudices which certain politicians foster against collegiate learning under a pretense of a very great devotion to common schools."[8]

Frustrated by attacks on his administrative leadership and by charges that he was alienating foreign groups in an attempt to Americanize the Lutheran church, Springer resigned in 1855. He suspected that much of his opposition was rooted in efforts by his colleague, Simeon Harkey, to undermine his authority. Writing in his journal, Springer deplored the "intrigue, vain egotism, vaunting self-importance and pedantic pretenses" displayed by "some of the little fellows strutting around me."[9] Harkey's appointment by the board as acting president did little to quiet Springer's suspicions.

Neither the personal tensions nor the financial crisis of the young university were solved by the brief interim incumbency of Simeon Harkey or the permanent appointment in 1857 of Dr. William Reynolds, former president of Capital University. The panic of 1857 paralyzed the fund-raising efforts of the sponsoring synods to ease the school's indebtedness. Faculty salaries were an entire year in arrears.

The Failure of an Ethnic Experiment

One of the reasons for moving the school further north was to accommodate the German and Scandinavian immigrant population. Both the Illinois and the Northern Illinois Synods therefore approved resolutions to add foreign language professors to the faculty. But neither the synod nor the university seemed able to raise the funds to pay the salaries for these professorships. The Northern Illinois Synod, in which the Norwegian and Swedish elements were most heavily concentrated, took the initiative in 1856, announcing its readiness to raise the funds for a Scandinavian professorship. Its resolution designated the Scandinavian professorship as a chair of theology and specified that its occupant should be nominated by the synod rather than the university board. Reflecting the theological conservatism of the Scandinavians, the synod also declared that its professor would be required to teach in conformity with the unaltered Augsburg Confession.

In view of the northern synod's announced intention to pay for the professorship, both the Illinois Synod and the university board concurred and in 1858 joined with the Northern Illinois Synod in electing the Reverend Lars P. Esbjörn to the new position.[10] Esbjörn, in turn, agreed to undertake a solicitation for an endowment to support the professorship.

Esbjörn was a university-trained pastor of the Church of Sweden who had led one of the first companies of Swedish Lutheran immigrants to western Illinois in 1849. Together with Paul Andersen, a Norwegian Lutheran pastor in Chicago, he represented the Scandinavian Lutheran congregations at the organization of the multilingual Northern Illinois Synod in 1851 and later became the founder of Augustana College and Seminary.

Esbjörn joined the faculty of Illinois State University at a particularly sensitive point in both the development of American Lutheranism and in the social and political development of the American nation. The issuance of Samuel Schmucker's "Definite Synodical Platform" in 1855 climaxed the extended controversy between the "American Lutherans" and the "Old Lutherans" over the issue of subscription to the unaltered Augsburg Confession. The decade of the 1850s also marked the climax of the "nativist" movement in the United States that directed suspicion and frequent attack upon "foreign" influences in American political and social life. The secrecy of such so-called "American" groups led to their popular description as "Know-Nothings," because when asked for information about their organizations, members responded, "I know nothing."[11]

Both Esbjörn himself and the Scandinavian students who came to Springfield to study under him complained of exclusive attitudes and behavior by the "American" element in the university community. Student organizations at the university were politically active, even successfully soliciting such prominent national figures as Stephen Douglas, Charles Sumner, Horace Greeley, and James Buchanan as honorary members of their societies. Literary societies that debated the current issues of slavery and secession and presidential politics excluded Scandinavian students from membership, and immigrant undergraduates were refused permission to organize societies of their own.[12]

Professor Esbjörn, elected by his synod as professor of theology, was assigned a variety of other courses, and complained that the teaching of secular subjects consumed 11 hours a week, leaving only 3 for theology. In addition, he was expected to give 4 hours of instruction in the Swedish and Norwegian languages each week.

More distressing to him, however, was the evidence, both in the synods and in the university, of a lax attitude toward the Lutheran confessions. When Esbjörn had joined the Northern Illinois Synod in the first place, he had protested its qualified adherence to the Augsburg Confession as a "mainly correct" exposition of scriptural doctrine. He suspected his faculty colleagues, Springer, Harkey, and Reynolds, all Gettysburg men whom he regarded as "New Lutherans," of straying from orthodoxy. With regard to the climate of the university, he wrote to his friend Eric Norelius, "I am not very satisfied here, either doctrinally or otherwise. Orthodox Lutheranism seems to exist more in theory than in practice, and the attitude of Americans toward foreigners sometimes sticks out."[13]

The second year had scarcely begun when his restlessness became quite apparent. In October 1859, he wrote to Eric Norelius that he felt as if he were "in a sort of Babylonian captivity," and found himself thinking of plans for establishing a separate school in Chicago. A little later he wrote, "We are anxious to get out of this cage and enjoy a little freedom among friends and countrymen, because no one knows how unhappy we are here."[14]

When President Reynolds learned that Esbjörn was sharing his critiques of other members of the faculty with his students and warning them of "un-Lutheran" communion practices in the local congregation, he went to Esbjörn's home and delivered a severe reprimand. The following day, March 30, 1860, Esbjörn submitted his resignation, effective immediately, and left Springfield shortly thereafter. With him went virtually all the Scandinavian students.

All efforts at reconciliation having failed, the pastors and delegates of the two Scandinavian conferences of the Northern Illinois Synod met in Chicago in April 1860, declared their support of Esbjörn, and announced their intention to form a separate Scandinavian Lutheran Synod. Organized June 5, 1860, at Jefferson Prairie, Wisconsin, the new synod was called the Scandinavian Evangelical Lutheran Augustana Synod. At the same time, the synod decided to establish its own school in Chicago and elected Professor Esbjörn as the Scandinavian professor in the new "Augustana Seminary."[15]

The Quest for New Beginnings

The loss of the Scandinavian students and the support of the Scandinavian congregations dealt a nearly fatal blow to the troubled university in Springfield. The outbreak of the Civil War in 1861 brought a further decline in student enrollment, and the following year President Reynolds resigned. Simeon W. Harkey again became acting president, while the board spent two years in search of a permanent successor. Meanwhile, personal and theological tensions persisted both in the faculty and the sponsoring synods. The breaking point was reached in 1867 with the suspension of the theological department of the university, and the dissolution of the Illinois Synod. Two new synods were formed, one largely German-speaking and confessionally identified with the "Old Lutherans." The English-speaking pastors and congregations reorganized as the Central Illinois Synod. Together with the Northern Illinois Synod, they remained loyal to the General Synod and shared control of the nearly defunct Illinois State University. The German group eventually joined the Missouri Synod.

In a final effort to save the institution the university board proposed sending a delegate to Springfield, Ohio, to suggest uniting the seminaries of Illinois State University and Wittenberg College and locating the school in Springfield, Illinois, as the Lutheran Seminary of the West. The Central Illinois Synod concurred and even agreed to pay half the expenses of its president, Ephraim Miller, as the official delegate. The effort, however, was unsuccessful; the Wittenberg board had no wish to move their college.[16]

Since no other recourse appeared available, the board of the university was obliged to close the school in 1868 and to offer the property for sale to liquidate the indebtedness. A temporary lease of the building to a Presbyterian group during 1868–1869 provided a few additional months of grace in which to seek a more favorable solution. The citizens of Springfield offered to assume the $15,000 debt if the church would establish a faculty of at least three professors and an endowment to pay their salaries. Based on previous performance, however, neither party seemed likely to fulfill such a commitment.

Another option was offered in 1869 by the Northern Illinois Synod which had operated a college in Mendota, Illinois, since 1857. Originally established as a women's seminary, the school had become coeducational by 1860. In 1867–1868 it enrolled 132 students, 73 female and 59 male. Citizens of Mendota, who had given the original campus and a $10,000 grant, offered additional land, buildings, and cash if the Lutheran church would "establish a first class college in our city and endow the same liberally as soon as practicable."[17]

The 1868 convention of the Northern Illinois Synod commended Mendota College and "its worthy principal and corps of able teachers." It expressed the hope "that now, as this has become a chosen point of concentration for our educational interest in the Northwest, there will be such unanimity and concert of effort in providing patronage for this institution as very soon to render it a power for good throughout our Church and the whole Country."[18]

The same enthusiasm for Mendota College was not shared by leaders of the Central Illinois Synod. President Ephraim Miller flatly rejected a request from the Northern Illinois Synod for joint support. To his own synod convention in 1869, he reported, "From the knowledge I had of the sentiments of members of this synod, as well as with the concurrence of judicious brethren whom I had opportunity to consult, I had no hesitation in declining to take any steps looking toward the object proposed by the president of the Northern Synod."[19] It is likely that both Miller and his "judicious brethren" wondered whether Illinois State University might have survived if the northern synod had been willing from the beginning to give its undivided support to the joint venture in Springfield.

In spite of conflict, frustration, and disappointment, the determination of the western synods to maintain their own theological school persisted. An intersynodical convention, expanded to include the English Synod of Iowa and the Synod of Southern Illinois, was called to meet on August 31, 1869, in Dixon, Illinois, to deliberate on Lutheran educational interests in Illinois and adjacent states. A convention committee report recognized the financial and moral obligations involved in the university in Springfield, but reluctantly agreed with the board's decision of the previous year, "to abandon it and tender it to our creditors."[20] However, neither this report nor the Mendota proposal that was also brought to the convention won general approval. The Dixon convention adjourned after adopting a report authorizing a commission of three representatives of each synod to take definitive action upon proposals for the location of a school.[21]

The Reverend Conrad Kuhl, pastor in Carthage, Illinois, was designated as convener of the commission. At his invitation representatives of four synods assembled on December 29, 1869, in Carthage, and elected Francis Springer as chairman. The commission received three formal proposals, two of which had already received some attention at Dixon. Both the Mendota offer and the offer of the Springfield citizens to assume the debt of Illinois State University were discussed and voted down.[22] The official representatives of the controlling synods thereby confirmed the decision made in 1868 by the board of trustees to close the university in Springfield.

Their action marked the end of a courageous attempt to weld together the several disparate elements of midcentury Lutheranism in mid-America. The faculty and students of Illinois State University included both "Old" and "New" German Lutherans. It was also sponsored by the Northern Illinois Synod, the first Lutheran synod to combine the multiethnic immigrant groups of the Midwest: Germans, Swedes, Norwegians, and Danes. Its significance lies not in its success or lack of it but in its character as a pioneer effort to unite groups of Lutherans who, after this historic attempt, would require another century to achieve that goal.

During its 16 years in Springfield, Illinois State University served about 2000 students. Its graduates entered the professions of law, medicine, and public service. One of its most distinguished alumni was John Hay, Lincoln's private secretary and biographer, subsequently United States ambassador to England and secretary of state. Of even greater significance in the life of the church on the western frontier was its contribution of 27 men to the Lutheran ministry.[23]

Early Years at Carthage

The third proposal, presented to the commission by the host community of Carthage was unanimously adopted in a night session on December 30, 1869. After discussing the nature of the anticipated institution, the commission pledged itself and the synods represented "to organize a faculty of instruction. . .sufficient to give instruction in all the classes usually taught in an American college." They also pledged the establishment and endowment of a theological department.[24]

Citizens of Carthage agreed to furnish a building site within the city and the sum of $35,000 for construction to be given in three stages over a three-year period as units of the building were completed. The synods agreed to establish an endowment of $100,000, also in three stages corresponding to the completion of the building units. Title to the property was to be conveyed by the stockholders to the synods when the endowment reached $50,000.[25]

On January 10, 1870, 11 residents formed an association and organized a joint stock company, which offered 3000 shares of stock at $100 per share. A seven-man board of trustees, elected by the stockholders in March, selected the site and authorized construction of the college building.

Meanwhile, the commissioners representing the synods also continued to meet. They decided to open a classical academy in September 1870, before the college building was ready. They appointed L. F. M. Easterday, a graduate and former faculty member of Illinois State University, as principal and instructor, assisted by the local pastor, Conrad Kuhl. The school opened in rented quarters with 16 students, including 4 women. As construction proceeded on the college building, enrollment in the academy increased, and by 1873 the commissioners were ready to reorganize it as a four-year college, while retaining the preparatory department.

The Reverend David Tressler, who had been appointed the previous year as an additional full-time faculty member, was named first president of Carthage College. A graduate of Gettysburg College and Seminary, he had served a pastorate at Lena, Illinois. In the fall of 1873 the college opened with 160 students and 6 faculty. The following year enrollment exceeded 200, and in June 1875 Carthage awarded its first four baccalaureate degrees.

In spite of these encouraging enrollments the financial position of the college remained precarious. The country entered a period of severe financial depression in 1873, and in each successive year operating expenses exceeded income. The synods were unable to raise the expected endowment of $50,000. Even the $35,000 claimed as endowment consisted largely of pledges that produced no interest. Because the funds promised by the citizens of Carthage for the building were only partially subscribed, the trustees were forced to borrow $10,000 at 10% interest to complete construction of the main college building. Student residences were also needed, and after an unsuccessful effort to finance them by the sale of scholarships, they too, had to be built with borrowed money. One of the few saving graces was Professor Easterday's mysterious success, in the face of possible claims by creditors, in transferring to Carthage the library and a considerable amount of furniture and equipment from the defunct Illinois State University.[26]

By 1879 the deficit had reached $3000, and the endowment was still short of the $50,000 required for the transfer of college ownership to the synods. President Tressler signed a personal note for $10,000, to bring the endowment up to the required level and undertook an extensive tour of churches in Illinois, Iowa, and Nebraska, seeking contributions for the college. Weakened by physical strain and exposure, he contracted pneumonia in February, 1880, and died at the age of 41.

Following Tressler's death the college seemed to be reenacting the sad experience of its predecessor institution. Financial distress coupled with internal dissension brought Carthage to the brink of dissolution. Tensions arose between the faculty and the commissioners over the selection of a Nebraska pastor, the Reverend J. A. Kunkelman as the new president instead of Professor L. F. M. Easterday, the faculty favorite. In a procedure which seems to have raised some questions among constituents, the commission was able to transfer ownership of the college from the board of trustees to the seven supporting synods. Thereupon, the Board of Commissioners voted its own dissolution, and governance of the college was assigned to a new 19-member board of trustees, with members elected by each synod and five elected at large.[27]

Confronted with the continuing financial crisis, the new board met in special session in December 1881 and asked the new president to lead a $25,000 campaign for endowment and debt relief. When President Kunkelman refused to "go on the road" as a fund-raiser, Professor Easterday agreed to take on the assignment. Even so, the effort was not successful, and in the summer of 1883 the president and the entire faculty resigned.

A new president, the Reverend J. S. Detweiler, was engaged, and a new faculty hastily assembled, but before the 1883–1884 school year had been completed they also resigned. In a special meeting in April 1884, the executive committee of the board accepted the resignations of the president and faculty and took steps to assure the reopening of the college for the ensuing school year. The results of their deliberation, however, were not revealed until the graduation exercises in May when five seniors received diplomas from the retiring president. At the close of the exercises in Trinity Lutheran Church President Detweiler announced that the college would cease operations.

Immediately following Detweiler's statement the secretary of the board came to the platform and informed the audience that the board of trustees had voted to continue operations. The college, he stated, would open as usual in September, and Dr. Edward F. Bartholomew, one of the faculty members who had resigned in 1883, would be the new president. Thereupon Dr. Bartholomew came to the platform and delivered a stirring appeal for renewed support of the college. The effect on the audience was described as "sensational."[28]

Although Edward Bartholomew remained in the presidency for only four years, his leadership in a most critical time spelled the difference between demise and renewal for Carthage College. During those years he was able to restore trust and confidence within the college community and among its church constituency. Fiscal deterioration was reversed and the long upward climb toward financial stability begun. Dr. Bartholomew's personal appearance before the newly organized Board of Education of the General Synod in 1890 with a request for assistance resulted in a $1000 grant for Carthage and the beginning of annual operational support from that body. In the area of curricular reform he introduced both the elective system and the use of credit requirements for graduation. After leaving Carthage in 1887 Dr. Bartholomew taught English and philosophy at Augustana College in Rock Island for 44 years. He died in 1947 at the age of 100.[29]

As successive presidents of Carthage would discover during the remainder of the century the upward climb was both long and steep. The classic slogan, *Carthago non delenda est* (Carthage shall not be destroyed), adopted by the friends and supporters of the college during these discouraging years, spoke to them more eloquently of a present plight than of a past historic event. When President Holmes Dysinger was inaugurated in 1887, the total enrollment of the college, including preparatory students, was only 75.

Four years later, however, it had reached 185 and by the turn of the century the 200 mark had been passed. Beginning in 1895 the generous benevolence of Henry Denhart, Washington, Illinois, banker and a member of the board of trustees, enabled the college to achieve financial stability and to expand its physical facilities. His offers of matching gifts encouraged continued support from the General Synod and made possible the achievement of a $250,000 endowment by 1909.[30] When the North Central Association began its listing of accredited schools, Carthage received full approval in 1916. During President Harvey Hoover's 17-year administration (1909–1926), a 50th-anniversary campaign increased the endowment to $675,000, one of the highest of any Lutheran college in America.

Mission to the Great Plains

As the Lutheran church moved beyond Illinois into the upper Midwest and the Great Plains, it continued to demonstrate two major concerns that had dominated its life since the days of Henry Melchior Muhlenberg, home missions and education. Both of these concerns had been expressed in the 1839 resolution of the Synod of the West, urging the establishment of a school to train pastors for the frontier regions of Indiana and Illinois. The founding of Hillsboro College and Seminary and its subsequent move to Springfield were attempts to serve an even wider constituency, including Scandinavians who were beginning to arrive in larger numbers by 1850. After the collapse of Illinois State University, the three Illinois synods and the English Synod of Iowa, all affiliated with the General Synod, moved to establish Carthage College, lest their territory be left without a school of higher learning.

The withdrawal of the Scandinavians to form their own independent synod was a prelude to a massive influx of immigrants from five heavily Lutheran countries of northern Europe: Norway, Sweden, Denmark, Finland, and Germany. Each speaking a different language, these groups organized their own congregations and church bodies. Their home mission programs sought to gather their own people and their educational efforts gave special attention to the preparation of pastors and teachers for their own congregations. The development of the wide-ranging Scandinavian network of educational institutions, mostly in the upper Midwest and the Great Plains, will be told in succeeding chapters.

The home mission thrust and its accompanying concern for the establishment of colleges and seminaries was also carried into the West by the older eastern Lutheran synods. The first missionary pastors from the Pittsburgh and Allegheny Synods entered Kansas and Nebraska in 1857 and 1858. As a result of these efforts of the General Synod, district synods were established in Kansas in 1868 and in Nebraska in 1871, serving largely English-speaking migrants from eastern states who had moved west to take advantage of the Homestead Act of 1862. German congregations were organized into the Wartburg Synod in 1872 and the German Nebraska Synod in 1890.[31]

The General Synod Founds a College

During these years of expansion missionary pastors were supplied either by Gettysburg Seminary or the theology department of Wittenberg College, both geographically far removed from the Kansas and Nebraska prairies. In 1885 the same appeal for a college and seminary that had been sounded by the Synod of the West 46 years earlier was made by the English synods of Illinois, Iowa, Kansas, and Nebraska. This time, however, it was directed to the convention of the General Synod in Harrisburg, Pennsylvania. A formal memorial requested that the synod create a board of education "to advance education in the West, Northwest and Southwest with system and efficiency."[32]

The petition was granted, and the General Synod became the first Lutheran church body in North America to establish a Board of Education. The board's initial membership consisted of nine men, four pastors and five laymen, with the retiring president of the General Synod, the Reverend Mosheim Rhodes, as its first chairman. Its first item of business was "the matter of the western college."[33]

A public advertisement of the board's intentions produced offers from nine cities and towns in Nebraska and Kansas. The city of Atchison, a boomtown of 30,000 on the Missouri River in northeastern Kansas, was growing rapidly as a commercial and trading center. It claimed that 80 passenger trains a day used its railroad depot. The "Atchison Boom Syndicate" promised $50,000 in cash for buildings, plus 25 acres of land for a campus, one-half the profits on the sale of 500 acres of land, and the assurance of 200 students.

In June 1887 the board accepted the Atchison offer and made immediate preparations for the opening of the college. Temporary facilities were made available in the Atchison Institute, a school operated by Mrs. Harriet Earhart Monroe, daughter of the pioneer pastor who had begun Lutheran missionary work in Kansas in 1857. Mrs. Monroe closed her school in favor of the new institution.

Within three months the Board of Education selected a name for the college, appointed the first board of trustees, applied for a charter, assembled a faculty, and named an acting president. A charter was granted in 1888 for Midland College of the General Synod of the Evangelical Lutheran Church in the United States of America. Dr. Rhodes served as acting president until a formal call was accepted by Dr. Jacob A. Clutz of Baltimore, general secretary of the Home Mission Board of the General Synod and a graduate of Gettysburg College and Seminary.[34]

Midland opened in September 1887 as a coeducational four-year college, with 101 students, 17 college freshmen, and 84 in the preparatory department. The main building promised by the city of Atchison was completed by January 1889 at the cost of $28,000 and dedicated in the fall of 1889, shortly after the arrival of President Clutz.

Midland College has the unusual distinction of being the only college in the entire 98-year history of the General Synod from 1820 to 1918 to be directly established by that body. All others were founded by individuals, groups, or district synods. The intent of the church for its college ''in the heart of the nation'' was incorporated into the preamble of its first constitution:

> The institution shall be in the broadest and truest sense a Christian College. It shall provide a liberal education amid Christian influences and by Christian methods. The Scriptures shall be read and taught. The college teachings must be specific without being narrow; loyal to the church without being bigoted. The highest mission of Midland is to develop the entire nature of its pupils, so as to lead to the highest womanhood and manhood.[35]

From Atchison to Fremont

The collegiate curriculum of Midland College included three distinct courses of study—classical, scientific, and literary—each leading to a bachelor's degree. The classical course required four years of Greek and three of Latin. The scientific course replaced Greek with laboratory courses in the sciences, and the literary course substituted German and French for the classical languages. No electives were permitted. An initial faculty of four was increased to seven, including three women, during the college's second year. Governance was entrusted to a self-perpetuating board of 15 trustees, two-thirds of whom were required to be members of General Synod congregations.

An annual grant from the General Synod supplemented college income from student tuition and private gifts. Several efforts were made to endow professorships. The largest single gift for this purpose resulted from the untimely death of a young pastor, George D. Gotwald, secretary of the board of trustees. Unable to make any substantial personal contribution to such an endowment, he undertook to pay the premiums on two insurance policies for which the college would be the beneficiary. Only a few months later the 28-year-old pastor was stricken with pneumonia and died, leaving a $24,000 endowment for the presidential chair of the college.[36]

The promising beginnings at Midland encouraged the General Synod to request the college to add a theological department in 1893. Two years later the Synod established the Western Theological Seminary as a separate institution on the Midland campus, but in 1909 asked that the seminary become an integral part of the college. Although retaining its name, first as Western, and later as Central Theological Seminary, it continued to function as a department of Midland College until 1966 when it was merged with the Lutheran School of Theology at Chicago.[37]

No event in the life of Midland College since its founding has exerted as great an influence upon its character and direction as its move from Atchison to Fremont, Nebraska, in 1919. Few of the great expectations of its association with the city of Atchison were realized. The boom of the late 80s collapsed in the early 90s and the population of the city actually declined. The Lutheran constituency in Atchison had never been strong, and by 1914 the general lack of community support led students to ask the board to consider moving the college "to a more favorable locality." The war against Germany in 1917 gave rise to a series of press attacks on the college, impugning the loyalty of some faculty and students. Some of the German seminary students were investigated by the Justice Department, and a German-born faculty member who had not yet become a naturalized American was interned. Under pressure from accusations President Rufus Peery called upon the Atchison Commercial Club to appoint a committee of responsible businessmen to make an impartial investigation into the patriotism and loyalty of the faculty and student body. The committee report publicly exonerated the college of the charges of disloyalty.

After the storm had subsided, President Peery's report to the college board called their attention to "insidious influences in this city working against us." He concluded with the question, "Can an institution prosper in a community, many of whose citizens and press take this attitude toward her?"[38]

In the midst of these discussions President Peery learned that it would be possible to purchase the buildings and campus of Fremont College, in

Fremont, Nebraska, a school owned and operated by a private citizen, William H. Clemmons. Clemmons had taken over a nearly defunct school in 1888, and had built an institution which had on occasion enrolled as many as 1200 students. Using as his model the Northern Indiana Normal School and Business Institute in Valparaiso, Indiana, of which he was an alumnus,[39] Clemmons offered to teach almost anything a serious student asked for, at low cost and without frills. In 1912 his faculty of 40, organized in 18 departments, offered preparation for teaching, business, law, medicine, pharmacy, home economics, public services, and music. In 1916 after nearly 30 years as president of the school, Clemmons was elected Superintendent of Public Instruction for the State of Nebraska. This added responsibility and the decline in enrollments caused by the war in 1917 led to his decision to sell the college.[40]

The proposed new location in Fremont offered great advantages to Midland College. The city was situated in the midst of strongly Lutheran territory, with 270 congregations within a 100-mile radius. The English and German Nebraska Synods offered to raise $300,000 if the college would move to Fremont. The city offered $25,000 toward the purchase of the school property. Additional bonuses would be the goodwill and community support bequeathed by Clemmons, as well as a potentially large number of students and faculty.

The Midland board reached its decision in June; three months later the college opened in its new location on September 1, 1919. Enrollments immediately rose to new heights. Although only 39 students transferred from Atchison, 99 college students registered in Fremont; 50 more enrolled in the academy. The influence of the new alliance, however, was mainly reflected in the 191 students enrolled in the new School of Commerce and the 232 who registered in the summer school. Only 9 faculty members, including 3 seminary professors, transferred from Atchison to Fremont; 20 new faculty members were recruited there.[41]

Prospect and Retrospect

The move to Fremont brought to a close the founding phase of Midland's history. As the college faced the 1920s both its character and its context had been substantially changed. Its base of community support had been broadened and strengthened by its move from Atchison to Fremont. The move had also resulted in the immediate multiplying of its enrollment, with the prospect of further increases in the years ahead. But the bulk of the increase was in areas of the curriculum which had received relatively little emphasis in the earlier Midland years. The character of the faculty also changed, increasing in size but leaning heavily toward the commercial and vocational disciplines. A strongly academically oriented school which on one occasion in 1896 had raised its entrance requirements and maintained them even in the face of decreased enrollments had merged with a school whose catalog cover carried the assurance to prospective students that they might "enter at any time."[42]

The merger of the college with the Fremont institution coincided with a church merger of major proportions. The General Synod which had created Midland College joined with the General Council and the United Synod of the South in 1918 to form the United Lutheran Church in America. A new Board of Education was created with responsibility for 16 colleges. Though Midland remained the only ULCA college west of the Mississippi, it no longer enjoyed the status it had held before 1918 as the special creation of its parent church body.

Much later in history another merger of Lutheran church bodies further extended the scope of Midland's relationships within the church and within its geographical area. When the Lutheran Church in America was formed in 1962 the Augustana Synod's Luther Junior College in Wahoo, Nebraska, was moved to Fremont, contributing both its tradition and its name to a greater Midland Lutheran College.

Almost exactly 100 years earlier a separation had taken place between the Scandinavians and the "American Lutherans" who had jointly supported Illinois State University in Springfield, Illinois. In their efforts to minister to Lutherans in the great inland empire of America, each of these groups had gone on to establish its own church structures and mission programs and its own colleges and seminaries. After the passage of a century the merger of 1962 brought the two streams together again. The uniting of Midland and Luther Colleges was a symbolic restoration of the institutional and ethnic break which had occurred in 1860 at Illinois State University in Springfield.

11 THE SWEDISH
DIMENSION

The Scandinavian Migration

Scandinavian migration to North America has a long history, dating at least to the 17th-century Swedish colony on the Delaware River and the Danish settlements in the Virgin Islands. Significant numbers of immigrants, however, did not appear until the middle of the 19th century, when circumstances in northern and western Europe turned the thoughts of thousands to the inviting opportunities of a new continent. Political restlessness, economic revolution, and religious dissatisfaction were endemic in Europe after 1815, and the Scandinavian countries shared in all those conditions. But for the Scandinavians who found their way to North America between 1825 and 1920, economic incentives outweighed all others.

Rural Scandinavia at midcentury was especially affected by changes in agricultural methods and in patterns of landholding. Farm consolidation drove tenant farmers and field hands off the land. Population increases, coupled with the continuing laws of primogeniture, forced even children of landowners to seek livelihood elsewhere. High taxes, low prices, and some extended periods of crop failure, such as that in Sweden from 1861 to 1869, pushed many marginal farmers over the edge.[1]

Political and social factors intensified the economic pressures. Scandinavia was a class society dominated by wealthy farmers and merchants, public officials, and clergy. Resentment of the superior privileges and social status of the official class was deeply rooted in the experience of small farmers, tenants, and workers who constituted the mass of common folk. The constitutions which had been adopted in Sweden in 1808 and Norway in 1814 were

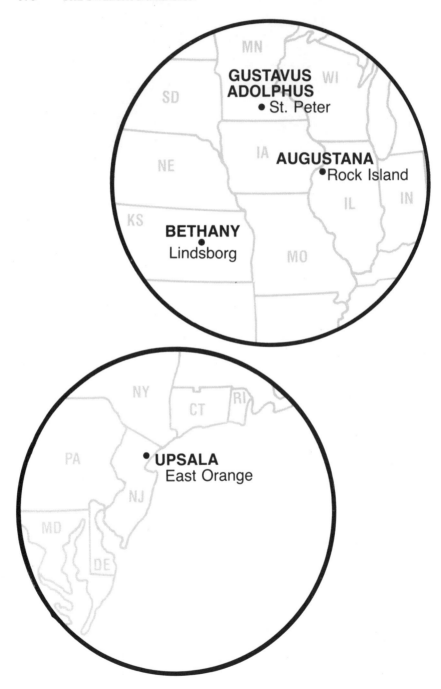

only promises of a democratic society not to be realized until late in the century. In the course of the struggle to achieve social and economic recognition many chose emigration as a more immediate and attractive option.

Since in all the Scandinavian countries the Lutheran church was the state religion, the clergy were by definition members of the governing class. The religious factor was therefore also closely related to the social and economic climate. Popular pietistic movements in both Norway and Sweden, which expressed themselves in small prayer meetings and devotional gatherings, often ran into official disapproval and hostility. The established church could invoke the anticonventicle laws which forbade public teaching of religion by other than officially ordained clergy. In some cases direct religious persecution drove individuals and groups to leave the country. In most cases, however, the religious factor was only one aspect of the general thirst for a climate which offered opportunity for a better and freer life.[2]

Emigration was only sporadic between 1820 and 1840. The numbers began to achieve significant proportion in the 1840s and increased steadily, reaching a peak of 105,000 in 1882. By 1920 more than two million Scandinavians had entered the United States and Canada. Their most favored destinations were the Great Lakes states and the northern Great Plains, though smaller groups settled at various times in New England, Texas, Canada, and the Pacific Northwest. Although the Norwegians were the earliest of the Scandinavians to begin the 19th-century migration to America and probably sent the greatest proportion of their population as emigrants, Sweden sent the largest Scandinavian group.

Several characteristics of the Scandinavian immigration from 1840 to 1860 were especially significant in shaping social and religious patterns in America. Most of those who crossed were farmers, and most settled in rural America. Great numbers had taken part in the pietistic revival movements and were accustomed to lay activity and even lay preaching in the church. In all three Scandinavian countries official church authorities opposed emigration, often denouncing it as an evidence of national disloyalty. Consequently, very few ordained clergy came to minister to the expatriates. Those who did come responded to urgent calls from small, struggling congregations, usually transmitted by individuals who had some personal connection with the pastor being called. In no case did the emigrant pastor represent an organized missionary concern on the part of the official church.

Lacking all ties with their mother church, therefore, the early Norwegian and Swedish settlers were left open to the proselytizing activities of American denominations, especially the Methodists and Baptists, but also Episcopalians and Mormons. The work of these denominations was made even easier by the eagerness of large numbers of the Scandinavian immigrants to adopt the English language.

In the absence of ordained European clergy the early Scandinavian settlers also hastened to develop their own pastors. Both Swedes and Norwegians sought cooperation with Lutheran synods of German origin. They sent their young men to already-established seminaries in St. Louis, Columbus, and Springfield, Illinois, until they could support their own schools of theology. In their eagerness for an education which would assist them in becoming Americans, they also founded academies and colleges for the general education of the laity.

Esbjörn and the Illinois Migration

Swedish emigration to America began during a period of religious upheaval in the homeland. The formalism and complacency of the Lutheran state church was first challenged through private devotional groups, often under the leadership of lay readers, called *läsare*. The 1840s and 1850s saw public revival meetings conducted throughout the country led by both lay preachers and awakened clergy.

Among the most influential revivalists were George Scott, an English Methodist who spent 10 years in Stockholm crusading for temperance and religious conversion, Carl Olof Rosenius, and Peter Fjellstedt, who established a school in Lund for the training of lay preachers. Most radical was a lay preacher named Eric Jansson who claimed divine authority as a prophet. After repeated confrontations with the Swedish authorities, he turned his back on the Old World in 1844 and led some 1500 disciples to establish a communal colony at Bishop Hill, not far from Rock Island, Illinois.[3]

Some voices were also raised among the Lutheran clergy for temperance and spiritual revival, but they received less than enthusiastic support from the officials of the church. One of these was Lars Paul Esbjörn. Already pastor of a small parish in northern Sweden, he had experienced a conversion in 1840 during a temperance rally led by Scott and an American Presbyterian, Robert Baird. His subsequent successes as a temperance speaker and evangelist, however, cost him election to several attractive parishes. Disappointed with the established church and burdened by an inner sense of responsibility for his deluded fellow countrymen who had followed Eric Jansson to America, Esbjörn began to consider emigration himself. "To seek out these [emigrants] with the gospel of Jesus Christ," he wrote in 1848 after his decision was made, "becomes a matter of conscience to one who, here at home, has neither the desired opportunity nor the liberty to proclaim it."[4]

Esbjörn's announcement encouraged others, both in his own and neighboring parishes, to follow his example. On June 24, 1849, a company of 146 persons joined their pastor on board a freighter bound for New York with a load of iron. Esbjörn thus became the first Swedish Lutheran pastor to lead a party of emigrants to America.

Upon arrival in New York the party was greeted by Olaf Hedstrom, a Methodist missionary who had welcomed Swedish sailors and emigrants in New York harbor since 1845. A land agent directed them to an inviting town called Andover, on the banks of an idyllic stream in western Illinois, not far from the Jansson colony at Bishop Hill.

The journey to the West was more taxing than the nine-week ocean crossing. River and canal boats were crowded and slow; delays were frequent; and an epidemic of cholera decimated the company. Esbjörn himself fell ill and was left behind in Chicago while his party struggled on down the Illinois-Michigan canal and a final painful 75-mile trek by horse-drawn wagon to Andover. Only then did they discover that Andover was little more than a dot on the open prairie. The weary travelers were greeted by Jonas Hedstrom, a brother of the New York missionary—also a Methodist minister—who persuaded most of them to accompany him to Victoria, 16 miles distant, where he assured them of good land and warm Swedish hospitality.[5]

When Esbjörn had recovered sufficiently to rejoin his party, he found its members scattered between Andover and Victoria. His plan to organize a congregation had to be postponed because of his continuing ill health. Moreover, when it became apparent to Hedstrom that Esbjörn intended to function as a Lutheran pastor and not as a Methodist, all signs of cordiality vanished.

Desperate for financial support, Esbjörn turned to Dr. Jonathan Blanchard, president of Knox College in nearby Galesburg, who recommended him for aid from the American Home Missionary Society of the Congregational Church. One of the conditions of the $300 salary grant was that in organizing congregations the custom of receiving members by confirmation would be replaced by "the stricter practices of American churches," which required positive evidence of conversion. This limitation, although not entirely foreign to Esbjörn's own pietistic bent, caused him to delay still further the organization of his first congregation in Andover. Although by March, 1850, there were 180 Swedes in Andover, he could identify only 10 persons, including himself and his wife, who after careful examination could qualify as truly regenerate Christians.[6]

Experiments in Lutheran Cooperation

The announcement in a Chicago newspaper of Esbjörn's appeal for aid from the American Home Missionary Society caught the eye of William A. Passavant, Lutheran pastor and editor in Pittsburgh. Passavant broadcast the plight of the newcomers from Sweden in the columns of his publication, *The*

Missionary. He called upon fellow Lutherans to join in assisting the new Scandinavian immigrants. Together with Dr. William Reynolds, president of Capital University, he made what he called a ''missionary journey to the Scandinavians of the West.''[7]

Following this visit Passavant urged the formation of a Scandinavian synod in Illinois and the establishment of a Scandinavian professorship to supply pastors for the growing settlements. Between April and July 1851 he also arranged for Esbjörn to visit several eastern synods to present personal appeals for funds to build churches for the Scandinavians in the West. Conventions of the Joint Ohio Synod, the Pittsburgh Synod, and the Pennsylvania Ministerium all received Esbjörn warmly and sent him on his way with generous gifts. The climax of his journey was a visit to Boston, where he met the famous Swedish singer, Jenny Lind, and received her gift of $1500 for the aid of her countrymen in Illinois. With these funds in hand construction began on churches in Andover and Moline and also in the colony of New Sweden, near Burlington, Iowa.

Passavant's suggestion of a Scandinavian synod appealed greatly to Esbjörn, and as early as July 1850 he broached the subject with the Norwegian pastors in Wisconsin and with Paul Andersen, the Norwegian pastor who had welcomed him when he first arrived in Chicago. Andersen, a graduate of Beloit College and a member of the Franckean Synod, favored the revivalist understanding of church membership. He was reluctant to be linked with the conservative Wisconsin Norwegians who acknowledged church members who were confirmed but not ''born again.'' Nonetheless, he was at least willing to discuss formation of a new church body with a group of ministers and lay delegates from both Scandinavian and German-American congregations in northern Illinois. On September 18, 1851, the Synod of Northern Illinois was organized, with 8 ministers and 20 congregations represented.

Having just returned from his eastern trip, Esbjörn was one day late for the meeting. During his series of visits in the East he had become fully informed concerning the current controversies in American Lutheranism and therefore reacted immediately to the new synod's conditional acknowledgment of the Augsburg Confession as ''mainly correct.'' To this he raised objection, insisting that ''the symbolical books of the Lutheran church contain a correct summary and exposition of the divine word.''[8]

During the years 1852 and 1853 two additional pastors arrived to bolster the spiritual ministry among the settlers, both of them to become leaders of Swedish Lutheranism in America. Neither had been sent by the Swedish church but came in response to calls issued by small congregations in Illinois. Tufve Nilsson Hasselquist became pastor of the Galesburg congregation in October 1852 and Erland Carlsson in Chicago in January 1853.

Esbjörn continued as pastor of the congregation in Andover until 1856 when he became the solicitor for an endowment to support a Scandinavian professorship at Illinois State University. Though times were hard in America in 1857, his efforts brought sufficient response to warrant the activation of the professorship in 1858. Esbjörn himself was elected to fill the position and began his work in Springfield in September.

The events of the ensuing two years, ending in his abrupt resignation from the faculty have already been described as part of a bold but ill-starred experiment in multilingual cooperation in Lutheran higher education (above, pp. 164-166). Even without Esbjörn's defection the experiment at Springfield might not have survived the decade of the 1850s, since serious tensions already existed between "Old" and "New" Lutherans in the Illinois synods supporting Illinois State University. But Esbjörn, who had left Sweden with a warm commitment to Methodistic pietism and had even sought to limit the membership of his first congregation in Andover to "born again" Christians, had within a few short years become such an orthodox Lutheran that he regarded conservatives such as William Reynolds and Simeon W. Harkey as unfaithful to Lutheran doctrine. His reaffirmation of Lutheran orthodoxy in 1851 was in part a reaction against the proselytizing activities of American Methodists and Episcopalians and in part the result of his early contacts with conservative eastern Lutherans such as William Passavant.

Less than a month after Esbjörn's resignation from the university faculty the Scandinavian conferences of the Northern Illinois Synod met in Chicago. Since 1852 such meetings had been held annually, apart from the general conventions of the synod, to deal with matters of special concern to the Scandinavians. It was this group which had nominated Esbjörn as professor, and it was to this group that he felt obligated to report the reason for his resignation.

Although the conference also listened politely to statements by both President Reynolds and Professor Harkey concerning Esbjörn's conduct, it seems clear that the secession at Springfield simply provided the occasion for a separation that had already been anticipated as both necessary and desirable. Esbjörn's explanation was accepted, and he was commended for his concern for the Scandinavian students at Springfield. The same meeting that endorsed his pullout from the university voted unanimously to withdraw from the Northern Illinois Synod and scheduled a meeting to organize a new synod on June 5, 1860.[9]

The Founding of Augustana

On the appointed day, pastors and delegates from 36 Swedish and 13 Norwegian congregations assembled in the Norwegian Lutheran Church in Jefferson Prairie, Wisconsin, and organized the Scandinavian Evangelical Lutheran Augustana Synod in North America. By adopting the Latin name of the Augsburg Confession as the official name of the synod, pastors and delegates left no doubt of the doctrinal position of the new body. Their approval of a constitution for a school of theology bearing the same name gave evidence of the high priority placed by the new synod upon the training of pastors to serve the growing number of Scandinavian congregations. It also placed Scandinavians in America squarely in the historic Lutheran tradition insisting upon a well-educated ministry.

The constitution of the seminary, drawn up by Esbjörn, provided for two departments: theological and preparatory. The faculty, which was to include three or more professors, at least one each of Swedish, Norwegian, and American origin, was to be elected by the synod.[10]

Augustana Seminary began its work in the schoolhouse of the Swedish Immanuel Lutheran Church in Chicago on September 1, 1860, with 21 students: 10 Swedes, 10 Norwegians, and 1 "American." As in most of the early Lutheran institutions of higher education in America, both European and American influences were evident. Since the basic purpose of the preparatory department was to provide a foundation for theological study, the classical languages were prominent. Nontheological subjects such as history and geography, mathematics and natural science, commonly found in the curriculum of the European gymnasium, were included in the preparatory department. Only in 1863, when the school received its charter, was the name of the institution changed to Augustana College and Seminary. American influences in the shaping of the collegiate program came largely from Gettysburg College, whose curriculum had also provided a model for Illinois State University, and several of whose graduates, such as William Kopp, Sidney L. Harkey, and Henry Reck, became early Augustana faculty members.

Like virtually every church-related college in America, Augustana had to struggle for financial survival. Although the college was founded by direct action of the 49 congregations of the Scandinavian Augustana Synod, the synod itself assumed no direct financial commitments. Even the salaries of professors depended upon voluntary contributions until adequate endowments should be established—a goal which had almost universally eluded Lutheran colleges. At Springfield Esbjörn had to solicit funds for his own salary. In August 1860, he complained that since arriving in Chicago he had received a total of $12 in salary, and "not . . . a single potato or turnip from the garden."[11]

Try as he would to retrieve what was left of the endowment funds he had collected for support of the Scandinavian professorship at Springfield, only a small part was returned. Likewise, funds Jenny Lind gave Capital University for support of a Swedish professorship had been preempted in that institution's struggle for survival. Finally, with nowhere else to turn, the New World looked back to the Old for help. Pastor O. C. T. Andrén was sent to Sweden to ask for offerings from Swedish congregations for the support of the new seminary. More than $10,000 was raised in this way, and the king personally donated 5000 books from the royal library.

Tufve Nilsson Hasselquist, president of the synod and pastor in Galesburg, Illinois, took the lead in handling this handsome gift. A graduate of Lund University in Sweden, Hasselquist had come to Galesburg in 1852 in response to the call of the small congregation organized by Esbjörn. A strong leader, he developed a large congregation in Galesburg and extended his influence among the Swedish settlements through the editing of a newspaper called *Hemlandet*. Like Esbjörn he was the product of an active Swedish pietism, but unlike Esbjörn he was also able to cultivate amicable relations with American churches while still maintaining his confessional Lutheran character.

In Galesburg he had been on friendly terms with Dr. Jonathan Blanchard, president of Knox College. From him he had learned that both the town and the college had been founded in 1841 as the focus of a colonization effort conceived by George Washington Gale, a Presbyterian clergyman in New York State. Even before the Swedish gift had been received, Hasselquist had written in *Hemlandet* of creating a Swedish colony modeled upon the successful Galesburg experiment.[12]

With funds now available Hasselquist enlisted the support of Erland Carlsson, Chicago pastor and newly elected chairman of the board, in an effort to relocate the seminary as the nucleus for a Scandinavian colony. Sharing the view of most pastors and educators of his time, Hasselquist considered large cities undesirable locations for educational institutions.

The Paxton Years

The synod convention in 1861 agreed to a colonization plan, but land offers in Iowa, Wisconsin, and Minnesota brought no enthusiastic response. At that point the Illinois Central Railroad approached the seminary board, proposing a location at Paxton, Illinois, 100 miles south of Chicago. The railroad offered 1000 acres at $6 per acre and a commission to the seminary of $1 for each of 30,000 additional acres which might be sold to settlers. A further commission of 50¢ per acre would be paid the seminary or its agent on the next 30,000 acres sold.

In June 1862, over strong objections, Hasselquist won synod approval of the move to Paxton. On the one hand, Eric Norelius insisted that Scandinavian migration was moving westward toward Minnesota rather than south from Chicago. On the other hand, Esbjörn saw Chicago as the future hub of the nation and the ideal location for the seminary. He wrote to his friend Norelius, "I believe that the area around the Great Lakes (especially Lake Michigan) will in the future become the most important section in America. Where else can you find such rich land, the enormous coal deposits, the inexhaustible forests, the rich ore, the limitless fishing, the possibilities for water power and transportation as are offered by Lake Michigan and the states of Illinois, Wisconsin and Michigan . . . ?" To Esbjörn, moreover, the use of the Swedish funds was sheer speculation, even "a breach of trust with the donors."[13] He resigned.

At the synod convention in June 1863, he delivered his final report on the seminary. He had made a journey to Sweden the previous year in an effort to secure a successor and also to seek an appointment for himself in the Swedish church. He was offered the pastorate in his home community at Östervala, but was unable to find a replacement for himself at Augustana. When the school moved to Paxton, the synod therefore asked its president, Tufve Hasselquist, to undertake the additional task of providing leadership for Augustana College and Seminary.

The first years in Paxton were pioneer years in every way. President Hasselquist was the only professor. Until the first building had been completed 23 people, including students, crowded together in the professor's farmhouse. Classes for the three Norwegian and seven Swedish students were conducted in a small schoolhouse which served both the congregation and the college.

Enrollments grew slowly; 15 were in attendance the second year. By 1868 the number had reached 50, of whom 12 were theological students and 17 were enrolled as college freshmen or sophomores. Also in 1868 Rev. Sidney L. Harkey, a brother of the former president of Illinois State University and also a Gettysburg man, arrived to fill the English professorship. August Weenaas came from Norway as the Norwegian professor.

But the prospects of permanence in Paxton had already begun to dim. Local citizens were not enthusiastic. The settlement was not growing. Increasing numbers of Scandinavian immigrants were finding Wisconsin and Minnesota more attractive. Signs of division in the long-standing alliance between the Scandinavian groups appeared at the church meeting in 1868. A request for relocating the school won little support. But a petition calling for formation of separate Norwegian and Swedish synods led to the appointment of a study committee to report the following year.

During the ensuing year the committee was undoubtedly influenced by the freely expressed views of the new Norwegian professor. A theological graduate of the University of Christiania (Oslo), in Norway, Weenaas was neither familiar with nor supportive of the American concept of a college which Hasselquist and Harkey were seeking to establish as the broad basis for theological study. Instead, he favored a narrower and more simplified theological course in the style of the Norwegian mission seminaries, which he deemed appropriate for the preparation of frontier pastors. Before the synod meeting in 1869, Weenaas and the Norwegians concluded that they wanted a separate seminary. A year later they proposed a separate synod as well. Without rancor, the Scandinavian Augustana Synod granted both their requests.[14]

New Beginnings in Rock Island

Meanwhile, the board of directors had been exploring possible new locations for Augustana College and Seminary. With or without the Norwegians, Paxton held little future promise. On the basis of an offer from Geneseo, a community near Moline, Illinois, the board recommended relocation and the synod convention in 1869 gave its approval. Several more years elapsed, however, before the actual transfer took place. The Geneseo offer was subsequently withdrawn, and the board decided instead on a tract of land between Moline and Rock Island which could be purchased for $10,000. General economic distress accompanying the financial panic of 1873 caused extended delays in the collection of funds both for the purchase of the land and the construction of a building. Only in September 1875 was it possible for the college to occupy its partially completed new facilities in Rock Island.

During the intervening years several other developments occurred which would significantly shape the future of the college. A new constitution clearly distinguished a four-year collegiate program, "similar to the course of American colleges generally"; a preparatory department, offering practical training "for various branches of business" and for college entrance; and a two-year course in theology. The board of directors was made up of four clergy and four laymen elected by the synod, and four citizens of the community who might be non-Lutherans, elected by the board. The president and the college faculty were also elected by the board, while the seminary remained under direct synodical control.[15]

The synod convention of 1874 took a historic action establishing an apportionment system of college support that would be used by the Augustana Synod throughout its history. The synod requested an assessment of 25¢ per year from each member of a congregation, 10¢ of which was designated for faculty salaries and 15¢ for student aid. Districts or conferences of the synod were assigned apportionments reflecting their total membership, and pastors were expected to see that apportionments were met in their congregations. College support would thus increase as the membership of congregations and synod increased. Additional goals for voluntary gifts to the building fund were also assigned to the conferences of the synod.

The festivities attending the dedication of the new college building in Rock Island reflected the ecclesiastical company in which the Augustana Synod had chosen to move. By coordinating its events with the convention of the

General Council at Galesburg in October 1875, it was possible to involve several leaders of eastern Lutheranism, especially Dr. William A. Passavant who, 25 years earlier, had been among the first to extend the hand of welcome to Esbjörn and Norelius.

Established at last in a permanent location in a growing community and surrounded by a substantial ethnic constituency, Augustana could begin to look beyond mere survival to broader goals of academic and cultural service. Its catalog for 1876-1877 noted 137 students in attendance, 19 in the seminary, 42 in the college, and 76 in the preparatory department.

Efforts to attract Swedish pastors to the faculty of the struggling institution in Paxton that had earlier been rebuffed now met with gratifying success. Three university-trained professors from Sweden accepted apppointments between 1876 and 1878. Among them was an eminent zoologist, Dr. Josua Lindahl, who established scientific studies at the college on a permanently high level. Olof Olsson joined the faculty in 1876. Trained in Sweden both as a pastor and a church organist, he led the group of immigrants who founded Lindsborg, Kansas, in 1869. To Augustana he not only brought his rich theology, but through his musical sensitivity he also made a unique cultural contribution both to the college and the community. After attending a presentation of Handel's *Messiah* in Exeter Hall in London in 1879, Olsson returned to establish a Rock Island tradition. Every year since 1881 Augustana College has presented Handel's great oratorio as a musical offering to the community.

During these years Augustana began to assume a role in supplying leadership for Swedish Lutheran higher education similar to that which Gettysburg College had long filled for the older tradition of German Lutheranism in America. Two members of Augustana's first graduating class in 1877 became presidents of Swedish colleges: Carl Aaron Swensson at Bethany and Matthias Wahlstrom at Gustavus Adolphus. Of Augustana's 25 graduates by 1882, 11 entered the ministry and 11 became teachers or professors.

Decades of Testing

The 1880s and 1890s were years of significant development for the college, but also years in which the unique role of Augustana as a synodical institution was severely tested. Beginning with the permanent establishment of Gustavus Adolphus College in St. Peter, Minnesota, in 1876, no fewer than seven schools were founded in various parts of the Augustana Synod. President Hasselquist acknowledged the role of these schools as ''feeders'' for Augustana, but when they aspired to collegiate status, they threatened the place of Augustana as the synod's focal point in higher education.

The accompanying drain on Augustana's financial support was felt especially in the 1880s, and no doubt crippled efforts to raise funds for a much-needed new building. Notwithstanding a $25,000 gift from P. L. Cable,

president of the Rock Island Railroad, the college was obliged in 1889 to dedicate an unfinished Memorial Hall and to shoulder a $30,000 debt.

College and seminary enrollments remained virtually unchanged during
the 1880s. An overall increase from 200 to 300 students reflected growth only
in the preparatory department and in new nonacademic programs in business
and music. At the same time critics within the synod deplored curricular
changes in the college which gave greater recognition to English and to natural
and social sciences. In 1890 the synod even raised the issue of moving the seminary to another location.[16]

These were difficult years for President Hasselquist, who had been a tire-
less advocate of synodical unity. Moreover, as a leader in both church and
college, he had exerted a powerful influence for the preservation of Swedish
language, literature, and music, and for the development of spiritual leadership
for the Swedish-American community. Yet throughout his long and distinguished ministry, he had maintained a refreshing openness toward the pluralistic cultural patterns of 19th-century America.

When Tufve Nilsson Hasselquist died in 1891 at the age of 75, the
Augustana Synod lost its most revered leader. "No one," in the judgment of
one of the synod's most discerning observers, had "so influenced the heart and
mind of the Augustana Synod" in its formative years.[17]

The decade of the 1890s was no less trying. The humane and sensitive
Olof Olsson, pioneer founder of the Lindsborg settlement in Kansas and
long-term professor at Augustana, succeeded Hasselquist as president in 1891.
His successful staging of the Uppsala Jubilee in 1893, commemorating the
300th anniversary of the decree which permanently established Lutheranism in
Sweden, drew 20,000 celebrants to the campus, but could not obscure the fact
that this was also the year of a nationwide financial disaster. The college debt
rose to $70,000.

Further curricular changes, which raised academic standards, opened the
way for electives, and offered a clear choice between a classical and a scientific
course, brought the college into closer touch with current American collegiate
practices. As the decade drew to a close, prosperity finally returned to the
country and the college was even able to begin the building of an endowment.

Never a man of robust health, the president asked in 1900 to be relieved of
his strenuous duties. On May 12, 1900, shortly after the board granted him a
leave of absence Olof Olsson died, at the age of 59. According to his own evaluation, his years at the presidency had been "times of Americanization," necessarily accompanied by turmoil and criticism. Another assessment of his role
in that process described him as a leader with "sensitivity to the needs of the
common man, to the meaning of education for an immigrant people, to the
needs of the church in the United States."[18]

The Rise of Regionalism

One of the unique characteristics of Swedish Lutheranism in America has been its relative freedom from doctrinal schism. Other Lutheran groups have had major controversies that have produced internal divisions and created new synods, often with separate theological seminaries and colleges to represent differing points of view. Except for the defection of the Mission Covenant group in 1885, the Augustana Synod maintained its structural integrity from its founding in 1860 until 1962, when it merged with other synods to form the Lutheran Church in America.[19] The synod also maintained a single theological seminary throughout its history, thereby further assuring its Swedish ethnic identity and its theological stability. The proliferation of academies and colleges in the Augustana Synod during the 1880s was the product of a growing regional self-consciousness among Swedish settlements and the eagerness of Swedish immigrants to secure the basic education that would enable them to make their way in the new American scene.

As the volume of Swedish immigration increased, the synod approved the formation of geographical conferences rather than independent synods. The earliest of these ''expansion'' conferences was the Minnesota Conference, organized in 1858. Swedish migration had begun there in the early 1850s, and settlements were established at Chisago Lake, Vasa, and Red Wing, not long after the Andover colony in Illinois. Both the Kansas and Nebraska Conferences were direct outgrowths of post–Civil War expansion, stimulated by the Homestead Act of 1862 and the railroad land boom. Each of these conferences developed a college during the halcyon years of the 1880s, as did the New York Conference in 1893.

The first display of regional self-consciousness with respect to educational institutions was touched off in Minnesota during the discussion over the permanent location of Augustana Seminary. Leading spokesman for Minnesota was Eric Norelius, the synod's first home missionary in that territory. He had emigrated from Sweden in 1849 as a young lad of 17 and been befriended by Lars Esbjörn, who directed him to the newly established Capital University in Ohio. His first contacts with Minnesota came in 1853, as a teacher in the Swedish summer school in the new settlements in the St. Croix Valley. At the urging of Dr. William Passavant, special friend of the Scandinavians in the Midwest, he returned in 1856 and spent a year as a circuit rider among the growing Swedish settlements. Norelius was convinced that the spiritual needs of the Swedes in this territory demanded the establishment of a special program of mission activity. When Passavant and ''Father'' C. F. Heyer, veteran foreign and home missionary, proposed the organization of an independent Minnesota Synod, Norelius was tempted to cooperate. Alarmed at this display of independent regionalism, the Swedes in the Northern Illinois Synod hastened to propose the formation of a separate Minnesota Conference in 1858.

When the Augustana Seminary board decided to move the institution to Paxton, Norelius and his colleagues saw it as further evidence that the Illinois leadership of the synod regarded the pioneer Minnesota settlements as "stepchildren" "who must take things as they came."[20] After returning from the synod meeting in 1862, the pastor of the largest Swedish congregation in Minnesota wrote to Norelius that there was "a desire among some within the congregation to have our own school in Minnesota."[21]

By October, when the Minnesota Conference convened, the prospect had been widely discussed among pastors and lay delegates, and Norelius had even suggested a plan. His own congregation in Red Wing authorized a Christian day school for its own children, but specified "that older persons from other places might attend, receive instruction, and prepare themselves for higher studies elsewhere." Neither a theological seminary nor a college was contemplated. Before they adjourned, the 11 pastors and delegates of the conference passed a resolution asking "Brother Norelius" "to assume the duty of teaching those young men whom our congregations may send to him, that they may be trained and prepared to teach school both in Swedish and English."[22]

Minnesota's First Academy

Brother Norelius agreed, and the first student joined the Norelius household in Red Wing in late September. Others straggled in after the fall harvests and, though no records were kept, Norelius later recalled that he had instructed 11 students in a one-room school "in connection with the congregational school in Red Wing," during the winter of 1862–1863.[23] Some lessons were given in Swedish and some in English, and in the absence of adequate books and supplies, instruction was quite informal. The mixture of parochial school children and adults in their 20s and 30s challenged the pedagogical skills of Norelius, but final public examinations in April drew praise from visiting pastors, both for the teacher and his students.

In keeping with the tentative character of the school, its first year concluded without either formal organization or official name. In the synod meeting of 1863 where Norelius reported on his work during the year, the school was referred to as the *Minnesota Elementar Skola*. When it was made clear that there was no intention to challenge Augustana, but that the school would function as a preparatory school, the synod approved a constitution assigning responsibility to the Minnesota Conference, but under synodical supervision. The first board of directors was nominated by the Minnesota delegates and elected by the synod. Norelius became the first board chairman.

Having won initial approval from the synod, the Minnesota Conference next faced the decision of where to locate their school on a more permanent basis. Three sites were proposed—St. Paul, Vasa, and Carver. Following the democratic procedures of the frontier the matter was submitted to the vote of congregations, and the village of Carver, 25 miles southwest of St. Paul, was selected.

Neither the founder nor the first president of the Minnesota Preparatory School brought a background of Swedish university training to their educational venture. Andrew Jackson, who headed the relocated school at Carver, had studied in the secondary schools of Sweden, but upon the death of both parents in 1852, had gone to sea. After deserting ship in New York, he changed his name to Jackson, spent several years in a variety of jobs, including a lumber mill and a bar, and finally made his way to a Swedish settlement in Wisconsin. Following a spiritual conversion he taught school and served on occasion as a lay preacher in western Minnesota. After studying for one year in the new Augustana Seminary in Chicago, he returned to the Minnesota frontier in 1862 just as the Sioux Indian uprising in the Minnesota River Valley forced the evacuation of most of the settlers, including those among whom he had ministered.[24] Jackson was present at the final public examinations for the school in Red Wing in 1862, and Norelius recommended him as teacher for the newly constituted school at Carver.

One of the strong assets of the school during its years in Carver was the presence of substantial Swedish congregations nearby, especially at East Union where the school was actually located. The original log church served as the temporary location of the school, and after the congregation erected a new facility in 1866, it was remodeled to serve as the main building for the academy. The teaching program retained much of the informality of the Red Wing school. The age levels and educational experience of students varied widely. Very few students remained from the beginning of the term to the end. Swedish and English instruction was emphasized, and until 1870, Norwegian as well. Other subjects included American history and geography, sacred history, arithmetic, and music. A few students were able to receive rudimentary instruction in German, Latin, and Greek.

At first the school was known simply as "Jackson's School." But in 1865 the Conference bestowed upon it the title St. Ansgar's Academy, to commemorate the 1000th anniversary of the death of St. Ansgar, the missionary who brought Christianity to Sweden.

Aside from the modest student tuition of $1 per month, the school depended upon gifts from individuals and congregations. The Augustana Synod contributed $100 during the first year but reduced its support by $50 during each of the two succeeding years. The Minnesota Conference maintained a small education fund to assist prospective pastors and church school teachers. The local pastor launched an imaginative venture in institutional financing by building a flour mill on the local stream. However, his hopes of providing an annual $1000 income for the school were disappointed. The Mission Mill Company produced debts rather than profits and it was sold to pay its creditors.

As the decade of the 1870s opened, the viability of a separate school in Minnesota appeared doubtful. East Union showed no signs of becoming a support community. The withdrawal of the Norwegians from the Scandinavian Augustana Synod in 1870 reduced the academy's base of support in Minnesota, both in enrollments and financially. The pending transfer of Augustana College and Seminary from Paxton to Rock Island would further tax the limited resources of the entire synod, including those of the Minnesota Conference.[25]

From Academy to College

In 1872 the Minnesota Conference appointed a committee to consider an endowment for St. Ansgar's Academy. The committee's report in 1873 touched off discussions which gave a new direction to the entire educational program of the conference. The possibility of an independent Minnesota Synod was once again suggested. Norelius assailed the narrow view which would concentrate Swedish educational efforts in a single institution of higher learning. "Unless a school is built and maintained in every state where a considerable number of Swedish countrymen have settled, he declared, "the young people will seek their education in the public institutions, and the church will miss the opportunity of training them for the church and the kingdom of God."[26]

Norelius recommended that St. Ansgar's Academy be moved from its rural setting and relocated in East Minneapolis near the University of Minnesota. Students at a reincorporated institution to be called Gustavus Adolphus Literary and Theological Institute could then take a full college course at the university. The institute would offer subjects preparatory to the university and also college-level courses in Christianity and the Swedish language and literature. Among schools said to be following this pattern of education, similar to the European gymnasium, Norelius cited the recently established Augsburg Seminary in Minneapolis. On the strength of the promise by John S. Pillsbury to donate a block of property near the university, the Conference voted in the spring of 1873 to relocate its school in Minneapolis.

But by September the financial crisis of 1873 that demolished the dreams of so many American colleges held the Midwest firmly in its grip, and the Minneapolis plans were shelved. The conference meeting which reached this decision was held in St. Peter, a small but enterprising town 60 miles southwest of Minneapolis. Capitalizing on the disappointment over the failure of the Minneapolis offer, five prominent citizens of St. Peter—only one of whom was a Swedish Lutheran—offered a guarantee of $10,000 and 10 acres of land if the school were to be relocated in their city.

Recognizing the "hand of God" in this timely opportunity, the Conference voted at its next convention to accept the invitation and appointed a committee to select an appropriate site. In May the charter of Gustavus Adolphus College was signed by the ministers of the Minnesota Conference. The local press hailed the new college as destined to be "the great central educational institution of the northwest."[27]

But the panic of 1873 was no respecter of promises. In both 1875 and 1876, while a handsome and enduring structure of native Kasota stone was rising on a hill higher, it was said, than Zion's Hill in Rock Island, the grasshoppers were munching away at the farmers' harvests. With pledges unpaid and building costs soaring well beyond estimates, the new college in St. Peter began its life burdened by a substantial debt. In his dedicatory address, delivered in both Swedish and English, Eric Norelius looked well beyond such mundane hazards to long-term purposes of a college. "People whose minds are exercised by the lofty and various thoughts of the Bible and our Christian religion," he said, "will not be satisfied by bread and meat alone. They crave intellectual culture and the true development of all the faculties of man. This, then, is the way in which we account for the existence of this institution. It is yet in its mere infancy."[28]

These remarks of the founder were indeed future-oriented. A new location, a new building, and a new charter did not immediately produce an institution of collegiate calibre. Of the 51 students who attended during the first year, those from the East Union school were placed in the "second class" and all the new ones in the "first class." Only gradually, as new classes arrived, was any distinction made between high school, college prep, and normal courses. Students came and went irregularly.

Most of the classroom instruction was handled by the new president, the Reverend J. P. Nyquist, a product of Dr. Fjellstedt's mission school in Sweden who had been ordained in 1869 after one year of study at Augustana Seminary. He had served parishes in Indiana and Illinois without distinction and was an itinerant missionary in Michigan when he received the letter inviting him to accept the presidency at Gustavus Adolphus. His colleague was A. W. Williamson, a local resident with a master's degree from Yale and formerly principal of an academy in Ohio. Williamson taught English, mathematics, philosophy, United States history, and geography, and made it possible for the school to appeal to American students. Unfortunately, the Conference passed a resolution in 1880 requiring that all teachers accept the Lutheran confessions.

Since he was a Presbyterian, Williamson was dismissed but was immediately rehired by Augustana, where he served with distinction for 25 years.[29] During the Nyquist years Gustavus Adolphus remained an institution of high school rank. Only with the advent of President Matthias Wahlstrom in 1881 was the transition to collegiate grade begun.

The road to collegiate status for Gustavus Adolphus, as for most Lutheran colleges established on the midwestern frontier, was a long and difficult one. Their constituencies were mostly immigrant farmers or tradesmen with limited educational backgrounds. Basic instruction both in their own languages and in English was required before higher levels of study could be undertaken. Public high schools in most areas were not yet available.

Even after collegiate departments were established primary and preparatory departments furnished the largest number of students. Of the 182 students enrolled at Gustavus in the fall of 1883, 76 were either in the subpreparatory or preparatory classes.[30] In 1885 the senior class in the academy was designated as the freshman class in the collegiate department. A sophomore class was added in 1886, but not until 1888 was it possible to induce enough students to continue so that a junior and finally a senior year could be offered. The first baccalaureate degrees were awarded to eight graduates in 1890, 28 years after the first students arrived at Pastor Norelius' home in Red Wing in 1862.

During these crucial years of transition the curriculum of the collegiate department developed according to the standard classical tradition, with strong emphasis on languages and only modest exposure to the natural sciences. The trend toward electives reached Gustavus Adolphus only after the turn of the century. But enrollments were nearly doubled in the late 1880s by the establishment of music and commercial departments.

President Wahlstrom himself was a graduate of Augustana and he drew on his alma mater for faculty additions. In an effort to strengthen the "American emphasis," he also brought to the faculty several Lutheran professors from the East, graduates in most instances of Muhlenberg College. Graduate programs of both Swedish and American universities provided growing academic strength as Wahlstrom's 23-year administration drew to a close in 1904.

The Minnesota Conference continued to be the source of both students and financial support. The per capita assessment system, adopted by the synod for Augustana, was employed by the conference for Gustavus Adolphus, assessments varying from 25¢ to 37½¢ per confirmed member. Private solicitations for debt reduction were conducted among congregations and individuals, and President Wahlstrom on one occasion sought the help of Minnesota senator Knute Nelson in approaching Andrew Carnegie for a capital gift. The pious senator advised against seeking help from such tainted sources, warning that it would be "catering too much to the mammon of unricheousness [sic]."[31]

Before Wahlstrom's presidency ended, the college faced still another attempt at relocation, once again in Minneapolis. The issue was raised by the need of a new building for the college. As in 1872 glowing promises of support were offered by prospective donors in the Twin Cities, only to be withdrawn when the major gifts failed to materialize. Its permanent residence in St. Peter thus finally confirmed, Gustavus Adolphus turned to its 20th-century task of seeking academic maturity in the rapidly moving stream of American collegiate developments.

The Beginnings of Bethany

The beginnings of organized Swedish migration into Kansas and Nebraska after the Civil War set the stage for the establishment of two additional educational institutions of the Augustana Synod—Bethany Academy in Lindsborg, Kansas, and Luther Academy in Wahoo, Nebraska. Both schools were founded through local initiative and became focal points for strong regional and local loyalties. Begun as high schools, both eventually sought and attained collegiate status, Bethany as a four-year institution and Luther as a junior college.

The story of Bethany begins with the founding of the Swedish colony of Lindsborg, Kansas. On April 18, 1868, a group of Swedish immigrants in Chicago organized the First Swedish Agricultural Company, and purchased 13,160 acres in central Kansas from the Union Pacific Railroad. They invited Olof Olsson, an energetic young pastor in the Church of Sweden, to join them as their pastor. Already restive under state church restrictions on his ministry in Sweden, Olsson accepted the call and in May 1869, with 250 of his parishioners, boarded a steamship for America. More than 100 of his fellow immigrants followed him to Lindsborg and became the nucleus of the colony in the Smoky River Valley.[32]

Six weeks after his arrival Olsson organized Bethany Lutheran congregation. During the seven years of his pastorate, this 28-year-old pastor was the acknowledged leader of the community. Within two weeks of his arrival he applied for United States citizenship. Within a year he was elected superintendent of public instruction in newly organized McPherson County and established the first eight public school districts. Elected to the Kansas state legislature he sponsored bills to protect immigrant labor from exploitation by employers and to protect farmers from the encroachments on their lands by the great cattle drives from Texas to the railhead at Abilene, Kansas.

In 1876 when Olsson was called to a professorship at Augustana College and Seminary, he recommended Carl Aaron Swensson, a young seminary graduate as his successor. Though only 22 years old, Swensson promptly demonstrated unusual powers of creative leadership and a strong personal commitment to Christian education. At his first annual congregational meeting in December he noted that the land originally given to the congregation by the First Swedish Agricultural Company had been designated as a gift "for church and school purposes." His recommendation that a part of the land be laid out in lots and that one-half of the proceeds of the sales be set aside for the founding of a Swedish school was enthusiastically endorsed by the congregation.[33]

The school opened in October 1881, in the sacristy of Bethany Lutheran Church. J. A. Udden, a recent graduate of Augustana College and later an eminent geologist, was responsible for all subjects except Bible and religious history. These were taught by Swensson himself. Only 10 students, both boys and girls, enrolled in the first classes of Bethany Academy, but before the year was over the number had risen to 27. Before the second year began, Swensson had purchased the public schoolhouse for $500, moved it to a "park" adjoining the church, and enlarged it to provide three classrooms. A faculty of five was required to accommodate the expanded enrollment of 92 students.

During the summer of 1882 congregations of the Smoky Hill District of the Kansas Conference joined the Lindsborg church in pledging support to the school. A board of directors was chosen and in September 1882, just one year after its organization, Bethany Academy received a charter from the State of Kansas.

By the beginning of the third year in October 1883, a new steam-heated brick and stone building providing classrooms, dormitories, and dining room had been erected at a cost of $5000. An expanded curriculum offered normal, classical, and scientific courses and the board passed a resolution "that in our school the Swedish and English languages shall be considered equally important."[34]

In 1884 the Kansas Conference of the Augustana Synod resolved to "adopt Bethany as its child," and assigned a specific geographical territory for its support. The same convention also decided that the congregations in Nebraska should support the newly established academy at Wahoo.

Riding High in Kansas

The early years of the 1880s were "boom years" in Kansas and Nebraska. Almost unlimited farm land was available from the richly landed railroads or through the federal government's Homestead Act. Easy credit terms encouraged farmers not only to purchase tools, livestock, and houses, but often to assume heavy mortgages for the purchase of more land than they could handle. Unusually generous rainfall produced bounteous harvests on the rich prairie soil.

The growth and prosperity of Bethany Academy was in part a reflection of boom times and in part an expression of the eloquent optimism of its youthful and enthusiastic founder. He reported conditions in the newly completed building as so crowded that at morning prayers the speaker had to stand in the doorway in order to be heard by the entire student assembly. Bethany, Swensson told the conference, needed expanded facilities.

The responses bore witness both to his promotional zeal and the high spirit of the times. Swensson himself described a school festival at which lots were auctioned to raise funds for a new building:

> We assembled in the Normal lecture room. We sang one of our soul-stirring hymns, united in prayer, and then our Treasurer, Mr. Sundstrom, took the auctioneer's stand. I almost trembled. Would we fail or would we succeed? The first lot was offered. It brought upwards of $100.00. Good! Everybody looks very cheerful. Now for a corner lot, $200.00. Good! Good! Now for the remainder of that half block. Mr. Jaderborg of Enterprise bids $1200.00, $1400.00, finally $1500.00 for that half block. Now we couldn't control ourselves any longer. There was clapping of hands and tears of rejoicing. Now, once more. Mr. P. G. Hawkinson, $100.00; Mr. Sundstrom, $765.00; Mr. Peterson of St. Mary's, $500.00; Mr. Berg, $550.00; Mr. Lincoln, $500.00; Mr. John A. Swenson, $450.00.[35]

On the strength of such responses, the board engaged an architect and contracted for immediate construction of the biggest building in Kansas. Its 5 stories held 10 recitation rooms, a library, a museum, a dining hall and kitchen, the president's office and the resident professor's suite. In addition there were included 103 rooms for students and a chapel with seating capacity of 805, furnished with first-class opera chairs. Swensson presided at spirited dedication ceremonies in June 1887.

But that summer drought ended the Kansas boom. The sun beat down on parched fields. The rains which had produced bountiful harvests failed to appear in 1887 and for several seasons thereafter. Crop failures brought mortgage foreclosures and bank failures as eastern capital fled. The flow of westward moving farmers was halted, even reversed. One newspaper cartoon displayed a tattered wagon and driver, eastward bound, bearing a rudely lettered sign, "In God we trusted; in Kansas we busted!"

Bethany Academy had its building; it also faced serious problems of survival under a burden of debt and several thousands of dollars in unpaid pledges. In answer to Swensson's earnest appeal Olof Olsson returned to Kansas to solicit funds for Bethany in 1888. Although an investment company in Salina came through with a loan of $40,000, prospects dimmed as the entire country entered a period of hard times, ending in the panic of 1893. Creditors clamored for payment of bills. College salaries fell in arrears and were paid by promissory notes called "Bethany script."[36]

A variety of funding efforts, some born of desperation, was undertaken. A Chicago development company offered $25,000 in return for assistance in promoting the sale of 1000 lots in Belt City, near Chicago. When the venture collapsed in the panic of 1893, those who had purchased lots charged Swensson and his colleagues with betrayal. A gift of 25,000 shares of Colorado mining stock turned out to be worthless. Sweden's King Oscar II authorized his nation's churches to take up an offering for the Kansans, but it yielded only $809.78. Yet through these years of near disaster the school survived under the doughty leadership of Carl Aaron Swensson. His often-repeated remark, "I morgon blir det bättre" (tomorrow it will be better),[37] reflected his own firm faith in God and the future, and inspired in the Bethany constituency a willingness to make personal sacrifices in order to advance the welfare of their school.

As a school originally intended to serve the needs of a single congregation and its neighboring communities Bethany quite naturally developed a strong local constituency, subsequently broadened to include the Kansas Conference. Its rapid expansion worried the leadership of the Augustana Synod, especially President Hasselquist, who feared that conference-supported schools would weaken financial support for the synodical institution at Rock Island. Swensson, however, like Norelius in Minnesota, resented the centralizing tendencies of the synod.

Terms such as "extravagance" and "recklessness" crept into Hasselquist's communications, while Swensson deplored the lack of understanding which the synod president displayed concerning work "in the West." The "hard words" from Rock Island, he suggested, came "perhaps because we did not blindly bow down before the Latin idol and outworn methods."[38]

By whatever methods, Bethany did indeed appear to constitute a potential rival for Augustana. In the short span of six years Bethany's enrollment had risen to more than 300, and its original two-man faculty had increased to 15. By 1887 the curriculum had been expanded to include a teacher-training program and a commercial course. When the construction of its imposing new building was accompanied by the announcement of plans for a four-year college course, it was clear that Bethany did not intend to remain as a "feeder" school for Augustana.

These fears were not allayed when in 1889 the Kansans formally renamed their school Bethany College and Carl Swensson, its board chairman from the beginning, assumed the presidency. Even while struggling to maintain the solvency of the school Swensson insisted upon expanding both curriculum and facilities. In spite of the already-existing indebtedness he persuaded the board to start work on a new dormitory for girls and a 4000-seat auditorium to accommodate the annual presentation of the *Messiah*. When the first four baccalaureate degrees were awarded in 1891, there were 33 students enrolled in the collegiate department. The total enrollment, including normal and college preparatory departments, music conservatory, commercial and art departments and model school, was 334.

As Swensson added one school after another, it seemed clear that he intended to elevate Bethany into nothing less than a university. The normal department became the School of Pedagogy. The commercial department became the College of Business. The conservatory became the College of Music and Fine Arts. In 1902 a two-year Law School opened, requiring a bachelor of arts degree for admission. In its first year 23 students enrolled. In 1904 it was expanded to three years; it continued to function until 1911. A Graduate School offered master's and doctor's degrees. Candidates could choose from 118 courses in 19 departments.[39]

The college catalog of 1901 described the philosophy and purpose of the school in terms which reflected the expansive climate of "Young America" at the turn of the century.

> In spirit Bethany College believes without reservation in the Bible and the Constitution. It is orthodox in faith; sound in its patriotism; broad in its principles. Bethany believes in hard work on the part of professor and student alike as conditions of success. Its desire is to give to the young people of Kansas the best and most reliable, liberal, and Christian Education of today.

In its first decade as a degree-granting college, Bethany had graduated 90 men and 13 women. Of the Bethany classes of 1898–1902, 21 members continued their education in graduate studies at Yale.

The founding era of Bethany College came to an abrupt end with the sudden death of Carl Swensson on February 14, 1904, at the age of 47. The flamboyant and charismatic founder of the college was traveling in Los Angeles, California, when he was stricken with pneumonia.

His death brought to the presidency of Bethany 31-year-old Ernst F. Pihlblad, a member of Bethany's first graduating class, who would guide the course of the college over a span of 36 years. After the expansive and often stormy years of Swensson's leadership, it became Pihlblad's special task to stabilize the institution both financially and academically, to define its primary purpose and give it substance as a Christian liberal arts college. His inaugural address gave promise of the blending of faith and culture inherent in such a purpose.

> To develop the individual physically, mentally, morally, and spiritually; to teach him his proper place in the universe, his relations and duties to himself, his fellowmen, and his Maker, and to impart to human life that indescribable charm, ripeness and maturity that we call culture, this I hold to be the purpose of the college. The college should train the man for the highest of all arts, the art of living, and that irrespective of what his profession or calling may eventually be.[40]

The Swedish Academy Movement

Although overshadowed in its early years by its brash neighbor to the south, Luther Academy in Wahoo, Nebraska, also exemplified the educational initiative characteristic of Swedish immigrant communities. Founded in 1883, Luther followed the example set by Bethany two years earlier. It was initiated by a group of pastors and laymen, representing 17 congregations, to serve local needs for parish and community school teachers. A strong element of local self-consciousness was evident in the simultaneous move to establish a separate Nebraska Conference as a support base for a Nebraska school. Luther's growth in the 1880s and 1890s was impeded by serious financial problems, but it emerged in 1909 as a normal school and junior college and served its Nebraska Conference constituency until its merger with Midland College in 1962.[41]

Both Bethany and Luther were part of what less friendly critics have called the "college mania" of the 1880s and 1890s among the Swedes.[42] Actually, Swedish Lutherans in America established no colleges at all in those two decades. The schools they established were rather a part of an "academy movement" that had both religious and cultural roots.[43] Early settlements were always in need of teachers both for the public schools and for the church schools or "Swede Schools," as they were often called. Even more important was the eagerness of the immigrants to press beyond the common schools for a general education which would enable them to make their way successfully in the society and economy of their new homeland.

Unlike many of the Germans, the Swedes were generally supportive of the public schools. Neither their parish schools, generally held during the summer, nor their academies were regarded as competitors, but as supplements to the developing public systems. Even Augustana served this purpose through preparatory departments at Paxton and Rock Island that outnumbered both college and seminary enrollments until nearly the turn of the century.

As more Swedish settlements sprang up, academies such as Bethany and Luther arose to meet local needs. A total of eight such Swedish Lutheran academies came into being before 1900, four in Minnesota, and one each in Kansas, Nebraska, Illinois, and New York. As the public high schools became more numerous, academies either expanded their programs to the collegiate level, while retaining a preparatory department as long as financially feasible, or closed altogether.[44]

A Swedish College for the East

Only one other academy founded by the Swedes before the turn of the century survived to achieve collegiate status. Founded in Brooklyn by the New

York Conference, Upsala was also the only school to be established by direct action of a conference of the Augustana Synod. Sporadic discussions throughout the 1880s crystallized under the leadership of an energetic conference president, Gustaf Nelsenius, in 1893.

In a burst of Swedish national pride the conference convention chose to name its infant school after the largest university in Sweden, and thereby also to commemorate the 300th jubilee of the Uppsala Decree, establishing Lutheranism in Sweden. They elected Lars Herman Beck, born in Sweden and trained at Gustavus Adolphus College and Augustana Seminary, as the first president of Upsala College. Shortly before his election Beck completed his doctorate at Yale. In order to accept the presidency at Upsala he turned down an invitation from Yale to return as a lecturer on Scottish philosophy.

The school opened on October 3, 1893, in the basement of Bethlehem Lutheran Church in Brooklyn with 16 students in attendance. Dr. Victor Hegstrom, also a Yale Ph.D, joined Beck to teach languages, and Dr. James Brown, a physician, taught mathematics and science. Other part-time teachers rounded out a faculty with exceptionally high academic qualifications.

During its second year the school moved to more commodious quarters in St. Paul's Church in Brooklyn. The New York Conference drew up a constitution placing responsibility for the election of all board members, the president, and the faculty in the hands of the conference convention. A New York State charter, granted in 1895, required the school to change its name to the Upsala Institute of Learning until its endowment and curriculum warranted the use of the term *college*. Only when Upsala moved to New Jersey did it reinstate its original name. Actual collegiate programs were first introduced in 1902 and the first graduates won baccalaureate degrees in 1905.

During the five years of Upsala's sojourn in Brooklyn, enrollments varied between 75 and 93. Although permanent quarters were desperately needed, the conference was unwilling, during those depression years, to take any steps "until sufficient means have been secured." Meanwhile the president and board investigated possible sites in Brooklyn, Staten Island, Westchester, and New Jersey, most of which would depend upon real estate developments for their financing.[45]

In 1898 the New Orange Industrial Corporation of New Jersey offered 14 acres of land for a campus and agreed to give the college $50 for each of the 2000 lots it intended to sell. With a free campus site and a possible $100,000 building fund and endowment dangling before them, the board accepted title to the 14 acres and made plans to move to Kenilworth.

Promises, however, were not fulfilled. Only a few lots were sold, largely through efforts of the college itself. The promoters paid only a small sum to the college, not nearly enough to undertake any construction. Meanwhile, the entire college operation carried on in a farmhouse that had been the office of the development company. The president rented a company-owned house as his residence.

Under such circumstances the board had to undertake a building project on its own, largely on borrowed funds. By early 1900 the college was able to dedicate a building which accommodated classrooms, a chapel, library, and a student dormitory. During the two decades of Upsala's sojourn in Kenilworth a few other buildings were added, but the location was never satisfactory and probably hindered the growth of the college. The conference, however, resisted all attempts to move it until 1929 when a major fund drive made possible the purchase of properties in East Orange as the permanent location of the college.[46]

The Founding Years

A brief span of 33 years separated the founding of Augustana College and Seminary in 1860 and Upsala College in 1893, the first and last units of collegiate rank to be established within the Swedish Augustana Synod. During these years something like a tenth of the homeland's population poured into the United States and spread across the continent. Although bearing a strong Lutheran heritage, these newcomers had no experience in the ways of a free church in the American tradition. In the process of adapting to the New World many were drawn away into aggressive American denominations.

The establishment of their own seminary and synod, however, provided a nucleus around which to rally the increasing flow of Swedish immigrants. At the same time the geographical distances separating Swedish settlements in Illinois, Minnesota, Nebraska, and Kansas necessitated organization into regional conferences, a process which was implemented as early as 1862 and greatly expanded after 1870.

Swedish congregations readily embraced democratic principles of church government as a welcome contrast to the original patterns of the Swedish state church. In other respects, too, Swedish immigrants demonstrated their eagerness to become active participants in a new society. They were open to the public schools, and often participated in establishing them. Their own academies were intended to hasten the process of popular education by providing teachers both for the common schools and for parish summer schools.

These factors created problems for a synod which was struggling to achieve its identity and maintain its unity. Early disagreement over the location of the synod seminary and college weakened the position of synod leaders such as Tufve Hasselquist and Erland Carlsson, who regarded Augustana College and Seminary as the core and rallying point of synodical unity. Beginning with the move of Augustana to Paxton, the issue of decentralization became the dominant issue during the entire period of college founding in the Augustana Synod.

After 1862 pastors and laymen of virtually every new conference established one or more schools, not to challenge Augustana but to provide local opportunities for Christian and general education. As the regional schools grew in number and in size, however, they tended to erode the base of support for the single synodically supported institution in Rock Island.

Part of the hope of Tufve Hasselquist and others was that Augustana might also become a center of Swedish culture, even a university which would inspire the support of the entire synod and the loyalty of all Swedish Americans. However, as one regional school after the other aspired to collegiate status, this hope faded. The fragmentation of resources of the Augustana Synod was dramatized by the nearly fatal burden of indebtedness which every institution, including Augustana itself, incurred as they all sought to expand during the 1890s.

Nevertheless, these schools, scattered throughout the Swedish settlements, were able to maintain a much closer identification with local Swedish immigrant communities than might have been possible if Hasselquist's dream had been realized. Since both academies and colleges were founded very soon after the initial waves of immigration, they served a large number of communities as conservators of the Swedish language and culture. They also served as vehicles for aiding a transition into a new social environment and as continuing sources of leadership for church and society. Together with other agencies of Swedish culture, they helped to establish an ethnic community, widely scattered geographically, but culturally identifiable in these founding years as "Sweden in America."[47]

12 EARLY NORWEGIAN COLLEGES

At the head of the great popular migration of Norwegians to America stands the romantic figure of Cleng Peerson. Likened by some to Henrik Ibsen's soldier of fortune, Peer Gynt, who first dreamed of lands across the seas and finally visited them, Peerson was both pathfinder and publicist for his countrymen.[1]

He had already traveled widely in Europe when in 1821 a group of Norwegian Quakers near Stavanger commissioned him to visit America to investigate possible sites for settlement. After three years of exploration Peerson returned to Stavanger, recommending a site on the shores of Lake Ontario not far from Rochester, New York. Leaving his friends to prepare for their voyage, Peerson returned to New York in 1824, secured the land, and began construction of dwellings for the colonists. On July 4, 1825, in a 54-foot sailing vessel called the *Restauration*, the 52 pioneers of 19th-century Norwegian emigration set sail from the port of Stavanger.[2]

Fourteen weeks later they landed in New York and, after being detained by American authorities for entering port with an overloaded ship, followed Peerson via the newly opened Erie Canal to their new home in Kendall, New York. From the outset most of the settlers were not satisfied. Land was expensive; debts mounted. After a few years reports of better and cheaper land encouraged them to move further west. Again Cleng Peerson led the way. His explorations in 1833 took him through Pennsylvania, Ohio, Indiana, and Michigan before he finally reached the valley of the Fox River in northern Illinois.

On this fertile prairie land was planted the first permanent Norwegian set-tlement in the Midwest. After 1834 the tone of letters to the homeland changed dramatically. One Kendall settler whose letters were widely read and who had moved to the Fox River wrote in 1835 that since he had arrived he had gained more than he had during all the time he had resided in Norway.[3] Such reports, publicized in newspapers in Norway, kindled the ''America fever.'' Economic opportunity beckoned, and venturesome spirits responded in increasing numbers.

The Fox River colony became the major point of origin for almost all of the later Norwegian concentrations that in the course of time fanned out to the north and west into Wisconsin, Minnesota, Iowa, and the Dakotas. Beginning in 1838 Norwegians moved into southeastern Wisconsin, with Jefferson Prai-rie as a focal point. The settlement of Muskego in 1839 opened another center for the growing influx of immigrants. Northern Iowa and southern Minnesota opened in the early 1850s. A caravan of 40 covered wagons set out from Rock Prairie, Wisconsin, in 1853, with Iowa as its destination. By 1860 the United States Census reported 11,893 Norwegians in the newly organized state of

Minnesota. Following the Civil War and the quelling of the Sioux Indians in 1862, the Norwegians spread into the James River Valley in South Dakota and later into the Red River Valley and North Dakota. By the turn of the century 335,726 persons of Norwegian birth were living in the United States.[4] By 1925 the total emigration from Norway to America had reached 750,000.[5]

Varieties of Norwegian Lutheranism

Economic factors, especially the desire for land ownership, primarily motivated the Norwegian migration to America. Religious conditions in Norway, however, significantly influenced the patterns of religious organization and practice which emerged among those who crossed to America. In Norway the clergy of the Lutheran state church, as part of the official class, regarded emigration as a desertion of the fatherland. They did all they could to discourage it. From 1825 to 1844 no ordained clergy of the Church of Norway accompanied emigrants to their new homes in America.

On the other hand, many emigrants felt a certain sense of relief in being freed from the frequently officious presence of the state church clergy. Indeed, most of the early immigrants who came to Illinois and Wisconsin were products of the lay-oriented revival movements in Norway, inspired by Hans Nielsen Hauge in the early 19th century. Like the Puritan dissenters who had founded New England, they were quite accustomed to lay leadership in preaching and teaching.[6]

Religious life in the earliest midwestern Norwegian settlements depended largely upon the exercise of lay leadership. Both in the Fox River settlement in northern Illinois and the Muskego settlement in southeastern Wisconsin, lay preachers moved about, conducting preaching services and prayer meetings in private homes and cabins. There was a considerable loss, especially in northern Illinois, to the Mormons, Methodists, and Baptists, but religious life in the Haugean manner was nevertheless carried on without the aid of ordained clergy. The most authentic embodiment of the Haugean spirit among the early lay preachers in America was Elling Eielsen (1804–1883), a dynamic and single-minded evangelist who arrived in the Fox River settlement in 1839.[7] He wasted no time in erecting a building that would serve both as a residence and an assembly hall. Through his vigorous preaching he was able to restore a Lutheran focus to the religious life in the Fox River settlement. From his headquarters at Fox River he visited all the Norwegian settlements in Illinois and Wisconsin and even journeyed on foot to New York to get copies of Luther's Catechism printed in English. In 1843 he moved to Wisconsin and continued his visitations there, although his reception among the more moderate and churchly Haugeans at Muskego was less than cordial.

To provide a greater degree of order and substance to their religious life, lay leaders at Muskego sent a request in 1841 to Haugeans in Norway for a teacher of religion. The call was answered by Claus L. Clausen, a 23-year-old Dane who had seriously considered overseas missionary work in Africa. While en route from New York to Milwaukee he chanced, during a stopover in Buffalo, to meet Pastor J. A. A. Grabau. Grabau expressed grave concern over the absence of ordained clergy among the Norwegians. When Clausen arrived in Muskego, members of the community urged him to seek ordination in order that the children might be confirmed and Holy Communion celebrated. In September 1843, after examination by the Reverend L. F. E. Krause, a German Lutheran pastor recommended by Grabau, Clausen was ordained. He thereby became the second Norwegian-Lutheran pastor in America, Elling Eielsen having requested and secured ordination two weeks earlier from the Reverend Francis A. Hoffman, a German-Lutheran pastor in Illinois. Neither Clausen nor Eielsen had received formal theological training.[8]

During its first half-century in America, Norwegian Lutheranism was plagued by almost continual internal conflicts and divisions, both doctrinal and personal. At the root of these dissensions was the controversy which the early emigrants had hoped to leave behind them when they left Norway, the conflict with the state church system and its official clergy. With the unannounced arrival of the Reverend J. W. C. Dietrichson in Muskego in August 1844, the stage was set for a new chapter of the old conflict.

Dietrichson was the first ordained clergyman sent by the Church of Norway; his commission instructed him to assess the religious situation and to establish the Church of Norway among its members ''in exile.'' After preaching in Muskego he traveled through the Wisconsin settlements and decided to settle in a pastorate in Koshkonong, west of Muskego. From this location he set out to introduce in all the congregations the liturgy and discipline of the Church of Norway, including formal membership in the local congregation and a commitment of spiritual obedience to the pastor.[9]

Dietrichson won few friends with his imperious and often tactless manner, but he did lay substantial foundations for an organized church structure, including the draft of a synodical constitution. After six stormy years he returned to Norway. Beginning in 1848 a succession of university-trained clergy began to arrive in response to calls issued by newly organized congregations.

For nearly a century of its history, Norwegian-American Lutheranism developed as variations of the two contrasting traditions represented by Elling Eielsen and J. W. C. Dietrichson. The Haugean wing was lay-oriented, strongly congregational and democratic in governance, nonliturgical, emphasizing personal, experiential religion. The Church of Norway wing was clergy-led, formal in structure and governance, doctrinally disciplined, strongly liturgical.

In the free church setting of America each of these groups was free to organize itself separately. The Haugean group, though able to flourish as an unstructured movement within an ordered state church structure in Norway, soon found that in America some organization was necessary to maintain its identity and provide for the full spiritual needs of congregations. For this reason Eielsen himself sought ordination and in 1846 organized the first synod among Norwegians in America, the Evangelical Lutheran Church in America, popularly known as Eielsen's Synod. In 1853, following the arrival of several more clergy from Norway, the state church pastors also organized a synod, the Norwegian Evangelical Lutheran Church in America, commonly known as the Norwegian Synod.[10]

Paramount among the differences between these two groups was their view of the ministerial office and the necessary preparation for the preaching of the gospel. The Norwegian Synod stood directly in the historic academic Lutheran tradition which required a university level course in theology based upon thorough classical preparation. All six pastors present at the constituting convention of the synod met this standard. Their philosophy of higher education would later find expression in the founding of Luther College in Decorah, Iowa.

Pastors of Eielsen's Synod emphasized the religious training of children in Luther's Catechism and the Bible. But their Norwegian experience led them to associate the university with the class system and the academic study of theology as a barrier to a truly spiritual ministry.

Adventure in Cooperation

It is therefore ironic that the first organized efforts among Norwegian Lutherans in America to provide higher schools for the preparation of pastors and teachers occurred among the Haugean groups. Norwegian Synod pastors apparently anticipated a continuing supply of clergy from the Church of Norway, and when they first sensed the need of developing a local supply turned to existing seminaries of other Lutheran bodies, notably the Missouri Synod. Once the Haugeans had acknowledged the need of an ordained clergy in America, a series of circumstances brought them into closer touch with still other Lutheran groups who shared the same concern.

Among the associates of Eielsen in the mid-1840s were two young lay preachers. Ole Andrewson had been trained as a teacher in Norway before he came to Wisconsin in 1841. Paul Andersen arrived in 1843 and, after meeting Eielsen, enrolled in the recently opened Beloit College where he studied for two or three years. Both men were associated with Eielsen in the organization of the synod in 1846 but broke with him in 1848. During the next two years Andrewson was licensed and Andersen ordained by the Franckean Synod of

New York. In 1849 Andersen organized the first Scandinavian Evangelical Lutheran congregation in Chicago. Andrewson served a congregation in Norway, Illinois, in the Fox River settlement.[11]

In his strategic location in Chicago, Paul Andersen met and befriended many incoming immigrants, among them Lars P. Esbjörn who arrived in 1849. William Passavant, visiting Chicago in 1850 out of concern for the needs of Scandinavian immigrants, met with Andersen and suggested forming a Scandinavian synod. Although unwilling to invite cooperation with the conservative Norwegian state church pastors in Wisconsin, Andersen wrote to the Swedish pastor, Lars P. Esbjörn, and to the German-American, but largely English-speaking Illinois Synod, suggesting the formation of a multiethnic synod. The Illinois Synod responded favorably and agreed to release its pastors and congregations in the northern part of Illinois to join with the Norwegians and Swedes in a new Synod of Northern Illinois. On September 19, 1851, the new synod was organized at Cedarville, Illinois, with five German-American, one Swedish, and two Norwegian pastors. Among the 20 congregations represented, 11 were German-American, 5 Norwegian, and 4 Swedish.[12]

The new synod promptly pledged its support of the college and seminary of the Illinois Synod that was in process of being moved from Hillsboro in southern Illinois to the state capital at Springfield and rechartered as Illinois State University. The reason for its relocation was to provide more adequate service to the northern part of the state, which was receiving increasing numbers of Scandinavian and German immigrants.

The Norwegian congregations of the Northern Illinois Synod thus became full partners with the Germans and the Swedes in the support of Illinois State University. This venture constitutes the first formal entry of organized Norwegian Lutherans in America into the field of college and seminary education.

The university in Springfield, including its theology department, survived for 15 years, from 1852 to 1867. Between 1852 and 1861 seven Norwegian students received theological training and entered the Lutheran ministry either in the Northern Illinois Synod or the Scandinavian Augustana Synod.[13] Both the Norwegian and Swedish conferences of the Northern Illinois Synod concurred in the election of Pastor Lars P. Esbjörn as professor of theology and of Scandinavian languages. Norwegian congregations contributed to the endowment for his salary and to the synodical fund for the support of needy theological students.

Esbjörn's personal dissatisfaction over the theological and social climate at the university and his abrupt resignation in 1860 has been recounted in a previous chapter.[14] Both the Scandinavian and Swedish conferences of the synod supported his withdrawal, and both severed their ties with the Northern Illinois Synod. Esbjörn was elected first professor of the new Augustana Seminary with the clear understanding that a Norwegian and an English professor would be added as soon as possible. When the seminary opened in Chicago, 10 of the 21 students were Norwegians. After the first year, classes were conducted in the basement of the Norwegian church. Two local pastors, Abraham Jacobson and C. J. P. Peterson, assisted Professor Esbjörn with the teaching responsibilities.

The quest for a Norwegian professor continued after the school was moved to Paxton, Illinois, in 1863. During 1866–1867 Johan Olsen, a young graduate of the University of Christiania (Oslo) who was studying theology at Paxton, assisted in language instruction. At last, in 1868 August Weenaas arrived from Norway as the first regular Norwegian professor of theology.

The Norwegian Separation

Although he was received cordially by the faculty and students, Weenaas was immediately sensitive to the minority position of the Norwegians. He also found himself in disagreement with the educational philosophy of Professor Sidney L. Harkey, his American colleague who was in charge of the preparatory department.[15] Restless almost at once after his arrival, Weenaas began to suggest to members of the synod's Norwegian Conference the desirability of a separate school. With the support of several pastors who also felt Paxton was too far removed from the center of Norwegian settlement, he brought the proposal before the very next synod convention in 1869. The synod gave its consent, elected a separate board, and gave to its members the task of finding a suitable location for a new Norwegian seminary.

A building housing a private academy in the village of Marshall, Wisconsin, not far from Madison, was purchased for $4000, under circumstances reminiscent of the purchase of the Hillsboro Academy in 1847. The agreement was signed with the provision that the academy continue to operate in the same building. On September 1, 1869, Augsburg Seminary and Marshall Academy opened with August Weenaas as president and professor of theology and J. J. Anderson as principal of the academy.[16]

The founding of Augsburg Seminary in Marshall marked a significant change of direction for higher education among Norwegian Lutherans. It terminated 19 years of ethnic cooperation with English-speaking German Lutherans and Swedish Lutherans, in which Haugean Norwegians had been active since Paul Andersen's initiatives in 1847. It moved major Norwegian Lutheran activity in higher education out of Illinois into Wisconsin, into more heavily Norwegian territory, thereby further narrowing its ethnic focus. Part of Weenaas's reason for urging a separate institution was his discomfort with Augustana's preministerial program. Weenaas's model was the mission school of Norway which stressed a practical preparation of pastors rather than the kind of American collegiate curriculum that was developing at Augustana in Paxton. The move to Marshall solved that problem for him but delayed for several years the emergence of liberal arts colleges in the Norwegian synods.

With the establishment of their own seminary in 1869, it was inevitable that the Norwegians in the Scandinavian Augustana Synod would also seek to organize a separate synod. When they presented their request the following year at the synod meeting in Andover, Illinois, it was granted without objection, thus terminating the long-standing association of Norwegian and Swedish Lutherans.

No sooner had the Norwegian pastors and delegates met to begin organizing a new synod than they fell out among themselves. One group went off to start the Norwegian-Danish Augustana Synod. A second element formed the Conference of the Norwegian-Danish Evangelical Lutheran Church in America. Weenaas sided with the Conference, and students at Augsburg Seminary supported their professor. The Norwegian-Danish Augustana group, though the smaller of the two, claimed to be the legitimate successor of the previous synodical connection and regarded the Conference as a breakaway group.[17]

Shortly after the opening of the school year, J. J. Anderson, principal of the Marshall Academy, appeared in Weenaas' office with a letter from the Reverend O. J. Hatlestad, president of the Norwegian-Danish Augustana Synod, ordering him to hand over the keys to the building and vacate the seminary operation. Rather than offer a legal challenge, Weenaas complied. He and his 20 seminarians rented a 10-by-18-foot attic room from a neighboring farmer. For two years "Cooper's Attic" served as classroom, chapel, and student center for Augsburg Seminary. Twelve of the students moved into the Weenaas residence; the rest found rooms wherever they could. At the end of the first year Weenaas, his salary yet unpaid and debts accumulating, was ready to close shop. Only the persistence of his students persuaded him to continue for another year.[18]

Haugeans in Higher Education

Elling Eielsen also had been thinking about the need for training pastors. By seeking his own ordination and supporting the organization of a synod, he had acknowledged that church life in America could not prosper without some formal structure. Not long after Paul Andersen and Ole Andrewson left him to join with Germans and Swedes in supporting Illinois State University, the pioneer Haugean leader sponsored a venture of his own into the field of higher education. At the synod meeting in 1854 Eielsen moved that in view of the great need for pastors, a seminary should be established "for the instruction of talented young people in the knowledge most necessary for the performance of said office."[19]

The synod approved Eielsen's motion and purchased a large house and 40 acres of land at Lisbon, Illinois. As first professor they chose P. A. Rasmussen, a young man who had come from Norway in 1850 to teach parochial school at Lisbon. Although he had only a common school education in Norway, he was able to translate Johann Arndt's *True Christianity* from German to Norwegian. Pleased with his preaching and teaching, the people at Lisbon wanted him to be ordained as their pastor in 1853, but he decided instead to spend a year in study under Dr. Sihler at the Fort Wayne seminary of the Missouri Synod. Following the 1854 meeting of Eielsen's Synod Rasmussen opened the school at Lisbon with three students. Theological differences, however, caused him to leave the synod, and Eielsen's short-lived venture into higher education ended abruptly in May 1856.[20]

Nine years later Eielsen's followers tried again. From 1865 to 1867 Andreas Aaseröd, trained in Norway as a teacher, operated a preparatory school near Cambridge, Wisconsin, enrolling 20 students and even offering instruction in Latin. When he resigned in 1867, a group of Haugeans in Red Wing, Minnesota, won synod approval to open a school in their city. But even after the sale of the Cambridge property, funds were not adequate to complete the building they had planned. In the midst of their disappointment Trinity Lutheran congregation in Chicago came forward with an offer to incorporate a school building in the construction plans for their new church. Red Wing supporters were still not ready to yield. Seventeen votes were cast in the synod meeting for each site. The tie was broken in favor of Chicago by the biblical device of casting lots—probably the only instance in Lutheran history in which a college location has been determined by this method.

In August 1871, the cornerstone of Hauge's College and Eielsen's Seminary was laid. Eielsen himself delivered a stirring address describing the need of Christian and civil enlightenment for the development of true Christians and useful citizens. In spite of its promising beginning this institution also failed, in 1877. Poor crops in the country and the aftermath of the great Chicago fire of 1871 so weakened the financial support base that it became impossible to continue. Both building and debt were left to Trinity congregation.

By 1875 the thoroughgoing "lay system" of Eielsen's Synod had given way to a more structured type of churchmanship. That year its convention adopted a new constitution and changed the name of the synod to Hauge's Synod. Eielsen and a few pastors withdrew, retaining both the name of Eielsen's Synod and the Old Constitution of 1850, while the majority continued the organization as Hauge's Synod.[21]

But Red Wing was to have its day after all. In 1878 a layman of that city, Hans Markussen Sande, mortgaged his farm for $10,000 to buy a building and site. In September 1879 the Red Wing Seminary, comprised of a prep school

and a seminary, opened. It endured for nearly 40 years as the educational institution of Hauge's Synod—until three Norwegian synods merged in 1917 to
form the Norwegian Lutheran Church of America. At that time the seminary
was moved to St. Paul, the college department was merged with St. Olaf
College, and the academy department of St. Olaf was moved to Red Wing.

From Marshall to Minneapolis

While August Weenaas and his students were huddled in Cooper's Attic
in Marshall, Wisconsin, uncertain whether their patience and resources would
last another year, the Norwegian-Danish Conference rallied its forces and
made the bold and far-sighted decision to reestablish Augsburg Seminary in the
city of Minneapolis. Conference leaders recognized that the center of Norwegian immigration was moving north and west from its original base in Illinois
and southern Wisconsin. By 1870 the population of Minneapolis had grown to
20,000. The move also challenged the common prejudice among midwestern
Lutherans against locating institutions of higher education in large population
centers. As early as 1871 synod president Claus Clausen had spoken favorably
about moving the seminary to a university city to eliminate the expense of
maintaining a separate preparatory department and to develop the English
competency of prospective clergy. Weenaas also supported this position and
actually enrolled six of his most promising preparatory students at the Universities of Wisconsin and Minnesota in 1871. Although the practice was not continued after the relocation, proximity to the state university was one of the advantages anticipated in the move to Minneapolis. As a result of the synod's decision, Augsburg College in later years would enjoy a unique position as the
only four-year Lutheran college of liberal arts in this major metropolitan center
of Scandinavian culture. Ole Paulson, pastor of Trinity Lutheran Church, enlisted local support among church and civic leaders for Augsburg's relocation
in Minneapolis.

With the future expansion of the seminary in mind, the 1873 Conference
commissioned President Weenaas to visit Norway in search of additional professorial talent. His success was immediate. Twenty-nine-year-old Sven
Oftedal, who joined the faculty in the fall of 1873, was a gifted, creative, and
controversial theologian. He had studied both in the University of Christiania
(Oslo) and in continental universities, and identified strongly with those
seeking to reform the church and democratize Norway's political life. After
only a few months in America he published an "Open Declaration," charging
the Norwegian Synod clergy with "anti-Christian" tendencies and with blight-
ing the potential contribution of the Norwegian laity to the cultural development of the Midwest. In addition to his professorial duties, he assumed the pas-

torate of Trinity Church, the chairmanship of Augsburg's board of trustees, and within four years won election to the Minneapolis Board of Education.

He also recommended that two additional Norwegian professors, Sven Gunnersen and Georg Sverdrup, be invited to join the faculty. Both accepted and began teaching in the fall of 1874. Gunnersen eventually returned to Norway, but for the next 40 years the colorful team of Sverdrup and Oftedal was virtually synonymous with the history of Augsburg Seminary. Sverdrup served as president for 30 years, and Oftedal as board chairman for 36 years. Professor Weenaas described the three recruits as a "new triumvirate, in which Sverdrup was the mind, Gunnersen the heart, and Oftedal the spirit."[22]

Georg Sverdrup came from one of the great liberal reform families of Norway. His great-uncle, Georg Sverdrup, presided over the assembly at Eidsvold in 1814 which gave Norway its first modern constitution. His father was a prominent clergyman and a member of the Norwegian parliament. His uncle, the leader of Norway's Liberal Party, became prime minister in 1884, and Georg's older brother served as minister of church and education.[23]

The Augsburg Plan

With forceful leadership of this kind it is not strange that Augsburg's history should be marked by both creativity and controversy. Both characteristics were evident in the comprehensive educational program which was formulated in 1874 and implemented after Weenaas returned to Norway and Sverdrup assumed the presidency in 1876.

The Augsburg Plan provided for a preparatory school with three departments. A one-year common school class served all who needed preparation for advanced work. The second level consisted of two parallel college-level departments: a Greek Department and a Department of Practical Studies. Courses in both departments were of four years duration and led to the B.A. degree. The Greek Department prepared its graduates for the three-year course in theology which constituted the third level of the program. The practical course, omitting Greek, Latin, and German, but substituting mathematics, history, science, and English, sought "to impart the knowledge that the practical life demands of an educated man."[24]

An interpretive statement prepared by the faculty stated the educational rationale for the new program. In keeping with historic Lutheran tradition, the faculty acknowledged responsibility for the general education of both clergy and laypersons. While recognizing the preparation of pastors as the primary concern, the statement clearly affirmed a further obligation "to reach the farmer, the worker, and the business man . . .. We must seek to encourage everyone, irrespective of occupational or professional status, to adopt a liberal cultural outlook . . ., and we must educate school teachers, officials, and legislators."[25] In the fulfillment of this broader educational mission in society the practical department was expected to play a key role.

A Norwegian-American institution such as Augsburg also carried special responsibility to preserve the Norwegian heritage of its constituents and to help them "find their place in the emerging nation." For this reason the curriculum of the practical department included both Norwegian and American history, language, and literature, thereby assisting the educated Norwegian American to become bilingual "both in speech and culture."[26]

Unfortunately, the practical department failed to develop and was dropped after two years because of insufficient enrollment. This left the pretheological course as the only remaining collegiate element in the Augsburg system. Although nontheological students were not excluded from the Greek department and a bachelor of arts degree was awarded after four years, the Greek department and the theological seminary course were increasingly viewed as a single unit.[27] The beginning preparatory department, originally a one-year course, continued to operate and was gradually expanded until it became a four-year high school in 1910.

The rapid physical growth that might have been expected at Augsburg after its move to Minneapolis did not take place. In a city heavily populated by Norwegians, a broad educational program with an English language emphasis ought to have succeeded. Instead, the restricted curriculum limited enrollments. In 1878, the first year of a full college program, 49 students were enrolled in the Greek department. Five graduated in 1879; two in 1882, and six in 1884.

Some of the potential support in the Conference's rapidly growing family of congregations became apparent in 1877 when the indebtedness incurred through building construction reached $16,000. At this point Sven Oftedal organized a campaign among the congregations of the Conference and within three weeks 30,000 individuals responded with $18,000 in cash. Even more important was the sense of ownership that resulted. After the campaign, Oftedal recalled, "The farmers got the habit of calling it 'Our School.' "[28]

By the mid-80s sufficient support had developed in the Conference to bring a $50,000 endowment campaign to a successful conclusion. Annual enrollments, too, had risen to an average of 142 students between 1885 and 1890.

These positive evidences of church support might have encouraged a new attempt to implement the original goals of 1874. Sverdrup, however, had reached a firm decision to focus on the preparation of pastors and had taken steps to integrate the faculty of the Greek department and the theological seminary. By 1885, 80% of the students in the Greek department were committed to continue their studies in theology. It was Sverdrup's conviction that church reform, his major goal, could be achieved only by educating a "new breed" of clergy, committed to a congregation-oriented ministry and a clear and simple presentation of the gospel without abstruse doctrinal interpretation. He envisioned Augsburg as the seminary of a united Lutheranism embodying these principles.[29]

Sverdrup's energies, which might have exerted a strong liberalizing influence in the development of Lutheran college education, aimed instead at the promotion of a particular pattern of theological education. In his report to the Conference convention in 1884, he recommended that in the future more than in the past, Augsburg should seek to become "exclusively" a divinity school. Finally, he came to see the preservation of the unified theological program as conducted in Augsburg Seminary, from the preparatory school through Greek department and theological studies, as essential to the welfare of the church. His insistence upon this would have a significant influence on the development of college education among the Norwegian Americans after 1890.

Norwegians Move West

When August Weenaas turned over the keys of the Marshall Academy to J. J. Anderson in 1869 and withdrew with his students to "Cooper's Attic," the Norwegian Augustana Synod, with only seven pastors—largely of the older Haugean persuasion, was left with an "American style" academy at Marshall and a $4000 debt on the building. The synod convention announced its intention to maintain the academy and pay the debt. They chose a new board of trustees, including such veteran pastors as Paul Andersen and Ole Andrewson. In a hopeful bid for outside support they elected as chairman of the board the long-time friend of the Scandinavians, William A. Passavant.[30] Professor J. J. Anderson continued to serve as principal of the academy until 1874 when the synod turned its operation over to local residents on a rental basis.

Since the academy had not been meeting the urgent need for ministerial candidates, the synod issued a call to Rev. David Lysnes, pastor of a rural parish near Decorah, Iowa, to undertake private instruction of theological students. In addition to his pastoral duties Lysnes conducted classes in his parsonage for two years until 1876, when the synod asked him to bring the seminary program to Marshall in order to utilize the facilities of the academy building.[31] At that time the school was named Salem Seminary and reorganized under Lysnes' direction with two departments, theological and preparatory.[32]

Meanwhile, the Norwegian Augustana Synod had been considering an even more drastic move to a completely new location in western Iowa, following the prevailing flow of Norwegian settlement. The specific opportunity arose through a chance visit to a meeting of the seminary board in Milwaukee in 1880 by James Wahl, a Lutheran resident of Canton, Dakota Territory. As commissioner of immigration for the Dakota Territory he was interested in encouraging the movement of settlers to the West. Through his mediation offers were made by both Canton and the neighboring town of Beloit, just across the Big Sioux River in Iowa.

With the added personal assurance from the president of the Chicago, Milwaukee, and St. Paul Railroad that its western line would shortly be completed to Canton, the synod approved the board's recommendation to move the school. When Canton residents could not agree whether to donate land on the east or the west side of town, the synod accepted the Beloit proposal instead. Beloit offered 20 acres of land and a public school building on condition that the school be opened no later than April 1, 1881.

Only with the help of the resourceful James Wahl and Emelia Hatlestad, daughter of the synod president, who possessed a teaching certificate, was it possible to meet the April 1 deadline and open the school. The regular faculty and a trainload of equipment from Marshall were blockaded by the mountainous snowdrifts which made the blizzard of 1881 a living legend in the West for years to come.

Nor was it easy to take leave of Marshall. Led by the town's most affluent property holder, who opposed the move of the school, citizens of Marshall withheld all assistance, even refusing to sell necessary moving supplies such as rope and boxes. With the help of the Milwaukee Railroad, James Wahl secured teams and wagons to transport property from the school to the railway station. When the school bell was removed and lowered to the ground, a crowd gathered and the local sheriff appeared with legal papers. Only after two years of litigation did the bell follow the school to Beloit.[33]

After its arrival in Beloit the school came to be known as Augustana Seminary and Academy. Under Pastor Lysnes' leadership 11 students enrolled in the seminary department, and the response to the academy was large enough to warrant the construction of a dormitory after the first year.[34] When it seemed imperative to provide even more space, a new offer came from a group of Canton citizens who had purchased a defunct hotel at a sheriff's sale. They were prepared to give the building to the synod if the academy were moved to Canton and if the synod would establish and maintain a college in Canton for at least 10 years.[35]

The synod accepted the offer in 1884 and the move was made. In recognition of the condition attached to the gift, the institution was named Augustana College. Under the direction of President M. D. Miller, a graduate of Thiel College who had also headed the preparatory department at Beloit, 67 pupils were enrolled. During Professor Miller's administration virtually all students were enrolled in academy or normal school courses. A few students undertook introductory college work; one man was awarded a bachelor's degree in 1886 and continued his studies at the seminary in Beloit.[36] Augustana College would experience two synodical mergers of Norwegian Lutherans—in 1890 and 1917—and a final relocation in Sioux Falls, South Dakota, before it emerged in 1920 as a four-year, degree-granting institution.

The St. Louis Connection

The Norwegian Synod, representing the High Church wing of Norwegian-American Lutheranism, established its first educational institution, Luther College, in 1861. Although not the first involvement in higher education by Norwegian Lutherans in America, Luther represents the most direct translation of the academic traditions of Norwegian Lutheranism from Norway to America. The Norwegian Synod was organized in 1853 under the leadership of ordained pastors of the Church of Norway. All of them were educated in the classical European tradition of Latin school, gymnasium, and university, extending from the Wittenberg of Luther and Melanchthon to the Scandinavian universities of Sweden and Denmark and, after 1813, to the Royal Frederik University in Christiania (Oslo). These same pastors were the moving spirits in establishing a system of ministerial education that would maintain academic and doctrinal integrity and also supply the congregational needs of their growing synod.

To the keen disappointment of the courageous clergy and spouses who had been willing to exchange the security and comfort of a Norwegian parsonage for a primitive cabin in Wisconsin or Iowa, new recruits from the mother church were not easy to win.[37] By 1859 only 12 Norwegian pastors were on hand to serve the synod's 48 congregations and the multitude of outlying preaching stations.[38]

At one point the synod explored a possible affiliation with the newly established University of Wisconsin, through which the university would provide the classical preparation and the synod would establish an independent professorship in theology. If a school of their own, however, was still beyond reach, most pastors and laymen found a cooperative arrangement with some existing Lutheran seminary a more appealing alternative. Consequently, in 1855 the synod appointed two pastors, Nils O. Brandt and Jacob A. Ottesen, to visit the seminaries of the Joint Ohio, Buffalo, and Missouri Synods and report their impressions and recommendations to the church council. At Capital University they found an imposing building but an unstable faculty. The hierarchical tendencies in the Buffalo Synod made Martin Luther College even less attractive. For the two Missouri Synod schools at Fort Wayne and St. Louis, however, Brandt and Ottesen had only praise. There they found warmth and fervor and a "burning zeal" for "pure and genuine Lutheranism." Instruction was thorough and rooted in the original biblical languages, Moreover, they were impressed with the size, structure, and discipline of the Missouri Synod.[39]

Their report was well received by the church council, and a recommendation was prepared for the synod convention in the fall of 1857. On October 10 the synod recorded its intent "to establish its own Norwegian Lutheran institution of learning" as soon as possible, and called upon congregations and pastors to begin a concerted effort to gather $50,000 in a "University Fund." The resolution, however, left open the possibility that "it might seem preferable" at a later date "to promote a union with the Missouri Synod and not to establish our own institution." In such an event the fund would be used "for the extension of the selected German institution."[40] Until a final decision should be reached, the synod designated a portion of the interest for the establishment of a Norwegian professorship at Concordia College in St. Louis. Pastor Ottesen, secretary of the synod, described the undertaking as "the most significant one that our young church has had to deal with."[41] With prophetic foresight he might also have seen this beginning of a close association between the Norwegian Synod and the Missouri Synod as one of the most significant factors in shaping the course of Norwegian Lutheranism in America for the next 60 years.

Staffing a Norwegian professorship at Concordia Seminary was no easier than securing Norwegian pastors to serve frontier congregations. After two rejections and a letter from a Norwegian theologian discouraging further attempts, the church council turned to Lauritz Larsen, one of the synod's promising young pastors. Larsen had responded to one of six calls to vacant American parishes advertised in Norway and at the age of 26 had come with his wife and infant daughter to the Rush River parish near Hudson, Wisconsin, late in 1857. Encouraged by his fellow pastors he accepted the new assignment; in November 1859, two years after the synod's decision, he began his work in St. Louis.[42]

Eight Norwegian students had preceded him and were already enrolled in several levels of the preparatory department. None was advanced enough to be a seminarian. Not until 1863 did the first Norwegian theological graduate complete his work at Concordia. Larsen himself had hardly settled in St. Louis when the Norwegian Synod's pastoral conference, overwhelmed by the ever-increasing need for pastors, urged their new professor to visit Norway in person to plead for help. Larsen agreed and spent several months in a virtually fruitless mission. Only two months after his return to St. Louis, the Civil War broke out. Concordia College and Seminary were temporarily closed and Larsen and his family and the Norwegian students returned to their homes.[43]

The Birth of Luther College

There was never any doubt concerning the position of the Norwegian immigrant on the issues of slavery and freedom that dominated American politics during the 1850s. In choosing America as their new home virtually all of them had responded to the shining promise of personal and economic freedom. They were therefore ardent opponents both of slavery and secession.

When students returning from St. Louis intimated that the Concordia professors harbored views sympathetic to slavery, the Norwegian-language press in Madison, Wisconsin, asked Lauritz Larsen to respond. After some hesitation he prepared an article in which he substantially endorsed the southern scriptural argument affirming that slavery in itself is not a sin. Since slavery is nowhere condemned but actually accepted and implicitly supported in the Bible, the basic issue for Larsen was one of biblical faithfulness. He buttressed his newspaper response by attaching a translation of an article on "The Christian and Politics" from the official Missouri Synod organ, *Der Lutheraner*.[44]

Nine days later, on June 26, 1861, the Norwegian Synod met for its annual convention. There was general agreement that the synod should proceed immediately to open its own school. Even the normally controversial question of location was resolved by a virtually unanimous vote in favor of Decorah, Iowa, following a carefully prepared and convincing plea by the local pastor, Ulrik Vilhelm Koren.

A committee report authored by the clergy recommended the resumption of the relationship with Concordia until sufficient money had been raised to construct a college building. Lay delegates strongly opposed the continuation of the Missouri connection because of the slavery controversy.[45]

After a spirited discussion of "what the Scriptures teach regarding slavery," synod leaders drew up a declaration they hoped would win unanimous acceptance. Instead, it failed to win a majority of the lay vote and stimulated instead the issuance of a counterdeclaration by the more vigorous lay opponents. At the conclusion of the discussion on slavery a motion to establish a school without delay was approved by a large majority.

Thus the institution later to be called Luther College came into being in the early days of the American Civil War. It emerged as the direct result of the conflicting views of clergy and laity in the Norwegian Synod on the subject of chattel slavery, one of the most profound moral and political issues ever to face the American nation. In the process of creating an institution of higher learning the laity of the church reminded the clergy of the intimate relationship between the Christian faith and public responsibility.

Events moved quickly after the decision had been reached to open the "Norwegian Lutheran School for the Education of Ministers." On September 1, 1861, Lauritz Larsen began a presidency that spanned 41 years. Friedrich A.

Schmidt, a pastor from Baltimore, Maryland, who was fluent in English and recommended by C. F. W. Walther, president of the Missouri Synod, became the second professor. Instruction began in a vacant parsonage at Halfway Creek, near La Crosse, Wisconsin, the initial enrollment of 5 increasing during the year to a total of 16. When a pastor was secured for the parish in June 1862, the school vacated the parsonage and moved to Decorah. The St. Cloud Hotel provided temporary facilities while the main college building was under construction. Contributions for this purpose had been accumulating since 1857 in the so-called University Fund, but the final cost of $75,000 exceeded both projections and immediate resources. Dedication was scheduled for September 1, 1865, but an unusually cold winter and late spring snows delayed the completion of the building until October 14, 1865.[46]

Dedication festivities drew a crowd of 6000 to the new campus, including most of the synod's ministerium. The sessions of a pastoral conference following the dedication were interrupted by a student strike. Protests were directed against crowded student accommodations and particularly against "the tyrannical and aristocratic lust of the professors," which extended to the sawing of professorial wood and the shining of ministerial shoes. The leader of the protest, 19-year-old Rasmus B. Anderson, was summarily expelled. Twenty-four years later, after Anderson had become a distinguished professor of Scandinavian studies at the University of Wisconsin and United States minister to Denmark, he received his diploma as a graduate of the Luther College class of 1866.[47]

Eighty-one students were in attendance when the first classes met in the new building. Enrollment rose steadily thereafter, exceeding 100 for the first time in 1868. By 1874 there were 229 on campus, a mark not surpassed until 40 years later.

From Gymnasium to College

Meanwhile the faculty also increased to meet the needs of an expanding student body. In 1874, the year of peak enrollment, there were nine professors.[48] The two early sources of recruitment were the Royal Frederik University in Oslo, Norway, and Concordia Seminary, both of which supplied professors in the 60s and 70s. Larsen, however, was eager to avoid dependence on European sources. "We need fresh forces," he wrote to synod president Herman Amberg Preus, "while everything imported from Norway invariably has to be more or less recast."[49] The first faculty member trained in an American college, Andrew A. Veblen, a graduate of Carleton College and a brother of the noted economist Thorstein Veblen, joined the faculty in 1877. Beginning in the early 80s Larsen was able to draw on some of Luther's own graduates who had undertaken studies at the new American graduate schools at Johns Hopkins and Cornell.

From its beginning in Halfway Creek Luther College maintained a conscious identity as a classical preparatory school modeled after the European Latin school and gymnasium, a pattern familiar to President Larsen from his own experience as a student and teacher in Norway and reinforced by his observations as a professor at Concordia in St. Louis. The purpose of the school had been unmistakably defined as the preparation of young men for the study of theology. From 1866, when its first class of seven graduated, until 1881, 90 of Luther College's 128 graduates entered the ministry. Since the synod did not establish its own theological seminary until 1876, virtually all of these graduates continued their studies at one of the seminaries of the Missouri Synod before ordination. Several of the nontheological graduates of the college's strong classical program undertook advanced studies in European and American graduate schools.

In 1866, shortly after the completion of the new building, President Larsen visited several colleges and universities in the interest of broadening his own understanding of American higher education. On his itinerary were the Universities of Wisconsin and Michigan, Beloit and Oberlin Colleges. He took note of the superior facilities and equipment and the increased emphasis on the natural sciences in these institutions. But the method and quality of instruction in the classics, except at Michigan, he found appalling. He described Oberlin as "the pinnacle of Yankee humbug and conceit,"[50] but at Michigan and later at Johns Hopkins he established enduring relationships for Luther College.

The Luther curriculum was very similar to that of Concordia in St. Louis, with its sequences of Latin, Greek, and German, except that Luther offered Norwegian instead of French and gave considerable emphasis to English. Students advanced in Latin school fashion, from *sexta* through *prima* levels, and obtained a bachelor of arts degree after six years. Curricular changes at Luther did not come easily. In order to bring the college into closer conformity with the general format of American colleges, Larsen proposed lengthening the course from six to seven years and separating the preparatory and collegiate departments. His proposal to the church council in 1879 was referred to conventions of the synod's three districts, one of which deferred action because "the arguments of the faculty were not convincing."[51] Only after two years was Larsen able to convince the synod convention that the basic preministerial purpose would not be altered by giving separate identities to the three-year academy and four-year college courses.

No less difficult was the language question. Norwegian was the language of both classroom and campus during the 60s. The first catalog, published in 1872, was in Norwegian. When the second appeared in English 11 years later

Larsen ventured the remark that "we have lived ourselves into our new surroundings and are beginning to feel at home in this country."[52] During the 70s the president was obliged to answer attacks from those who thought Americanization was progressing too slowly. In the 80s he had to defend the college against those who deplored too rapid an introduction of English. Veblen claimed English had virtually replaced Norwegian as a campus language by 1881.[53] By the mid-80s at least as many class hours were conducted in English as in Norwegian. Though he himself never acquired fluency in English, President Larsen encouraged its introduction into the college and commended the value of a bilingual education. In adopting English as its main medium of instruction the college was well in advance of its parent synod. As late as 1916 more than 75% of the synod's congregations continued to use Norwegian in their worship services. Until 1922 the minutes of the Norwegian Lutheran Church of America were published only in Norwegian.

As the first of the Norwegian Lutheran colleges to grant baccalaureate degrees and to send its graduates on into both theological and graduate studies, Luther also became the source of supply for leadership of other Norwegian Lutheran educational institutions. It contributed the first two presidents of St. Olaf College and 10 of its first 14 faculty members between 1874 and 1887. The first presidents of both Concordia College in Moorhead, Minnesota, and Pacific Lutheran University were graduates of Luther.

Years of Theological Conflict

Because of the close relationship between college and synod, faculty members became deeply involved in the theological controversies that marked the life of the Norwegian Synod during the late 19th century. Curiously, the slavery issue was revived from 1866 to 1869 and caused sharp conflicts within the membership of the synod and some loss of support for the college. Its alliance with the Missouri Synod brought the Norwegian Synod into the Synodical Conference in 1872, an association of conservative Lutheran synods unable to establish fellowship with the General Council in 1867. Of most momentous effect for the Norwegian Synod was the controversy over predestination which broke out in the Synodical Conference and caused the withdrawal of the Norwegian Synod in 1883. The synod itself, however, was internally divided on this issue, so deeply that in 1887 about one-third of its pastors withdrew to form the Anti-Missourian Brotherhood. The concern of this group for theological education led to steps which would have far-reaching effects upon the further development of Lutheran collegiate education.

13 LATER NORWEGIAN COLLEGES

The Issue of the Common School

In his *True Account of America*, written from Illinois in 1838, Ole Rynning touched a responsive chord in the minds of his emigration-minded countrymen when he commented that in the United States public education "is within reach of all." Directing his words to "peasant and commoner" in Norway, Rynning called attention to the American practice of allotting one section of land in each township for the support of public schools. Two such schools, he reported, had already been established in the Fox River settlement in Illinois.[1]

For the Norwegian immigrants America promised not only abundant land and economic independence but also a new kind of life, free of class restriction and open to all kinds of personal opportunities for themselves and their children. This was a time when Americans, too, viewed education and the free public school as the key to opportunity and progress. "District schools" could be established and directed by local communities, and Scandinavian immigrants took full advantage of the opportunity. Children generally received religious instruction within the congregation. Parochial schools, staffed by the pastor or by a teacher employed by the congregation, met for varying periods of time, mostly during the summer.

With the advent of the state-church clergy who founded the Norwegian Synod in 1853, the district schools in the Norwegian settlements came under severe criticism. As early as 1858 the president of the synod, Herman Amberg Preus, assailed such free schools as "religionless" and educationally inferior, and because the English language was used for instruction, destructive of the

225

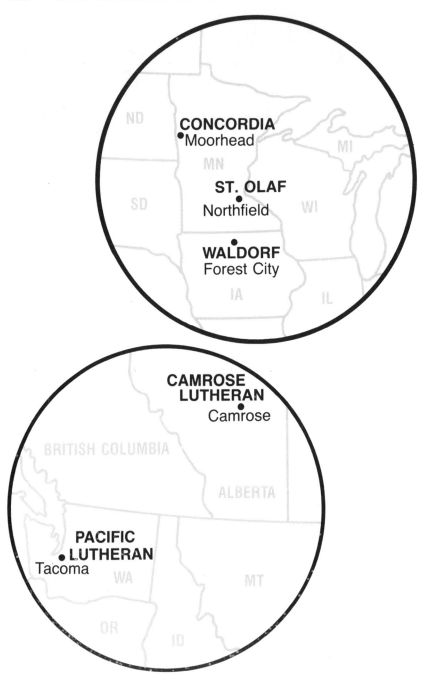

Norwegian heritage. Ready and often vehement responses strongly supporting English instruction for children came from the laity and especially from the Norwegian immigrant press. The influence of the Missouri Synod among the Norwegian clergy became especially apparent after 1866 when several pastors advocated a system of parochial schools to replace the public school.[2]

The controversy reached a climax in 1869, when Rasmus B. Anderson and several Norwegian-American editors organized the Scandinavian Lutheran Education Society in Madison, Wisconsin, to support "genuine public education among the Scandinavian people in this country."[3] There will be no good schools at all, Anderson declared, "if every little nationality and church party puts up its own."[4] To achieve a role for Norwegian Americans in the American cultural context Anderson proposed instead the appointment of Scandinavian teachers and professors in American higher schools. Such persons would be able to assist and guide students from Norwegian immigrant communities attending American schools and universities. These young people would subsequently return to their communities as teachers and leaders.

Excluded from the initial meeting of the Education Society by a parliamentary maneuver, supporters of the parochial schools met the following day under the leadership of Pastor H. A. Preus. They, too, acknowledged the importance of preparing qualified teachers for district and parochial schools, but opposed the appointment of Scandinavian professors at state universities as the means of achieving that objective. Preus proposed instead that English instruction be given at Luther College to prepare Lutheran teachers.

More significant for the development of Lutheran higher education among the Norwegians was his suggestion to the Madison meeting to erect "smaller high schools . . . in localities convenient to the large and old Norwegian settlements, e.g., at Koshkonong, Wisconsin, in Goodhue County, Minnesota, etc. . . . We could begin on a moderate scale," he said, "and broaden our program as the interest becomes livelier. With the establishment of several such schools higher education may become a general advantage rather than the privilege of a few." Such schools would form "a link, a transition stage, between the elementary school and the various institutions in which the young person will seek the final preparation for the particular earthly calling or life's work which he intends to enter." They would also offer religious instruction so young people might have fuller knowledge of Scripture and Lutheran doctrine. Thus young people could be fitted to "fulfill their duties as Christians and citizens and work for the blessing of church and state." Moreover, while Preus was not quite ready to advocate coeducation, he recommended that "we should also consider providing our girls with an opportunity for more enlightenment than is generally the case now."[5]

The debates over the "school question" and the meetings in Madison in 1869 in particular were of great significance in shaping the course of educational history among the Norwegian Lutherans. It became clear that the Norwegian laity supported the American public school in preference to a system of parochial education. However reluctantly, the Norwegian Synod clergy recognized this and turned instead to the promotion of a system of secondary schools in which religious instruction might be given in close association with a curriculum of general studies.

The Academy Movement

Beginning in the early 1870s Norwegian Lutherans, led by the Norwegian Synod, launched an "academy movement" that resulted in the formation of more than 75 secondary and normal schools from the Midwest into Canada and the Pacific Northwest.[6] Supplementing the publicly supported "common schools," they offered the opportunity to young Norwegian immigrants to equip themselves for productive involvement in the society and economy of their new country.

The academies were established to serve a different purpose from the classical schools preparing young men to study theology. Yet they shared fully in the educational tradition established by Luther himself when he called for schools to provide educated merchants and businessmen, "people who can do more than simply add, subtract, and read German."[7] The academy movement among the Norwegians had its counterpart among both their Swedish and Danish cousins who embraced the common school even more heartily than the Norwegians. As the public high schools of the upper Midwest grew in number and quality during the early 20th century, however, the church academies declined; with the coming of the Great Depression of the 1930s, they virtually disappeared. The most durable and enterprising of them developed into collegiate institutions. Among the present four-year Lutheran colleges of Scandinavian background in the United States, Gustavus Adolphus, St. Olaf, Bethany, Concordia, Pacific Lutheran, and Upsala originated as church academies rather than theological preparatory schools.

One of the first to act upon the principles enunciated by H. A. Preus in Madison was Bernt Julius Muus, Norwegian-born pastor in Goodhue County, Minnesota, the founder of St. Olaf College. An outspoken opponent of the public school, Muus described it as an institution "which because of its essential principle must work in opposition to the kingdom of God."[8] While he was not willing under all circumstances to declare resort to the common school a sin, he denounced it as a dangerous influence from which youth should be guarded.

During 1869 and 1870 Muus conducted a private school in his parsonage at Holden, but a shortage of both pupils and money compelled him to discontinue instruction after only two terms. Four years later, however, when the synod convention met in his parish, he made a plea for church schools and induced Harald Thorson, a prosperous Lutheran businessman, to offer five acres of land and $500 in cash if the synod would establish and operate an academy in the village of Northfield, Minnesota.[9]

From Academy to College

When the synod took no action except to thank Thorson for his generous offer, he and Pastor Muus determined to move independently. Together with the resident pastor in Northfield, Rev. N. A. Quammen, they laid their proposal before a group of Northfield citizens who expressed "much interest" in having the institution located in their community. Thorson's initial gift of $2000 encouraged other pledges, and within a few days $5400 had been raised. Though Muus and Quammen spoke only Norwegian, the local newspaper's report nevertheless "construed" their expressions "to be favorable to locating their College" in Northfield. The Northfield representatives, almost entirely "Yankee" professional and business people, responded with enthusiasm and extended to their "Norwegian brethren" a cordial invitation to locate their college in Northfield. One of the businessmen was applauded when he said his experience with the beginnings of Carleton College, also founded in Northfield some eight years earlier, gave promise of equally cordial support for the new school.[10]

Less than three weeks later, on November 6, 1874, articles of incorporation were drawn up for St. Olaf's School. Its stated general purpose was "the advancement in education of pupils, from fifteen years of age and upwards, as a college" and the preservation of its pupils "in the true Christian faith." Although at the outset there was no official relationship with the church the Articles stated the intent "to give this school in the charge of the Synod" whenever the synod should be willing to accept it.[11] Meanwhile, the five incorporators of the school, one pastor, one merchant, and three farmers, served as its governing board. One of their first and most notable decisions was to establish their school as a coeducational institution.

On the same day that the articles of incorporation were signed, the board invited Thorbjörn Nelson Mohn, pastor in St. Paul and a graduate of Luther College and Concordia Seminary, to become the first principal. St. Olaf's School opened on January 8, 1875, in temporary facilities purchased from the Northfield Board of Education.

Both Muus and Mohn delivered addresses at the dedicatory ceremonies. Muus spoke in Norwegian and emphasized the social dimension of education, describing it as a sharing of accumulated experience from one generation to another for the common good. Mohn spoke in English, stressing the role of education and the Christian faith in the development of responsible American citizenship among Norwegian immigrants. Both leaders voiced the lay-oriented educational emphasis characteristic of the Scandinavian colleges rooted in the academy movement of the late 19th century.

Thirty-six students enrolled for the opening term. During the year their number increased to 50, including 12 women. The curriculum consisted of grammar school subjects and high school subjects. English was the medium of instruction in all subjects except religion, history, and Norwegian.[12]

By 1878 the new Main Building stood completed and the school moved to a 30-acre tract west of the town, but not before students and faculty had shared the excitement of the daring attempted bank robbery in Northfield that ended the fabled careers of Jesse James and the Younger Brothers in 1876.[13]

Conflict of quite a different sort characterized the life of St. Olaf during the remainder of Mohn's 25 years as principal and president. Between 1860 and 1900 theological and ecclesiastical controversy split Norwegian Lutheranism into at least nine different synodical entities, each of which at some point operated its own seminary and accompanying preparatory school. Although St. Olaf was not a theological school nor affiliated with any synod, it too, became involved during the 1880s in the divisive debate on the issue of predestination.

Pastors of the Norwegian Synod were drawn into the controversy because of close ties with the Missouri Synod, in whose seminaries most Norwegian Synod pastors were trained until 1876. Followers of Professor C. F. W. Walther claimed that the individual believer is predestined *unto* faith, solely on the basis of God's grace and the merit of Christ. Their opponents insisted that when speaking of God's predestination of the individual believer one must understand that predestination takes place *in view of* his faith which has been foreseen by God.[14] Norwegian Synod pastors who disagreed with Walther and charged him with Calvinistic tendencies were called "Anti-Missourians." Both Muus and Mohn belonged to this group. Passions reached such intensity in 1883 that the Norwegian Synod withdrew from its association with Missouri in the Synodical Conference.

Still not satisfied by this action, about one-third of the Norwegian Synod pastors broke away from their own synod to form the Anti-Missourian Brotherhood. At Muus' suggestion they organized an independent theological seminary representing their views and persuaded the St. Olaf Board of Trustees to permit the use of its classrooms. In consideration of a $1200 annual contribution from the Anti-Missourian Brotherhood, St. Olaf also agreed to open a college department, starting in the fall of 1886 and adding one class each year. At its meeting in June 1889, the St. Olaf board changed the name of the institution to St. Olaf College, altered Mohn's title from Principal to President, and prepared to graduate its first baccalaureate class of five members in 1890.[15]

During its three-year sojourn on the St. Olaf campus, the Anti-Missourian seminary maintained a separate existence. With the introduction of the college department in 1886, however, several changes occurred in the program and personnel at St. Olaf itself. Enrollment rose to 135 in 1887. The curriculum was expanded and enriched to provide the classical base for theological study. Among the new faculty members was Albert Egge, who brought to the college its first Ph.D. degree, earned in 1887 at Johns Hopkins.

The Augsburg–St. Olaf Controversy

The Anti-Missourian Brotherhood did not organize itself as a synod but chose instead to seek union with other Norwegian Lutheran synods. Through its initiative the first step in that direction was taken in 1890, arresting at last the long process of fragmentation among Norwegian Lutherans. Joining with the Norwegian-Danish Conference and the Norwegian Augustana Synod, they formed the United Norwegian Lutheran Church in America, thereby reducing the number of Norwegian synods to three. To the great joy of its supporters, St. Olaf College was designated as the college of the new church, providing it for the first time a formal church affiliation.[16]

Meanwhile, Norwegian Lutherans were also discovering for the first time the institutional problems which may accompany the merging of synods. According to the articles of union of 1890, Augsburg Seminary was clearly designated as the divinity school of the new United Norwegian Lutheran Church. It absorbed the two smaller seminaries of the Norwegian Augustana Synod at Beloit, Iowa, and the Anti-Missourian school in Northfield, Minnesota.

Since St. Olaf had not been formally affiliated with any of the three merging groups, the question of its adoption as the official college of the United Church had not been a part of premerger discussions, but was taken up only at the opening convention of the new church. Although the resolution was enthusiastically approved, shadows of forthcoming conflict were already apparent in the discussions on the convention floor.

Under Georg Sverdrup's leadership Augsburg Seminary had developed the concept of a nine-year divinity school, combining beginning preparatory, college, and theological studies in a single integrated program. Adoption of a separate four-year baccalaureate institution such as St. Olaf as *the* college of the church represented to him a direct threat to Augsburg's preparatory program and to its basic philosophy of theological education[17]

Unfortunately, suspicions arose that a conspiracy was in process among supporters of St. Olaf and other long-time opponents of Sverdrup and Oftedal to destroy Augsburg's preparatory and college departments. In the months following the convention charges and countercharges filled the columns of the Norwegian-language press. Gradually, controversy shifted from the question of the nature of a divinity school to the educational quality of Augsburg and St. Olaf. Friends of Augsburg assailed St. Olaf for its humanism and rationalism, "its luxurious facilities, its doctors of philosophy, its masters of arts, and [its] deficits." St. Olaf supporters branded Augsburg as a "humbug" institution offering piety as a substitute for intellectual rigor and scholarship.[18]

Further complications arose when the United Church learned that the transfer of property from one nonprofit corporation to another would encounter legal difficulties under Minnesota law. As a solution to this problem two Minneapolis lawyers suggested a plan whereby the delegates to the United Church convention would convene at different times as the corporations of Augsburg Seminary and St. Olaf College, thus giving the United Church ownership and control of both institutions. At the recommendation of a "college committee" appointed by the synod, both the United Church and the St. Olaf board of trustees accepted the so-called Pattee-Bacon plan. The Augsburg board, however, under the direction of its chairman, Sven Oftedal, acted instead to enlarge the Augsburg corporation, adding members who would support the maintenance of its established pattern of education.[19]

In spite of a referendum among the congregations of the United Church reflecting a readiness to designate Augsburg as its only institution of higher education if ownership were transferred to the church, Augsburg supporters were not convinced that their educational program would be permanently maintained. In a final effort to end the controversy, the 1893 Convention rescinded its earlier action recognizing St. Olaf as the college of the United Church and pledged to support and maintain Augsburg if the Augsburg board would accept the Pattee-Bacon plan. Even this assurance failed to convince Sverdrup and Oftedal. Both resigned as professors of the church while retaining their positions on the Augsburg faculty.[20]

An organization called the Friends of Augsburg developed into an association of congregations that functioned as a *de facto* church body within the United Church and eventually seceded in 1897 to become the Lutheran Free Church.[21] The 1893 convention of the United Church instructed its officers to find a new location for the synod's divinity school if the Augsburg faction remained adamant. Accordingly, they rented a building in Minneapolis, formerly a macaroni factory owned by a local citizen named Zacharias, and opened a new seminary and preparatory school in September 1893. Subsequent graduates of this seminary were informally known as "macaroni prester" or "Zachariter."

In a concluding effort to assert the authority over Augsburg which it presumed to have inherited from one of its predecessor bodies, the Norwegian-Danish Conference, the United Church Convention in 1896 elected a new board for Augsburg and brought suit in the Hennepin County Court to secure control of the Augsburg property. Its case was sustained by the County Court, but an appeal by Oftedal's board to the Minnesota Supreme Court determined that ultimate control rested with the Augsburg board rather than with the United Church convention. Both parties finally agreed to a settlement in 1898 under which the United Church yielded all claims to the buildings and real estate of the seminary. A $49,000 endowment gathered by the Norwegian-Danish Conference was assigned to the United Church, together with a portion of the seminary library.[22]

The original cause of the decade-long controversy, namely, the issue of the nature and pattern of a divinity school, was settled for the United Church in 1899 when it relocated its seminary in a new building in St. Paul, Minnesota, and reinstated St. Olaf as its official college. Augsburg Seminary continued as the divinity school of the Lutheran Free Church under Sverdrup's integrated program. While its preparatory department continued to award a bachelor's degree at the completion of six years of pretheological study, the development of a distinctive liberal arts collegiate program at Augsburg was delayed for several decades and full accreditation was not achieved until 1954.

The College of the Church

The reinstatement of St. Olaf as the college of the church at the convention in 1899 was greeted with jubilation at the college. It marked the end of the most critical span of years in the college's history. Having launched its college program in 1886 in response to the needs of the church and having contributed its leadership to the formation of the United Church, it was a bitter blow to be "thrown out like a criminal," as President Mohn once put it.[23] Nor could a worse year have been chosen to be deprived of a regular annual financial grant than 1893, the year of the great national economic disaster. Enrollments declined, salaries had to be cut, and the full-time faculty was reduced from 11 to 7. Each year the board faced the question of whether or not to continue the college program or even to keep the school open. Professor H. T. Ytterboe devoted six years from 1893 to 1899 traveling among the Norwegian Lutheran congregations of the Midwest soliciting funds but also building goodwill and confidence in the mission of St. Olaf.[24]

Moreover, although St. Olaf's School was established independently of church affiliation, to provide a general education for both boys and girls, its college program was called into being to support the theological program of the Anti-Missourian Brotherhood and later the United Church. Even during its years of "exile" most of its graduates went on to study theology. Upon its reinstatement as the college of the United Church in 1899, it affirmed as its "special purpose" the preparation of young men for theological study "in order that they may become ministers or missionaries of the church."[25] These commitments to the higher education of both laity and clergy placed St. Olaf firmly in the historic Lutheran educational tradition and also paved the way for its significant contribution to the development of the modern American liberal arts college.

There is little doubt that the church controversy of the 1890s had an adverse effect on St. Olaf's academic growth. But as the new century opened the troubling issues were laid aside. Prosperity returned to the nation and the college entered a period of exceptional growth. New and vital leadership was provided by John Nathan Kildahl, who served from 1899 to 1914 as the second president of St. Olaf College. Born in Norway, Kildahl was educated at Luther College and the seminary of the Norwegian Synod in Madison, Wisconsin. He had been a pastor in Chicago for 10 years before being elected by the United Church convention in 1899. One of the most effective preachers of the church, he combined a doctrinal orthodoxy with warm evangelical pietism. His election by the convention which reinstated an official relationship with St. Olaf was a clear affirmation of the intent that St. Olaf should be, in fact as well as in name, "the college of the church."[26]

In the fulfillment of this expectation, as in many other respects, Kildahl placed his personal stamp upon St. Olaf College. Few men in its history have commanded the confidence and respect that he inspired in both church and college communities. His pastoral qualities were evident in his encouragement of campus religious life, through worship and through organized student activity.[27]

At the same time he presided over a period of physical expansion and academic growth. Enrollments increased from 184 in 1899 to 545 by 1914. New buildings, not only dormitories but also a library and a chapel, were built. Some of the most distinguished names in St. Olaf's history were added to the faculty; Carl August Mellby, social scientist, in 1901; F. Melius Christiansen, father of the choral tradition at St. Olaf, in 1905; and Ole Edvart Rølvaag, distinguished novelist and author of *Giants in the Earth*, in 1906. Curricular changes were introduced. While the classical course was maintained, additional tracks were opened, including a scientific and a literary course. Individual course offerings increased from 30 in 1899 to 114 in 1914, and new departments of biology, economics, political science, sociology, and education were established.

During the 15 years of Kildahl's administration St. Olaf emerged as a self-conscious, coeducational college of liberal arts, an instrument for the interpretation of Norwegian-American culture and a devoted servant of the church. Kildahl resigned in June 1914 to accept a professorship in theology at Luther Seminary in St. Paul just as World War I was about to begin.

Chosen by the church convention to lead the college through the next years of uncertainty and change was Lauritz A. Vigness, president of Pleasant View Luther College in Ottawa, Illinois.[28] His brief administration coincided with the war years, ending in 1918. Also, during his term of office, the merger of three Norwegian synods, forming the Norwegian Lutheran Church of America, numbering one-half million members, was consummated. Broadened resources in the new church and new opportunities opening for higher education in postwar America invited St. Olaf into a decade of significant achievement in the 1920s.

Augustana and the United Church

The junior partner in the synodical merger of 1890 was the Norwegian Augustana Synod with only 41 congregations, compared with 379 congregations in the Norwegian-Danish Conference and 268 in the Anti-Missourian Brotherhood. It had only two educational institutions, a theological seminary at Beloit, Iowa, and Augustana College in Canton, South Dakota. According to the articles of union, the seminary became part of Augsburg Seminary in Minneapolis, while the school in Canton continued to function under the new ownership of the United Church.

An expanded constituency of 688 congregations offered more favorable prospects for the future of Augustana College than at any time since its move to the West in 1881. With the election of a promising young faculty member named Anthony G. Tuve as president and an immediate increase in enrollment from 55 to 116 in 1890, these expectations seemed well-founded. Their spirits also buoyed by the brightening prospects, Canton businessmen and neighboring congregations offered $10,000 toward a new dormitory to house the expanded student body. The new parent church body agreed to sponsor a general appeal for an additional $5,000 toward a $20,000 building, provided no funds were taken from the synodical treasury. The synod's board of trustees authorized the construction, and in a flush of optimism President Tuve even made plans for the expansion of the college curriculum beyond the first two years.[29]

Then suddenly, in the fall of 1893, disaster struck. Severe drought took a heavy toll in the harvest fields. Financial resources of the farmers dried up with their crops. The entire country fell under the shadow of the panic of 1893 and the depression that followed. Resources of the United Church were depleted. In addition, the church was struggling with the bitter controversy over Augsburg and St. Olaf. In 1893 the United Church had severed its ties with St. Olaf in an unsuccessful attempt to prevent the defection of Augsburg Seminary. Faced with the necessity of establishing another seminary and preparatory department while also struggling with the general financial crisis, the trustees of the United Church requested Augustana to discontinue its college department. They also advised President Tuve that the church was unable to provide any further support for the academy.[30]

Rather than close the school entirely, Tuve offered to lease the academy personally and to seek private support. In 1895 he was able to organize a group of local pastors and representatives of congregations as the Augustana College Association. The synod, however, retained ownership and supervision and agreed to pay insurance on the building and to cover any operation deficit up to $500. In 1899 when better times returned, the trustees of the church gave cautious permission to add a much-needed building, but only on condition that no synodical expense be incurred.[31]

Under the patient and persistent leadership of President Tuve, members of the Association rallied strong local support for the Canton school. By 1903 they were able to dedicate a substantial multipurpose structure at a cost of nearly $50,000. Curricular offerings were also expanded. Academy courses stressed college preparation and a normal department offered opportunities to qualify graduates for state certification at several levels. As in most church academies at the turn of the century, commercial and business courses drew substantial enrollments. In 1910 the Association voted to reintroduce college work on the freshman and sophomore levels, including courses in English, religion, history, science, modern languages, and Greek. By 1918, enrollment had risen to 324.[32]

Anthony Tuve concluded 25 years as president of Augustana in 1915, on the eve of another synodical merger with more turbulence in store for Augustana than the realignments of 1890. In 1917 the United Church, the Norwegian Synod, and Hauge's Synod formed a single church body, uniting 90% of the Norwegian Lutherans in America. As in 1890, one of the complex problems was the so-called school question. A single theological seminary was established in St. Paul, Minnesota. St. Olaf and Luther both became colleges of the Norwegian Lutheran Church of America. The college department of Hauge's Synod at Red Wing, Minnesota, was moved to St. Olaf in exchange for St. Olaf's academy department. The college department of the Norwegian Synod's Park Region Luther College was moved to Concordia in Moorhead, Minnesota.

A Tale of Two Cities

Most controversial was the proposed merger of Augustana College in Canton and the Lutheran Normal School, operated by the Norwegian Synod in Sioux Falls since 1889. Both their geographical proximity—they were only 20 miles apart—and their overlapping programs spoke convincingly for consolidation. The issue of the location of the merged institution, however, ignited a controversy which alternately burned and smouldered for nearly two decades.

The fierce loyalty of the Canton supporters was rooted in the long struggle by members of the Augustana College Association to keep their school going with minimal support from the church. The Sioux Falls school, with alumni numbering about 2000 former students and graduates, had the added support of a larger city that could offer a potentially greater constituency for a future college. Both groups offered generous financial inducements.

In 1918, one year after the merger, a special convention called to deal with the "school question" received recommendations from the synod's newly elected Board of Education to consolidate the two schools and to establish a single junior college and normal school in Sioux Falls.[33] Unable to reach agreement, the convention referred the matter to the synod's board of trustees and the Board of Education and authorized them to act. The joint boards reaffirmed the earlier recommendation and, over the strenuous objection of the Augustana Association in Canton, announced the immediate opening of a consolidated school in Sioux Falls to be known as Augustana College and Normal School. Furniture and supplies were transferred from the school in Canton and the building was offered for sale to the Canton Board of Education.

Meanwhile, an informal meeting of South Dakota District pastors and laymen in Canton offered a compromise proposal. They concurred in the establishment of a four-year college in Sioux Falls and recommended a local campaign to raise a $200,000 endowment to support it. If the campaign for the college were successful, the church would agree to the operation of a separate normal school at Canton.[34] The South Dakota District endorsed the proposal and the church boards accepted it. The $200,000 endowment was promptly raised, and the Canton Normal School opened in the fall of 1920 with an enrollment of 172 students. In Sioux Falls the combined Augustana College and Normal School also opened, and a new president, Dr. C. O. Solberg, former professor of English and Religion at St. Olaf College, undertook the development of a four-year college program. Fifteen freshmen and one sophomore enrolled. The following year all classes were represented, and in 1923 Augustana College awarded its first baccalaureate degree.[35]

Meanwhile, however, since both schools continued to offer academy and normal school courses, competition persisted. Finally in 1925, acknowledging frustration and failure, the Board of Education of the Norwegian Lutheran Church turned both schools over to the South Dakota District and offered the District an annual subsidy of $15,000 if it would assume the responsibility of settling the school question. A district committee recommended that the synod deed the properties to a corporation to be called the Augustana College Association, which would operate both schools under one board and one president. After 1926, under the direction of the Association, all advanced normal training was transferred to Augustana College in Sioux Falls, and all academy level work was assigned to Augustana College Academy in Canton.[36]

In 1932, in the throes of the Depression, enrollments in the academy dropped so low that the president recommended that it be closed. In a final display of local determination born of long experience, the people of the Canton area rose again to its defense. Reorganized as the Augustana Academy Association, they and their school not only weathered the Depression but continued as one of the few survivors among Norwegian Lutheran academies until 1971.

Schools of a New Generation

From 1890 to 1920 Norwegian Lutheranism in America experienced its most rapid expansion. Immigration from Norway reached its peak in the 1880s and continued at a high level into the 90s. Following a brief decline as the result of the economic depression, it surged ahead into the 20th century until World War I. Between 1890 and 1920, 350,000 Norwegian immigrants entered the country.

Since land was more difficult to obtain in the older settlements in Illinois and Wisconsin, the stream of settlers flowed west and north through Iowa and Minnesota into the Dakotas and the Red River Valley, along the route of the Northern Pacific Railroad into Montana and the Pacific Northwest, and northward into the prairie provinces of Canada.

The churches followed the settlers. In three decades Norwegian Lutheran synods ordained 1507 pastors and organized more than 4000 congregations, mostly in these newly settled areas.[37] During the same period Norwegian Lutherans established more than 40 academies, normal schools, and Bible schools.[38] These numbers reflect the active presence of several competing Norwegian Lutheran synods in the same geographical territory. They also bear witness to the enthusiasm of the Norwegian settlers for an education that would equip them for life in the new land and the eagerness of their pastors to provide young people with a higher education that would undergird both their Christian faith and their Norwegian heritage.

However, only three of these schools eventually emerged as permanent baccalaureate institutions, surviving the gradual expansion of public high schools, the rigors of economic depression, and the consolidation of parent church bodies. These are Concordia College in Moorhead, Minnesota; Pacific Lutheran in Tacoma, Washington; and Augustana College in Sioux Falls, South Dakota. Two other academies achieved status as two-year junior colleges: Waldorf in Forest City, Iowa, and Camrose College in Alberta.[39]

The Norwegian Concordia

Concordia College was established in 1891 in Moorhead, Minnesota, in the heart of the rich valley of the Red River of the North, on the boundary between Minnesota and North Dakota. Together with its twin city of Fargo across the river in North Dakota, Moorhead was part of a commercial and trading center that served some of the most productive agricultural land in North America. Fargo-Moorhead was also a major terminal for steamboats on the Red River and the point of departure for the Northern Pacific Railroad as it thrust across the Great Plains toward the mountains and the western ocean. Thanks to the coincidence of the Norwegian outpouring into the northern plains and the eagerness of the Northern Pacific and the Great Northern railroads for settlers along their tracks, North Dakota, even as late as 1980, could still claim the highest percentage of Lutherans in its population of any of the United States.

In its early days, however, neither Moorhead nor Concordia College had any general mandate from Norwegian Lutherans as an educational center. Moorhead itself enjoyed a dubious if somewhat exaggerated reputation as "the wickedest city in the world," dating from its beginnings in the early 1870s as a tent town for Northern Pacific railway construction crews and assorted camp followers. After North Dakota entered the union in 1889 as a "dry" state, saloon keepers operated four-seated "jag wagons" offering "dry" Fargoans free transportation across the Red River to Moorhead saloons.[40]

When the Norwegian Lutheran pastors' conference agreed that the time was ripe for the establishment of an academy in the Red River Valley, it was the time-honored system of community bidding that finally brought Concordia to Moorhead. Grand Forks and Fargo, North Dakota, made offers, as did several communities in Minnesota. But the availability, at a bargain price, of a substantial building erected 10 years earlier by the Episcopalians and vacated when their school was forced to close, gave Moorhead the needed advantage.

After carefully assessing potential local support, a group of three pastors and nine laymen organized the Northwestern Lutheran College Association on April 14, 1891, and purchased the Bishop Henry Whipple Academy building for $10,000. This group functioned as the Concordia College corporation for more than 30 years until they were finally able to place the institution under direct church control.

They named their school Concordia, not in recognition of historic 16th-century Lutheran confessional documents, but in gratitude for the concord and harmony which had been achieved through the merging of three synods in 1890 to form a United Norwegian Lutheran Church. Although called a college, Concordia functioned as an academy from its beginning.[41]

Classes began in September 1891, under the leadership of the principal, Ingebrikt F. Grose, a graduate of Luther College who had served as professor of English at St. Olaf College for the previous five years. Only 12 students were present on the opening day, but by Christmas the number had risen to 50 and before the year ended 200 boys and girls were crowded into Bishop Whipple Hall.

The initial faculty consisted of Principal Grose, who taught English, and Elmer D. Busby, who taught science and mathematics. Busby was a graduate of Thiel College, no doubt recommended by Rev. George H. Gerberding, pastor of an English-speaking mission church in Fargo and himself a Thiel graduate. Gerberding was an active member of the Norwegian Lutheran pastoral conference and one of the incorporators of Concordia. A descriptive passage in his later memoirs indicates his admiration for the strong impulse for higher education that he observed among the Norwegian immigrants:

> "How they love education," he wrote. "How they will plan and how ready they are to sacrifice and to suffer that their children may have an education. I actually saw large families living in sod shacks on the open prairie sending a boy or a girl to Concordia College."[42]

The initial curriculum at Concordia offered three courses of study. The commercial course included bookkeeping, business practice, arithmetic, English grammar and reading, letter writing, and penmanship. The practical course offered English language, rhetoric and literature, Norwegian, algebra, geometry, U.S. history, geography, civics, and some science. The classical course prepared for college entrance and supplemented the practical course with German and Latin. Catechetical classes were formed to prepare teachers of religion for the Norwegian parochial schools, and instruction was offered to all students in piano and organ. A particular inducement for new immigrants were the special classes in English, a service which Concordia continued to offer until 1917.[43]

In order to offer these courses two additional faculty members were added during the first year, each of whom would play a significant role in the early development of the college. Hans H. Aaker was invited to teach the commercial courses. He had studied at Luther College and Valparaiso University, taught at the Willmar Academy in Minnesota and had practical experience as operator of a general store. When Professor Grose resigned in 1893, preferring the classroom to the administrator's office, Aaker became principal of Concordia and, capitalizing on the general popularity of the commercial and practical business education in the 1890s, tried to change Concordia into a business college. In 1902 when the members of the association objected to this and also to his involvement in local and state politics, he resigned and opened his own business college in Fargo.[44]

The second new addition was Rasmus Bogstad, a young Norwegian-born pastor in Kindred, North Dakota, a few miles southwest of Fargo. Invited to teach religion and Norwegian, he became instead the college's most effective field representative and fund-raiser. Traveling by horse and buggy or by train in all kinds of weather, he visited farmers and pastors, soliciting both dollars and students with remarkable success. As the second year began enrollment reached 200 students and the costs of the original building and necessary dormitories had been met. In the throes of the depression of the 1890s Bogstad almost single-handedly kept the school solvent.

When Aaker resigned in 1902 the board of directors invited Bogstad to become Concordia's principal. Under his leadership the business school image gradually receded. The college preparatory course was given greater emphasis; full-year enrollments increased. Bogstad convinced his reluctant board that a $50,000 main building was both necessary and possible and raised most of the needed funds himself, climaxing his efforts with a capstone grant of $12,500 from Andrew Carnegie.[45]

Bogstad was one of the first Norwegian Lutheran educators to employ the techniques of promotional advertising. While the Main was under construction, he printed 10,000 folders for distribution in connection with fund-raising and student solicitation. Offering its first courses on a junior college level during 1907–1908, Concordia also became the first Norwegian Lutheran school to reach an enrollment of 500 students.

Bogstad's efforts to move Concordia toward collegiate status were not universally welcomed. A proposal placing the academic program in the hands of a dean and freeing the president to raise funds and represent the school to the public received only lukewarm response from the board. At the conclusion of a leave of absence, Bogstad resigned in 1910, leaving to his successors the completion of the transition for which he had laid the groundwork.

At this point Johan Arnt Aasgaard (1876–1966) became president of Concordia. The new president was a graduate of St. Olaf College and Luther Seminary in St. Paul. As the first recipient of a scholarship from the United Norwegian Lutheran Church, he had spent a postgraduate year at Princeton Seminary. Under his able and determined administration the collegiate program received fresh encouragement. In the fall of 1916 a senior class of five men and one woman was organized in anticipation of the college's first baccalaureate event in the spring of 1917.[46]

Of even greater importance to Concordia's academic future were the preliminary discussions of the syodical merger of 1917 among Norwegian Lutherans. Park Region Luther College, an academy of the Norwegian Synod in nearby Fergus Falls, Minnesota, established in 1882, had also developed a collegiate program and had awarded its first bachelor's degrees in 1912. Backed by the assurances of continuing support from the business community of Moorhead, President Aasgaard won the consent of a special education committee of the merging churches to consolidate the programs of the two schools. In the outcome, Park Region retained its well-established academy program while transferring its small collegiate program to Concordia. In return, Concordia's normal, parochial, and special English courses were moved to Park Region. Not yet ready to stake its entire future on the success of a baccalaureate program, Concordia retained its academy for another 10 years until the increase of small-town public high schools rendered it uneconomical. Concordia's greatest gain through consolidation was the acquisition of six members of the Park Region faculty who brought much-needed strength to academic courses in English, history, mathematics, chemistry, and the classics.[47]

The combining of the college programs of Park Region and Concordia established the direction of Concordia's future academic development, but the goal of a strong liberal arts program was yet to be achieved. Even in 1919 only 131 of the 550 enrolled were college students. The college library needed expansion. An adequate endowment was needed to qualify for accreditation. When President Aasgaard resigned in 1925 to become president of the Norwegian Lutheran Church of America, Concordia College was well on its way toward these goals.

Waldorf in Iowa

Waldorf College was the result of a contest between two groups of civic promoters in a small Iowa town. In the wake of a successful campaign to make Forest City the county seat of Winnebago County, both groups built new hotels to accommodate the anticipated influx of outside visitors. It became quickly apparent that one hotel was sufficient, and the ''Waldorf'' was forced to close. Before its scheduled demolition the local Lutheran pastor, Christian S. Salvesen, took an option on the property for possible use as a college.[48]

Pastors and members of surrounding parishes formed a local association and purchased the hotel at a minimal price. With Pastor Salvesen as president and a faculty of five, the school opened as an academy in September 1903. By the year's end 125 students were enrolled. Two years later it was recognized as one of the official academies of the United Norwegian Lutheran Church.

Throughout successive church mergers Waldorf remained under the governance of an association of congregations in the area surrounding Forest City. In 1920 it became a two-year junior college, one of the earliest in the state of Iowa. Waldorf has enjoyed a unique distinction as an ''administrative training school'' for college presidents, three of its presidents having later become presidents of St. Olaf College.

Camrose in Canada

The northwesterly movement of Norwegian immigrants and farmers from Minnesota, Iowa, and the Dakotas continued into the prairie provinces of Canada during the early years of the 20th century. Concentrations were heaviest in the newly created provinces of Saskatchewan and Alberta, where by 1916 nearly 400 Norwegian Lutheran congregations had been established.[49]

The presence of five separate Norwegian Lutheran groups, each sending pastors from the neighboring midwestern states to establish new congregations, and the openness of many congregations to lay preaching reduced the pressure for additional clergy supply. The earliest educational ventures among the Norwegians were therefore not pretheological schools but high schools to provide the youth with opportunities beyond the elementary levels. Many Norwegian settlers had come from communities in the United States where they had become accustomed to the English language, and their children had already been exposed to American district schools. As in the midwestern communities from which they came, they were eager to establish church academies.

The initiative for the first school in Camrose, Alberta, came from the United Norwegian Lutheran Church in the United States on the recommendation of its home mission superintendent, the Rev. Olaf Glasoe. A representative of the church was sent to Canada to promote the school, and the city of Camrose eagerly offered a free and spacious tax-free site for the erection of a high school.

In an exemplary action of Lutheran cooperation, pastors and lay delegates of both United Church and Hauge's Synod congregations were invited to join in support of the school. The Alberta Norwegian Lutheran College Association was organized and in October 1911 steps were undertaken for the opening of Camrose College. A building with five classrooms, offices, residence and dining facilities for 65 students and two teachers was dedicated in June 1913, at a cost of $28,000.[50] An almost identical sequence of events occurred under similar auspices when the Saskatchewan Lutheran College Association was organized in 1911 to establish a Lutheran academy in Outlook, Saskatchewan.

Enrollments at both schools were maintained at satisfactory levels during the early 1920s, but the adding of one year of university-level instruction at Outlook in 1928 failed to stem the decline of the high school, and the rigors of the economic depression forced its closing in 1936. The high school program at Camrose was able to survive the depression and in 1939 began a gradual transition toward junior college status.[51] Having achieved recognition by the University of Alberta in 1969, Camrose Junior College has continued to enrich and expand its curriculum in an effort to secure full recognition for a four-year liberal arts curriculum.

Pioneering in the Pacific Northwest

At about the same time that plans for Concordia College were taking shape in the Red River Valley, a meeting of Norwegian Synod pastors in

Decorah, Iowa, took note of the educational needs of Norwegian Lutherans in the Pacific Northwest. In response to requests for help from pastors on that western frontier the conference in Decorah adopted a resolution urging Pastor Bjug Harstad, president of the Minnesota District to visit "the brethren on the Coast" and assist them in establishing a Lutheran high school. The pastors indicated their readiness to contribute to such an effort through personal donations but "without in any way making the Synod responsible."[52]

Having founded three academies while serving pastorates in North Dakota between 1878 and 1889, Harstad had both the experience and the zeal for such an undertaking. Within two weeks he was in Seattle conferring with local pastors concerning possible locations and sources of support.

Previous to his arrival a real estate promoter who had a large block of land in an outlying section of Tacoma had made a proposal to the local pastors. He offered to donate a 100-acre tract of land if a school were located in his development. In addition construction funds would be supplied through payment of a 10% commission on all lots sold, plus a $10,000 bonus if 1000 lots were sold. Harstad and the local committee accepted this proposal.

After organizing a corporation optimistically styled "The Pacific Lutheran University Association" and naming Harstad as president, they launched a publicity program to assist the developer in the sale of lots. The Association publicized its goals and promoted the school through a Norwegian-language newspaper called *The Lutheran University Herold.*

By May 1891, with confidence running high, plans were completed and excavation begun for a five-story building large enough to accommodate 248 students. The sale of lots began auspiciously. Some were even purchased by pastors and other friends in the Midwest during a synod meeting in Iowa addressed by Harstad, but substantial sums still had to be borrowed to continue construction. Cost estimates rose ominously from $20,000 to $30,000 while the building was under construction.[53]

Meanwhile, Harstad was also elected president of the school. Trustees of the Association laid plans for the educational program and began to assemble a faculty. Students were offered four options: a normal course, a business course, a scientific course, and a classical course for college preparation.

The opening of the school, however, was dependent upon the completion of the building, and continuing financial problems caused repeated delays in the construction process. Only on October 14, 1894, three years after ground was first broken, was it possible to dedicate the buildings. Classes began two weeks later with 30 pupils in attendance, a number which increased to 75 by Christmas.

Much of the problem in those years of uncertain survival was caused by the collapse of land values and the general economic depression which followed the panic of 1893. Lots ceased to be marketable, and those who had made their investments before the collapse were left with virtually worthless land and in many cases bitter resentment toward those who had sold them the land. The Association was left with a partially completed building, far too large for its immediate needs, and a mountainous $37,000 debt.

In 1895 an appeal was made to the Norwegian Synod to take over the school, but after a full discussion of its financial status the synod was unwilling to assume the obligations involved. Pledges of $14,000 from several pastors and congregations and the assumption of $10,000 of the indebtedness by the Pacific District prevented the closing of the school. Disconsolate at the thought that he had been a party to a land-promotion scheme in which many good and trusting people had lost money, Bjug Harstad made one final effort, bizarre in retrospect, but a clear sign of his eagerness to set things right. From February 1898 to August 1899 he tramped and camped through the gold fields of the Yukon in a fruitless quest for the bonanza which would pay all the bills.[54]

With the opening of school in the fall of 1897, Nils Joseph Hong of Willmar, Minnesota, a 31-year-old graduate of Luther College, joined the faculty, and the following year became principal and president. During the opening decade of the new century he provided steady leadership for the school, slowly building both a loyal alumni constituency and a reputation for sound high school training.

Perils of Proliferation

While Pacific Lutheran Academy was striving to pay its debts and achieve academic respectability, Norwegian Lutherans in the state of Washington undertook several other educational ventures. Between 1902 and 1909 three more schools were established by competing Lutheran synods, each with limited resources and small constituencies. Although these efforts finally converged in the support of a single collegiate institution, this early fragmentation seriously limited the Lutheran impact on higher education in the Pacific Northwest.

In 1907 members of the Lutheran Free Church established Bethania College, a small academy that led a marginal existence in the city of Everett until its closing in 1917. When in 1902 the United Norwegian Lutheran Church urged its Pacific District to establish a school in the Pacific Northwest, members responded by forming college associations in two cities, Spokane and Everett. Columbia College in Everett opened in 1909 as an academy in direct competition with Bethania in the same city.[55]

Spokane College, located in a growing city on the eastern edge of the state, began under the most favorable circumstances, offering a full four-year college course at the outset. Within a year after the organization of the Spokane College Association in 1905 citizens of Spokane had contributed $18,000. A

$52,000 neoclassical brick building was erected on a site donated by the Washington Improvement Company in a residential section of the city. During its first year the college enrolled 189 students and engaged 24 faculty members. Its first president was Dr. Paul M. Glasoe, a former chemistry professor at St. Olaf College. In addition to a standard four-year academy Spokane College offered a full liberal arts curriculum and operated a law school which quickly achieved a strong reputation in the community.[56] The Spokane Public Library established a branch at the college which numbered 38,000 volumes in 1910. Plans were announced in 1909 for a $200,000 endowment.

In 1908 the Reverend C. F. Johnson, pastor of the large Lutheran church which had provided much of the local support for the college, resigned as president of the board of trustees of the college corporation. He objected to the organization of a new congregation near the college, fearing that the membership of his own congregation would thereby be diminished. His resignation not only undermined much of the Lutheran support for the college but also raised questions within the community concerning the seriousness of the Lutheran commitment.

With the loss of local Lutheran support the officers of the corporation sought to broaden their community base. They created a College Council of 32 businessmen as advisers, and, while stressing the college's Christian character also proposed that it be independent of denominational control. When the corporation's plan was broached to officials of the United Church, they flatly rejected it. Within a year Dr. Glasoe resigned to return to St. Olaf, and community interest in the college faded. Reduced to junior college and later to academy status, Spokane College was closed by the church in 1929 as an economic liability.[57]

The Emergence of Pacific Lutheran University

The lack of unified Lutheran support of higher education in the Pacific Northwest, evidenced in the loss of Spokane College, was further dramatized in the vacillating efforts of the Norwegian Lutheran Church of America to consolidate its educational resources in that region after the merger of 1917. It was clear that the new church intended to maintain only one school on the Pacific coast, but both Pacific Lutheran Academy and Columbia College expected to be the favored choice. When the Tacoma Commercial Club pledged $25,000 by August 1, 1917, the church selected Pacific Lutheran Academy and ordered the closing of Columbia College in Everett.

Uncertainty over the fulfillment of the pledge, however, caused the church leadership in Minneapolis to hesitate. Their delay revived the hopes of Everett supporters who reopened their school for the 1917–1918 year.[58] President Hong also reopened the academy in Parkland (suburban Tacoma) in September, but advised the president of the church that without assured church funding the survival of the school was doubtful. At the end of a precarious year Hong resigned, in hopes of facilitating the negotiations, but also in frustration over the lack of decisive action by church leadership.

In the summer of 1918 the Board of Education and the trustees of the church decided to support the Everett location, but a year later reversed their decision again. Not until 1920, after Pacific Lutheran Academy had been closed for two years, was the matter resolved by a decision to establish a hospital on the Columbia College site and to form a new college association to operate the academy at Parkland.[59]

Fortunately, the consolidation process was completed on the threshold of a period of economic prosperity and growth. Under the leadership of a new president, Pastor O. J. Ordal, the first college-level courses were added in 1921. Increased enrollments filled the dormitories and deficits disappeared. Staunch faculty members were added who would serve the college for several decades, and in 1925 the college launched a drive for a $250,000 endowment.

It was the task of a new president, Dr. O. A. Tingelstad, who took office on the eve of the Great Depression, to lead Pacific Lutheran once again through years of deficits and discouragement but also of crucial academic growth.[60] Dr. Tingelstad was a graduate of Luther College, an ordained pastor, and one of the few Lutheran college presidents with an earned doctorate. Even under the stress of the Depression, enrollments grew in response to curricular enrichments. Third-year programs in both liberal arts and normal training were added in 1932.

Even more important than the financial assistance which they provided were the bonds of cooperation established in these years with other Lutheran church bodies. When Spokane College closed in 1929, the Joint Ohio Synod transferred to Pacific Lutheran both the faculty and financial support which it had contributed since 1914. In 1933 the Columbia Conference of the Augustana Synod voted $6500 to the college and elected its first representative to the Pacific Lutheran board of trustees. The development of such broad-based relationships, a particular contribution of President Tingelstad, laid the foundation for the unified Lutheran approach to higher education in the Pacific Northwest which had been so patently missing between 1890 and 1920.[61]

In other respects, too, the college seemed to be compensating for its precarious early history. In 1937 the "Choir of the West" began its long and distinguished tradition in choral music under Professor Gunnar Malmin. Athletic teams of the late 30s and early 40s became the "giant killers" of the Pacific Northwest. In 1940, with an enrollment of more than 500 students, Pacific Lutheran graduated its first bachelor of arts and in 1944 achieved full regional accreditation as a four-year liberal arts college.

The coming of World War II, however, brought the recovery of Pacific Lutheran to a halt. As men left the campus for military service, enrollment declined to 265, the lowest figure in a decade. Faculty salaries fell into arrears. Obligations to local merchants remained unfulfilled. When President Tingelstad retired in 1943 after a 15-year incumbency, the college once again faced a crisis of survival.

The task of reviving the flagging spirits of faculty and constituents and restoring the fiscal credibility of the college devolved upon the Rev. Seth C. Eastvold, who assumed the presidency in the summer of 1943. Bringing to his task resources of boundless energy, business acumen, and promotional skill, Eastvold was able to turn the course of the institution away from disaster and start it on its way to economic stability.[62]

His leadership style was often controversial, productive of high praise and bitter criticism both within and outside of the college. But in the golden year of postwar national affluence and educational expansion he was able to draw the financial and community support to Pacific Lutheran which prepared the way for its later emergence as a strong Lutheran presence among the educational institutions in the Pacific Northwest. In 1960, as the Eastvold administration drew to a close, the college was reorganized as a small university, reclaiming the name originally attached to its founding association in 1980.[63]

14 COLLEGES
OF THE DANES
AND THE FINNS

Although the Danes hold the distinction of having placed the first Lutheran pastor, Rasmus Jensen, on North American soil, on the shores of Hudson
Bay in 1619, far fewer of their countrymen found their way to America in the
19th century than either their Swedish or Norwegian cousins. Only 10% of the
total Scandinavian immigration to the United States between 1820 and 1920
was Danish in origin. Not only were the Danes fewer in numbers but they came
later than other Scandinavians. By 1860 only about 5000 Danes had entered the
country while Sweden and Norway had already sent more than 36,000.[1]

The population increase which all European countries experienced in the
19th century because of improved diet and disease control also affected
Denmark. But because of the earlier arrival of industrialization, the factories of
Copenhagen and other Danish cities were able to absorb the increased numbers
of young men and women. The reclamation of moorlands in western Denmark
also provided jobs for more farm laborers, further alleviating the pressures to
emigrate.[2]

After 1860, however, many of the same economic factors which stimulated earlier emigration from Sweden and Norway began to operate in
Denmark. Farm workers were no longer able to find employment. Wages were
dismally low. Small landholders were frustrated by the lack of opportunity to
expand.

An additional factor was the political unrest produced by the war with
Prussia and Austria in 1864. Denmark lost the provinces of Schleswig and Hol-
stein to Prussia; between 1867 and 1871 many young Danes residing in these
provinces migrated to America to avoid Prussian military service.

249

These factors, combined with the availability of free land under the United States government's Homestead Act and the promise of unlimited opportunities in America produced a marked increase in emigration after 1862. Between 1860 and 1870 more than 17,000 Danes entered the United States. Numbers increased to 88,000 between 1881 and 1890 and by the early 1920s had reached 300,000.

Religious Currents in Denmark

Except for the Mormon converts who left Denmark to join their new community of faith in Utah, the religious impulse was not an important factor in Danish migration to the United States.[3] However, the internal tensions and conflicts which troubled the Church of Denmark, especially during the years of active emigration, crossed the ocean with the emigrants and exerted a determining influence upon the shape of Danish Lutheranism in America.

One faction represented the followers of Bishop Nicolai Frederik Severin Grundtvig (1783–1872).[4] Following his own deep spiritual struggle, he first raised his voice in 1825 against the rationalism and indifference of the Danish clergy and in support of the "godly gatherings" of pious laypeople that were proscribed by both church and government. His quest for a clear and simple witness to faith led to his "matchless discovery" of Christ himself as "the Word" who lives in his church and nourishes it through his "living word," in the Apostles' Creed, the Lord's Prayer, and the sacraments. For him the Bible was a sacred source-book of the faith but was not to be identified with the true "Word of God." "We shall not stand on the Bible and search for faith," he wrote, "but stand on faith and read the Bible."[5]

Grundtvig's emphasis upon a "living faith" led him also to a strong affirmation of the positive potential of human life, created by God and redeemed by Jesus Christ. In contrast to the otherworldliness of the pietists, he stressed cultural as well as spiritual awakening. As the "father of the Danish folk-school," he regarded education as an instrument for developing enlightened, cultured, and sensitive human beings, rather than the means of assuring a livelihood. By the time of his death in 1872 he had become Denmark's most influential figure, but his views aroused opposition both within the church and among the increasingly vocal antireligious professionals in Denmark.

After Grundtvig's death new spiritual leadership was provided by Vilhelm Beck, an outstanding preacher and the leader of the pietistic Inner Mission Movement. While Grundtvig emphasized the objective nature of the baptismal covenant, the Inner Mission people stressed the subjective elements in Christianity such as conversion and sanctification. They also held a narrower view of culture and a more pessimistic view of human nature and the natural world.

These two streams of Danish religious thought and practice were transmitted to America during the most active periods of Danish migration. While both could exist within the broad embrace of the Danish state church, it was almost inevitable that in the free-church climate of America, they would establish separate organizations and educational institutions.

Danish Churches in America

The first Danish pastor ordained in America was Claus L. Clausen, who came to the Norwegian congregation at Muskego, Wisconsin, as a teacher in 1843 and was called as their pastor shortly after his arrival. Although he never joined the Danish church groups that were later organized, he was the first to confront Danish church authorities with the need for pastors to serve Danish immigrants in America. His visit to Denmark in 1867 resulted in the formation in 1869 of the "Commission for the Furtherance of the Proclamation of the

Gospel among Danes in America,'' a body that, though independent and private, received financial support from the state. During the next 10 years the Commission sent 23 missionary pastors or candidates to America.[6]

The first efforts to coordinate Lutheran work among their countrymen in America were made by two missionary pastors, Adam Dan and Rasmus Andersen in 1872. Together with a group of laypersons in Neenah, Wisconsin, they organized the Church Mission Society "to gather our countrymen . . . into congregations and give them spiritual service through word and sacrament.''[7] Two years later they changed the name of the society to the Danish Evangelical Lutheran Church in America, seeking thereby to identify their "intimate connection . . . with the Danish National Church . . . from which they have not separated themselves by going to America.''[8] In 1879, however, under "the contagious influence of the American spirit," the "Danish Church," as it was more commonly known, adopted its own constitution, thereby establishing its independence from the Church of Denmark. By that time it numbered 5000 members in 65 congregations served by 17 pastors.[9]

When it became apparent that most of the men being sent to America by the Commission were Grundtvigians, the Inner Mission in Denmark began to send young men of their own group to the Norwegian-Danish Conference. Not only was Danish-born Claus Clausen a cofounder of this body, but the Conference had also clearly indicated its rejection of Grundtvig's views on biblical authority. Between 1872 and 1884, 10 young Danes sent by the Inner Mission studied at Augsburg Seminary, the theological school of the Conference. Most of them were called to serve the rapidly growing Danish settlements in western Iowa and eastern Nebraska. Although relations between the Norwegian pastors and their "Danish brethren" remained cordial, interest in organizing a separate Danish church grew as new congregations were established. In 1884, with the cordial approval and blessing of the Norwegian-Danish Conference, an amicable separation took place. At a meeting in a rural parish near Blair, Nebraska, nine pastors and 19 congregations organized the Danish Evangelical Lutheran Church Association in America. To distinguish it from other church organizations that also employed the term "Danish" in their names, this group was known as the "Blair Church.''[10]

Beginning with these two early Danish church organizations a complex sequence of divisions, mergers, and realignments took place that finally drew the line clearly between the Grundtvigians and the Inner Mission Danish Lutherans. Efforts of the "Danish Church" to incorporate both views within its membership failed. When a new constitution was proposed in 1893, pastors and congregations favoring the Inner Mission emphasis withdrew to form the Danish Evangelical Lutheran Church of North America, more commonly known as the "North Church." In 1896 the North Church and the Blair Church

merged to form the United Evangelical Lutheran Church of Am
In 1960 the UELC joined Norwegian and German synods to be
The American Lutheran Church.

The "Danish Church," much reduced in size but relieved at last of its in-
herited burden of conflict, maintained its Grundtvigian identity, yielding only
to the forces of acculturation by changing its name in 1952 to the American
Evangelical Lutheran Church (AELC). In 1962 it joined synods of Swedish,
Finnish, Slovak, and German heritage to form the Lutheran Church in
America.[11]

The Folk-School Tradition

While both groups of Danish Lutherans in America established theological seminaries and colleges, the most distinctive educational contribution of
the Danish tradition was the folk school. Although their emphasis upon the development of an enlightened and responsible citizenry and their inclusion of a
wide variety of disciplines echoed some of Luther's love of the liberal arts,
such schools did not fall within the traditional patterns of European higher
education.

In content, method, and purpose they were also unique in the American
scene in the late 19th century. Contrary to the rising emphasis upon the practical and vocational in both secondary and higher education, they sought instead
to introduce students to great ideas and personalities in history and literature
and thereby to awaken both mind and spirit. Rather than books and recitations
they made extensive use of the lecture as a means of instruction. They set no
examinations, established no grades, awarded no diplomas. Their openness to
both men and women and their focus on adult education anticipated the future.

Since most of the early leaders among Danish immigrants were products
of such schools in Denmark, it was quite natural that the first educational institutions they established in America followed the model they knew best. Beginning in 1878 in Elk Horn, Iowa, a scattered network of folk schools marked the
location of Danish settlements from Michigan to California. Only a few, however, survived more than a brief time. Faced with the necessity of developing a
native ministry for the increasing number of Danish congregations, both Danish Lutheran groups turned to the educational pattern adopted by other immigrant churches, the theological seminary and its accompanying multipurpose
preparatory schools.[12]

For the first decade of its life the "Danish Church" had been supplied
with clergy by the Commission in Denmark. Most of their pastors had been
trained in mission schools or at the Askov Folk School in a special two-year
theological course designed to prepare young men for service in America. In
1886 the synod decided to establish its own seminary and invited Thorvald

Helveg, a graduate of the theological faculty at Copenhagen, to be its first professor. The building of an already defunct folk school at West Denmark, Wisconsin, was purchased, and the seminary opened in 1887 with five students. In an honest effort to maintain the inclusive stance of the Danish Church, Helveg insisted that a second professor be appointed to represent the Inner Mission emphasis. Peter Sorensen Vig, later to become one of the most eminent Danish-American historians, became Helveg's colleague. But the doctrinal and personal tensions which would eventually split the Danish Church developed to such intensity that in 1891 the synod requested both men to resign, and the seminary closed.[13] Not until the schism of 1893–1894 had brought about the withdrawal of the Inner Mission faction was the Danish Church able to initiate the actions which resulted in the founding of Grand View College.

Grand View in Des Moines

In the expansionist climate of the 80s and 90s the church had no lack of offers from communities eager to invite the planting of a college in their midst. Encouraged by some leading Danish residents of Des Moines, Iowa, a real estate promoter named D. H. Kooker offered a building site consisting of one city block and a promise of $100 profit for each of 100 specified building lots sold in the Grand View addition of the city. Although there were no Danish congregations in Des Moines, the synod was attracted by the prospect of a free site and a $10,000 building fund.

The original intention simply to restore the West Denmark theological school blossomed into a far more expansive plan to establish "The Danish Evangelical Lutheran Church's University." Although such a concept reached far beyond both the resources of the Danish church and the scope of a Danish folk school, it nevertheless expressed the serious intent of the founders to enrich the stream of Lutheran higher education in America with the distinctive contribution of the Danish heritage. According to a pamphlet published to attract funds for an endowment, "The free-born Danish spirit craves a home for the freedom of the spirit; a home from whose gables shall wave the banner of spiritual freedom and from whose windows the view shall be clear and unhampered."[14]

The $10,000 building fund was never achieved. Nevertheless, in spite of the nationwide economic depression, enough lots were sold and enough pledges paid to ready the first wing of the college building for occupancy in October 1895. Yet another full year elapsed while the church sought a president for the school. At last, in September 1896, under the temporary leadership of Pastor N. P. Gravengaard, a graduate of the West Denmark seminary, the "school in Des Moines" opened, with one full-time residential student. Eight others straggled in during the fall term.

There was no structured curriculum; each student chose his classes and the teachers provided instruction at the level of each student's competence. The more advanced preseminary students met as a group for several classes. At least half of the 34 students who registered for the Winter Term came, in the spirit of the folk school, simply to broaden their general knowledge and to share in a cultural experience. They took no examinations. Another characteristic feature of the folk school which carried over was the daily lecture hour, attended by all students and addressed by faculty and visiting pastors on topics of broad cultural interest.

The first elected president of the college, Rasmus Rasmussen Vestergaard, came from Denmark to assume his responsibilities in October 1897. He was an honor graduate of the University of Copenhagen and had given private instruction in Latin, Hebrew, and religious philosophy. With his arrival the theological seminary began to function and the first candidate graduated in 1901.

However, Grand View College, as it came to be known at this time, retained its folk-school character. Its advertisements described it as "The Danish-American Youth School." Its catalogs listed three departments: the Academic School, for teacher training; the English Department, offering a preparatory course, a commercial course, a shorthand and typewriting course, and a first-grade certificate course; and the Seminary. But it was the traditional Winter School, a three-month term conducted on the folk-school pattern, which accounted for most of the growth of enrollments in the years before World War I.[15]

When President Vestergaard resigned suddenly in 1902, he was succeeded by a faculty colleague, Benedict Nordentoft, also a theological graduate of the University of Copenhagen. Although he professed his intention to continue Vestergaard's educational policies, Nordentoft presently published an article criticizing the inadequacy of the theological preparation received by Danish-American pastors. Those trained in Denmark, he wrote pointedly, received a "full intellectual schooling" under "prolonged academic tutoring and a subsequent thoroughgoing theological study at the university for about six years."[16]

One of Nordentoft's colleagues, Carl P. Höjberg, himself a university graduate but an ardent defender of Grundtvigian educational philosophy, rose in defense of Grand View's more liberal, less structured preparation for theological study. In a burst of Grundtvigian eloquence, he pleaded, "Let the sap flow freely in the stem, so that the leaves feel it! Shall the green tree rejoice at the sight of withered leaves? Bloom, thou Danish beechwood, in the name of the Lord, and let each of your leaves become a tongue!"[17] Pastors and congregations of the Danish Church viewed Nordentoft's attack on the Danish-American system of theological preparation as a disparagement of the folk-school principle. Criticism became so intense that he resigned as president of Grand View in 1910.

The theological seminary at Grand View continued to supply the Danish Church with pastors throughout the remaining years of the synod's independent existence. In 1962 it merged with three other seminaries to form the Lutheran School of Theology at Chicago. Grand View College continued as a modified folk school, gradually assuming the character of an American secondary school. In 1924, it offered its first college-level courses; in 1939 it was recognized as a standard two-year junior college. After expanding to a three-year program in 1968 it finally gained accreditation as a four-year baccalaureate college in 1975.

Beginnings in Blair

The collegiate program of the United Danish Evangelical Lutheran Church found expression in Dana College at Blair, Nebraska. The emergence of Dana, however, was the result of the merging of two institutions of differing origins and purposes, Trinity Seminary of the Blair Church and Elk Horn College of the North Church.

When the Blair Church was organized in September 1884, one of its first official actions was to elect an education committee to lay plans for a theological school. When the committee was unable to secure a theological professor from Denmark, its members prevailed on the committee chairman, Anton Marius Andersen, a parish pastor and a graduate of Augsburg Seminary, to accept the appointment. During the previous year Andersen had moved his residence to Blair, one of seven preaching points in his rural parish. Because of its location at a Missouri River crossing and at the intersection of two railway lines, Blair was the acknowledged hub of transportation for northeastern Nebraska and western Iowa. In the two-story brick parsonage which he built, Andersen began theological instruction of four young men in the fall of 1884.[18]

When a local real estate developer offered a building site and half of the $6000 projected cost of a building, Blair was also chosen as the permanent location for Trinity Seminary. While instruction continued in the Andersen parsonage, a fund-raising effort was launched among the Danish congregations. In October 1886 an imposing four-story brick building containing classrooms, an apartment for the professor, and accommodations for 40 students was dedicated, debt free.[19]

As in other early Lutheran theological schools students varied greatly in age and academic background. Much of the instruction was therefore given on the preparatory level. Theological students serving as part-time instructors taught courses in English grammar, mathematics, and history. Enrollments were small and financial problems plagued the new seminary from the beginning. The Danish farmers who had shown themselves willing to provide funds for the erection of a building were far less keen to support the operation of the school which they felt ought to be self-supporting. Under the continuing burden of his parish duties and the heavy teaching load at the seminary, Andersen finally resigned in 1887. His $50-per-month salary was seven months in arrears.

After a year during which theological instruction lapsed for lack of a professor, Gottlieb Bender Christiansen, one of the six founders of the synod, accepted the position. His enthusiastic leadership brought an increase in enrollment and the synod responded by adding another wing to the building to accommodate the larger numbers. By 1896 a total of 327 students had attended Trinity, 23 of whom graduated in theology and entered the ministry.[20]

In 1896 the merger of the Blair Church with the North Church brought Elk Horn College into the new United Danish Church and with it two of the most colorful and controversial personalities of early Danish American Lutheranism. Kristian Anker was born in Denmark, attended folk schools, and received his theological training at the Askov school before emigrating to the United States in 1881. After serving briefly in south Chicago, he was called to the Elk Horn parish in western Iowa where the first Danish folk school had been established in 1878. Anker directed the school for 17 years, even rebuilding it after fire destroyed the building in 1887. In 1890 he bought the school from the Danish Church, intending to change it into a combination academy and normal college that would offer broader educational services to the community. Since there was no local public high school, Elk Horn College offered high school, business, and college preparatory courses for both men and women. It also conducted special courses in English for Danish immigrants.

Shortly before the schism in the Danish Church occurred in 1893, Kristian Anker sold the school to a group of pastors who subsequently became the nucleus of the seceding North Church. Anker himself remained in charge of the academy and college programs, but a theological department was added. P. S. Vig, whose outspoken anti-Grundtvigianism had earlier resulted in the controversy that closed the West Denmark seminary of the Danish Church, was called as professor.

Two years later a merger of the North Church and the Blair Church brought both the Elk Horn school and Trinity Seminary into the newly formed United Danish Church. It was quickly decided that two seminaries were not needed, that theological study should be concentrated at Trinity in Blair, and that all preparatory work should be given at Elk Horn. P. S. Vig was called to Blair as president and professor of theology while Anker remained in charge of the college at Elk Horn. However, since Vig had already agreed to teach at Elk Horn during the 1896–1897 school year, the synod agreed to move all instruction to Elk Horn and the building at Blair stood vacant for one full year. In 1897 Vig and the seminary returned to Blair.[21]

The Emergence of Dana College

Two years later, in the interest of economy, the synod also moved the academy and college departments from Elk Horn to Blair, thus bringing the two synodical schools together under the same roof. With this move in 1899 the identity of Dana College as a distinct institution emerged. A catalog issued in 1899 carried the name Blair College and Theological Seminary. Name changes occurred in three successive catalogs until in 1903 a convention report declared, "The name of the school of the synod shall be Dana College and Trinity Seminary."[22]

After three years as president of Trinity Seminary, the restless Vig returned in 1899 to the parish in Elk Horn. At the same time, when Elk Horn College moved to Blair, Kristian Anker became president of both college and seminary. During the next six years in Blair, Anker reorganized the academy and college programs, placing them on a broader basis than either a Danish folk-school or a purely pretheological preparatory school.

The combined institutions offered eight different departments, including the seminary, a four-year seminary preparatory course, a two-year college preparatory course, and a normal course. The college department listed a classical course leading to the B.A. degree and a scientific course leading to a B.S. degree. In 1899, however, only 4 of the 96 students were listed as degree students and even these did not proceed beyond two years. Dana awarded its first bachelor's degree in 1922.

In keeping with Anker's intention to prepare students for participation in American society, instruction in the college was given in English. "We realize," he wrote in the catalog of 1900–1901, "that every person living in this country should be able to fully understand and speak the adopted language."

When Anker left Dana in 1905, his letter of resignation identified the most persistent of Dana's problems during its early years in Blair. His basic complaint was simply that there were "too many running the school."[23] Governing authority for both the college and the seminary was vested in a "joint board," composed of the synod board of trustees and an institutional board of directors. In practice, however, even decisions involving small and petty problems of the school were made by delegates to the annual synod conventions.[24]

A further hazard to sound administration was the ambiguous relationship between college and seminary. From the beginning it was never clear whether they were separate institutions sharing the same campus or whether they were a single institution. Throughout the 57 years of their relationship, from 1899 to 1956, joint and separate presidencies alternated eight times.[25]

Part of the continuing problem was the great discrepancy in size between the seminary and the college. In early years from 1899 to 1910 seminary enrollment was very small, hovering between 4 and 11 students. During the same period college enrollment rose from 90 to 172. Only rarely during its years in Blair did seminary enrollment reach as high as 20. In his resignation letter of 1905 Vig explained that he could not "in good conscience continue each month to accept a salary in order to teach in a seminary that has as many teachers as it has pupils and no prospect of improvement in the next few years."[26] The necessity of utilizing seminary faculty to teach college classes also made administrative clarity more difficult, and led to personal tensions and frequent charges that the college was being favored over the seminary.

Moreover, during the first decades of the century there was no regular system of financial support. Delegates expected the school to pay its own way. Annual requests to the synod from the school at Blair for budgetary aid were only grudgingly received. In a burst of frustration President C. X. Hansen reminded the synod in 1912 that the college was not an investment company, paying dividends in dollars and cents, but the institution upon which the church depended to provide its lay and clergy leadership. Nevertheless, deficits continued to mount. Finally, in 1917 on the 400th anniversary of the Reformation, a massive appeal was mounted throughout the synod for the retirement of the accumulated debt of $60,000. The success of this effort opened the way for the physical expansion and the academic growth of the college during the 1920s.

However, basic uncertainties concerning institutional structure and purpose continued to hinder the development of Dana College. Proposals to separate the college and the seminary were periodically discussed, but were consistently resisted by the seminary. Finally, in 1956, in anticipation of the pending merger with the American Lutheran Church and the Evangelical Lutheran Church, the synod voted to relocate Trinity Seminary on the campus of Wartburg Seminary in Dubuque, Iowa. Meanwhile, Dana's efforts to secure accreditation met with repeated disappointment. Only in 1957, the year after its separate identity was finally established, was Dana able to attain the long-sought approval of the North Central Association.

The Divided Danish Tradition

Probably to a greater extent than in any of the other Scandinavian immigrant groups, the impact of the Danish tradition in the life of the church and in Lutheran higher education was weakened by internal division. Differing Lutheran emphases that found shelter under the broad canopy of the state church of Denmark were crystallized by strong-minded leadership into separate denominations in the individualistic free-church climate of America. Fewer in numbers than either the Swedish or Norwegian immigration, the Danes could ill afford the fragmentation which occurred.

The educational institutions they established remained small, with limited constituencies and resources. They have served their own support groups well, supplying pastors and lay leaders for the churches and facilitating the transition of a generation of immigrants into the American society. But, unfortunately, they have not been able to transmit effectively into the American experience the unique educational and cultural contributions of their Danish heritage.

The Coming of the Finns

Finnish immigrants were among the earliest and the latest of European Lutherans to settle in North America. As many as 75% of the Swedish colonists on the Delaware between 1638 and 1655 may have been "Swedish" Finns. By the 19th century when the vagaries of European politics placed Finland under Russian rather than Swedish rule, Finns played a role among the Russian colonists in Alaska. It was a Finnish Lutheran pastor, Uno Cygnaeus, who ministered to the settlement of Finns, Germans, and Swedes in Sitka from 1840 to 1845.[27]

In the years following the Civil War employment in the copper mines of northern Michigan, the ore docks of Lake Erie, and the construction crews of western railroads drew modest numbers of job-hungry Finns. But major migrations did not occur until the 1890s, and especially after 1899, when the "Russification" policies of Czar Nicholas II, begun in the 1880s, became oppressive. Faced with the loss of their constitutional freedoms, many of them displaced by economic changes accompanying industrialization, thousands of Finns left their homeland. Between 1893 and 1918, 303,460 Finns flocked into North America. The largest concentrations were around the Great Lakes, especially in northern Michigan, Wisconsin, and Minnesota, but Finnish settlers found their way into almost every part of the United States and Canada.[28]

The impact of the church in North America on this large group of Finnish immigrants was relatively small. Most of the Finns who emigrated between 1900 and 1914 were already alienated from the church in Finland. As farmers and laborers dispossessed through the agricultural and industrial revolutions of the late 19th century, they had found little sympathy from the established church, and many had turned instead to the popular gospel of socialism.[29]

Varieties of Finnish Lutheranism

Those immigrants who were sympathetic to the church carried with them a loyalty to one or another of the revival groups which had dominated Finnish religious life since the 1840s. While these groups operated as "movements" within the inclusive structure of the "folk church" in Finland, they became independent congregations or denominations in the free-church society of North America, competing with each other for the support of an already limited segment of the Finnish population.

Three such organizations were formed to minister to the spiritual needs of Finnish Americans. One stemmed from the strongly lay-oriented revival movement which arose in the 1840s among the Lapps and the Finns in northern Sweden under the preaching of Lars Laestadius. Several independent congregations of Laestadians in North America eventually formed a national body called the Finnish Apostolic Lutheran Church. Another group, the Finnish-American National Evangelical Lutheran Church, originated in 1898 as a reaction to the centralizing tendencies of the Suomi Synod. The National Church identified itself with a movement within the Church of Finland called the Evangelicals, and many years later, in 1965, became a part of the Lutheran Church–Missouri Synod.

Of the three groups the largest and most directly representative of the churchly tradition in Finland was the Suomi Synod. Its founder was Juho Kustaa Nikander (1855–1919), a graduate of the University of Helsinki, strongly influenced by the rising missionary movement within the Finnish church. He came to Calumet, Michigan, in 1885, as pastor for three congregations which had been served by Pastor Alfred Backman since 1876. Backman had returned to Finland in broken health after seven years of struggling with sectarianism, indifference, and outright enmity toward the church.[30]

Five years later 4 pastors and 16 laymen representing 9 congregations met in Trinity Church[31] in Calumet and organized the Suomi Synod. They adopted a constitution, rejecting sectarian exclusivism and affirming the evangelical Lutheran character of the synod. Pastor Nikander was elected president.

During its early years the synod based its missionary efforts among the widely scattered Finns in America on its claim to represent the extension of the traditional Church of Finland in North America. Indeed, between 1890 and 1930 more than 50 pastors of the Church of Finland served within the Suomi Synod.[32] That 34 of them returned to Finland suggests in addition that there was a considerable difference between the ecclesiastical climate of the mother church and the congregational democracy which flourished among the Finns in North America. It also made clear to synod leadership that for a dependable supply of clergy they must develop a local program of theological education.

Suomi College in Hancock

The first initiative for the founding of a school came through the columns of a religious periodical established by three Finnish pastors in 1889. Their initial appeal was for pastors and teachers for the summer church schools, but the prospect of training in English and other practical subjects that would provide young people with the tools for progress won even wider popular support. One of the decisions of the constituting convention of the Suomi Synod in 1890 called for the establishment of an academy and a seminary, and named a committee to select a location.[33]

Sites in Minnesota, Ohio, Wisconsin, and Michigan were considered. On September 8, 1896, the synod made its decision to open Suomi College in temporary facilities in Hancock, on Michigan's upper peninsula, in the heart of the strong Finnish constituency of the copper country. Juho K. Nikander, the synod president, was also elected to the presidency of the college, a position he held for almost 25 years.

The direction of the school was placed in the hands of an 11-member board. The educational program was essentially that of an academy, providing preparation for college and eventually for theological study but also offering practical business and commercial courses. The school was coeducational from the beginning, its opening enrollment including 15 boys and 7 girls. Most of the early teachers had both training and teaching experience in Finland. Local high school teachers gave some assistance as part-time instructors in English.

By the fall of 1904 seven young men had completed the full seven-year course at the college and were the first to enroll in the two-year theological course of Suomi Theological Seminary. By 1919, 28 pastors had been prepared for the Suomi Synod. For more than 50 years the seminary functioned as a separate department of the college. In 1958, in anticipation of the 1962 merger creating the Lutheran Church in America, it merged with the Chicago Lutheran Seminary at Maywood, Illinois.

A new era began in 1920 with the election of Dr. John Wargelin to the presidency. During the administration of the founding president, Dr. Nikander, Suomi was essentially an Old World institution using Finnish as its language of instruction and serving as a symbol of loyalty to the Finnish tradition in America.

Celebrating the new phase in its life, Suomi introduced a junior college program for the first time in 1923 and at the same time terminated its preparatory department. While it continued to operate strong commercial and music programs, its future focus would be on collegiate and seminary education.

Beginning in 1920 under Wargelin's leadership, Suomi expanded its horizons and sought to meet the standards of training for its faculty which were required for the recognition of its collegiate offerings. It sought financial stability through fund-raising campaigns for buildings and endowment. These steps were not undertaken without vigorous protests from those in the synod who wished to preserve Suomi as a symbol of the old Finnish heritage. As late as 1926 the synod convention passed resolutions specifying that all religious instruction be given in Finnish and that instructors hired should be able to speak Finnish, "as far as possible."[34]

The addition of the condition, "as far as possible," indicated that the Suomi Synod, too, realized that the old order had passed, and that its college was no longer able to serve as a Finnish bulwark against Americanization. It would continue, however, as a conservator of the Finnish-American heritage and an interpreter of Finnish culture far into the 20th century, maintaining close relationships with ecclesiastical and governmental agencies in Finland.[35]

But as a distinctive church-related American junior college, Suomi has also reached beyond its historic constituency to offer educational opportunities to young men and women of widely varied ethnic and national traditions. During the 1960s it developed cross-cultural programs involving black students from metropolitan Detroit and groups of students from the United States trust territories of Micronesia. Supplementing its own resources with a variety of church- and government-sponsored programs, Suomi has intentionally sought to enroll economically disadvantaged young people and to develop programs that enable them to qualify for further college study or for paraprofessional positions. As the only two-year institution affiliated with the Lutheran Church in America, Suomi receives its annual operational grant from a churchwide agency, the Division for Mission in North America, rather than from any single regional synod.

15 EMERGING PATTERNS IN LUTHERAN HIGHER EDUCATION, 1865–1914

An Age of Revolutions

The half-century between the Civil War and World War I was a period of revolutionary change in almost every aspect of American life. The nation emerged in 1865 from a war ending slavery and establishing the permanence of the Union. A northern victory, based in large part on industrial superiority, projected the nation into a period of unprecendented expansion. Under the leadership of a legendary generation of empire builders the continent was spanned by a network of railroads. Steel mills, oil wells and refineries, coal and copper mines became the hallmarks of industrial progress.

An agricultural revolution of equal proportion took place as the great West was flooded by waves of Civil War veterans, southern exiles, new immigrants, and fortune hunters. The government's generosity—expended equally upon railroad builders and individual settlers—brought land and people together. Grants to the transcontinental railroads represented the largest government subsidy ever given to private enterprise: 10 square miles of land for each mile of track laid and construction loans of $16,000 to $48,000 per mile. The Homestead Act of 1862 offered 160 acres of land to anyone who would settle on it for five years. Agents of the railroads opened offices in every eastern city and European seaport, offering free rail tickets to prospective purchasers of choice acreages—with assured access to markets.

In the later decades of the 19th and the early 20th centuries the midcentury immigrants from northern Europe were joined by Italians, Poles, Greeks, and Russians. These new arrivals congregated in the cities and became the labor force for mines, mills, and factories. Between 1860 and 1910 almost

23,000,000 immigrants poured into the United States[1] and the total population of the nation reached 92,000,000, a threefold increase in 50 years.

The years following the Civil War not only witnessed economic revolution and population explosion but deep social and intellectual ferment as well. The rural democracy of prewar America was threatened by a growing cleavage between the wealthy and the poor, both in cities and on farms. Social consciences were stimulated to demand economic and social reforms, while the Puritan ethic proclaimed that God's blessing rested upon the wealthy. And the growing power of the youthful nation was interpreted as a sign of God's favor and a divine mandate to enlighten and redeem the whole world.

Into this kaleidoscopic America came also the largest influx of Lutherans ever to enter the continent. Pre–Civil War migrations were small in comparison. After 1870 they streamed in by the hundreds of thousands. Great numbers of them mingled with their third and fourth generation Americanized cousins who had sold their Pennsylvania or Ohio farms and moved west to claim the benefits of the Homestead Act. Still others brought their skills and their will to work into the mines and factories. All of them enriched the ethnic mix and the cultural variety of their adopted land. Through their churches and their schools they gave institutional expression to the most cherished aspects of their Old World traditions.

Between 1865 and 1914 Lutherans established 26 schools in the United States and Canada which would persist into the late 20th century as collegiate institutions. The distinctive circumstances surrounding the origin of many of them have already been recounted. Notwithstanding their strong ethnic character and religiously oriented purposes, all of them were profoundly influenced by the powerful social and economic forces that were shaping their adopted land.

The Civil War itself had significant effect upon the 10 Lutheran colleges already in operation, some in the North and some in the South. The exodus of young men to military service cut deeply into the enrollments of all colleges and resulted in the closing of two southern schools, Newberry and North Carolina College. The buildings and campus of Gettysburg College sustained severe war damage. Newberry's physical plant was a total loss. Concordia College in St. Louis closed briefly and was moved to Fort Wayne, Indiana, for the safety of its younger students. Luther College in Decorah, Iowa, owed its founding in 1861 to the tensions over slavery which brought on the Civil War.

The expansion of the railroads in the post–Civil War period was a major factor in drawing Lutheran immigrants into the states of Minnesota, Iowa, Kansas, Nebraska, and the Dakotas. Railroads also played a direct role in the founding and location of several Lutheran colleges. An offer of land by the Illinois Central induced Augustana to locate in Paxton, Illinois, in 1863. An immigration agent with close ties to the Chicago, Milwaukee, and St. Paul Railroad invited the Norwegian branch of Augustana at Marshall, Wisconsin, to locate in Canton, in the Dakota Territory, in 1881. Founders of Midland College chose Atchison, Kansas, in 1887, because of that city's promise as a future rail center.

Few events in the economic life of the nation have had such direct effect upon the development of Lutheran colleges in the West as the financial panic of 1893 and the depression that followed. The panic was preceded by a period of economic overexpansion accompanied by a nationwide wave of land speculation. Schools as widely separated as Upsala in New Jersey, and Pacific Lutheran in Tacoma, Grand View in Des Moines, and Wartburg in Clinton, Iowa, acquired their campuses through real estate developers who promised them commissions on the sale of lots adjoining the college campus.

While each of these schools managed to survive the deflation of land values which occurred when the speculative bubble burst, they all labored for many years thereafter under the heavy burdens of construction debts and frequently the ill will of individuals who had responded to the sales programs sponsored by the colleges. Quite apart from land speculation, every college in the land suffered financially in the wake of the disaster of 1893.

The Revolution in Education

In the latter years of the century Lutheran colleges also shared in a revolution which profoundly altered the character and content of American higher education. The standard classical pattern which had dominated the curricula of American colleges from their beginning came under direct attack.

Under this curriculum college students were tradtionally faced with a prescribed sequence of courses, usually including four years of Latin and Greek, mathematics, rhetoric, natural philosophy, and a capstone course on mental and moral philosophy given by the president. Most Lutheran colleges established before the Civil War included some courses in science and a few offered limited options in modern languages. But because their founding purpose had been to provide a strong basis in biblical languages for the study of theology, all of them retained a central emphasis on the standard curriculum.

The leader of the postwar attack on the rigidly prescribed course of study was Charles W. Eliot, who became president of Harvard in 1869. Beginning in 1872 he announced that Harvard seniors would have full freedom of course selection. In 1884 he extended the principle to include sophomore and junior classes, and eventually, with the exception of a course in rhetoric, to freshman as well.

Eliot's action touched off a chorus of protest from defenders of the status quo who declared the elective system to be "about as wise as to allow a sick man to select his own medicines."[2] Nevertheless, with the exception of those schools that deliberately limited themselves to preministerial education, diversification gradually made its way into all college curricula, Lutheran as well as others. At first, fully prescribed courses parallel with the standard classical course were introduced. In 1874 Gettysburg College offered a bachelor of science degree for the first time, substituting chemistry for Greek. Roanoke's scientific course, established in 1880, omitted Greek and included courses in modern languages, mathematics, and natural sciences. Augustana in Rock Island announced three parallel tracks in the early 1880s: classical, scientific, and classical-mathematical.

One of the earliest Lutheran colleges to permit electives within the classical course was Wittenberg in 1883. By 1890 several others had given conditional approval, offering specified options to juniors and seniors. President Swensson of Bethany College assured the Kansas Conference of the Augustana Synod in 1896, "We have not fallen for the elective system." But a decade later, his successor acknowledged "pressure from the outside to follow the modern tendency by permitting some freedom of choice among areas and within subjects."[3] Theologically oriented institutions such as Augsburg and Luther resisted the trend until the early 1920s, and loyalty to a prescribed curriculum persisted within the Missouri system until after World War II.

The most revolutionary educational development between the Civil War and World War I was the rise of the modern American university. Its emergence was in part the expression of the demand of educational reformers that higher education serve the "real life" needs of a practical and democratic society. No public event signaled this demand more clearly than the passage of the Morrill Act of 1862 by the United States Congress. Through a direct federal subsidy of 30,000 acres of public land for each congressman and senator, states were encouraged to establish institutions of higher learning for the promotion of agricultural and mechanical arts. The new emphasis was upon usefulness rather than mental discipline, upon democracy rather than aristocracy in higher education, upon the sciences rather than the classical languages.

To this demand for vocational and utilitarian education was added the rising respect for the research-oriented German universities which since early in the century had been attracting increasing numbers of young American scholars. Returning with Ph.D. degrees from Leipzig and Berlin, Göttingen and Jena, they urged the adoption of the investigative methods associated with the new understanding of science.

The American university, however, did not emerge as a well-defined institution patterned after a European model. It developed primarily as a response to popular demands for advanced training in new fields of learning and service which the collges were unwilling or unable to enter. The German university supplied the impulse to include a graduate faculty of arts and sciences which would award the Ph.D. degree, but the American version of a university could include an undergraduate college, a school of business, a teachers college, a scientific institute, or a college of agriculture, as well as a graduate school of arts and sciences. The founding of Johns Hopkins University in 1876 as a graduate institution dedicated to the development of the Ph.D. degree was an attempt to re-create the German model in America, but it also felt obliged to include an undergraduate program.

Meanwhile, in the flush of educational expansion some small colleges also aspired to university status merely by the change of name or by the awarding of advanced degrees. Upon its achievement of full baccalaureate status in 1894, the Missionary Institute assumed the name of Susquehanna University. The awarding of master of arts degrees to graduates if after two or three years they were engaged in literary or educational endeavors was a common practice among colleges. By 1890 course requirements and often a thesis as well were introduced. From 1888 to 1910 Augustana College in Rock Island granted a total of 50 master's degrees. Between 1869 and 1900, Gettysburg College awarded 20 Ph.D. degrees; Thiel granted six.

But the influence of the university upon Lutheran higher education was not primarily as a structural model. The strong commitment of the older Lutheran colleges to theological preparation deterred them from venturing very far beyond a traditional four-year undergraduate program. However, as their collegiate enrollments grew and their curricula became more diversified they turned to the graduate programs of the new universities as resources for the training of new faculty.

Early Lutheran colleges were almost entirely staffed by clergy, many of whom were well qualified in ancient and modern languages, philosophy, mathematics, and—in several instances—also in the natural sciences. Even before the Civil War a few colleges were able to engage faculty with European doctorates. But after the American universities began to offer doctoral programs, increasing numbers of Lutheran college graduates found their way both to eastern and midwestern graduate schools and subsequently joined Lutheran college faculties.

One of the most significant effects of the new state universities, especially in the Midwest, was the promotion of the public high school as a clearly defined link in the American democratic system of public education. Beginning with the University of Michigan in 1870, midwestern state universities introduced a system of certifying public schools whose curricula would qualify graduates for college admission.

Four-year public high schools conforming to standards established by state universities developed rapidly after 1880, especially in the Midwest. Not

only did the four-year high schools add a second level abov
mon school to the American system of public education; th
growing reservoir of potential students for the new public u
private colleges as well. Small church academies and prepai
were no longer the only source for church college recruits. F
of midwestern Scandinavian Lutheranism which had chosen secondary schools
rather than parochial schools as the institutional focus of their religious education program, the rise of the public high school forced a painful reassessment
of educational policy. As enrollment in the academies declined, most of them
were obliged to close, while the most vigorous made a gradual transition to
two- and four-year colleges.

Even those schools which maintained the six- or seven-year German-style
gymnasium gradually adjusted both their structure and their terminology to
conform to the American distinction between high school and college. President Lauritz Larsen urged the separation of the preparatory and collegiate departments at Luther College in 1879 ''in order to comply with the general plan
of the American college.''[4] Augsburg extended its preparatory department to a
four-year course in 1910. In 1920 the Missouri preparatory schools abandoned
the terminology of the German gymnasium and began to describe its six-year
course as four years of high school and two years of junior college.

One of the issues which gained prominence in American higher education
through the influence of the German university was that of academic freedom.
As a necessary adjunct to scientific research and experimentation, the German
university professor asserted the right to *Lehrfreiheit*, freedom to expound his
findings even when they might seem to contradict generally accepted views.
The issue was not entirely foreign to American college experience. Conflicts
caused by the rise of Darwinian science resulted in the dismissal of a few faculty members by southern universities in the 1870s and 1880s, though there is no
indication that evolution was a controversial issue in any Lutheran college before World War I.[5]

Many of the new universities, however, which had been handsomely endowed by the philanthropy of the new industrial and banking fortunes were in
no position to defend their outspoken professors, especially social scientists.
Edward W. Bemis, economist at the University of Chicago, was dismissed in
1894 for attacking the railroads during the Pullman strike. Edward A. Ross, so-
ciologist at Leland Stanford, disapproved of coolie labor which had built the
Central Pacific Railroad, and, at Mrs. Stanford's insistence, was summarily
fired in 1900. Economic nonconformity was dangerous fare for university professors at the turn of the century.[6]

In a case receiving national attention in 1910 a Lutheran college president
took a strong stand for academic freedom in defense of a young history profes-

.r on his faculty. Herman J. Thorstenberg, a graduate of Bethany College with a doctorate from Yale, joined the faculty of Roanoke College in 1907. For his introductory course in American history, he selected a popular textbook by Henry W. Elson, a graduate and later president of Thiel College and holder of a Ph.D. from the University of Pennsylvania.

A freshman student, the daughter of Judge William Moffett of the 20th Judicial Circuit of Virginia, enrolled in the course. While confined to his home during a period of illness the judge picked up a copy of his daughter's history text and was incensed by the passages which he read concerning slavery, John Brown, and the Confederacy in the Civil War. Moffett complained to President John Morehead, also a Virginian, who discussed the matter with Thorstenberg; Morehead then advised Moffett that the professor would deal fairly with the sensitive issues. The judge was not satisfied. He withdrew his daughter from the class and from the college and assailed Thorstenberg in a series of eloquent but intemperate letters. Morehead stood by the right of Thorstenberg to select his own textbooks and tried to point out that a professor did not necessarily endorse everything within the covers of any assigned book. Moffett, however, enlisted the southern press, the Confederate Veterans, and the Daughters of the Confederacy in a bitter attack on Thorstenberg and Morehead and the college. Although Thorstenberg finally withdrew the text from class usage, he did so out of deference to community feelings, not in acknowledgment of the truth of Judge Moffett's charges.

The formal statement of President Morehead at the conclusion of the controversy failed to win plaudits from the constituents of Roanoke College, but it stands as one of the landmarks in the defense of academic integrity in American higher education: "There cannot be loyalty to the truth in scholarly work without freedom to investigate, to think, to review all phases of a subject—the truths, the half-truths, and the untruths about it—and to form and to express independent judgments. This is the principle of academic freedom."[7]

Student Life under Lutheran Auspices

Student life and activities on Lutheran campuses also underwent significant changes between the Civil War and World War I. Some of them were reflections of general trends among American colleges; others were expressions of the particular backgrounds and traditions from which both students and college came.

Shared with virtually all of American college education in the late 19th century was the paternalistic stance toward student behavior. From supervision of study hours and the use of the recitation method in the classroom to restrictions on unauthorized absences from dormitories and prohibitions on visitation of pool halls, bars, and theaters, student conduct was tightly regimented. Ten years after the Civil War Harvard was still listing eight pages of regulations, even prohibiting students from leaving the campus on Sunday without permission or loitering in groups anywhere on college property.[8] At about the same time, Concordia College at Fort Wayne listed 18 house rules, equally explicit, promulgated on the authority of the Fourth Commandment.[9] In a section of its 1888 catalog labeled "Discipline," Gustavus Adolphus College advised that "the authorities of the school endeavor to rule by love rather than fear," but gave assurance the "punishment will be the sure consequence of transgression." Stipulated transgressions included "dancing, card playing and other games of chance, the use of intoxicating drinks, profane and obscene language, smoking and chewing in the buildings, and visiting disreputable places."

Until the growing size of the student bodies brought about the appointment of additional supervisory personnel, eventually called deans of men or preceptresses and deans of women, the president or a faculty member was responsible for student conduct. Crowded and ill-equipped dormitories and barracks-style cuisine were as productive of student frustration and complaint in the 19th century as in the 20th. Student strikes and campus protests were frequent occurrences. At Gettysburg in 1861 Henry Warren Roth, a senior student and later president of Thiel College, led a boycott of graduation exercises because the faculty awarded honors to the second in the class rather than the first. In 1894 in the aftermath of a three-day student strike at Thiel the president was booed at the commencement exercises and pelted with "torpedoes" when he appeared on Main Street. The minutes of college faculty meetings in these years devote much greater space to cases of student discipline than to issues of academic substance.

On the more constructive side, student activity in the colleges of the 19th century found expression in a variety of voluntary organizations. Of special significance in every Lutheran college were the literary societies. Those at Gettysburg College, for example, actually preceded the establishment of the college itself, having been organized by the students of the Gettysburg Gymnasium in 1831. The purpose of the societies was partly social, but they were primarily intended to provide opportunity for reading, discussion, and debate on wide-ranging topics and for the cultivation of public expression. Colleges usually maintained at least two societies to encourage interaction and competition.

Students took great pride in furnishing and equipping the rooms made available by the college, and developed libraries which in the earliest years were often larger and more current than the college libraries. The weekly meetings of the literary societies provided a forum for the kind of independent thought and expression which was impossible in the recitation-bound procedures of the college classroom. The societies adopted constitutions, colors, and mellifluous Greek names such as Chrestomathian or Phrenokosmian. As the curricula of the colleges became more diversified and the classroom methods less rigid, the role of the societies became less important. By the 1920s most of the literary societies had either disappeared or been transformed into social organizations.

The national fraternity movement that became popular among American colleges in the 1830s made its initial appearance on a Lutheran campus in 1855 when a chapter of Phi Kappa Psi was established at Gettysburg College. Several other national fraternities organized chapters after the Civil War, at Gettysburg, Roanoke, Wittenberg, Thiel, and Susquehanna. The movement, however, did not win acceptance at most Lutheran colleges founded after 1865, largely because of the theologically based objections of the churches to secret societies. Citing the secrecy and ritualism employed by the fraternities as an adaptation of Masonic practice, boards of trustees and church conventions discouraged or prohibited the organization of national fraternities on their campuses. Nevertheless, in the colleges where they were already established, fraternities served an important role in the social life of the students, developing relationships which persisted beyond graduation into both the personal and professional lives of their members.

In addition to literary societies and fraternities student interests expressed themselves through a wide variety of organizations and activities. Augustana's Linnean Society, founded in 1891, gathered students interested in science. Each of the Scandinavian colleges developed organizations devoted to the culture of the land of their origin. St. Olaf had its Edda society in 1902; Bethany its Svea in 1899; Dana its Dannebrog in 1879.

Every Lutheran campus had its local religious organizations for Bible study, prayer, and foreign mission outreach. Beginning in 1867 at Gettysburg College, campus religious life found expression at several of the older Lutheran colleges through the YMCA, which had been organized in the United States in 1851. Wittenberg, Roanoke, and Carthage all established chapters before 1900. Through the intercollegiate department of the YMCA students at Roanoke became involved in the Student Volunteer Movement in 1886. Under the motto "The world for Christ, beginning at our own College," 38 Roanoke students committed themselves to Christian service. Two of them later became missionaries in India and three in Japan.

The strong musical tradition of the Lutheran church that became the hallmark of many Lutheran colleges during the 20th century found early expression through student choral and instrumental groups. The important place of music even in the earliest curricula for the preparation of parochial school teachers in the Missouri Synod fostered the formation of student choral groups. During the first year the teachers seminary was located in Addison, Illinois,

1864–1865, a student chorus walked several miles through the country to a church to give a concert.[10] A Silver Cornet Band established in 1874 was Augustana's first student musical group at the college, but the launching of the annual presentation of Handel's *Messiah* in 1879, a tradition still being honored, gave even stronger evidence of the appeal of music as a voluntary student activity. Although military and community bands were quite common in the early 19th century, the Luther College Band, organized by students in 1878, was one of the first college bands in America.[11] When F. Melius Christiansen came to St. Olaf College in 1903, his first musical venture was the refining of a voluntary student instrumental group into a disciplined concert band. It was not until 1912 that an organized choral group, making its first concert tour to Eau Claire, Wisconsin, was formally described as the St. Olaf Lutheran Choir.[12]

The Rise of Intercollegiate Athletics

There was, however, no aspect of extracurricular life which captured the enthusiasm of students as did athletics. Although the first recorded intercollegiate contest in America was a boat race in 1851 between the crews of Harvard and Yale on Lake Winnepesaukee, it was baseball that won general campus popularity in the decades immediately after the Civil War. One of the first Lutheran colleges "at bat" was Concordia in Fort Wayne, which in 1867 won a smashing 85–42 victory over the Athletic Baseball Club of Fort Wayne. The director of the college insisted that German terms be used in playing outside teams, but when he was presented with the 1868 English rule book and asked to translate it, he agreed to have the game played in English.[13] Most sports at Luther College were easily amenable to Norwegian, but the six teams which were fielded in 1877 also agreed that baseball had to be played in English. Andrew Veblen, brother of the economist Thorstein Veblen and a member of the Luther faculty, later credited the gradual Americanization of the college "partly to the influence of this, the national game."[14]

While it was never replaced, baseball was forced to yield center stage in the 1880s and 1890s to a national passion for football. Beginning as a kind of soccer or kicking game, it shifted to a modified version of English rugby with the kicking more or less subordinated to a running style. By the mid-80s football had become the standard intercollegiate sport. The resulting need for regulating athletic relations between colleges has been credited with introducing the practice of intercollegiate consultation to American higher education.[15]

Before the turn of the century Lutheran colleges were also scheduling intercollegiate contests. Gettysburg, Wittenberg, Susquehanna, Luther, Midland, Thiel, and St. Olaf fielded teams in the 1890s. Gustavus Adolphus,

Augustana at Rock Island, Concordia at Fort Wayne, and others followed in the early years of the 20th century.

Football, however, encountered a greater degree of opposition from college faculty, trustees, and church leaders than did the more gentlemanly game of baseball. The Synod of West Pennsylvania deplored the "serious interruptions of study," and also the "occasion of great moral evils" which accompanied all intercollegiate athletics.[16] In 1894 President Mohn at St. Olaf denounced football as "brutal." The Luther College faculty banned intercollegiate football in 1897 and did not reinstate it until 1919. Unimpressed by the prowess of the Augustana College football team in winning the Illinois Conference championship in 1905, the Augustana Synod convention instructed the college board to abolish all intercollegiate competition in football, basketball, and baseball.

Not all college authorities, however, were opposed to intercollegiate football. The older Lutheran schools in the East, closer to the nerve center of the sport, were able to avoid any ban on intercollegiate competition. A few presidents, such as Wittenberg's Samuel Ort, who himself had been a good rugby player in his college days, encouraged competition. John I. Woodruff, the Latin professor at Susquehanna, helped students organize their first football team in 1893, coached it, and occasionally filled in as right halfback. His colleague in Hebrew and biblical theology, Jacob Yutzy, held that football has "a most noble aim, a true purpose," namely, "to develop giants of Herculean physical strength" so that men could bear the burdens of life."[17]

There was, however, substantial cause for concern over the way the game was being played. In 1905, 18 American college students died of injuries received on the "battle fields." Even as staunch an advocate of "the strenuous life" as President Theodore Roosevelt was appalled. Brandishing his "big stick," he threatened to abolish the game entirely by executive order unless the colleges could play it "on a thoroughly clean basis."

By this time, however, most of the Lutheran colleges had placed their athletic programs under faculty control and were participating in collegiate conferences that established standards for the conduct of sports.[18] Several eastern schools employed professional coaches in the early 1890s. Thus, although critical voices were raised, none of the eastern colleges banned intercollegiate football.

In all the colleges, whether intercollegiate competition was permitted or not, sports of all kinds flourished. Students persisted in their demands for gymnasiums until trustees or church conventions responded. Basketball, track and field events, tennis, and gymnastics—all became popular both as intramural and intercollegiate sports.

In the face of growing pressures, bans on intercollegiate competition that restricted Lutheran colleges in the Midwest were gradually lifted. One of the staunchest supporters of the Augustana Synod's policy, President Peter Mattson of Gustavus Adolphus, reflected on the trend of the times. Weary of the battle, he wrote to synod president Eric Norelius in 1910, "I have more than once been ready to give up in the struggle against this worldly movement, intercollegiate athletics. There is dreadful pressure in this direction in our school world."[19]

The pressure continued to mount until in 1917 under Mattson's successor, O. J. Johnson, the ban of the synod was lifted. Gustavus Adolphus, like virtually every other Lutheran college, was ready to enter the "golden age of sports" which beckoned to American college education in the 1920s.

Lutheran Women in Higher Education

One of the most significant developments in all of American higher education in the late 19th century was the growth of collegiate education for women. This trend was evidenced not only in the expansion of the number of seminaries and colleges for women but most dramatically in the adoption of coeducation by an overwhelming majority of all institutions of higher learning. In 1865 only a handful of colleges were coeducational. By 1880, 30% admitted women, and 71% enrolled both men and women by 1900.[20]

Some of the earliest ventures in higher education for women were expressions of humanitarian movements of the pre–Civil War years that promoted such causes as women's rights, temperance, and antislavery. Oberlin College in Ohio enrolled four women in 1837 and thereby introduced coeducation to the American college scene. In 1838 the Pennsylvania legislature in a single omnibus bill simultaneously incorporated 25 female seminaries, investing each of them with degree-granting powers.[21] The Civil War itself summoned women into new roles in society, and the rapid expansion of the western frontier left little room for romantic legends concerning the "weaker sex." The establishment of the new public land-grant universities in the Midwest and the opening of college curricula to a variety of new disciplines offered educational opportunities not previously available to women. In many cases the needs of struggling colleges to bolster their enrollments also contributed to the growing attractiveness of coeducation.

The Lutheran concern for women's education antedates the Civil War. At least 14 female seminaries were in operation before 1860, scattered across seven states both in the North and the South. In the half-century following the Civil War about 20 more Lutheran seminaries and colleges for women were established, largely in the southern states. Most of them were founded privately by Lutheran pastors and laypersons and supported by tuitions and private gifts. In many cases they were recognized and recommended by Lutheran synods, but rarely were they under direct synodical sponsorship or control.

While most of the instruction was given on the secondary level, there were several schools that offered collegiate work and were authorized by state charters to grant academic degrees. Most of these did not exercise the privilege, but issued diplomas instead upon completion of prescribed courses of study. Until the introduction of accreditation procedures, the content of academic degrees varied widely among all colleges. One college for women in Pennsylvania, not Lutheran, felt it inappropriate for a female college to award a bachelor's degree and therefore bestowed upon its first two graduates in 1860 the degree of "Mistress of Liberal Arts" (M.L.A.).[22]

The first Lutheran college for women to grant the bachelor's degree was Irving College in Mechanicsburg, Pennsylvania. Founded by Methodists in 1856, it came under Lutheran direction in 1888. For more than 30 years it was governed by Lutheran trustees and served mostly Lutheran students. Between 1890 and 1920 it awarded 112 B.A. and 107 B.S. degrees. Elizabeth College, founded in 1897 in Charlotte, North Carolina, and later moved to Salem, Virginia, also granted more than 200 degrees before it was closed in 1922, when fire destroyed its main building.

Since the early motivation for higher education among Lutherans in America was the preparation of a learned clergy, the earliest Lutheran colleges began as all-male institutions. The first Lutheran school to adopt a policy of coeducation was the oldest of them all, Hartwick Seminary. In the fall of 1851 a new principal, the Reverend Levi Sternberg, established a "female department" in addition to the three-year preparatory and collegiate course and the theological course. With the enrollment of a class of 27 young women Hartwick became one of the first coeducational schools in the country. At the same time Sternberg appointed his sister-in-law, Charlotte Miller, as the first female member of the Hartwick faculty.

Thiel enrolled three young women in its initial class of five students in 1866 and thus became the first Lutheran college to begin operation as a coeducational institution.[23] When the Susquehanna Female College closed in 1872 the Missionary Institute opened its doors to women. Wittenberg followed in 1874. Gettysburg and Roanoke granted limited admission to women during the 1890s, but not until 1930 did Roanoke adopt a policy of full coeducation. Gettysburg delayed until 1935.

The Lutheran colleges of the Midwest that were primarily oriented to theological preparation remained as all-male institutions until well into the 20th century. Capital opened its doors to women in 1918, Augsburg in 1921, Wartburg in 1928. Luther yielded up "the old order" in 1936. After a one-year experiment with coeducation in 1881 Northwestern College returned its collegiate program permanently to an all-male status.[24] The Missouri Synod maintained an exclusively male system of education until 1919, when Concordia Teachers College at Seward, Nebraska, admitted the first females. Concordia Teachers College at River Forest did not admit women until 1938. Midwestern colleges such as St. Olaf, Bethany, Gustavus Adolphus, and Concordia in Moorhead, Minnesota, that originated late in the 19th century as academies with a focus on the general and practical training of immigrant youth were coeducational from their beginnings.

Mere access to higher education, whether through female colleges or through the expansion of coeducation, by no means assured women of equal opportunities in the educational system. In coeducational institutions the curriculum, especially courses leading to the baccalaureate degree, remained under male domination. A few courageous women undertook the classical course or one of the new literary or scientific courses which were becoming increasingly popular during the 1880s and 1890s. By far the largest number of women were attracted to the music departments and conservatories and to the normal departments offering one- or two-year courses preparing teachers for public elementary and secondary schools or for Lutheran parochial schools. Commercial courses in bookkeeping, accounting, and business skills blossomed, drawing female enrollments that in some cases enabled colleges to weather the depressed economic conditions of the early 1890s. In 1896, for example, Augustana College in Rock Island enrolled only 115 students in degree courses, but counted 287 in the music conservatory and school of business.[25]

The number of women completing degree courses remained very small during the entire period leading up to World War I. Among Lutheran coeducational colleges Carthage granted the first B.A. degree to a woman, Ida Harris, in 1874. She delivered the salutatory address in Latin. Thiel awarded degrees to four women in 1875. Midwestern schools which had begun as coeducational academies admitted women to college courses but awarded few degrees before 1914. In its first 16 college graduations from 1890 to 1905 St. Olaf awarded bachelor's degrees to 159 men but only six women.

Female faculty members teaching college courses in coeducational schools were also concentrated in music, art, and commercial courses. Wittenberg engaged its first female faculty member in 1887 when it opened its conservatory. During the following 13 years it employed seven women in music and seven in art. A few pioneer women graduates returned to teach English, Latin, or modern languages at their alma mater or some other Lutheran college. Dr. Inez Rundstrom, Augustana's first female graduate in 1887, continued her studies at Uppsala and Lund in Sweden and subsequently joined the faculty at Gustavus Adolphus. Four of St. Olaf's first six alumnae later became teachers at the college.[26]

College/Church Relationships

If the Lutheran churches and their educational institutions had been able to confer on the eve of World War I to review their life together during the preceding half-century, they would have had grounds for both amazement and gratification. The 50 years from 1865 to 1914 witnessed the greatest growth and expansion of the Lutheran church in North America since the first settlement of the continent. Lutheran immigrants from five European countries swarmed into the new land and spread across its vast territories, founding communities, churches, and schools. Twenty-six institutions of present or future collegiate rank had been established in the United States and Canada. Fourteen others founded before or during the Civil War were continuing to serve both old and new Lutherans.

All of them had served as conservators of the ethnic and linguistic traditions of their immigrant founders, but also as facilitators for the younger generation moving into the new American society. Among the Scandinavians of the Midwest who had quickly accepted the American common school, the Lutheran academies and colleges led the way in the adoption of English as the language of learning. The churches followed more slowly, retaining their European languages for worship and church affairs. Midwestern German groups committed to the parochial school and bolstered by the strong German nationalism of the later 19th-century immigrants clung tenaciously to their mother tongue until confronted by an equally aggressive American nationalism during World War I.

The five decades were marked not only by growth but also by tension, division, and conflict among the churches. Older issues of confessionalism gave way to new controversies over lodge membership and predestination. Norwegians and Germans, Danes and Finns disagreed among themselves and with each other. Neither the attempts of the General Council in 1867 nor of the Synodical Conference in 1872 had been able to gather the Lutheran family together. Even such closely knit bodies as the Norwegian Synod and the Missouri Synod were not able to avoid divisions. And the first successful step toward reunion by three separated Norwegian groups in 1890 was marred by a subsequent division creating the Lutheran Free Church.

In the pervasive theological controversies of the 19th century the institutions of the church were intimately involved. In almost every college the president was a clergyman and frequently himself a leader in the theological debates. Faculties and student bodies were almost entirely Lutheran. The question was never whether a college was estranged from the church but rather on which side of an "issue" the college stood. In some cases, as with St. Olaf and Augsburg in the late 1890s, the colleges themselves were the subjects of the controversy. Wittenberg and Gettysburg, the two colleges which had been most closely associated with the controversial "American Lutheranism" before the Civil War took positions during the 1890s which reflected a strengthening rather than a weakening of denominational loyalties. After an unsuccessful effort in 1893 by a few dissident trustees to unseat Dr. Luther A. Gottwald, a religion professor at Wittenberg College, for being too conservative theologically, President Samuel Ort and the board of trustees affirmed their support of Gottwald and the commitment of the institution to the unaltered Augsburg Confession.[27] In 1892, when Gettysburg College received a $25,000 grant to endow a chair in English Bible, President Harvey McKnight issued a document entitled "The Lutheran Status of Pennsylvania [Gettysburg] College." "Lutherans," it stated, "have never wavered in maintaining their charter-given majority [in the Board of Trustees] . . . and nothing short of a total, immoral, and incredible breach of trust can be conceived of as ever changing this well-established relation." Gettysburg College, with 32 of its 36 trustees and every faculty member a Lutheran, "is of the church, by the church, and for the church."[28] Much the same could be said of other Lutheran colleges.

The formal patterns according to which a Lutheran college related to a church or synod, however, varied widely. Some schools were founded by individuals or groups of Lutheran pastors and laity, others by direct action of a synod or conference. Whether trustees were self-appointed, elected by synods, alumni, or townspeople, care was always exercised in assuring Lutheran control. Ownership was variously vested in individuals, associations, stock companies, and synods.

Financial support during most of the 19th century was provided through private gifts, tuitions, and modest endowments. A few synods made annual grants to some colleges, but the practice was by no means universal. Beginning in 1874 the Augustana Synod, and later its conferences, supported their colleges through an annual assessment of 25¢ per member. Until 1890 none of the general bodies of older eastern Lutheranism undertook regular financial responsibility for their related colleges, though member synods of the General Council such as the Pennsylvania Ministerium and the Pittsburgh Synod contributed annually to Muhlenberg and Thiel Colleges. The Norwegian Synod allocated funds to Luther College on a regular basis from its founding in 1861, while St. Olaf, having no permanent church affiliation until 1899, depended entirely upon tuitions and voluntary gifts. Schools of the Missouri Synod were owned by the synod and directly supported from synodical funds. All Lutheran colleges solicited both church and community support for capital purposes, especially for initial land purchase and building construction.

In about 1890 all major American denominations began to develop systematic programs of college support, most of them distributing their grants through general boards of education. By 1921–1922 denominational support of colleges reached the highest level yet achieved in the history of American higher education. Among the Lutherans the first body to establish a board of education was the General Synod in 1885. Although its initial purpose was to establish Midland College as a service to its western synods, the board also continued to support both Midland and Carthage Colleges and in 1909 responded to the plea of its other related colleges to provide annual operational grants.

During the late 19th and early 20th centuries many colleges and universities also shared the largesse of America's new generation of philanthropists. Andrew Carnegie offered grants for essential expansion of facilities, and several Lutheran colleges successfully solicited his aid in financing dormitories and classroom buildings. In 1906 the Carnegie Endowment established a $10,000,000 fund to provide retirement benefits for college faculty, though its trustees imposed conditions that excluded colleges under church control. Of 615 schools surveyed, only 15 severed their ties with churches in order to become eligible.[29] Among Lutheran colleges only Wittenberg was able to meet Carnegie standards, asserting that no denominational tests were imposed by the college in admissions or in the choice of teachers or officers.[30]

In contrast Rockefeller's General Education Board, established in 1902 as an expansion of the American Baptist Education Society, announced as its policy "systematic and helpful cooperation with religious denominations" and before World War I distributed matching grants to 103 colleges, including several Lutheran schools. By 1925 it had expended $60,000,000 to strengthen the endowments of 291 colleges and universities.[31]

The National Lutheran Educational Conference

As the century drew to a close Lutheran educators for the first time were beginning to take a critical look at the complex of Lutheran colleges and academies which had grown up since the Civil War. Most schools had been founded to meet local needs, especially the preparation of pastors and teachers. With the exception of the Missouri Synod schools, however, almost all of them had expanded their programs and made some curricular adjustments in response to the elective system and to demands for scientific and practical courses. But Lutheran colleges of the 19th century generally remained loyal to the classical tradition.

One of the earliest calls for self-examination came from Dr. Franklin V. N. Painter, professor of modern languages at Roanoke College. In addressing one of the first general meetings of Lutheran college educators, in Philadelphia in 1898, Professor Painter lamented the fact that Lutherans had established more colleges than they could properly endow and equip. Episcopalians had one college for every 90,000 members; Baptists one for every 80,000; Methodists one for every 55,000. But Lutherans, thanks to their multiplicity of synods, had one for every 30,000 members. And many of them, he added, "are colleges only in name."

Painter was convinced that the Lutheran tradition in higher education, historically rooted in a university, was capable of making a deep impression on the intellectual and spiritual life of this country but only if it could maintain strong institutions of learning. The Lutheran ideal, he declared, "avoids puritanic narrowness and Catholic asceticism and subjection to authority" and "recognizes the validity of all men's faculties and divine gifts."[32]

His proposals for the improvement of Lutheran colleges sounded a fresh note in Lutheran higher education. He called for higher standards for faculty preparation, improved facilities and endowments, and cooperation to prevent duplication and waste. Weaker colleges could be converted to preparatory schools to feed the larger ones, and men's and women's colleges could be merged into single coeducational institutions.

Painter's observations stimulated Lutheran educators to call for a special college session at the Second General Conference of Lutherans four years later, in 1902 in Philadelphia. Representatives of Roanoke, Susquehanna, Wittenberg, Gettysburg College, and others heard President John Ruthrauff of Wittenberg echo Painter's plea for improved educational quality. Lutheran young people, he urged, "will not long be contented to study in inferior schools." Unless we make our colleges what they should be, "we shall drive our children into the purely secular schools of the state."[33] He had no doubt that resources were available; the question was whether the churches would direct their resources toward quality higher education or toward other purposes. It was a matter of priorities.

As the 19th century faded into the 20th, it became clear that Lutheran college presidents were increasingly concerned about educational issues as well as theological ones. In 1901 the General Council's newly appointed Standing Committee on Education headed by Dr. Theodore L. Seip, president of Muhlenberg College, called for the exploration of common attitudes which Lutheran colleges might develop "with reference to certain phases of newer education which are becoming an issue in modern educational discussions."[34] If the colleges were not to remain small parochial institutions, they would have to meet the competition of both state and private universities and offer educational opportunities of equal quality. They would need to share with one another their insights and experiences and marshal the educational resources of their tradition to face new issues and problems confronting the colleges, the culture, and the church.

The two Philadelphia meetings spurred those interested in greater cooperation among Lutheran colleges to push for a more inclusive and formal organization. On June 3, 1910, representatives of nine colleges and three seminaries of the Joint Synod of Ohio, the General Synod, General Council, and the United Synod of the South came together in Harrisburg, Pennsylvania. After listening to a paper by Professor A. J. Bowers of Newberry College on "The Advantages of an Association of the Educational Forces of the Lutheran Church," the group organized itself as the Lutheran Educational Conference, elected officers, and laid plans for future meetings.[35]

Sessions at Gettysburg in 1911 and Wittenberg in 1912 reflected the continuing concern of Lutheran college presidents over entrance requirements, standards of performance, vocational and technical training, faculty teaching loads, and fellowships for the advanced training of college teachers. Questions relating to Lutheran preparatory schools and theological seminaries were also discussed, but the primary concerns were college oriented. Lutheran educators had found a forum in which as Lutherans they could explore together the crucial issues of contemporary higher education. In so doing they also acknowledged that Lutheran higher education intended to be a full participant in the American educational scene. They were determined to strive toward the secular standards of academic performance, financial stability, and physical growth to which all colleges aspired.

Lutheran educators also recognized the need to share common concerns for church-related higher education with other denominations. In 1911 both the General Synod and the General Council took part in the organization of the Council of Church Boards of Education, an ecumenical group in which 13 denominations participated. Its purpose was "to promote the interests of Christian Education . . . through the exchange of ideas, the establishment of fundamental educational principles held in common by the churches of evangelical faith."[36] In 1915 the council promoted the organization of the Association of American Colleges for the advancement of liberal arts education. Eleven Lutheran colleges became members.

The distinctive character of the church-related liberal arts college, rarely a subject of discussion during the 19th century, became a major issue after World War I. College presidents, both in the forum of the National Lutheran Educational Conference and elsewhere, began to wrestle with the emerging concept of the modern church-related college in an increasingly secularized society. As each Lutheran church body formulated educational policies, it exercised great care in defining its relationship to its colleges with respect to governance, curriculum, and financial support. As secular educational standards became more formalized through state regulations, accreditation standards, and graduate school requirements, the churches, through their boards of education, also tended to formalize their standards for recognition and support.

The sudden plunge of the United States into the European war in 1917 and its emergence into the tempestuous decade of the 20s brought a host of new concerns both to colleges and churches. But the issue of advancing secularism in Lutheran higher education had come to stay, replacing the ethnic and theological issues which had dominated church and college relationships throughout the 19th century.

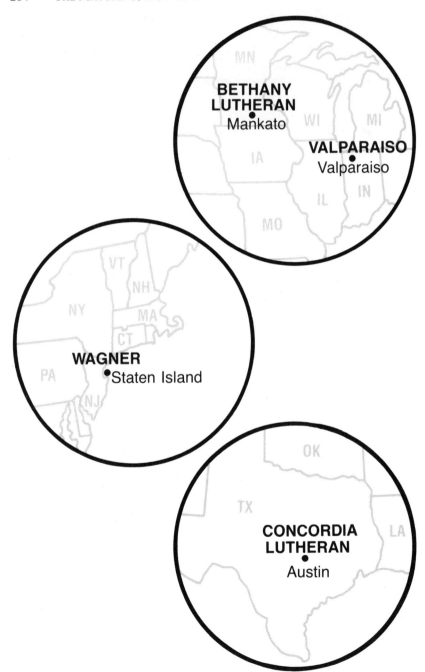

16 THE MATURING OF LUTHERAN HIGHER EDUCATION, 1914–1940

The Impact of War

For the Lutheran churches and their colleges the years between 1917 and 1920 constitute a significant historical watershed. At the 400th anniversary of the Reformation, Lutherans of America turned away from their schisms at last and began a process—still continuing in the 1980s—of coming together. The union of three Norwegian groups in 1917 brought into a single church body more than 90% of all Norwegian Lutherans in North America. In the following year the three estranged wings of colonial Lutheranism—the General Synod, the General Council, and the United Synod of the South—came together, buried their old quarrels, and merged 42 constituent synods into the United Lutheran Church in America.

These actions signaled that a multilingual European Lutheranism was moving to assert its identity as a confessional communion in the midst of the religious pluralism of America. They lent substance to the hope that the Lutheran church, by then the third largest Protestant denomination in America, might at last begin to exert influence in American church life commensurate with its size.

There is a degree of irony in the fact that the American commemoration of the anniversary of the German Reformation coincided with American entry into war against the nation which gave birth to the Reformation. Perhaps more than any other single factor World War I was responsible for forcing Lutheran churches in America to cut their cultural ties with Europe and become wholly American. A surge of national frenzy swept the country, calling into question the loyalty of anything "foreign," especially persons or practices relating to

Germany. So strong was the wave of hyper-Americanism that several mid-western legislatures passed laws banning the public use of any and all "foreign" languages, whether for instruction or worship. Zealots threw yellow paint on some German Lutheran pastors and subjected them to other personal indignities. Where such unjust attacks were made, Lutherans learned quickly to protest and found their protests sustained by constitutional guarantees of free speech. But the experience also made it abundantly clear that the Americanization of the Lutheran churches both in language and cultural orientation could no longer be resisted.

Though colleges were generally well ahead of churches in the process of Americanization, they also felt the wartime pressures. In several instances they too faced unfair charges of disloyalty. Midland College, affiliated with the General Synod, the strongest English-speaking wing of American Lutheranism, was one such victim. The hostile climate which developed in Atchison, Kansas, played a prominent role in the college's decision in 1919 to move to Fremont, Nebraska. Wittenberg, the most consciously "American" of Lutheran colleges, also carried the most German of names and accordingly was obliged to affirm its loyalty more vigorously. In his efforts to do so, President Charles Heckert invited former president Theodore Roosevelt to address a "War Chest" rally in the college chapel. Roosevelt, who had inveighed against "hyphenated Americans" took special note of the many stars in the college's service flag. Commending Wittenberg's high ideals, he saluted its "honorable position among educational institutions of the country" and deplored all discrimination and prejudice based on diverse nationalities.[1]

Enrollments in all American colleges suffered substantial decline because of the exodus to military service. When Uncle Sam cried "I need you," Lutheran students were as quick as any to answer the call. And on more than a dozen Lutheran campuses units of the Student Army Training Corps (SATC) provided opportunity to combine continued study with military training, thereby both serving a patriotic purpose and bolstering the sagging finances of the colleges. Still more significant in the long view was the introduction provided for Lutheran colleges to a relationship with the United States government. It was a relationship which would become increasingly intimate in future years.

The Drive for Accreditation

As they emerged from the wartime experience Lutheran colleges joined all of American higher education in a decade of unprecedented expansion and maturation. Enrollments rebounded after the war, rose year after year, and doubled between 1920 and 1930. This growth reflected in part the popularity which college education had come to enjoy as the public responded to broader and more practical curricula. Further stimulus came from the continued expansion of public high schools, turning out increasing numbers of graduates, both male and female, qualified for college entrance. The entry of women into public life, stimulated by wartime needs and by the passage of the Nineteenth Amendment, contirrued as one of the main social trends of the 20s, and was also reflected in expanded college enrollment. Wittenberg, one of the fastest growing Lutheran colleges during the 1920s, enrolled 468 women, 44% of its student population of 1059 in 1928.[2] St. Olaf, the only other Lutheran college to top the coveted figure of 1000, enrolled 1005 students in 1925,[3] of whom 453 were women. The average enrollment of only 345 students at the 13 four-year colleges of the ULCA in 1931, however, is a reminder that even at the conclusion of a decade of expansion Lutheran colleges remained comparatively small institutions.[4]

Still, virtually every college required additional faculty and expanded physical facilities. Dormitories, especially for women, gymnasiums to satisfy the popular enthusiasm for athletics and physical education, science buildings and libraries, and an occasional chapel, appeared in college requests to church bodies and philanthropic organizations. The 1920s witnessed the greatest expansion of college facilities in a century of Lutheran higher education.

The rapid physical expansion of colleges was accompanied by a growing concern for the content and quality of educational programs. While much of this concern was internally motivated, external forces such as the mounting competition for students and the influence of accrediting agencies helped to translate good intentions into positive improvements. The accreditation movement began in the late 19th century and was at first directed toward the secondary schools. State universities and regional associations established lists of high schools whose course offerings provided preparation judged essential for college entrance.

Lutherans were among the leaders in several of the early associations that set standards for colleges. Samuel Sprecher, president of Wittenberg College, was the first president of the Ohio College Association, founded in 1867.[5] President Theodore L. Seip of Muhlenberg was the first secretary of the College Association of the Middle States and Maryland when it was organized in 1887.

Since many colleges continued to accept students with less than a four-year preparatory course, the North Central Association voted in 1904 to deny membership in the association to colleges requiring less than 15 high school units for admission. In 1913 the North Central and subsequently other regional groups began publishing lists of colleges that met established standards of admission, faculty size and preparation, instructional facilities, library and financial resources.[6] The first Lutheran college to win accreditation as a member of the North Central Association in 1913 was Augustana at Rock

Island. Five others achieved similar recognition before World War I: Luther, St. Olaf, and Gustavus Adolphus in 1915; Carthage and Wittenberg in 1916.

Most general church boards were also eager to strengthen the academic quality of their related institutions and were therefore supportive of college efforts to secure accreditation. Some church leaders, however, especially in the conservative German synods of Iowa, Wisconsin, and Missouri tended to view outside accreditation procedures as an intrusion upon their independence. Only when graduates of their teachers colleges began to seek positions in the public high schools following World War I were curricular changes introduced to meet the standards required for state certification and ultimately for regional accreditation.[7]

In 1923 the North Central Association, the largest of the regional agencies, established as a minimum requirement for accreditation that by 1927 all colleges must have an endowment of at least $500,000. Larger colleges were required to have an additional $50,000 for each 100 students beyond an enrollment of 200. Since no Lutheran college, even including those already accredited, was able to meet that standard in 1923, a wave of financial campaigns followed.

To meet these needs in the 1920s Lutheran colleges for the first time sought the assistance of professional fund-raisers. Under the leadership of its new president, Rees Edgar Tulloss, Wittenberg College opened the decade in 1920 with an effort to raise $1,500,000, the largest fund-raising program ever undertaken by a Lutheran college. Tulloss was an aggressive leader, who by the age of 39, when he became president of Wittenberg, had earned a doctorate in psychology at Harvard, directed a naval radio school during World War I, and served as pastor of one of the largest Lutheran congregations in the country at Mansfield, Ohio. Nevertheless, he sought the services of C. H. Dreshman, a professional campaign director from New York, and appointed the Reverend Otto H. Pannkoke to be in charge of publicity. Pannkoke was a pastor of the Missouri Synod who had developed his skills as a director and publicist for the New York Reformation Quadricentenary Committee in 1917 and later, as director of the Lutheran Bureau, had aided in raising funds for postwar Lutheran relief activities in Europe. The Wittenberg campaign was oversubscribed. Receipts reached $1,900,000 and were further augmented by a $233,000 grant from the General Education Board of the Rockefeller Foundation.

As a result of the successes of the Wittenberg appeal and the earlier war relief efforts, Dr. Pannkoke's services were employed by more than 20 Lutheran institutions throughout the East and the Midwest.[8] Some Lutheran colleges undertook two and three financial campaigns between 1917 and 1927. The 13 colleges of the ULCA conducted 25 campaigns, seeking a total of $9,037,000. Ninety-four percent of this amount was actually pledged.[9] The stated purposes included buildings, debt reduction, and faculty salaries, but the main focus was endowments. Between 1921 and 1928 six of these schools also received a total of $848,333 from the General Education Board in support of endowments.[10] Colleges of the Augustana Synod and of the Norwegian Lutheran Church, as well as Valparaiso University, also conducted successful endowment campaigns during the decade under the able guidance of Lutheranism's first promotional genius.

Church Boards of Education

A further development of the 1920s, stimulated by the Lutheran mergers of 1917 and 1918, was the establishment of general church boards of education. Although each of the predecessor bodies of the United Lutheran Church in America (ULCA) had its own board before the merger of 1918, the responsibilities of the new ULCA Board of Education embraced all of the 16 collegiate institutions related to the constituent synods. To supervise its four senior colleges the Norwegian Lutheran Church established a general board in 1917. Other Lutheran bodies followed suit, the Iowa Synod also in 1917, the Augustana Synod in 1923, the American Lutheran Church in 1930. The Missouri Synod system operated under direct synodical control and did not establish a board for higher education until 1944.

The functions of general church boards varied widely, depending on the polity of the church body itself and upon provisions of individual college charters with respect to governance. In the case of the ULCA, where colleges continued to relate primarily to constituent synods rather than the central body, the board's role was advisory. However, it provided annual grants to the colleges, supplementing the support from individual synods. Through its full-time executive and additional staff the board was also able to offer a wide variety of direct services to the colleges and to the church. In 1926, for example, it commissioned a comprehensive survey of the facilities, resources, and programs of all the colleges related to the ULCA. In the interest of professional objectivity the study was conducted by Teachers College, Columbia University. On the basis of this survey, published in three volumes in 1929, a total of 391 specific recommendations were submitted to the board, of which 184 were subsequently implemented by the colleges.[11]

In church bodies of more centralized polity, where actual ownership of institutions was vested in the church, church boards exercised wider powers, including the allocating of annual operating grants to the colleges. The newly formed board of the Norwegian Lutheran Church of America nominated candidates to the church convention for election to permanent positions on the faculty, established faculty rank and salaries, and conducted annual inspections of each school. The new board faced a special problem because of the large number of academies and normal schools brought into the new church by the three merging Norwegian bodies at a time when public high schools were already beginning to dominate secondary education. Though instructed by the church convention to merge schools in both South Dakota and Washington State, the board experienced strong local resistance to its actions in 1918–1920. Nevertheless, between 1918 and 1930 it was able to mediate the closing or merging of 10 academies. Another group of 10 succumbed to the rigors of the Great Depression between 1932 and 1937.[12]

While the synodical mergers of 1917–1918 substantially reduced the number of competing Lutheran church bodies in North America, both doctrinal controversy and structural division persisted into the 1920s. The familiar themes of church fellowship, confessional faithfulness, and membership in secret societies were supplemented by new differences on ecumenical attitudes and the verbal inerrancy of the Scriptures. Among some of the German-American bodies, however, understandings were reached which in 1930 led to the formation of the American Lutheran Church (ALC), a merger of the Joint Ohio, Iowa, Texas, and Buffalo Synods.[13]

Among these bodies only the Iowa Synod had established a board of education before the merger. But the urgent need for both a policy and a structure for higher education in the new church made the creation of a general board imperative. In all three merging synods the development of higher education for the laity had historically been subordinated to theological training. Exclusive of its two theological seminaries, only one of the eight institutions of higher education acknowledged by the ALC at its organizing convention in 1930, Capital University, was qualified to award a baccalaureate degree.

The new board was assigned the responsibility to develop a program of higher education for the new church and to supervise it once it was in place.[14] Its initial reports reaffirmed ministerial preparation as the primary task of the church in higher education, acknowledging the need for only a limited measure of lay education.[15]

Continued discussion of educational philosophy, however, yielded to more immediate concerns over financial solvency as the Great Depression of the 1930s tightened its grip. As a partial remedy for the fiscal crisis the board recommended closing or merging most of the smaller institutions. The schools at Clinton and Waverly, Iowa, and St. Paul, Minnesota, were combined into a single four-year liberal arts college. Wartburg College, located at Waverly, was to become the western counterpart of Capital University in Columbus, Ohio. Two junior colleges were retained, one in Seguin, Texas, and one in Regina, in Canada, both of which would eventually develop into four-year baccalaureate institutions.[16]

In this process of consolidation schools and colleges surrendered their individual institutional charters and lost their separate incorporations. Ownership of all institutions was vested in the American Lutheran Church; local boards of regents were elected by the church convention. All policy decisions affecting finances required approval by the synodical board of trustees. Early in 1931, after slashing allocations to all of the colleges, the trustees adopted a pay-as-you-go plan that restricted expenditures to available cash income and thereby placed the burden of maintaining impoverished institutions on faculty and staffs.[17] Even after the Depression had yielded to a resurgent wartime prosperity, all capital expansion at ALC institutions was expressly forbidden. Only in 1945 did the church authorize a fund appeal that netted $1,675,000 to provide for the plant needs of its six colleges and seminaries. During virtually the entire life of the ALC (1930–1960) its board of trustees maintained a "no debt" policy, eschewing even 4% government loans for dormitory construction.[18]

If the ALC board of trustees kept a tight grip on the purse strings, the synod's Board of Christian Higher Education also left little room for independent educational decisions by the colleges. The board established uniform policies for hiring, compensation, and promotion of college faculty, directed that persons nominated for membership on boards of regents should be "actually ALC-minded Lutherans," and even determined the length of the school year.[19]

Missouri's New Look

For the tightly knit educational system of the Missouri Synod, the decade of the 1920s marked the beginning of the end of more than a half-century of isolation from American educational influences. The fierce attacks on German churches and schools and pastors during World War I forced a redirection of synod loyalties from the Old World to the New and brought about significant changes in policy and practice.

The most dramatic evidence of change was the abandonment in 1920 of the old German gymnasium pattern for preparatory schools in favor of the American system of four-year high schools and two-year junior colleges. In planning a new curriculum to conform to this change, a committee received instructions to "take into consideration the accreditation demands of the various states where the colleges are located."[20]

This action by the synod opened the way for more changes in the system. English came into wider use as a medium of instruction. Traditional Latin class names were dropped in favor of the English equivalents.[21] *Primaners* became college "sophomores."

Patterns of classwork and study also changed to conform to American ways. Instead of the old-style 30 to 32 classroom hours per week required in the gymnasium, junior college students spent no more than 15 to 18 hours in the classroom but were expected to spend much more time in outside reading and preparation. The first major curriculum study since 1908, including a full statement of aims and objectives, was brought to the synod in 1926 and finally implemented in 1938. Latin and German were deemphasized; the natural and social sciences were strengthened; and Greek was moved from high school to college.[22]

In spite of continuing resistance from more conservative church leaders who viewed accreditation procedures as a secular intrusion, Concordia Teachers College at River Forest sought and received approval of its normal program by the State Department of Education in Illinois in 1919. The wave of certification laws for teachers following World War I increased the pressure on the synod to meet standards prescribed by other states as well. By 1926 the boards of control and the Professors' Conference of the synod urged that all synod schools seek accreditation.[23]

Structural changes came more slowly. As colleges were added to the Missouri system, they came under the same direct synodical control that had been adopted for Concordia College in 1850. The synodical convention was responsible for all operations. A local board of control carried responsibility for the oversight of property but beyond that had little authority.[24]

In 1917 a new synod constitution created a synodical board of directors that for the next 30 years exercised stringent control over finances, educational policies, selection of personnel, and location of all educational institutions. After 1923 these functions were carried out by a Committee on Colleges selected from the membership of the board. The measure of its educational vision was reflected in an administrative bulletin issued by the committee in 1929. "Our colleges and seminaries must be conducted as 'poor man's schools,' " it declared. "Every one connected with the administration must be imbued with the spirit of economy . . . as one aim of the school." Nor should extracurricular activities be allowed to "strain the resources of the boys. . . . Is it really necessary to publish college papers and class books?" Some allowance needed to be made for recreation and diversion, the committee admitted, "but great moderation is undoubtedly necessary in these matters also."[25]

During the 1920s both internal growth and institutional expansion in the Missouri system continued. Enrollments in the colleges had not been seriously depressed by World War I and reflected the general upward trends of the 1920s, with an increase of 33%. However, in 1930 only two schools, in River Forest and Milwaukee, had enrollments of more than 300, including both high school and junior college students.[26]

Nevertheless, in the absence of any synodical planning board, convention delegates agreed to the establishment of two new schools, one in Canada and one in Texas. The congregations of western Canada petitioned the synod for a school in 1920 and delegates responded with an appropriation of $125,000 to build it in hopes of developing an indigenous ministry for Canadian congregations. The school opened in Edmonton, Alberta, in October 1921, with 35 students.[27] The Texas petition in 1923 pleaded the large size of the state as grounds for establishing a school in Austin and reminded the synod of the need to prevent boys from enrolling in "sectarian and atheistic schools" where "they are exposed to the danger of doing shipwreck to their faith." The 1923 convention appropriated $50,000, to be supplemented by $30,000 from the Texas District and charged its new board of directors to work out details with district representatives.[28]

An additional institution of junior college standing, indirectly related to the Missouri Synod as a co-member of the Synodical Conference, also came into being in the 20s. Bethany College in Mankato, Minnesota, was affiliated with the Evangelical Lutheran Synod, more often referred to as the "little Norwegian Synod," made up of pastors and congregations that regarded the Norwegian merger of 1917 as a betrayal of Lutheran orthodoxy. Without a school of its own during its first decade, students from "little synod" congregations were welcomed by Missouri's Concordia College in St. Paul, Minnesota.

In 1926 a Lutheran college for women operated by a private association in Mankato faced bankruptcy and possible sale to Roman Catholics. The synod purchased the property and opened Bethany College as a coeducational four-year high school and two-year junior college. Under the leadership of its scholarly president, Dr. S. C. Ylvisaker, the school became an important focal point, and after the adding of a theological department, an independent source of clergy supply for the small and intensely conservative Norwegian Synod.[29]

The Depression of the 1930s had a profound effect on the entire Missouri system, moving it still further toward patterns and practices in common usage among American colleges. Between 1925 and 1935 enrollments dropped by more than one-third. Fewer parents were able to meet transportation and maintenance costs for their children to attend high school or junior college away from home. To fill unoccupied space in dormitories and classrooms institutions began to solicit nonprofessional students as well as those preparing for church vocations. Faced with this crisis the synod reluctantly approved limited curricular changes to accommodate "general" students, both male and female. In 1935 Concordia at Bronxville expanded its college curriculum and in 1938, together with Concordia at Oakland, California, opened its doors to women. The synod also approved coeducation at River Forest in 1938.

These emergency measures had immediate and far-reaching effects. No schools were closed, but by 1940 nearly one-third of the students in the two teachers colleges were women and more than one-third of the entire enrollment in the 10 preparatory schools were "general," or nonprofessional, students; by 1946 it stood at 40%.[30] The following year the synodical convention officially approved the introduction of lay education in the synod colleges. Although the central educational emphasis of the Missouri Synod remained unchanged, the all-male system devoted exclusively to the training of church professionals for 90 years had been irretrievably breached.

The Rebirth of Valparaiso

One of the most significant educational developments of the 1920s in the Missouri Synod and possibly in all of American Lutheranism, was the rebirth of Valparaiso University under Lutheran auspices in 1925. Founded in 1859 as a Methodist college, it was transformed by Henry Baker Brown in 1873 into a proprietary institution known as Northern Indiana Normal School and Business Institute. His nationwide publicity program announced "no frills" instruction in almost any field, whether business or medicine, law or telegraphy, for anyone with a will to work and determination to succeed. A special appeal was made to immigrants, for whom Brown extended generous credit allowances. In its halcyon years from 1900 to 1910, during which it assumed the name Valparaiso University, the school enrolled 5000 students. It operated centers in both Chicago and Valparaiso, and was described by George Kennan in *McClure's Magazine* as an "educational miracle." Among its distinguished alumni were Senator George W. Norris of Nebraska, General Walter Bedell Smith, and radio commentator Lowell Thomas.[31]

World War I, however, cut deeply into its enrollment and with the death of the founding president in 1917 the school failed to make a postwar recovery. Management and financial problems dogged its path in the early 1920s. In 1923 as it teetered on the brink of collapse, Indiana officials of the Ku Klux Klan reportedly reached an agreement to purchase the campus, but the offer was withdrawn when the national offices of the Klan failed to give its approval.

In the spring of 1925 the Reverend George F. Schutes, pastor of Immanuel Lutheran Church in Valparaiso, unofficially suggested to leaders of the Central District of the Missouri Synod that the nearly bankrupt institution be purchased and converted into a Lutheran university. Under the leadership of a Fort Wayne pastor, John C. Baur, a group of pastors and laymen organized and incorporated the Lutheran University Association with a view to acquiring Valparaiso University for the Lutheran church. From June through September, 1925, events unfolded in almost dizzying sequence. The Central District of the synod endorsed the idea. The association negotiated a purchase price of

$176,000 and borrowed the funds for a down payment. The services of Dr. O. H. Pannkoke were engaged to conduct a campaign for $833,000 to cover the purchase and establish a half-million-dollar endowment. When classes began on September 26, 1925, the 66-year-old Valparaiso University had been launched into a new life as a Lutheran institution.

The tasks of transition were monumental. The entire transaction had been achieved in about three months. Only the ownership changed. The campus was run-down. A heap of blackened ruins still cluttered the site of a burned-out building. A new president had to be found, and faculty replacements secured. Students, especially Lutherans, had to be recruited. Above all, accreditation had to be sought.

The first president, Dr. W. H. T. Dau, professor at Concordia Seminary and former president of Concordia College in Conover, North Carolina, was inaugurated in September 1926 and served only one year. More active in the earthy tasks of resurrecting the university was John C. Baur, who served first as business manager and then, in 1927–1928, as acting president. Under his leadership within four years a virtually bankrupt institution with a decaying campus, a faculty without a single Ph.D. and with no financial subsidy from the church became a fully accredited university, including colleges of liberal arts, engineering, law, and pharmacy.

The coveted goal of accreditation had scarcely been achieved before the nation was plunged into the Great Depression. A new president, Dr. Oscar C. Kreinheder, took office in May 1930 and for the next decade battled to preserve the solvency of the university. Enrollments dropped from 600 to 400. Programs were curtailed and faculty salaries drastically reduced. During these difficult years, however, the internal structure of the school was strengthened. As its Lutheran character became more evident, the university won acceptance among the congregations of the synod while retaining its institutional independence under the direction of its operating association.

As the depression relinquished its grip, the Second World War loomed with more hazards for a still unstable institution. In 1940, however, Dr. O. P. Kretzmann assumed the presidency of Valparaiso. His inaugural address pointed the way to the future of the university as a recognized leader in Lutheran higher education in the 20th century. His 28 subsequent years in office did much to achieve that goal.

The courageous and imaginative action of the group of men who established Valparaiso as a Lutheran university constituted the restoration of a dimension in the educational agenda of the Missouri Synod which had lain virtually dormant for nearly a century. The original prospectus for the "log college" in Altenburg, Missouri, in 1839 had endorsed higher education of the laity for service to the community. C. F. W. Walther himself had entertained similar hopes for Concordia College in St. Louis. But across the years the urgency of parochial education and careful preparation of the clergy had dominated synodical policy.

The founding of Valparaiso University was an expression of a fresh impulse within the Missouri Synod released by the breaking of old cultural ties to Europe to bring the rich resources of its tradition into the mainstream of American higher education. Though its founders explicitly chose to organize independently of the synod, there was never any doubt of their intent to build a Lutheran university in partnership with the synod. When the synod sensed this intent, it offered its support and found in the university a strong and helpful colleague. The university, in turn, was able to devote itself to the fulfillment of its primary mission, defined by its distinguished president, O. P. Kretzmann, as "a voluntary association of free men and women in a community which is dedicated to a two-fold task: the search for Truth and the transmission of Truth, free and unbroken, to those who are born later in time."[32]

College Expansion in the East

The founding of Valparaiso University was by no means an isolated phenomenon, either in American higher education in general or in Lutheran circles. All of higher education experienced an era of great expansion during the 1920s, both in the size and the number of institutions. The general economic prosperity of the decade and the growing popularity of the "college experience" contributed to this growth. The continued expansion of the public high schools produced an increasing number of applicants for college entrance each year. Among Lutherans these developments brought about the closing of many academies and hastened the transformation of others into collegiate institutions.

Among those making this transition in the 1920s were some of Lutheranism's oldest as well as its youngest schools. Hartwick Seminary, founded in 1797, had operated since 1815 as a theological school and preparatory academy near Cooperstown, New York, occasionally offering a year or two of collegiate instruction as well.[33] In 1926 under the energetic leadership of a new president, Charles R. Meyers, the seminary board proposed a financial campaign of $500,000 to provide buildings and endowment for a "Greater Hartwick." The seminary was to be modernized and the college expanded to a four-year baccalaureate program. The New York Synod gave its unanimous approval and the omnipresent Dr. O. H. Pannkoke was engaged to manage the campaign.

In the course of solicitation the city of Oneonta offered to guarantee $200,000 and a tract of land if the college would relocate within its limits.

Within 10 days a house-to-house canvass raised $208,000 that, together with a successful synod campaign, provided Hartwick College with cash and pledges of $637,000 for facilities and endowment.

The college opened in Oneonta in the fall of 1928 in temporary quarters with a freshman class of 38, and by the end of the semester had enrolled a total of 235 students. At its first commencement in June 1932, 73 students received bachelor's degrees. But, the Depression settled in before the young college could gain stability. By 1929 stock values had plummeted. Many of the pledges were irredeemable and Hartwick College struggled through the hard times with a handful of students and a single building on its Oneonta campus. Only after World War II did Hartwick emerge under the leadership of President Frederick Binder as a strong and fully accredited liberal arts college.

Less fortunate was the historic old Hartwick Seminary which moved to Brooklyn in 1930 and later to Manhattan. In 1941 it concluded its 144-year history in the parish house of St. John's Lutheran Church on Christopher Street, in the same neighborhood where John Christopher Kunze had served as its first professor of theology in 1797.[34]

Another Lutheran college in New York State which began a new chapter in its life during the 1920s was Wagner College. Founded in Rochester, New York, in 1883 to maintain a supply of German-speaking pastors for the New York Ministerium, it was conducted as a six-year German gymnasium until 1918, even publishing its annual catalogs in the German language.[35] Originally chartered as the Lutheran Pro-Seminary of Rochester, New York, it was renamed Wagner Memorial Lutheran College in 1886 in recognition of a $12,000 gift by John G. Wagner, a Rochester businessman, given in memory of his deceased son who had hoped to become a Lutheran pastor.[36]

By 1900 the demand for German-language ministry had begun to decline, and suggestions were made both for broadening the curriculum and for moving the college to a more favorable location. In 1916 a special synod meeting resolved to raise $100,000 to relocate Wagner College in suburban Staten Island in New York City. Through the efforts of Pastor Frederic Sutter, a college trustee, the synod purchased the former estate of the Cunard family, a 38-acre tract with four buildings, overlooking New York Harbor.[37]

The transition to Staten Island constituted a virtually new beginning for Wagner College. It completely revised its structure and curriculum, replacing the six-year gymnasium with a four-year college and a four-year high school. A new faculty and student body had to be assembled, since only one professor and 16 students followed their college to New York City. The Lutheran pastors and congregations of Staten Island, under the enthusiastic leadership of Pastor Frederic Sutter, formed a supportive local constituency, and both enrollments and financial resources slowly developed.[38]

In the mid-20s a successful appeal for $500,000 enabled the construction of a main college building. The first college class was graduated in 1928 and the coveted regional accreditation was achieved in 1931. When in the following year the high school department was closed and coeducation introduced, Wagner had completed its transformation to a four-year American liberal arts college. Enrollments reached 250-275 in the late 1930s, but major growth did not occur until after World War II.

Joining the ranks of Lutheran schools that emerged as independent baccalaureate institutions in the 1920s was also a Canadian college. Waterloo College, in Waterloo, Ontario, began in 1914 as a high school and preparatory school for the theological seminary founded in 1911 by the Canada and Central Canada Synods. Beginning about 1920 graduates of the high school department were invited to enroll for additional course work beyond the high school level. This advanced program, recognized as the Waterloo College of Arts, began to offer a full year of university level courses in 1923.

Under the Canadian system of higher education private or denominational schools of higher education were free to affiliate with provincially supported universities and thereby to expand the educational opportunities available to their students. In 1925 Waterloo College chose to affiliate with the University of Western Ontario, a small provincial university in London, Ontario, newly reconstituted as a part of the expanding Canadian higher education emphasis of the 1920s. Through this relationship Waterloo College was able to offer a full collegiate program and to graduate its first baccalaureate class in 1927. As a four-year liberal arts college, supported by the Canada Synod of the ULCA, it offered a variety of general and preprofessional majors and also supplied the synod's seminary with well-qualified candidates for theological study. In the years of even more intensive educational expansion in the 1950s, Waterloo College developed into a small, fully recognized independent Lutheran university.[39]

The Descent of the Depression

The golden years of American higher education which had brought enrollments, endowments, and enthusiasm to college campuses all across the country came to a jolting halt in 1929. The pall which settled over the land when the Great Depression followed in the wake of the stock market collapse enveloped colleges and universities as well as businesses and farms. Student enrollments declined sharply. Sources of financial support, whether churches or individual donors or public treasuries, withered. Debts incurred during the construction boom of the 20s remained to haunt college presidents and trustees, while operating deficits mounted. Faculty members had to be dropped, and the salaries of those fortunate enough to be retained often went unpaid.

As the depression tightened its grip on the national economy, survival was the major aim for most small colleges. Fortunately, the early experiences of many of these schools had provided training in frugality and the brief prosperity of the 1920s had enabled them to gather new resources before the clouds descended. Federal assistance programs such as the National Youth Administration (NYA) provided funds for the part-time employment of students, enabling many to remain in college who would otherwise have joined the ranks of the unemployed.

Inevitably, many institutions closed. Most noticeable in Lutheran ranks was the demise of most of the remaining academies and normal schools. Several junior colleges either closed or were merged with other collegiate institutions. All degree-granting Lutheran institutions operating in the 1920s, however, survived the rigors of the depression.

Two promising Lutheran educational ventures conceived during the golden years of the 1920s foundered under the impact of the depression before they were fairly launched. Long-cherished hopes of Californians for a Lutheran educational institution in their midst seemed about to be realized in 1928 when a 100-acre site for a projected new Los Angeles University was dedicated on the oceanside at Santa Monica.[40] But construction funds failed to materialize. Ground was never broken, and Californians waited 30 more years for a Lutheran college.

After a fire destroyed the building of Elizabeth College in Salem, Virginia, in 1921, the only remaining Lutheran degree-granting women's college, the Board of Education of the ULCA undertook the establishment of a national Lutheran college for women in the vicinity of Washington, D.C. Leadership for the project was provided by Mary Markley, the first female executive of a denominational board for higher education in America. Nine member synods of the ULCA promised support of a campaign for $1,000,000. A 189-acre tract of land was purchased in 1926 and the college was incorporated the following year. Several substantial bequests were received, and brochures containing architect's sketches for the campus of Grace College were prepared and distributed. But as the Depression deepened, support from synods and individuals dwindled and eventually ceased. By 1934 the project was reluctantly abandoned. Assets of more than $100,000 were invested by the Board of Education to provide college scholarships for "worthy young women of the church."[41]

A Time for Assessment

There were also some positive benefits to individual colleges and to Lutheran higher education as a whole that resulted from the depression. The loyalty of college faculty, an often unheralded factor in the shaping of the Lutheran college, was once more attested in their willingness to share both financial stringencies and increased workloads. The faculty at Wittenberg, for example, cooperated with the local YMCA in the Springfield Free-Time People's College, offering a variety of college courses without charge to local high school graduates unable to attend college because of economic conditions; 375 students enrolled.[42]

Of even longer range significance was the revival of educational self-analysis stimulated by the economic crisis. Just before World War I Lutheran college leaders, especially in the East, had begun to draw their institutions together, both denominationally and ecumenically, to affirm their special character as church-related colleges. The formation of the Lutheran Educational Conference in 1910, the Council of Church Boards of Education in 1911, and the Association of American Colleges in 1915, all reflected concern over the pervasive secularism and the hostility toward liberal and church-related education fostered by the modern universities.

Effective attention to these concerns by the colleges, however, was almost immediately diverted by the involvement of the nation in World War I. No sooner had peace been restored than the colleges were caught up in the feverish 20s. Enrollments boomed; money flowed freely; facilities expanded. Educational goals were defined in terms of accreditation standards and enrollment dollars. The agendas of the National Lutheran Educational Conference in the 20s ranged from publicity and finance to college-seminary relations and student social life. Little attention was paid to the historic goals and purposes of Lutheran higher education. Still riding the crest of prosperity in 1928, Conference leaders projected an all-Lutheran fund appeal as the theme for a Higher Education Year in 1930 commemorating the 400th Anniversary of the Augsburg Confession.[43]

By the time the conference met in March 1930, the economic collapse had intervened and the fund appeal had been set aside—in the ULCA for 20 years. In its place the conference agenda for 1930 introduced themes that would stimulate self-examination and productive debate among Lutheran educators for the next half-century. Dr. Otto Mees, president of Capital University, opened the conference with an address on "A Philosophy of Christian Education as Concerns our Church Colleges," and President Henry W. A. Hanson of Gettysburg College concluded with a presentation on "The Future of the Liberal Arts College."

A few months later, on the actual anniversary of the Augsburg Confession, five midwestern Lutheran synods compacted together in an association called the American Lutheran Conference, which they hoped would eventually lead to organic merger. Among them were the newly merged American Lutheran Church, the Augustana Synod, the Norwegian Lutheran Church of America, the Lutheran Free Church, and the United Danish Evangelical Lutheran Church. Together they counted 6,680 congregations, but in view of the collapsed national economy, their immediate concern was the plight of the 12 senior colleges and 8 junior colleges for which these congregations and churches were ultimately responsible.

One of the first actions of the conference was to appoint a Commission on Higher Education to discuss common strategies. In 1933 and 1935 the commission organized research groups, made up of college presidents and professors who spent several weeks in study at the Universities of Chicago and Minnesota under the chairmanship of Dr. O. H. Pannkoke and with faculty advisers from the host universities. The results of the 1933 workshop were published as a study of "Trends and Issues Affecting Lutheran Higher Education."[44] The 1935 workshop proposed a two-year "Christian General Education Curriculum" for possible adoption by the colleges of the American Lutheran Conference.[45] A further outcome of the workshops was the organizing of the Lutheran Faculties Conference, which met in 1935 for the first time, to discuss the findings of the commission. Subsequent annual meetings of the Lutheran Faculties Conference were limited in early years to colleges of the American Lutheran Conference. After the interruptions of World War II faculty groups on several midwestern campuses undertook extensive inquiries into the role of the liberal arts in Lutheran higher education.

Having returned to the basic concerns over the character of church-related and Lutheran higher education that brought about its formation in 1910, the National Lutheran Educational Conference continued to examine them in its annual meetings after 1930. Dr. Karl Ermisch of Augsburg Seminary gave the keynote address in 1931 on "The Fundamental Principles of Education in the Lutheran Church." The following year the Conference heard a paper on the "Distinctive Function and Service of the Lutheran College of the Future." Beginning in 1932 joint sessions were held for three successive years with its organizational colleagues of prewar years, the Council of Church Boards of Education, and with a new ally, The Liberal Arts College Movement.

As the 1930s drew to a close and the grip of the Great Depression began to loosen, the community of Lutheran colleges emerged from a period in which wartime dislocation, exhilarating prosperity, and economic disaster had all been crowded into two short decades. Traumatic as these years had been, they had brought the colleges to a degree of maturity not previously experienced.

For a large part of the group, representing the more recent streams of European immigration, the experience of World War I compelled a decisive break with European languages and cultural ties, and an intentional affirmation of identity with American culture. For all colleges the war had involved institutional participation in a major national experience to which they contributed both men and facilities.

As the result of the great upsurge in the popularity of higher education both before and after the war, Lutheran colleges were larger and stronger. They were academically more mature as the result of enthusiastic participation in both the letter and the spirit of the accreditation movement. They had become more closely knit as self-consciously Lutheran institutions through an association which reached across synodical lines. They had become identified with a well-defined movement in American higher education to advance the liberal arts in opposition to the rising strength of specialization and secularization. Both within the church and in the secular arena Lutheran colleges had established channels for independent expression.

The new age in which they would seek to fulfill their responsibilities in church and society was destined to be no less traumatic than the troubled times from which they had just emerged. Another war even more overwhelming than the last was about to break. When it was over the world of higher education would never be the same.

17 HIGHER EDUCATION'S NEW AGE, 1941–1960

The Colleges and the War

When the bombs dropped on Pearl Harbor on December 7, 1941, and the nation was plunged into World War II, American college campuses were even less prepared for it than were the armed forces of the United States. If the totalitarian upsurge in Europe in the late 1930s had produced among Americans a strong sense of their country as the bulwark of democracy, their determination not to become embroiled again in Europe's conflicts seemed equally strong. While Congress rushed to pass neutrality legislation and Lutheran educators extolled the virtues of democracy, campuses were engaged in a vigorous peace movement marked by fervent antiwar pronouncements and demonstrations.

In 1937 students at Thiel College carried a wooden coffin inscribed "Victim of a Future War" through the streets of Greenville, Pennsylvania, and concluded their march with a ceremonial burial of the coffin at the foot of the college flagpole.[1] Even after the Nazi invasion of Norway, St. Olaf College students shrugged off as "war-mongering" the impromptu plea for patriotism that President L. W. Boe delivered at the conclusion of commencement exercises in 1941.[2]

Only a few months later, on the "day of infamy," the surprise Japanese attack shocked the American people as never before in their history. The national climate changed abruptly. Political differences were set aside in an immediate demonstration of national unity. American industry mobilized. Peace rallies ceased and young men by the thousands flocked to enlistment centers. Colleges and universities offered both manpower and facilities for the nation's defense.

In response to government suggestion most colleges made provision for accelerated study, enabling students to complete their college work in less than the usual four years. Reserve programs in some colleges allowed students to continue their regular courses of study and to enter active service after graduation.

The readiness of educational institutions to support fully the national mobilization, however, in no sense lessened the impact of the exodus of male students which inevitably followed. Especially hard hit were colleges too small to handle the military training programs offered by the army or navy. Newly established Hartwick College lost more than half of its 273 students and by 1943 had only 20 men left on campus.[3] Having reached its highest enrollment in 1942 with 587 students, Augustana in Sioux Falls saw its student body shrink to 220 by the second semester of 1943–1944, only 43 of them men.[4]

For schools able to serve as centers for the variety of military training programs, much of the financial strain was alleviated. Moreover, in dealing with government agencies and with a more diverse group of students than previously known, the colleges gained valuable experience in preparation for the postwar decades.

At St. Olaf a Naval Pre-flight Prep School occupied two dormitories, dining and athletic facilities, and 25 classrooms, and employed several college faculty.[5] Wittenberg made room for an Army Air Force Training School which maintained a steady contingent of 700 cadets on campus and introduced a total of 2800 men to the college during the war years.[6] Without the presence of a na-

val V-12 unit to utilize its resources, Muhlenberg, a men's college, mi̇
have faced disaster. Of its total enrollment of 576 in 1943–1944, 44.
servicemen, all of them encouraged to participate fully in all college activities.
As a special bonus the strapping men of V-12 produced for Muhlenberg
College a national reputation in athletics. Their presence was a financial blessing as well. Of the total college budget of $671,121.25 in 1943–1944,
$426,107.36 represented reimbursements for the care and feeding of navy
trainees.[7]

The Return of the GI's

The most profound effects of World War II on American higher education
came afterwards. To enable the returning servicemen to make an appropriate
readjustment to civilian life, the Congress passed in 1944 what came to be
called the "GI Bill of Rights." Any veteran who wished to undertake some
form of schooling could draw on a tuition credit of up to $500 and a $65 to $90
monthly living allowance. Most of the returning GI's who took advantage of
the offer chose to take short-term training courses promising early employment. No fewer than a million, however, returned to complete a course interrupted by the war or entered college for the first time.

Startling was the contrast as the flood of veterans washed over American
campuses. By comparison, the increased enrollments of the 1920s seem insig-
nificant. Instead of the 220 students on its campus in January 1944, Augustana
College in Sioux Falls was inundated by 927 students in the fall of 1946. There
were shortages of everything: classrooms, chairs, books, supplies. In one
small cubicle at Augustana which served as an office for an entire department,
faculty members jested that there was a professor in every desk drawer.

Fortunately for the colleges, the eagerness of both the government and the
people of the United States to demobilize the armed forces quickly vacated military installations in every part of the country. Harrassed administrators grate-
fully moved surplus buildings to campuses and reconditioned them as dormitories, classrooms, and laboratories. It was a rare campus which could not
display at least one or two barracks or Quonset huts fulfilling civilian duty as
dormitories, housing ex-GI's now responding to alarm clocks rather than
bugles.

The massive entry of the GI's to the college scene was only the start of the
revolution that transformed American higher education after World War II.
Close behind followed a surge of new public policy, setting off waves of educational legislation that rolled through American society for the next 40 years.
In 1948 President Truman's Commission on Higher Education proclaimed a
new goal: "higher education for all." With this it became national policy that
Jacksonian rather than Jeffersonian principles would henceforth govern access

to American collegiate education, as had long been true in the public schools of the land. Already struggling to cope with a record student population of two million in 1948, the nation's colleges and universities learned that they must be prepared for four million by 1960. Congress lent them a helping hand with legislation extending additional support, mainly for college housing, but also for some academic facilities to aid institutions in handling veterans.

Crisis of Funds and Facilities

From 1946 to 1950 Lutheran colleges were strained to the limit to meet the extraordinary demands placed upon their resources. Expanded enrollments required expanded services and personnel, and operational costs rose with postwar inflationary trends. The Korean War drew off another generation of younger students in 1950, and enrollments slumped while costs continued to rise. A new GI Bill for Korean veterans in 1953 providing lump-sum benefits rather than separate grants for tuition and living costs shifted the flow of new veterans to public institutions where lower tuition costs left a larger balance for living expenses. Moreover, the temporary barracks buildings which had saved the day for private colleges in 1947 and 1948 offered poor competition for the attractive new buildings which meanwhile had mushroomed on every state college and university campus.

Recognizing the crisis confronting their colleges, both in finances and facilities, Lutheran church bodies responded with great generosity, increasing annual appropriations and engaging in capital campaigns on their behalf. In 1950 the United Lutheran Church in America launched its long-postponed Christian Higher Education Year (CHEY), originally planned as a commemoration of the 400th anniversary of the Augsburg Confession in 1930. Their colleges cataloged as major needs nine chapels, four gyms, three science halls, ten libraries, one heating plant, and one president's residence. The appeal netted almost $7,000,000.[8] The American Lutheran Church estimated in 1958 that $5,000,000 would be available for its schools by 1960.[9] The Evangelical Lutheran Church, having raised more than $1,500,000 in 1948–1949 in a Christian Education Appeal, distributed an additional $300,000 cost-of-living bonus to all its college faculty in 1951.

Annual grants from the churches also increased. From a figure of $45,000 in 1948, the Pittsburgh Synod progressively raised its annual grant to Thiel to $74,540 in 1956, $120,000 in 1960, and $210,000 in 1970.[10] The Pennsylvania Ministerium sponsored six capital appeals for Muhlenberg between 1946 and 1960, raising nearly $3 million, while increasing its annual subsidy from $43,000 in 1950 to $300,000 in 1966.[11]

During the mid-50s philanthropic organizations also added their support. In 1955 the Ford Foundation distributed $5,415,000 to 28 Lutheran colleges, largely for support of faculty salaries. The following year it joined the Carnegie Foundation in launching the National Merit Scholarship program.[12] Funding from a new source also became available to colleges in 1953, when a United States Supreme Court decision legalized gifts by corporations to private education.[13]

By 1960 most Lutheran colleges had broken out of the emergency status which prevailed after the Korean War and had begun to share in the largesse of America's most affluent decade. With the help of their supporting churches and through financial campaigns among alumni and friends, almost every college threw up new buildings, enlarged its budget, and raised the pay of its faculty. Government loans financed several dormitories, but chapels at Texas Lutheran, Gustavus, and Pacific Lutheran; science buildings at Luther and Thiel; field houses and gymnasiums at Concordia (Moorhead), Muhlenberg, and Augsburg, and entire campuses at Concordia Senior College and California Lutheran were built with church grants and private gifts. Between 1943 and 1963 the number of buildings on the campuses of both St. Olaf and Wittenberg more than doubled, from 14 to 30.

Education and National Defense

Beyond the benevolent intent of the United States government to bring the blessings of higher education to a broader range of the American public, as expressed by the Truman Commission in 1948, was a policy not heretofore applied to American higher education. An all-consuming effort to contain and combat Soviet communism dominated American foreign policy and public life during the years from 1946 to 1963. To this end the nation placed its military establishment on a wartime footing, forged new alliances, pursued loyalty investigations, fought an Asian war, developed the H-bomb, and geared its economy to the demands of a Cold War. In this context all of American education was summoned to public service.

Frightened and shamed by the success of the Russian Sputnik in 1957, national leadership demanded a wholesale revamping of public school curricula. President Eisenhower told the American people that the nation's most crictical problem was a shortage of scientists. Using National Education Week as a platform he asked every school board and PTA in the nation as a "special order of business" to scrutinize their school curriculum and standards and to ask "whether they meet the stern needs of the era we are now entering." Both the kind of revisions he had in mind and the reason for their importance were clear in his reminder that "when a Russian graduates from high school, he has five years of physics, four years of chemistry, one year of astronomy, five years of biology, ten years of mathematics and trigonometry, and five years of a foreign language."[14]

The focus was not alone on elementary and secondary education. If science and mathematics were to be taught effectively in public schools, well-prepared teachers would be needed. Colleges and universities must supply them as well as the thousands of research scientists and engineers needed to fuel the cold war.

When in 1958 Congress passed the National Defense Education Act, the very title of the legislation announced that higher education was to be used as an instrument of public policy for the furtherance of national manpower needs, for defense, and the achievement of foreign policy goals. New billions were allocated for student grants and loans, university research in science and technology, foreign-language study, teacher training, and, especially after 1963, construction of academic facilities.

By the time this sweeping science-oriented legislation was passed, colleges and universities of the land were again bursting with students. The twofold GI bulge had largely passed. But the impetus it had given to college education, now reinforced by the national emphasis on education for defense and fueled by the huge population explosion generated by the wartime baby boom, drove college enrollments to unprecedented levels. By 1960 more than 3.6 million students, an increase of 35% since 1955, were crowding onto all campuses, and within the next decade the numbers would reach nearly 8 million.

Confronted by this overwhelming flood of students and by a national manpower training program directed toward noneducational goals, the entire higher education establishment faced both physical and philosophical problems. Even an unlimited government treasury could not immediately supply the trained personnel needed to administer and to teach. But beyond this loomed the specter of government control of the educational structure for its own ends.

Even more pointed was the dilemma of the church-related liberal arts colleges. Their goals were student-oriented. The courses they offered were neither technical nor specialized. Eager to serve their country and the men who had risked life and health in its defense, these colleges had made their faculties and facilities available to educate a volume of students which public institutions could not possibly have accommodated alone. In so doing many extended themselves beyond their capacities, endangered standards of quality, and adjusted curricula to accommodate the government requirements for national defense and technical development at the expense of traditional offerings in the liberal arts.

In some instances, as with schools of the American Lutheran Church prior to 1960, both financial conservatism and sensitivity to possible government encroachment kept them from requesting any federal grants or loans, though they had welcomed the returning GI's as students. Schools of the Missouri system, as church-worker institutions, were not eligible for federal funds. Gould Wickey, Executive Director of the National Lutheran Educational Conference, circulated a memorandum to all member colleges warning that federal support "may make the definition of the purpose of the institution more difficult." Federal grants, he noted, tend "to be project oriented within a single discipline and therefore tend to intensify the already serious fragmentation of the intellectual life of the campus."[15]

Campus Climate in the Fifties

When the initial shock waves produced by the swarming of the GI's had subsided, college leaders had time to catch their breath and look down the road at what lay ahead. The GI invasion had been only a "curtain raiser." After a temporary dip during the Korean War in 1950–1953, enrollments continued to rise far beyond any previous levels. Not only did the GI Bill offer opportunity to the veteran; it set an example for all of America. If a college education was good for the GI, why not for every high school graduate? Even before the education frenzy which swept the nation after Sputnik, it was clear that American higher education would never again be an elitist preserve.[16]

Nor would the character of student bodies at Lutheran colleges ever again display the homogeneous pattern that had prevailed, especially on midwestern campuses, as late as 1945. Not only had many of the colleges doubled or even quadrupled in size, but neither faculty nor student body resembled the college communities of days gone by. In a very real sense, by responding to the need for facilities to educate the nation's war veterans and by joining in government programs that enabled them to do their part, all American colleges and universities had become "public" institutions. Many pastors and church leaders honestly wondered whether such a role could be compatible with the traditional understanding of the colleges of the church as agencies created primarily to prepare clergy and lay leadership for congregations and to buttress the faith of the young. The matter was of sufficient concern to the Evangelical Lutheran Church in 1948 to lead its Board of Christian Higher Education to appoint a commission to visit each of its college campuses to ascertain whether these tasks were being properly carried out.

It is quite likely that the climate of Lutheran campuses did undergo substantial changes in the postwar decades. The GI's, whether veterans of World War II or Korea, selected their colleges less for religious reasons than for geographical, financial, and educational reasons. Many of them displayed evidences of their exposure to the roughness of military life. On the other hand, many were mature men, often with families of their own, and they were neither interested in youthful "collegiate" activities nor were they as impressionable as their younger counterparts. Younger faculty candidates, too, with freshly-earned master's or doctor's degrees were often quite differently oriented from the faithful "old guard," many of whom had served their college through years of struggle and depression with single-minded commitment.

It might have been equally appropriate to express concern over the younger generation of students who flocked into college during the late 40s and 50s in the shadow of their older GI colleagues. These were the young people who by the mid-50s were being called the "silent generation." They were described in 1957 by a widely heralded study, based on data gathered between 1949 and 1954, as "gloriously contented both in regard to their present day-to-day activity and their outlook for the future." Ready to conform to the social and economic status quo in the expectation of a good and rewarding job at the end of the college years, they coasted through an affluent decade without challenging anything. "Perhaps," mused analyst Philip Jacob, "these students are the forerunners of a major cultural and ethical revolution, the unconscious ushers of an essentially secular, self-oriented society."[17]

A Time of Self-Assessment

As they faced these prospects, leaders and supporters of Lutheran colleges turned to serious examination of their educational goals and the resources available to achieve them. Virtually every college came forth with a 5- or 10-year master plan, often with the help of professional consultants. Campus designs were prepared and studied together with projections of enrollments, assessments of faculty needs, curricular expansion, financial resources. Faculty committees debated at great length the nature of liberal arts education and its relation to the Christian character of the college.

As far back as the early 30s most church-related colleges had rallied to an organized Liberal Arts Movement that resisted prevailing trends toward specialization and vocationalism in American higher education. The General Education Program of the 1920s at Columbia University and the Harvard Report on General Education in a Free Society in 1945 gave heart to their battle against fragmentation and specialization. Many Lutheran college faculty saw the emphasis on technology that marked the new mass thrust in higher education as a particular challenge to the kind of education most Lutheran colleges had traditionally offered.

At a meeting of the Lutheran Faculties Conference in 1950 at Augustana College in Rock Island, Illinois, a study group of faculty members from several midwestern colleges was formed to consider the question, "Is there a Lutheran Philosophy of Higher Education?" This group, representing a variety of disciplines and changing both in size and makeup over a 10-year period, met periodically to discuss papers prepared by its members. In 1960 the distillation of their work was published in a volume called *Christian Faith and the Liberal Arts*. Their study came down unequivocally on the side of the humanities and deplored the technical and utilitarian emphases of modern secular education.[18]

A second faculty-related effort, at St. Olaf College, dealt with the subject of integration in the liberal arts. Citing Dietrich Bonhoeffer's ideal of the "whole man" who has found a common denominator for both thought and life, this faculty self-study attempted to discover the integrating qualities and materials around which a truly liberating curriculum could be built. Their findings, published in 1956 in a volume entitled *Integration in the Christian Liberal Arts College*, led to the strengthening of interdisciplinary studies in the St. Olaf curriculum.[19]

Still another proposal was structural in character. In 1955 Dr. Orville Dahl, executive secretary of the board of higher education of the Evangelical Lutheran Church, circulated a plan to federate the educational institutions of the church in a transcontinental Lutheran University of America.[20] Dahl's proposal derived from findings of a workshop at the University of Chicago, conducted by the Commission on Higher Education of the American Lutheran Conference in 1933 under the shadow of the Great Depression. Looking ahead to an increasingly unified Lutheranism in America the Commission had urged closer cooperation and coordination among the colleges of the church in the interest of both economy and effectiveness.[21] Dahl's proposal found little support among the ELC's strongly individualistic colleges poised on the threshold of higher education's most affluent decade.[22] Several of them found it more in keeping with their liberal arts character to join other like-minded institutions in regional consortia, sharing such services as library resources, lecture series, and other activities that would broaden opportunities available to their students, without loss of institutional independence. St. Olaf became a member of the Associated Colleges of the Midwest in 1958, and other Lutheran colleges joined similar regional groups during the following decade.

Three colleges, however, chose during this decade to change their names and their structure and to declare themselves Lutheran universities. In 1959 and 1960 Wittenberg, Pacific Lutheran, and Waterloo Colleges joined the three other Lutheran institutions which had long carried the university title: Valparaiso, Capital, and Susquehanna. In no case, however, had these institutions fulfilled the long-cherished but unattained dream of a national Lutheran university of comparable stature with those of other major denominations in North America.[23]

New Ventures in Wisconsin and California

Lutheran educators looked in other directions to meet the expanding opportunities of the 50s. In 1953 the Northwest Synod of the ULCA set out to establish a new liberal arts college in the state of Wisconsin. Before the decade was over church and college leaders had solved their problem by moving Carthage College from Carthage, Illinois, to Kenosha, Wisconsin. Not only did the college thereby gain a spectacular campus location on the shores of Lake Michigan but won direct access as well to a state whose population was 20% Lutheran and which had no four-year Lutheran liberal arts college.[24]

California was also inviting territory.[25] On the suggestion of Dr. J. C. K. Preus of the Evangelical Lutheran Church, the boards of education of the ELC, the United Lutheran Church, and the American Lutheran Church undertook a joint feasibility study in 1954. Their findings, presented in a 63-page document, concluded with the statement that "the Lutheran church would be refusing to face its responsibility in higher education if it did not plan for future service in the California area."

The three bodies, joined by the Augustana Synod and the Danish-background UELC, formed a separate corporation called the California Lutheran Educational Foundation (CLEF). The foundation was empowered to solicit funds from churches and individuals and to proceed with the organization of a college. Its board of regents elected Dr. Orville Dahl as director of the foundation in 1957 and later as first president of California Lutheran College.

Between 1957 and 1959 under Dahl's energetic and imaginative leadership, a 100-acre ranch site was secured in Thousand Oaks, a community near Los Angeles on the threshold of a California-style residential boom. Church bodies made financial contributions of $400,000 and with additional loans and gifts a campus "Centrum" of eight buildings was completed at a cost of $1,300,000. The college opened in September 1961, with an initial enrollment of 302 students, and a faculty of which 40% held the Ph.D. degree. By the following March, California Lutheran College had received full regional accreditation by the Western Association of Colleges and Secondary Schools. Its unique character as the only Lutheran college jointly owned and operated by more than one church body was reflected in its unique pattern of governance. College regents were elected by a specially constituted convocation with representatives proportionately assigned to the five participating church bodies.[26]

Reassessment in the Missouri System

The schools of the Missouri Synod were not as seriously affected by wartime dislocations as other Lutheran colleges. Since their students were mostly of high school or junior college age, few left for military service. Boys certified as pretheological students or as teacher candidates received the same exemption from military service as theological students. The number of returning veterans who enrolled in the junior college programs of Missouri schools at the close of the war was not large. Enrollment increases after World War II were nevertheless substantial. Trends begun with the admission of general education students and women in the late 30s and 40s accelerated. A serious shortage of elementary parochial school teachers called for a vigorous recruitment program by the synod, resulting in the doubling of enrollments in its two teachers colleges by 1950 and a fourfold increase in the decade following. Total attendance of college-level students in the 12 colleges of the Missouri system increased from 1,613 students in 1950 to 3,558 in 1959.[27]

In 1940 Dean Theodore Hausmann of Concordia College in Bronxville was commissioned to conduct a thorough study of the educational structure of the synod. The Hausmann Report of 1943 analyzed the effect of the "emergency" measures of the late 30s which introduced both lay education and limited coeducation into the schools. Hausmann's recommendations became the basis for a sweeping reorganization of the Missouri system. As a start, the synod in 1944 established the Board for Higher Education as a permanent agency and in 1947 granted it virtual autonomy in the supervision of its national educational program.[28] Dr. Martin J. Neeb became the first full-time executive secretary in 1945 and a new era opened for Missouri's educational program. Under Dr. Neeb's leadership the colleges laid stress on regional accreditation, sound financial policies, and more adequate library and laboratory accommodations for the colleges. Warning against a "deterioration of spiritual tone" in the colleges, Neeb also urged the provision of full-time resident guidance and counseling service for students.

With central formulation of educational policy came the demand for local freedom in administrative detail. Individual institutions were given freedom to prepare and administer their own budgets. Local boards of control received authority to choose faculty members on recommendation of the president. For the first time the president of the college became the chief executive officer of his institution, responsible to his local board of control in accordance with the prevailing pattern among American colleges. As the synod began its second century of service, Dr. Neeb observed appreciatively that "after extensive delay" it had recognized "the application of technical competence as a crucial factor in its academic policies."[29]

In addition to the administrative changes adoped in 1947 the synod convention of 1950 approved significant structural and curricular changes affecting the entire system of secondary and higher education. With the admission of women to the program of teacher education, enrollments at River Forest and Seward had more than doubled between 1943 and 1950. To relieve these pressures, the synod authorized two-year pre-teacher-training programs at four of the preparatory schools: Fort Wayne, St. Paul, Oakland, and Portland. On an experimental basis the high school course at Concordia in Fort Wayne was discontinued and only the junior college program retained. Students could enter from any high school with only two years of Latin, two years of German, and no Greek, thus for the first time admitting students to a pretheological course without a heavy emphasis on classical languages.[30]

To cap the changes, Missouri also introduced the senior college concept. This came about as a response to the frequently expressed complaint that the ministerial training program in the Lutheran Church–Missouri Synod was not as comprehensive as that of other Lutheran synods and that it did not require a full four-year college course for admission to the seminary.

An earlier effort in 1938 to add a year to the seminary course at St. Louis and to grant a B.A. degree at the end of the second year had not been well received. A second possible option was to turn one or more of the existing preparatory schools into four-year colleges. In 1947, however, the synod directed the Board for Higher Education to carry out a plan retaining a distinct two-year preministerial course at all existing prep schools and creating a separate "senior college" embracing the last two years of the standard American college course and offering the B.A. degree. Under the plan, reaffirmed in 1950, the synod would establish a fully accredited four-year preministerial course and at the same time enable its St. Louis seminary to meet the accreditation standards which called for a B.A. degree as prerequisite for admission to theological study.

Concordia Senior College opened in 1957 in Fort Wayne, Indiana, in a handsome complex of buildings designed by the Finnish architect Eero Saarinen, erected at a cost of $2,750,000. In assessing the project the Board for Higher Education confirmed the growing trend in the Missouri system to adjust its structure to meet the demands of contemporary educational practice. "The longer our Church works in the American scene," it declared, "the more necessary it becomes for us to approach the national educational pattern which influences the American public so that our workers will be well equipped to understand the environment in which they do their work."[31]

Church Mergers and College Relations

If the colleges of the Lutheran church emerged from the dislocations of the war and its immediate aftermath into an era of unprecedented growth and prosperity, the same can be said of the Lutheran churches themselves. The 1950s were a time of religious "boom" or of renewal in all of American religious life. Church membership in the United States rose to 70% of the population. In 1955 it was estimated that just under one-half of the population attended religious services in a typical week.[32] Although Billy Graham and Oral Roberts kept the revival of the 50s within the traditional American pattern of the mass rally and the "call to personal decision," mainline denominations employed a variety of new devices to extend their mission and ministry and to deepen the spiritual life of their congregations.

Lutheran churches, historically dependent upon immigration and large families for their increase, reached out in neighborhood canvasses, well-organized membership drives, stewardship education, evangelism programs, and "PTR" (Preaching-Teaching-Reaching) meetings. As membership expanded, hundreds of neat English Gothic churches blossomed in the suburbs. At its peak one church extension program produced one new congregation every 54 hours.[33] Leading the way, the conservative Missouri Synod grew from 1,400,000 members in 1945 to 2,500,000 in 1960, an increase of 56%.

The churches grew not only in numbers but also in affluence. They shared their largesse generously in overseas relief programs, improved pastors' salaries, and churchwide benevolences. As has already been described, their bounty included Lutheran colleges as never before.

The postwar years also brought further progress toward church unity. As the 19th century had been marked by the proliferation of Lutheran synods, the trend of the 20th had been toward cooperation and unification. Significant mergers had taken place in 1917, 1918, and 1930, and a cooperative National Lutheran Council had emerged out of the common service activities of eight church bodies during World War I. World War II had given further stimulus to cooperative efforts, both to serve members of the armed forces and to aid war-ravaged European churches and refugees at the war's end. American churches that had thus learned to know each other better opened dialogs that led to two broadly inclusive mergers in 1960 and 1962.

The American Lutheran Church, formed in 1960, brought together three ethnic groups: The Evangelical Lutheran Church, of Norwegian origin; the American Lutheran Church, of German parentage; and the Danish-background United Evangelical Lutheran Church. The Lutheran Free Church, another Norwegian group, joined in 1963. In 1962 the Lutheran Church in America united five ethnic strains: the multifaceted United Lutheran Church in America, of largely German origin; the Augustana Church, of Swedish background; the Finns of the Suomi Synod; the Danes of the American Evangelical Lutheran Church; and the Slovak Zion Synod. More than two-thirds of all Lutherans in North America were thereby brought into two major bodies of nearly equal size. Members of the Synodical Conference, largely made up of the Missouri and Wisconsin Synods, constituted the third large association of Lutherans.

These mergers brought 9 colleges and 2 junior colleges into The American Lutheran Church (ALC), and 18 colleges and 3 junior colleges into the Lutheran Church in America (LCA). Although the mergers did not directly influence the internal operation of related colleges, they did affect the patterns of relationship with each other and with the new church bodies. Each college brought the traditions, constituency, and patterns of governance and financial support developed within its own church. In the predecessor bodies of The American Lutheran Church most of the colleges had been established by direct action of church bodies. A few had been founded and operated by local or regional associations of Lutherans who elected the college trustees. All were accustomed to receiving annual financial support from central synodical treasuries. Colleges of the old American Lutheran Church had been very closely controlled by a synodical board of education. The corporations of both Luther College and St. Olaf College were identical with the biennial convention of the Evangelical Lutheran Church, while the corporations of Pacific Lutheran University, Concordia College, and Augustana College were substantially identified with district conventions of the church.

In the new American Lutheran Church these governing structures, closely identified with the structure of the church itself, were maintained. Supervisory authority was assigned to a Board of College Education. Elected by the church convention, it determined the annual financial allocations to the colleges and maintained representation on all college boards.

The formation of the Lutheran Church in America posed a more complicated problem. Each of the two smaller synods, those of the Danes and the Finns, brought a single junior college into the merger. The Augustana Church had 4 senior colleges supported by the geographical conferences of the synod. The 14 colleges and 1 junior college of the ULCA were all individually related to local synods.

In the new Lutheran Church in America the local synodical structure was maintained, but new synod boundaries were drawn and colleges were matched with synods on the principle of at least one college per synod. These realignments made serious changes in the traditional geographic constituencies of several of the schools and in some cases narrowed their base of financial support as well.

The Constitution of the LCA expressly stated that the relations of the church to the colleges, including governance, should, with limited exceptions, be "sustained entirely through the synods." Wide variety, however, prevailed in the degree to which synods participated in board elections. Colleges which had been established by synod actions or had become synod-owned provided for election by the synod conventions of most if not all trustees. Others, established by associations of Lutherans but not owned by synods, had fewer synod-elected trustees. By 1962 all LCA colleges were receiving annual grants from their related synods. The newly created Board of College Education and Church Vocations was given advisory powers, the power to grant supplementary financial aid to colleges and to establish standards upon which the LCA would recognize the colleges as related to the LCA and to the synods.[34]

The patterns of church relationship thus established by the two new church bodies in 1960 and 1962 were substantially different, each reflecting the historical antecedents of its constituting churches and their colleges. Variety also persisted within each of the new structures. Nevertheless, new channels of cooperation and interaction were opened, both among the new groups of colleges associated through each merger and between the newly constituted boards of college education.

Fifty Years of Lutheran College Cooperation

While most of American Lutheranism was engaged in the process of regrouping, Lutheran colleges were celebrating the 50th anniversary of their pioneer venture in inter-Lutheran cooperation. In 1960 the National Lutheran Educational Conference assembled in Boston to commemorate the event under a future-oriented theme: New Dimensions in Lutheran Higher Education.

Just two years earlier, in a move which reflected heightened confidence in the usefulness of the organization to its membership, the NLEC had established its own office in Washington, D.C., and appointed its first executive secretary.[35] Dr. Gould Wickey, the new executive, had served for 30 years as executive secretary of the ULCA Board of Education and earlier had been professor at Concordia College in Moorhead, Minnesota, and president of Carthage College. Few Lutheran educators have been so effective in drawing together the diverse strands of Lutheran higher education. In a long and distinguished career he had served as spokesman, interpreter, and publicist for Lutheran college cooperation. His leadership promised strength and stability for the Lutheran Educational Conference and its 64 member institutions as they entered the stormy decade of the 60s. The selection of a Washington location recognized that in the future, relations with the United States government would assume an increasingly important role in the development of Lutheran higher education.

18 THE SIXTIES: DECADE OF TESTING

Agenda for Unrest

In one of the papers presented at the 50th anniversary meeting of the National Lutheran Educational Conference in 1960 Dr. Conrad Bergendoff observed that in 1910, the year of its founding, no one could successfully have predicted the coming of World War I, the Great Depression, the growth of communism, the splitting of the atom, or the orbiting of man-made satellites in space. Any self-appointed prophet for the much shorter span of the 1960s would have been equally hard put to foresee the kaleidoscopic series of events which shook the foundations of society during those 10 years and subjected American higher education to its severest test.

Before the decade had run its course the nation would have seen four presidents in office: one retiring in dignity, one assassinated, one rendered politically impotent by promotion of an unpopular war, and one newly elected, but destined to resign in disgrace before his second term expired. International relations would be dominated by a cold war against communism—whether in Berlin, Cuba, or Southeast Asia—and would cost the nation more than 200,000 casualties. A struggle for equal rights for blacks and for women, launched amid bitter white opposition in the South in the 50s, would erupt into riots and violence, the burning of northern cities, and assassinations of its most articulate leaders. A generation of youth—black and white—the product of the nation's greatest population boom, kept out of the labor market, drafted for an unpopular war, and disillusioned with the plastic affluence of a society which had no place for them except in school, registered its frustration in protest

against all established authority, whether government, family, or the current code of social mores.

Education's Golden Years

The college enrollment explosion of the two previous decades was repeated in the 60s as the postwar baby boom reached college age. Between 1960 and 1970 the number of students in American colleges and universities increased at the rate of about a half-million a year, a number equivalent to the entire higher education population of 1920, reaching a total of 8.5 million by 1970. By far the largest increase was in the public institutions, which by 1970 enrolled 75% of all college students.

A whole new echelon of two-year public community colleges sprang up across the nation. In 1962 the state of Florida announced its intent to put a community college within commuting distance of 99% of the state's citizenry. California operated 70 such schools in 1963 and planned for 22 more in the immediate future. More than 800,000 students swarmed into the 700 community colleges already operating in the country in 1962.[1]

Many states established hierarchies of public institutions or expanded existing ones, such as the giant systems of New York, California, and Wisconsin. State colleges became universities, and teachers colleges added courses and programs in every conceivable field. Private colleges continued to perform their public services, straining facilities and faculties to accommodate more than two million students, one-fourth of the national total by 1970. In 1966, 36 Lutheran four-year colleges and 18 junior colleges enrolled 78,364 students, an increase of 54% since 1960 and more than 100% since 1956.[2]

No decade in American history has equaled the 60s in the mass of educational legislation which rolled through the Congress of the United States and through state legislatures. The Higher Education Act of 1963 made grants and loans available for classrooms, libraries, and laboratories. A Health Professions Educational Assistance Act in 1963 provided funds for establishing health professions training programs. The Economic Opportunity Act of 1964, a part of President Johnson's "war on poverty," provided grants and work-study funds for lower income families. The Higher Education Act of 1965 established the category of "developing institutions," funded programs of library assistance, community services, and a National Teacher Corps. The International Education Act of 1966 offered grants to colleges and universities to establish and operate programs of international studies. Amendments to all the preceding legislation in 1968 expanded federal programs and continued their operation into the 1970s.

New Buildings and New Dollars

All of these programs were made available to both public and private colleges, with the limiting proviso that funds not be used for religious purposes. Every Lutheran college whose policies did not render it ineligible became deeply involved in a variety of federal and state grants or loans; classroom buildings, libraries, science facilities, student centers, and dormitories blossomed. Open excavations and construction scaffolds were standard exhibits on every campus tour. In a single period of 20 months in 1965–1967 the 19 colleges of the LCA received federal grants and loans for building construction in the amount of $29,949,644 and additional program grants of $1,524,790.[3] During these affluent years sponsoring church bodies and college development offices were also extending themselves to provide facilities and operating resources for their expanding institutions. The Missouri Synod carried the full cost of all capital construction on its college campuses, totaling $44,000,000 between 1955 and 1965. The largest single expenditure was the purchase of a 200-acre campus for a new junior college in Ann Arbor, Michigan, and the construction of a complete complex of college buildings at a cost of more than $6,000,000. The Lutheran Ingathering for Education (LIFE) campaign of The American Lutheran Church distributed $10,419,708 to its 12 colleges from 1965 to 1975, largely for capital construction. From 1956 to 1966 capital gifts to 19 LCA colleges totaled $58,058,222, of which over $14,000,000 came from church sources.[4]

With increased enrollments, larger faculties, and expanded facilities, costs of operating the colleges rose accordingly, and with them student tuition and fees. By 1970 the annual bill for tuition, board, and room at the average four-year Lutheran college exceeded $2500, a 120% increase since 1959.[5] Church bodies also responded with more generous annual operational subsidies. Colleges related to the LCA, for example, received grants of $3,278,051 in 1966–1967, compared to $1,619,976 ten years earlier.[6] The Missouri Synod, which covered more than 40% of the educational costs of its colleges, raised its subsidy from $5,788,123 in 1963 to $9,192,572 in 1970.[7]

Church subsidies helped to some extent to keep student costs down, but more than half the students in Lutheran colleges required further financial assistance. In 1969–1970, 28 senior colleges distributed a total of $22,243,000 in financial aid through grants, loans, and campus employment, an increase of 461% since 1959–1960. Most of this came from government sources, but about $6,000,000 came from college operating funds at the expense of enrichments in their educational programs.[8]

During these years of physical growth and expansion Lutheran colleges also developed internally. Faculties increased in numbers and also in the quality of their preparation. Of a total of 4,153 full- and part-time teachers at 32 senior colleges 37% had earned doctorates in 1970. Three colleges, Muhlenberg, Gustavus Adolphus, and Wittenberg, reported more than 50% holding Ph.D. degrees.[9] Library facilities expanded on most campuses. Four schools had chapters of Phi Beta Kappa: Gettysburg, Augustana (Rock Island), St. Olaf, and Muhlenberg.

With the increased volume of student applications several Lutheran colleges were able to exercise greater selectivity in admission. Nineteen of the 22 colleges using the Scholastic Aptitude Test (SAT) in admissions procedures reported median verbal scores above 500.[10] While raising the academic quality of their student bodies, Lutheran colleges also raised questions for the first time among pastors and congregations whose sons and daughters failed on this account to gain entrance to the college their church supported.

Of Calendars and Curricula

In their efforts to enhance the quality and attractiveness of their academic programs, the colleges engaged in a variety of new ventures, some of which were experimental in character. The traditional two-semester academic calendar was subjected to careful reexamination and, beginning with Gustavus Adolphus in 1963, 14 Lutheran schools adopted the "four-one-four" pattern, with two terms of equal length separated by a four-week "Interim" in January. Such a one-month term encouraged the development of special courses stimulating the creativity of faculty and capturing the imagination of students—even offering the opportunity for study abroad and off-campus experiences in other colleges or in nonacademic settings.

Interdisciplinary courses, independent study, and honors programs for superior students were introduced. Two of the most innovative and enduring experiments were undertaken by Valparaiso University and St. Olaf College. In its fuller development of a university structure Valparaiso created Christ College in 1966 as a separate and highly selective college of liberal arts within the university. Students became members of the college by invitation and were offered special courses in composition, literature, history, religion, philosophy, and integrated courses in "General Studies" while fufilling graduation and major requirements in other undergraduate colleges. As suggested by the name of the college, its intention was also "to establish the relevance of Lutheran theology to the liberal arts in every area."[11]

St. Olaf established its "Paracollege" in 1969 with an initial selected group of about 75 freshmen. These students were given freedom to take or audit regular courses, work independently, or study under the direction of a faculty tutor. Progress was dependent on successful completion of examinations. The intention was to provide opportunity for independent, individual learning within the existing curricular and faculty structure.[12]

One of the positive by-products of the wartime experiences of the American public was a rekindled interest in international study and travel. Instead of a resurgent isolationism, such as occurred after World War I, American interest in postwar reconstruction after World War II was followed by a wave of overseas travel facilitated by the general affluence of the 50s and 60s. When St. Olaf College conducted a survey during the 60s, it discovered that more than half of its entering freshman class had already had an overseas experience.[13]

With their cultural roots deeply embedded in the languages and traditions of several European countries, Lutheran colleges have always maintained relationships with persons and institutions in their lands of origin. Faculty have been drawn from abroad; immigrant youth have always been among their students, though in decreasing numbers. Languages have been taught and cultural ties nourished, especially among midwestern German and Scandinavian schools founded in the late 19th century.

Efforts to develop a broader international consciousness or to encourage attendance by foreign students, however, had been rare. Roanoke College provided a notable exception before World War I by enrolling nearly 100 students from Japan, Korea, Mexico, Puerto Rico, and other West Indian islands, as well as 35 Choctaw Indians from Oklahoma.[14] Before World War II foreign mission boards of the Lutheran churches had placed some African and Asian students in Lutheran colleges in an effort to develop leadership in mission churches. A Scholarship and Exchange Program initiated in 1957 by the Lutheran World Federation and the National Lutheran Council placed from 50 to

100 students each year in Lutheran colleges. Under the direction of Dr. Ruth Wick during the 1960s, this program made a significant contribution both to ecclesiastical and to political leadership in several emerging African and Asian nations.[15] In 1962–1963, 234 overseas students studied at Lutheran colleges in the United States; by 1979 the number had risen to 750.[16]

Academic courses in international relations had been included in the curricula of Lutheran colleges well before World War II, but the postwar decades brought a wide variety of new programs, curricular and extracurricular, emphasizing better understanding of other peoples and cultures. Area studies such as the Near East Program established at Thiel in 1958, the Latin-American Program of Augustana (Rock Island), Asian studies at Gettysburg and Gustavus Adolphus, and many others gained great popularity. Nearly every Lutheran college offered the opportunity to spend the junior year, a summer, or a January term in an overseas program. Wagner College even established its own student center in Bregenz, Austria. Several colleges such as Wittenberg, Augustana (Rock Island), and Luther created Offices of International Studies to coordinate and direct the variety of programs offered to their students. In 1970 one-half of the graduating class of St. Olaf College had participated in a foreign study experience during their college years.

Beginnings of Black Higher Education

It was only in the late 60s that Lutheran colleges began to face seriously their social and educational responsibilities for the education of the black minority in the United States. A survey conducted in January 1965 by the Lutheran Students Association of America reported the following counts of black students at Lutheran schools in the North: Augsburg, five; Augustana (Rock Island), "between five and ten"; California Lutheran, three; Carthage, "three-fourths of one percent of our students"; Concordia, Moorhead, only one; Dana, four; Gettysburg, three; Luther, eight; St. Olaf, "about six"; Susquehanna, "only two"; Texas Lutheran, one; Upsala, "from thirty to forty"; Wartburg, five; and Wittenberg, "perhaps twenty."[17]

With the exception of the Missouri Synod, none of the Lutheran churches had undertaken any effort to include the black minority or to provide educational opportunities for them. Only one black student is known to have attended a Lutheran institution prior to 1867. Daniel Payne, a product of Dr. John Bachman's ministry in Charleston, South Carolina, studied at Gettysburg Seminary in 1835 and was subsequently ordained by the Franckean Synod. He later became a bishop of the African Methodist Church and president of Wilberforce University.[18]

No institutional ventures for blacks were undertaken until after 1900 when the Synodical Conference opened schools in New Orleans and Concord,

North Carolina, to prepare teachers and pastors. The New Orleans school closed in 1925, but Immanuel College, founded in Concord in 1903 and moved to Greensboro in 1905, eventually included a four-year high school, a normal department, and a four-year pretheological program. After 1930, until it was closed in 1960, Immanuel College operated as a coeducational junior college.

In 1916 the Board of Colored Missions of the Synodical Conference sent Rev. Nils Bakke to central Alabama as a mission organizer. By 1922 there were enough mission stations scattered through Alabama, Louisiana, and Mississippi, for Bakke to organize a training school for teachers in Selma, known as Alabama Lutheran Academy and College. The school was compelled to cut back its program during the depression, but in 1947 the junior college division was reopened.[19]

During the 50s Lutheran civil rights activists urged the closing of both the school in Selma and Immanuel College in Greensboro as "outmoded" segregationist institutions.[20] After conducting open hearings on this matter in 1960 the Synodical Conference determined to close Immanuel, transfer its library and equipment to Selma, and turn the administration of the school over to the Missouri Synod. Since 1962 the school in Selma, now known as Concordia College, has functioned as a junior college of the Missouri system, serving almost entirely black students. As late as 1946 there were only two blacks in the entire white college preparatory system of the Missouri Synod. The only other Lutheran synods to take an interest in black education in the South were the Joint Ohio Synod, during the 1920s, and its successor, the American Lutheran Church, from 1930 to 1951. Instruction in the schools sponsored by these bodies, however, was not conducted on the collegiate level.

Among Lutheran colleges Upsala was the pioneer in breaking the color barrier. After its move from Brooklyn to East Orange, New Jersey, in 1924, nine black students enrolled between 1925 and 1929. In January 1947, President O. P. Kretzmann personally escorted the first two black students at Valparaiso from the railroad station to the campus to enroll in the university's Lutheran Deaconess School. A National Lutheran Council questionnaire circulated by Ervin B. Krebs revealed that in 1952, with the exception of Upsala, Capital, and Wartburg, most Lutheran colleges had either no blacks at all, or at most, one or two.[21]

Significant changes in attitude and practice in both churches and colleges, however, occurred in the wake of Supreme Court decisions and the civil rights struggle. Immediately after the school desegregation decision in 1954, nine synods of the ULCA went on record indicating their support. The Missouri Synod convention in 1956 resolved that its institutions, agencies, and offices make no distinctions based on color in their entrance requirements or employment policies.[22] By 1957 a college poll revealed that nine colleges had adopted official policies against discrimination and most had opened their classrooms to blacks "by common consent" rather than official action.[23]

The early 60s witnessed sit-in demonstrations in the South, the Freedom Ride Campaign, James Meredith's fight for admission to the University of Mississippi, the historic 1963 March on Washington addressed by Martin Luther King Jr., and the Civil Rights Act of 1964, prohibiting discrimination in public accommodations and employment. By 1965 when Dr. King led the march from Selma to Montgomery to claim voting rights for Alabama blacks, student involvement in the civil rights crusade had reached national proportions. Thirty-one members of the Valparaiso University community, including two faculty members, traveled to Selma to join the march. The Rev. James Reeb, a Unitarian minister from Boston and a graduate of St. Olaf College, was beaten to death by four white men in Birmingham while on his way to a meeting the evening following the march. The first student political protest demonstration at Valparaiso occurred as an expression of sympathy for the family of the murdered minister.[24]

In the face of mounting racial tensions and the minimal enrollment of black students in Lutheran colleges in 1965, it was not sufficient simply to "admit" blacks. Active recruitment and assistance programs were hastily devised, and early in 1968 the LCA Board of College Education and Church Vocations commissioned an Educational Opportunity Study by Louis W. Bone.[25]

Bone visited 14 campuses, assessing the efforts being made to recruit, accommodate, and teach black students. In response to his recommendations the board allocated funds to encourage special programs for economically deprived students, college counseling services for minority youth, programs for teachers of minority groups, and "Opportunity Grants" of $500 for Afro-American and Native American students.

Black Activism on Lutheran Campuses

About 1966, following the riots in Watts and the assassination of Malcolm X, the goals of the "black revolution" changed from integration to "black power."[26] Black students on several Lutheran campuses began to make demands similar to those by their counterparts at secular colleges and universities. An organization of black students at Wittenberg won its demands for a separate residence, a black student adviser, and a budget for black student activities by temporarily withdrawing from the college and joining the black community at nearby Antioch College in Yellow Springs, Ohio. In a more serious confrontation early in 1968 involving the shooting of a black student by a campus security guard, the Wittenberg campus was virtually immobilized for a 48-hour period. At Wagner a group of black and Puerto Rican students occupied a campus building and held Dr. Harold Haas, the academic dean, in his office for eight hours to dramatize their demands for more black student enrollment and representation on the faculty.[27] At Upsala a building housing the history department was occupied by students demanding courses reflecting the Afro-American experience.[28]

In contrast, however, most Lutheran colleges located in rural or small-town settings enrolled few blacks and had little or no experience with black activism. In efforts to sensitize their predominantly white student populations, many of these colleges conducted forums, invited minority speakers, and inaugurated faculty and student exchanges with black colleges in the South. Luther, Wartburg, Gustavus Adolphus, St. Olaf, and Concordia (Moorhead) all conducted such exchange programs. Luther established an Upward Bound program in 1966 from which several black students were recruited for college study.[29]

Lutheran colleges which made serious efforts at the recruitment of black students were confronted by two hard facts. Black youth were most often from poor families and many were academically unprepared for college education. To meet these problems colleges tried a variety of remedial and financial-aid programs assisted in part by federal and state funding.

Church departments of higher education provided assistance as well. The 1968 convention of the LCA designated a part of an emergency churchwide appeal for minority scholarships. Its Board for College Education and Church Vocations funded a wide variety of projects submitted by the colleges for aiding minority students. Among these was the Timothy J. Still Program at Upsala College for recruiting high school dropouts from Newark, New Jersey, and other nearby communities.[30] In 1970 The American Lutheran Church inaugurated the National Scholarship and Grant Program for Minority Students. During its first 10 years 1,764 awards totaling $1,029,687 were made, mostly to black students attending colleges of the ALC.[31]

By the early 1970s, as black enrollments at Lutheran colleges rose, campus and curricular changes began to appear. Black students at Thiel College formed an association in 1969 and established Unity House as a residential and cultural center.[32] Courses in Afro-American history and culture, black literature, and majors in minority studies appeared at several colleges, but most schools sought to broaden existing courses to include multicultural emphases. Luther College established a separate Department of African and African-American Studies, which was being maintained as recently as 1984.

The continuing effects of the ''black revolution'' have been evident both in the enrollments and the curricula of Lutheran colleges. While many of the courses and activities generated as immediate responses to the tensions of the late 60s have disappeared, a wide variety of other cross-cultural programs has been introduced which has continued to broaden the horizons of later generations of students. When compared with the virtually all-white character of most Lutheran campuses in 1965, the 2,247 blacks in attendance in 1984 represent a significant increase.[33] A few schools in urban locations have been able to maintain substantial black enrollments. Of Upsala's 1,046 full-time students in 1984, 26.5% were black.[34]

Internal Campus Protests

While racial issues persisted throughout the 60s as a major cause of campus tension and conflict, students rallied to a bewildering variety of other causes as well. Among these were nuclear testing, environmental pollution, the new morality, parietal rules, campus food services, curricular inflexibility, participatory democracy, the Vietnam War, the ROTC, and the military draft. Accompanying and often motivating the protests was an almost indefinable mixture of frustration and resentment with the seemingly arbitrary authority embodied in the ruling institutions of society—whether government, school, family, or church. While such feelings were not confined to the student population, they found their most articulate expression on college campuses in protests and demonstrations ranging from peaceful sit-ins to strikes and violence.[35]

The first of the major campus uprisings—at Berkeley in 1964—was directed at the university itself, in protest at the inept handling of a dispute over the distribution of campus literature. Although it had few parallels either in immediate cause or in the extent of disruption it produced, the Berkeley revolt exposed issues which were basic to much of the campus unrest of the 60s. Local circumstances differed widely, depending on the location, size, and character of the instituion. But young people in general and students in particular were increasingly impatient with institutions which seemed insensitive to them as persons.[36]

There was ample evidence of impersonality in such massive academic bureaucracies as the University of California, whose president Clark Kerr described them as "multiversities." But even in smaller colleges the assignment of student numbers to correspond with IBM registration cards conveyed a similar message in less strident terms. The network of regulations surrounding campus and dormitory life seemed unduly paternalistic, and academic requirements correspondingly inflexible. It was against such restraints on student freedom that organized protests and demonstrations were directed on most residential campuses across the country. Studies conducted by the Educational Testing Service found that in 1964–1965 dormitory regulations and food services were issues of protest at one-fourth to one-third of all four-year colleges.[37]

Socially conservative Lutheran campuses had traditionally acknowledged their responsibility *in loco parentis* and had dutifully regulated dormitory hours for women students. Prohibitions against women smoking, social dancing, and the use of alcohol were common, especially in midwestern colleges. All such regulations came under student attack. Under student pressures dormitory hours were drastically extended or eliminated entirely. Coed dorms and intervisitation rights won limited approval, and the longstanding Norwegian taboo on social dancing at St. Olaf and Augustana was lifted.[38]

Both mandatory attendance at chapel and all-college convocations became casualties in the concerted drive to eliminate all requirements. Even in schools which had maintained voluntary but traditional chapel programs, attendance dropped, and in some cases the chapel was maintained only with difficulty.

Strong demands for student autonomy focused on due process in handling student discipline, privacy of student rooms, and independent administration of student-activity funds. Beyond autonomy in the conduct of their own affairs, students sought membership on faculty committees and campus councils and in some cases won representation on the governing boards of the colleges.[39]

In addition to demands for new courses meeting standards of "relevancy," they pressed for elimination of comprehensive examinations, and substitution of "pass-fail" for conventional grades. In a reversal of roles, students developed systems for evaluation of faculty and often published results in the campus newspaper. In campaigning for many of these innovations, students resorted to demonstrations, marches, placards, sit-ins, and direct appeals to the president of the college or the board of trustees.

War-Related Campus Protests

Beginning in 1965 with the bombing of North Vietnam by the United States, a new focus was provided for student protest. The war in Vietnam seized center stage for young American men and women for the remainder of the decade and eventually undermined the confidence of the American people in its national leadership. Following an alleged provocation by North Vietnamese gunboats in the Gulf of Tonkin in August 1964, President Johnson increased the number of American troops in Vietnam to 185,000 and doubled the monthly draft quota. College students responded with an initial series of peaceful "teach-ins," petitions, and demonstrations. These later gave way to open draft resistance and antiwar protests reaching far beyond college campuses. A climax of national dissent in early 1968 forced President Johnson to decline renomination. Following the assassination of Martin Luther King Jr. in April, black militancy exploded. Riots occurred in 110 cities, including the nation's capital where fires raged throughout one whole section of the city.[40] Before the summer was over Robert Kennedy, too, had been felled by an assassin's bullet, and a riot-ridden Democratic convention in Chicago had nominated Hubert Humphrey for the presidency.

After 1968 the incidence of campus protests of all kinds continued to rise. In 1969–1970, 80% of all four-year colleges reported protest incidents over some issue.[41] More than half of them were war-related, but even the internal bouts between students and college administrators over interdormitory visitations or faculty evaluation were conducted in a climate of nervous tension over national issues. The prospect of being drafted for service in Vietnam hovered like an evil spirit over every campus. Most campuses observed a national Vietnam Moratorium on October 15, 1969. Classes were canceled while students and faculty gathered for memorial services, prayers, lectures, discussions, and debates. In the spring of 1970 when President Nixon announced that American troops had crossed the Cambodian frontier, a new wave of protests swept the country. An "Anti-War Week" at St. Olaf College in late April concluded with an overnight student occupation of the administration building and an accompanying demand for the dismantling of the college's ROTC unit. A prompt and reasoned response to the students by President Sidney Rand promising speedy completion of a review of the unit's status ended the sit-in after 24 hours. In a gesture of confidence probably unique in the chronicles of campus protest, the students swept and mopped the corridors of the occupied building before they left.[42]

President Nixon's announcement triggered more tragic developments on larger and more volatile campuses. A special presidential commission headed by former Governor Scranton of Pennsylvania reported that in the four days following the announcement 20 new student strikes had begun each day.[43] Some were peaceful; others were marred by stone-throwing, violence, and altercations with police. In an effort to maintain order on the campus of Kent State University the Ohio National Guard was called. Shortly after noon on May 4, for reasons yet unclear, the troops opened fire on the students, leaving four dead and nine wounded on the campus green.

Students at Valparaiso University were also engaged in a strike at the time, and the news from Kent State raised existing tensions to an even higher pitch. On the night of May 5-6, after the conclusion of an extended nocturnal discussion between college leaders and protesting students, a fire broke out in Kinsey Hall where the discussion had been held. The building and an adjoining structure were burned beyond repair.[44]

The tragedy of Kent State and its counterpart 10 days later at Jackson State College in Mississippi stunned the campuses and seemed to exercise a sobering influence on the whole country. It also opened the way for soul-searching and for critical review of responsibility for the disasters of the previous six years as well as an assessment of the damages which had been sustained. It was clear that public confidence in the whole system of American higher education had been profoundly shaken. Both student behavior and the indecisive way in which student insurgency had been handled by some college administrators were severely criticized. Less attention was given to root causes, such as the war itself, the social malaise affecting the entire nation, and the almost impossible enrollment and financial pressures to which the educational structure of the country had been subjected during the preceding 20 years.

Lutherans Lose Two Colleges

Although Lutheran campuses experienced relatively few severe protests and only minimal violence, the nationwide decline in confidence in colleges and their leadership was nonetheless shared by their constituencies. Their concern came into sharper focus when at the close of the decade the governing boards of two Lutheran institutions took steps to sever official relationship with the church. Hartwick College was affiliated with the Metropolitan and Upper New York Synods of the Lutheran Church in America and Waterloo Lutheran University with the Eastern Canada Synod. In both cases the decisions were strongly influenced by public policy developments of the 60s that prompted institutional dependence on government while correspondingly weakening relations with the church.

Although Hartwick's Lutheran roots reached back to 1797, the college itself was one of the youngest of the four-year institutions related to the Lutheran Church in America, having been chartered only in 1928. After weathering the Depression and World War II it shared both the benefits and the hazards of rapid expansion in the 1950s and 1960s. Between 1959 and 1968, under the able presidency of Frederick M. Binder, enrollment increased from 450 to 1550 students. During the same period nine new buildings and a $5 million endowment were added to the college's assets.

In 1968 the state of New York made available direct financial grants to private colleges independent of church control. To become eligible for the so-called Bundy grants of $400 per graduate, the trustees of Hartwick College voted to disassociate the college from its two affiliated synods.[45] Since board membership included more than a dozen synod-elected members, and the resolution of disassociation was prepared by the president of the Upper New York Synod, the decision can scarcely be termed a unilateral college action. The Bundy money doubtless provided the immediate impulse for the separation, but the ease with which it was accomplished strongly suggests that during the

hectic decade of the 60s neither college nor synodical leaders paid serious attention to the nourishing of mutual relationships.[46]

The change in the status of Waterloo Lutheran University was consummated in November 1973, when it became a provincial university and
adopted a new name, Wilfred Laurier University, in honor of Ontario's first
prime minister. Developments leading to this final step, however, began in
1956 when the president of Waterloo College, Dr. Gerald Hagey, attempted to
create a new university with associated faculties in science and engineering to
supplement the arts faculty of Waterloo College. The Lutheran board of governors, fearful of losing control of the college, rejected his proposal. Dr.
Hagey then resigned as president of Waterloo College and proceeded to establish the "associated faculties" as a separate provincially supported university.
The Lutherans, in turn, secured a new charter for their college, thereafter to be
known as Waterloo Lutheran University.[47]

During the 60s Canadian colleges and universities experienced expansion
similar to that of their American counterparts. Under the presidency of Dr.
William Villaume, Waterloo Lutheran University continued to operate its original faculties of arts and theology, but added a School of Business, a School of
Graduate Studies, and a Graduate School of Social Work. By 1973 enrollment
exceeded 4000 students and the annual operating budget was $8 million.

In 1967 funding by the Canadian federal government that had been largely
responsible both for operations and for the extensive capital expansion of the
university was terminated. Under new procedures the province of Ontario,
which had a long-standing policy of not giving grants to church-related institutions, became responsible for university funding. However, after extended ne-
gotiation the province agreed to grant subsidies to such institutions equal to
50% of the grants to provincial schools. As a condition for receiving even this
limited support, Waterloo Lutheran University was not permitted to add any
new programs nor to increase its student tuition.[48]

Under these conditions and facing the heretofore untried option of seeking
private support for both operations and capital expansion, the board of governors saw little likelihood of competing successfully with its provincially supported neighbor, Waterloo University. The willingness of the province of
Ontario to entertain a request for the acceptance of Waterloo Lutheran University as a provincial university, with full compensation to the Eastern Canada
Synod for its investment, seemed an attractive solution. The board's recommendation was adopted by the synod in 1973 over the strong objections of a
group of pastors and laity organized as a Committee for an Independent WLU.
Under the terms of the transfer in 1973 the Eastern Canada Synod received
$3,100,000 and retained full ownership and control of the seminary, which
continued to operate as a federated college of Wilfred Laurier University.[49]

...ipt to the Sixties

...story over 200 years provided very few ex-
...disassociation of Hartwick and Waterloo from
...ppraisal of the general health of college/church
...e 60s. The enormous growth in student population,
...strength since World War II had progressively de-
...e of the colleges on the church. The pursuit of govern-
...ts had occupied the energy and attention of college offi-
...expense of attention to synod activities and congregational
...es of many an alumnus or lay supporter, the colleges were no
longer the familiar places where "prexy's" office was always accessible and
every homecoming was a kind of family reunion.

By the end of the decade a large part of the constituency tended to see all
campuses as capitals of disorder. Though highly overdrawn in the case of a majority of Lutheran campuses, the image of long-haired, free-wheeling students,
seemingly without respect either for parents or professors, demanding a role in
running the college and forcing concessions from harrassed college administrators, undermined much of the old-time confidence in alma mater and its
leadership.

Nor was the faculty the closely knit homogeneous unit of days gone by.
Diversity in academic and social background and religious profession of the
expanded faculties created a more cosmopolitan campus climate, but stirred
discussion among both pastors and laypersons concerning the "critical mass"
that would assure a college of a Lutheran character.

While enrollments at Lutheran colleges increased by 54% between 1960
and 1970, the percentage of Lutheran students in attendance declined from 66
to 49.[50] Required chapel disappeared at almost all colleges and new curricula
often reduced religion requirements to one or two courses or even an option
among other choices in fulfilling a distribution requirement.

Moreover, the churches themselves, shaken by the social earthquakes of
the 60s, had lost much of their earlier confidence and optimism and were uncertain of their strategies. The religious boom of the 50s had collapsed. Church
attendance slumped. Both the newly merged LCA and ALC were already beginning to consider plans for reordering their internal structures. The erosion of
social mores so apparent on college campuses also afflicted the youth in congregations and even some of their parents. Beginning in the late 50s a theological shift, especially calling into question the popularly held literalist view of
the Scriptures, had taken place among conservative Lutheran seminaries of the
upper Midwest. These views met sharp resistance among pastors and congregations and caused even greater dismay when they were reflected in the religion departments of several colleges of the former ELC. A confrontation at

Luther College in 1962 resulted in the replacement of the entire religion faculty.[51]

Finally, the crisis of the cities became a reality to the churches after the urban debacles of 1967 and 1968. When the LCA convention of 1968 voted spontaneously for a two-year, $6,500,000 emergency campaign for urban concerns, it signaled a new era in budget priorities for the church. Thereafter institutional grants, including annual college subsidies, were regularly curtailed in favor of specific social programs for minority concerns and urban ministries.

These developments, bridging the 60s and 70s, subjected college/church relationships to a greater strain than at any previous time. Nevertheless, in spite of the strongly secularizing influences of public policies in the 60s, the increasingly pluralistic character of college constituencies, and the social revolution which enveloped both colleges and churches, their virtually unbroken ranks speak eloquently of the strength and resilience of the Lutheran tradition in higher education.

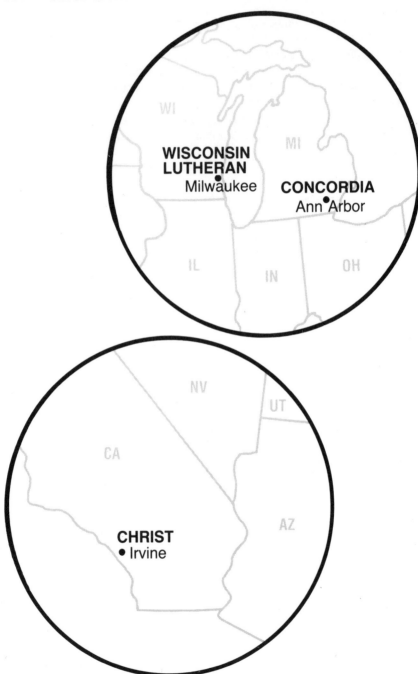

19 THE QUEST FOR NEW DIRECTIONS, 1970–1980

A Time of Troubles

The final report of the Carnegie Commission in 1973 described the transit of American higher education from the 1960s to the 1970s as a move from a Golden Age to a time of troubles. In so doing it was not seeking to minimize the campus traumas still fresh in the nation's memory.[1] Indeed, the sense of national relief as the violence subsided and the demonstrations tapered off after the tragedies of Kent State and Jackson State might well have been viewed as the end of troubles rather than the beginning. President Kingman Brewster of Yale spoke of an "eerie tranquillity" that pervaded college campuses during the academic years 1970–1971 and 1971–1972.[2] The storms seemed to have passed.

The commission's judgment was made from a longer perspective in which the student revolution itself might be seen as an introductory phase of a multifaceted "time of trouble" whose roots reached back into the Golden Age of affluence in the late 50s and early 60s. During those years, as enrollments soared and money from both public and private sources flowed freely, colleges added new facilities, programs, and course offerings. Such developments meant additional expenditures, and these, plus debt service and growing rates of inflation, produced sharp increases in the cost per student. While enrollments in Lutheran senior colleges increased by 54% between 1960 and 1970, cost of operation rose 223%. Deficits began to appear as early as 1965 and, when Francis Gamelin made his extensive study of Lutheran colleges in 1970, 16 of the 28 senior colleges were "in the red," one with an accumulated deficit of $700,000.[3] It was no comfort to the Lutherans that a year later, after

335

completing a study of 500 colleges and universities across the country for the Association of American Colleges, William W. Jellema reported that "most colleges in the red are staying in the red and many are getting redder, while colleges in the black are growing grayer."[4] The "new depression in higher education" had indeed arrived, and only by severe economies involving cutbacks in program and personnel and by reluctantly imposed tuition increases were college presidents able to stave off an expected wave of college closings. Timely expansion of state programs of student aid and the launching of the Basic Educational Opportunity Grants program (later called Pell Grants) by the federal government in 1972 helped to bolster the sagging numbers of college applicants and increase institutional income from student tuitions.

Students in the Seventies

Maintaining adequate enrollments became a major problem in the 70s, especially for private colleges whose budgets depended heavily on student tuitions. The pool of potential students did not begin its predicted decline until later in the decade. But the end of the military draft and the widespread popular decline in the value attributed to a college education reduced the number of applicants. Exceptions were the community colleges whose short-term, vocationally oriented courses were especially attractive to young people eager to enter the job markets. Lutheran colleges reflected this trend, especially in the first half of the decade, most showing a decline in enrollment between 1972 and 1975. Through strengthened recruitment efforts, however, the losses were retrieved and by 1980 the total enrollments of the 29 colleges of the ALC and LCA showed a small increase over 1970. Thereafter enrollments began to reflect the decline in the number of persons in the traditional college-going group of 18- to 21-year-olds.[5]

The students who entered the colleges during the 70s were not only more difficult to recruit than their older brothers and sisters of the 60s. The new generation came with different attitudes and interests. They pursued their own personal goals with greater intensity. Grades became more important as necessary documentation for advanced study. The college experience was valued in terms of the job opportunities it could open.

On the positive side, students were not subjected to the same external tensions. The explosive issues of the Vietnam War and the draft had subsided. The institutions to which the students came were more receptive and relaxed. Many of the goals of the campus crusades of the 60s had been achieved and were being honored by the colleges. Students were being treated as adults. There was greater flexibility in the curriculum and greater opportunity for individual student initiative. Students continued to participate in decision making, both in matters relating to campus life and curriculum. Their concern over social issues such as racial justice, the environment, and women's rights, were pursued with serious purpose but through more conventional channels.

Public Policy and the Tuition Gap

The serious financial crisis as the new decade began brought home to the colleges with alarming clarity the degree of their dependence upon the policies and programs of the federal government. Federal policies had opened higher education to millions of young men and women and helped to provide facilities, educate faculty, and underwrite curricular enrichment for both public and private institutions.

But as the costs of operating these expanded programs mounted, the burden fell most heavily upon the private colleges. Both public and private higher education were heavily subsidized, but increased costs in public institutions were largely absorbed by the taxpayers. Private institutions, dependent on limited endowments and private gifts, could meet the added cost only by increasing student tuition.

As the differential between the modest tuition at public institutions and that of private colleges widened, more students gravitated to public colleges and universities. In 1950 an equal number attended public and private colleges. By 1960 the proportion had shifted to 41% private and 59% public. By 1970, 25% and by 1980, 22% of the 12 million college students were enrolled in private institutions.[6]

In the face of this financial crisis the federal government responded to the call for help, indirectly aiding the colleges by offering loans and grants that enabled students to choose the institution they wished to attend.

Recognizing the fiscal dangers threatening the entire private sector Lutheran educators drew up a formal statement in 1972 on *Public Policy and Church-Related Higher Education.* Its intent was to alert Lutherans to "the effect of public policy on their institutions and the possibility of exercising their influence as citizens" in preserving the dual system of higher education in the United States, and more specifically, the survival of Lutheran higher education in its present form.[7] Their plea was officially endorsed by the boards of college education in both The American Lutheran Church and the Lutheran Church in America.

A major feature in the development of Lutheran higher education since 1970 has been its clear recognition of the importance of exerting direct influence on the development of public policy in higher education on both state and national levels. Lutheran college presidents have therefore monitored closely the actions of their respective state legislatures and the course of education legislation in the Congress of the United States. They have maintained membership in college associations with permanent staff in Washington, such as the National Association for Independent Colleges and Universities (NAICU), the Council of Independent Colleges (CIC), and the American Council on Education (ACE), and have been active in state associations of independent colleges. The office of the secretary of the Lutheran Educational Conference of North America, with the support of an advisory public policy committee of college presidents, has served both as ear and voice for Lutheran higher education in Washington.

The major issue since the passage of the Educational Amendments of 1972, under which the program of Basic Educational Opportunity Grants (BEOG) has been coordinated, has been the nature and extent, and the principles on which public financial aid is made available to students. In 1981–1982 more than 40% of the $140,000,000 in student costs at 18 LCA colleges were paid by students with funds received under federal or state-sponsored programs of financial aid.[8]

The Colleges and the Courts

In the early 70s the massive program of federal aid to church-related higher education was subjected to its first judicial test. In the early development of higher education in America no distinction was made between "public" and "private" institutions. Private institutions, many of which were church related, received public funds well into the 19th century, and public policy provided indirect support through local tax exemption.

Following World War II the size and extent of government programs of aid both to students and institutions inevitably raised the issue of the constitutionality of aid to church-related colleges. At specific issue was the right of four Catholic colleges to receive construction funds under the Higher Education Facilities Act of 1963. The challenge was based on the so-called establishment clause of the First Amendment of the United States Constitution that prohibits Congress from passing any law respecting the establishment of religion. In a landmark decision in the case of *Tilton vs. Richardson* in 1971, the Supreme Court upheld the legislation under which the grants had been made and laid down three criteria for determining whether certain governmental programs violated the Establishment Clause of the First Amendment. The Court asked three basic questions concerning each program under review: (1) Does the statute establishing the program have a secular legislative purpose? (2) Does the statute have a primary effect that neither advances nor inhibits religion? (3) Do the statute and its administration avoid excessive government entanglement with religion? Under these guidelines the Supreme Court has since examined and approved the constitutionality of federal and state programs for construction grants, institutional aid, and student-aid programs without which church-related higher education in its present form could not have survived.[9]

The nation's commitment to the goal of equal opportunity, demonstrated in part by improved access to higher education, led also to the passage of a series of civil rights statutes directly affecting higher education. Beginning with the Civil Rights Act of 1964 and including such subsequent legislation as the Discrimination and Employment Act of 1967, these laws prohibited discrimination against students and faculty on the basis of race, sex, religion, handicap, and age, and provided access to the courts to challenge adverse decisions.

In consequence of these laws Lutheran colleges, as all others, have been obliged to scrutinize their constitutions and bylaws, catalogs, faculty handbooks, personnel policies, campus regulations, and disciplinary procedures in order to be sure their decision-making processes are fair and reasonable rather than arbitrary and capricious. In keeping with the equal opportunity requirements of the federal government colleges have also made efforts to increase the numbers of ethnic minority persons on college faculties. In 1982, 88 persons of minority groups were employed as full-time faculty members (3.2%) in 29 Lutheran colleges. Efforts to increase female representation on faculties, however, have met with meager success. While the proportion of female students increased from 49% in 1970 to 54% in 1982, only 25% of faculty members in these colleges were women.[10]

Lutheran colleges, in company with most others, have also been involved in litigation over issues arising from civil rights legislation. Court decisions have been both favorable and unfavorable to the colleges. Lenoir-Rhyne College litigated one of the early cases regarding alleged sex discrimination against a female faculty member. Augustana College in Sioux Falls was charged with religious discrimination in the dismissal of a student. In both cases the college procedures were sustained. Muhlenberg College litigated a very significant case in which a federal court not only reinstated a dismissed faculty member, but awarded tenure without a specific review of merit by the faculty and administration.[11]

The unionization of college faculties also won the sanction of the United States government's National Labor Relations Board during the 1970s. The movement arose partly as a result of the oversupply of qualified college teachers existing at the time of the financial crisis in higher education. As a means of establishing job security during institutional retrenchments, many faculties turned to labor unions as collective bargaining agencies. By 1974, 338 institutions, mostly public universities and colleges, had chosen this route. Faculties in Lutheran institutions, as in most private liberal arts colleges, generally rejected unionization as incompatible with their professional character. Only two Lutheran colleges, Wagner and Luther College in Canada, established bargaining units. Several others rejected unionization by faculty vote.[12]

Redefining Church/College Relations

Much of the restive climate of Lutheran college/church relationships during the 1970s was the outgrowth of the unsettling experiences of both churches and colleges in the 1960s. As described in the conclusion of the preceding chapter tensions developed that weakened mutual confidence, altered support patterns, and in two instances resulted in the complete severing of relationships. During the 60s, more than in any previous period in their history, the life of the colleges was shaped by external forces, notably public policies and the national climate of protest and social revolution. The same external forces also had an enormous impact upon the congregations and leadership of the Lutheran churches, one effect of which was to divert the focus of social ministries from institutions to programs of direct social action.

Moreover, each of the major Lutheran bodies was experiencing its own internal problems. As the climax of a period of openness in inter-Lutheran relations the Lutheran Church–Missouri Synod had joined the new Lutheran Council in the United States of America (LCUSA) in 1967. Synod conservatives, however, critical of what they deemed unionistic trends, rallied to elect Jacob A. O. Preus as synod president in 1969, and for the greater part of the 1970s conducted a systematic effort to rid the synod of alleged liberalism. The central issues were the verbal inspiration and inerrancy of the Bible and use of higher criticism in the interpretation of Scripture. As president of Concordia Seminary in St. Louis, Dr. John Tietjen became the focal point of the controversy. His suspension led to the withdrawal of a large majority of the seminary faculty and student body and an eventual break in the synod itself, resulting in the loss of about 3% of its congregations. In the process several district and college presidents and faculty also resigned. By the time the tumult had ended in 1979, the synod was firmly in the hands of conservative leadership, with little inclination for extending inter-Lutheran cooperation.[13]

Both the Lutheran Church in America and The American Lutheran Church were attempting during these years to weld their newly merged structures into smoothly functioning church bodies. The American Lutheran Church, more homogeneous in structure and less urban in character, had fewer problems in consolidation and less tension in college/church relations. The decline in percentages of Lutheran students in the colleges and the action of several college boards expanding their membership to include non-Lutherans raised the anxiety of some pastors that the colleges "were growing away from the church." The Board of Education was called upon in 1972 to respond to concerns over "irresponsible student minorities tainting some ALC colleges." But church constituencies generally observed the growth and expansion of their colleges with pride and satisfaction.

The Lutheran Church in America, with historically and structurally diverse components and a much heavier concentration of congregations in urban centers, experienced greater problems in developing unity of purpose and program. Sharp differences in the understanding of church/college relationships appeared in responses to a 1966 study document prepared by the Board of College Education and Church Vocations.[14] The board therefore appointed a 30-member Council on the Mission of LCA Colleges and Universities, made up of educators, church leaders, pastors, and laypersons from all parts of the church. In late 1969 the Council completed a statement that won acceptance by the 1970 convention of the LCA. The statement pointed to four major areas of responsibility for a Lutheran college: (1) the fostering of the intellectual growth of its students; (2) the encouragement of Christian life and learning; (3) service to the church; and (4) service to society.[15]

To merit official recognition by the church, colleges were expected to meet certain basic requirements: (1) Their institutional goals must reflect a commitment to Christian life and learning. (2) College documents must affirm that a relationship exists with the Lutheran Church in America. (3) The college must be regionally accredited. (4) The college must maintain and uphold academic freedom for students, faculty, and administration.

Colleges might also expect certain things of their church. Through its official documents the church should acknowledge its relationship and its responsibility to provide regular financial support. It should encourage its members to attend a church-related college and should foster understanding and support of the mission of the colleges among the church constituency.

Finally, the statement offered a procedure by which colleges and their supporting synods might develop covenants setting forth mutual expectations and commitments. Such written agreements aimed to encourage interaction between synod and college, and could be periodically reviewed and updated. The Board of College Education and Church Vocations provided counsel and assistance in the covenant-making process and sent visiting teams to each college to determine compliance with the church's standards of recognition.

The Mission Statement of 1970 and the covenant process became the bases for a concerted effort in the LCA during the 1970s to interpret the relationship of the colleges and the church in the new social context. The task was not a simple one. In the merger of 1962 both historic and geographic support bases of nearly every college had been changed, and in many cases seriously damaged, as new synodical boundaries were drawn and colleges reassigned on the mechanical principle of at least one college for each synod. The general alienation produced by campus unrest and violence was more pronounced where new college/synod ties had not yet become established. When in 1972 under the leadership of a new church president the internal structure of the

LCA was reordered, college concerns were assigned as a minor responsibility of the wide-ranging Division for Mission in North America (DMNA).

A major task of the DMNA through its Department for Higher Education during the 70s was the effort to interpret college education in the LCA as a critical ministry of the church in a new age. A joint commission representing DMNA and a newly created Council of LCA Colleges, an organization of the college presidents, developed programs addressing three major concerns: student recruitment, fund-raising, and church relations. Technical expertise was made available to the colleges in admissions and development. A special committee undertook the development of a new statement setting forth the theological rationale for the church's involvement in higher education.

At the same time the commission sponsored a major survey of the images and expectations of LCA colleges held by the various constituencies of each college: faculty, students, administrators, trustees, pastors, alumni, and parents. Individualized statistical data were made available to each college and synod.[16] The general results were published by DMNA in 1976 and later widely circulated in a popular interpretive version to the entire clergy roster of the church and to all college faculty and trustees.[17]

The rationale statement, "The Basis for Partnership between Church and College," was adopted by the Biennial Convention of the LCA in 1976. Together with the survey data it became the focus of six regional conferences on higher education, bringing together representatives of colleges and their supporting synod.

Based on Luther's doctrine of the orders of creation and preservation, the statement affirmed the integrity of the educational task of the college as a God-ordained ministry carried out in close partnership with the church. While cherishing this relationship and celebrating the common concerns of college and church for God's people and for God's world, the statement drew a distinction between the primary functions of the church as the mediator of the means of grace and the college as an educational institution.

The American Lutheran Church also developed a statement of self-understanding strongly emphasizing the integral relationship of its colleges as extensions of the church. Defining them as "the church in mission in higher education," the statement affirmed a redemptive and reconciling role for education, in addition to its investigative and creative dimensions.[18]

During the 1970s the efforts of the higher education agencies of the LCA and the ALC to reemphasize the importance of colleges within the church were enhanced by a cordial spirit of interchurch cooperation. Frequent interstaff consultations helped to develop joint service programs for the colleges. Conferences of college deans, chaplains, and business officers became annual events. Trustee development seminars were conducted. Statistical data were exchanged and a joint faculty registry established. Colleges of both the LCA and LC–MS participated in an extended program of management audits administered by the ALC Division for College and University Services (DCUS).

Early experience in the joint ownership and operation of California Lutheran College opened the way for further cooperative institutional relationships. Regional LCA synods became participants in the support and governance of two ALC institutions, Texas Lutheran College and Pacific Lutheran University, and two colleges of the Evangelical Lutheran Church of Canada, Camrose College and Luther College in Regina. The ALC established a supporting relationship with the LCA's Carthage College.

A committee representing the DCUS and DMNA met over several years with the express intent to develop fuller cooperation among the colleges and a common understanding of the relationship of church and college. Such conversations prepared the way for the establishment of a new network of 29 colleges and universities as a part of the projected new Lutheran church in 1988.

Missouri's Decade of Decision

Because of their primary character as schools for the preparation of church workers, the colleges of the Missouri system were not as directly affected by government educational policies and programs as other Lutheran institutions. Other external factors, however, such as economic inflation, demographic changes, and social unrest influenced the development of Missouri colleges, as all others, during the 60s and 70s. Internal conflicts and divisions within the Missouri Synod itself resulted in the loss of a considerable portion of the synod's educational leadership, thereby taking a heavy toll on the academic vitality of the system.

Of greatest significance for the Missouri system were the persistent challenges to the single-purpose character of the higher education program. The major contributing factor was the growing rate of admission of "general," or non-church-worker, students to the preparatory schools and teachers colleges. Further, the innovative senior college at Fort Wayne, opened in 1957, failed to function as planned. It was intended that the synod's standard theological course would begin with basic training in one of the preparatory schools and after two years of junior college work, would continue at Concordia Senior College at Fort Wayne for the two final college years. Equipped with an approved bachelor's degrees and command of the biblical languages, graduates would qualify for admission to Concordia Seminary in St. Louis for three years of theological study.

The "practical" seminary at Springfield, Illinois, originally intended to provide a briefer and less demanding theological training for men with limited academic background, during the 1950s began to raise its standards of admission. When it admitted candidates with bachelor's degrees from secular colleges and universities, Concordia Seminary in St. Louis joined the movement to produce more pastors by admitting graduates, whether from the Senior College in Fort Wayne or not. It thus became possible for students to enter either seminary of the Synod without attending a college of the Missouri System.

Changes in the teacher-education program contributed still further to the erosion of the system. With the increase in demand for teachers in the Missouri parish schools, Concordia College–St. Paul won synod permission in 1962 to join Seward and River Forest as the third teachers college and to award a four-year bachelor's degree. Although the baccalaureate program at St. Paul was intended to prepare teachers only, some graduates also applied to the seminaries at Springfield and St. Louis and were admitted.

By 1970 the traditional structure of the system had been changed. One after another, the preparatory colleges applied for and were granted permission to become four-year institutions. In 1975 a new four-year institution, Christ College, opened in Irvine, California. By 1981 only St. Paul's in Concordia, Missouri, and Concordia in Selma, Alabama, remained as junior colleges.

With four-year graduates of other colleges bypassing Fort Wayne on their way to the seminaries, the senior college had lost its distinctive mission. Enrollments dwindled. Finally, in 1977, it closed. The senior college program was transferred from the Fort Wayne campus to Concordia College in Ann Arbor, Michigan, thereby transforming the Ann Arbor institution also into a four-year college. The erstwhile "practical" seminary in Springfield, Illinois, returned to Fort Wayne, where it had originally been established in 1846 by Wilhelm Loehe to train missionary pastors for German immigrants.

During the 1960s and 1970s the colleges were authorized to prepare students for a variety of new ministries in the church: social workers, directors of Christian education, parish assistants, and lay ministers. The greatest increase in enrollments, however, was among non-church-work students, majoring in nursing, computer science, business, public school teaching, and a variety of preprofessional courses. Total college enrollments remained at approximately the same level throughout the 70s, but the proportion of non-church-work students continued to increase, reaching 50% in 1984. Since the synod subsidy to each college was based on the percentage of church-work students enrolled, financial support from the synod correspondingly decreased. In 1970 the synod covered 40.5% of all institutional expenses; in 1972, 37%; and in 1975, 27.5%. Consequently, the colleges were obliged to compete with each other for the limited supply of potential church-work students and also to increase tuition and step up efforts to recruit more general students.

Recognizing the strain on the colleges, as well its own financial limitations, the synod gave reluctant approval to the changes in the system that were already too far advanced to be reversed. In resolutions reflecting both frustration and uncertainty concerning future directions, the convention of 1977 requested each college to prepare a report to the synod stating the college's own view of its mission and philosophy and its plans for achieving its mission. "The four-year colleges," according to synod resolution, "need not be single-purpose institutions but should be encouraged to develop programs consistent with their resources and strengths, synodical needs, and local concerns. . . ." Such programs, however, were to be submitted to the Board for Higher Education for approval.[19]

Two years later the board described the vigorous and comprehensive examination to which it had subjected the faltering educational system. It had scrutinized all the traditional policies and procedures, "including the role of individual schools, methods of funding, faculty selection, curriculum determination, governance relationships, and previously adopted planning propositions and operating principles."[20] But even after an additional biennium of study, the new "system-wide model" hoped for by the synod failed to emerge. Instead, in 1979, the Board for Higher Education offered a series of "postulates" as guides for continued planning. It commended the endorsement of higher education for the laity, based upon Luther's definition of vocation and occupation. It encouraged recognition of the unique character of each institution, its local environment and leadership, and recommended a governance system for the colleges, providing "coordinated opportunities" as contrasted to "explicit control."[21]

The synod convention, however, responded with its own set of planning principles. Reaffirming the primacy of its historic tradition, the synod called for the redoubling of efforts to recruit church vocations students. Determined not to "turn schools loose" to pursue their independent interests, it confirmed the authority of the Board for Higher Education to approve all new college programs.[22]

On the threshold of the 1980s the Missouri Synod thus faced the task of reconciling its historic commitment to church professional education with the demands of faithful stewardship of facilities, funds, and personnel. The resolution of this crucial problem was entrusted in 1983 to a presidential Commission on Synodical Higher Education, with a mandate to review the mission and purpose of the synod's schools, propose new structures and programs to fulfill the broader educational opportunities open to the synod and its colleges, and to report its findings in 1986.[23]

LECNA Views the Future

The high point in inter-Lutheran cooperation in North America was reached on November 16-18, 1966, in Cleveland, Ohio, with the formation of the Lutheran Council in the United States of America (LCUSA) and a corresponding Lutheran Council in Canada. For the first time all major Lutheran bodies in both countries formally joined in organizations to carry out programs of common interest. Through its newly created Office of Educational Services in Washington the council agreed to provide full logistic support for the National Lutheran Educational Conference.

Under a new constitution and a new name, adopted in 1967, the Lutheran Educational Conference of North America (LECNA) continued to elect its own officers and conduct its own annual meetings as it had since 1910. All the colleges of the Lutheran Church–Missouri Synod now joined as active members. Upon the retirement of Dr. Gould Wickey in 1968 the educational representative of the Lutheran Council in Washington assumed responsibility as LECNA's secretary and treasurer. With its new format and more inclusive membership, LECNA served Lutheran higher education as a common forum and cooperative agency through two critical decades, deepening the sense of community among college presidents and their institutions.

The theme of the LECNA Annual Meeting in 1971 was one which lay very close to the heart of college leaders throughout North America: "Resources for the Future." Dr. Albert G. Huegli of Valparaiso University opened his presidential address to the conference with words all his colleagues understood: "College presidents today live in the future. The past is history and the present is bleak. Only the future seems to hold promise."[24]

To meet that future the officers of LECNA invited Francis C. Gamelin, Executive Director of the Central States College Association, to analyze the status and prospects of Lutheran higher education. On the basis of a comprehensive statistical review of the strengths and weaknesses of the 44 Lutheran colleges and universities, Gamelin called for the development of a master plan. Reminding the assembled presidents of the financial malaise that was affecting all of higher education and producing operating deficits in almost half of their own institutions, he urged inter-Lutheran college cooperation, coordination, and even consolidation as a possible means for significant survival.[25]

In response to his appeal, members of LECNA voted to establish a Commission on the Future. The commission in turn appointed three working groups: (1) a committee on Master Planning to investigate possible ways of closer cooperation among the colleges, (2) a committee to inform and advise the colleges on matters of public policy, and (3) a committee on Liberal Learning to study the curricular implications of recent changes among students and in the society. In January 1973 the members of LECNA took the unprecedented step of assessing themselves $10,000 annually for three years to support the commission's work and to provide staff leadership. Additional funding by church boards of higher education and by Lutheran Brotherhood enabled the commission to pursue its work over a three-year period.[26]

Several publications resulted from the work of the Commission on the Future. Allan Pfnister, Professor of Higher Education at the University of Denver, compiled a review of current trends in American higher education and their implications for Lutheran higher education.[27] Francis Gamelin prepared a study of the ways in which Lutheran colleges expressed their mission as church-related colleges.[28] A final report of the commission in 1976 included summaries of all committee reports and recommendations for further cooperative activities.[29]

The advisory committee on public policy continued to monitor legislative trends and provide counsel to college presidents. Additional funding enabled LECNA to establish a Curriculum Consultation Project continuing the work of the Committee on Liberal Learning. Over a six-year period 16 colleges invited teams of faculty and administrators from other Lutheran colleges to review their curricula in relation to the stated goals of their colleges.[30]

LECNA also provided a forum during the 1970s for exchange of information on continuing efforts within the church bodies to clarify and strengthen church/college relationships. The outcomes of surveys assessing these relationships in both the ALC and the LCA provided themes for LECNA annual meetings in 1973 and 1977.[31]

A Point of Perspective

At the midpoint of the 70s a new and refreshing theme captured the attention of the entire nation. Beginning in 1963 with the assassination of a young and greatly admired president, America had experienced one of the most depressing eras in its history. Internal conflicts such as had not been experienced since the Civil War were followed by national disappointment and disillusion over the scandals of Watergate and the consequent resignation of another president. The observance of the bicentennial of the birth of American national independence in 1976, therefore, came as a welcome opportunity to celebrate the nation's history, restate its pristine values of life, liberty, and human dignity, and summon all Americans to a time of renewal.

Lutherans, too, responded in 1976 in reflections upon the nation's religious heritage and upon the Reformation roots of Lutheran theology and education.[32] As the decade drew toward its close, the appeal for perspective in dealing with both present and future concerns of Lutheran higher education was expressed with increasing frequency. A possible enrollment crisis loomed in the United States Census Bureau projection that the number of 18-year-olds in the population would decline by 19% between 1980 and 1990. The heavy reliance of Lutheran colleges on tuition income to meet increasing costs of operation seemed likely to increase their dependence on government student-aid programs and render competition with tax-supported colleges more acute. For some Lutheran colleges the issue would be simple survival, for others, economic elitism; and for all, the question of their identity as church-related institutions.

In quest of the perspective needed to meet these issues, Lutheran educators turned instinctively to Luther himself, his biblical foundations, and his theology,[33] and to an examination of the manner in which his educational tradition has been transmitted through changes in time, geography, and culture to our own day.[34] This volume is, in part, the product of their quest. On the basis of this theology and the witness of history Lutheran educators may with confidence summon both churches and colleges to the reaffirmation and renewal of their mutual covenant.

EPILOG

Lutheran higher education is an odyssey of 400 years, reaching from the medieval world of the 16th century to the threshold of the 21st. It is much more than the history of a group of educational institutions with denominational affiliation in the United States and Canada. Nor can it be limited to the story of any single institution with a life history of 100 years or more. Each of these is a part, but only a limited part of a powerful educational tradition rooted in the theology of Luther and Melanchthon. Since the Reformation, the Lutheran tradition has continued to exert its pervasive influence through the churches and universities of northern Europe. It has in turn been enriched by the religious and cultural contributions of both Europe and North America.

The most influential educational vehicle of that tradition in North America has been the Lutheran college, an institution not native to Germany or Scandinavia but adapted from the American environment. Originally established to provide the classical preparation for theological studies, Lutheran colleges almost immediately welcomed students preparing for other professions or simply seeking a broad general education.

The initial focus of Lutheran higher education in America was thereby enlarged in accordance with Luther's doctrines of Christian vocation and the priesthood of all believers to give greater emphasis to providing society with teachers, homemakers, lawyers, doctors, and a well-informed citizenry. Called through Baptism to discipleship, the Christian serves God and neighbor through every honest profession and thereby fulfills his or her role as a citizen of both the earthly and the heavenly kingdoms.

Interwoven with their basic roles in the preparation of leadership for church and society, Lutheran colleges have served uniquely in the cultural transit of ethnic groups from European to American society. Not only have they provided instruction for thousands of immigrants, but they have also been conservators of traditions and customs that have enriched the culture of America.

Lutheran colleges have made special contributions in music and the arts. The choral tradition established by F. Melius Christiansen and the St. Olaf Choir has been multiplied in schools and colleges and churches throughout the country. The schools of the Lutheran Church–Missouri Synod have enriched the tradition of Lutheran church music. From the art studios of several colleges have emerged gifted artists and architects whose work continues to bring beauty and grace into churches and communities.

In the American higher education community, which has fallen increasingly under the domination of the scientific and technological approach to knowledge, the Lutheran tradition has been a countervailing force, affirming the centrality of humane values and a curriculum which honors the study of religion, literature, history, and the arts. Since the time of Martin Luther himself the Lutheran tradition in higher education has been hospitable both to the liberal arts and to professional studies. Lutheran colleges in North America have been faithful to this tradition, but have also stoutly supported a broad foundation for all professional training.

For thousands of young men and women who have attended the colleges of the Lutheran church there has always been the opportunity for spiritual nourishment as well as intellectual stimulation. The worship of God and the open proclamation of the gospel in the midst of the academic community is an essential expression of the Lutheran tradition in higher education.

Throughout their history in North America the institutions of higher learning which have carried the Lutheran name have also maintained their loyalty to the Lutheran church. In 1985, 50 colleges in the United States and Canada affirm their identity as Lutheran institutions. They are the current expressions of the irrepressible Lutheran commitment to learning, rooted in the love of the gospel, a sense of the mind as a gift of God, and of the world as God's creation in which the people of God explore their vocation. Whether explicit or implicit, this is the essential quality of Lutheran higher education.

LUTHERAN COLLEGES AND UNIVERSITIES IN NORTH AMERICA

	Location	Founding date
Gettysburg College	Gettysburg, Pennsylvania	1832
Roanoke College	Salem, Virginia	1842
Wittenberg University	Springfield, Ohio	1845
Carthage College	Kenosha, Wisconsin	1847
Muhlenberg College	Allentown, Pennsylvania	1848
Capital University	Columbus, Ohio	1850
Wartburg College	Waverly, Iowa	1852
Newberry College	Newberry, South Carolina	1856
Susquehanna University	Selinsgrove, Pennsylvania	1858
Valparaiso University	Valparaiso, Indiana	1859
Augustana College	Rock Island, Illinois	1860
Augustana College	Sioux Falls, South Dakota	1860
Luther College	Decorah, Iowa	1861
Gustavus Adolphus College	St. Peter, Minnesota	1862
Concordia College	River Forest, Illinois	1864
Northwestern College	Watertown, Wisconsin	1865
Thiel College	Greenville, Pennsylvania	1866
Augsburg College	Minneapolis, Minnesota	1869
St. Olaf College	Northfield, Minnesota	1874
Bethany College	Lindsborg, Kansas	1881
Concordia College	Bronxville, New York	1881
Concordia College	Mequon, Wisconsin	1881
Midland Lutheran College	Fremont, Nebraska	1883

St. Paul's College	Concordia, Missouri	1883
Wagner College	Staten Island, New York	1883
Dana College	Blair, Nebraska	1884
Dr. Martin Luther College	Mankato, Minnesota	1884
Concordia College	Moorhead, Minnesota	1891
Lenoir-Rhyne College	Hickory, North Carolina	1891
Pacific Lutheran University	Tacoma, Washington	1891
Texas Lutheran College	Seguin, Texas	1891
Concordia College	St. Paul, Minnesota	1893
St. John's College	Winfield, Kansas	1893
Upsala College	East Orange, New Jersey	1893
Concordia Teachers College	Seward, Nebraska	1894
Grand View College	Des Moines, Iowa	1896
*Suomi College	Hancock, Michigan	1896
*Waldorf College	Forest City, Iowa	1903
Concordia College	Portland, Oregon	1905
*Camrose Lutheran College	Camrose, Alberta, Canada	1911
Luther College	Regina, Saskatchewan, Canada	1913
*Concordia College	Edmonton, Alberta, Canada	1921
*Concordia College	Selma, Alabama	1922
*Bethany Lutheran College	Mankato, Minnesota	1926
Concordia Lutheran College	Austin, Texas	1926
California Lutheran College	Thousand Oaks, California	1959
Immanuel Lutheran College	Eau Claire, Wisconsin	1959
Concordia College	Ann Arbor, Michigan	1963
*Wisconsin Lutheran College	Milwaukee, Wisconsin	1973
Christ College	Irvine, California	1976

*Two-year colleges

NOTES

Chapter 1: Reformation Roots (pages 11-20)

1. Friedrich Paulsen, *The German Universities and University Study* (New York: Longmans Green & Co., 1906), pp. 14-15.
2. Ernest G. Schwiebert, *Luther and His Times* (St. Louis: Concordia Publishing House, 1950), pp. 254-257.
3. Walther I. Brandt, Introduction to Luther's address "To the Councilmen of all Cities in Germany that they Establish and Maintain Christian Schools," *Luther's Works*, vol. 45 (Philadelphia: Fortress Press, 1962), pp. 342-343.
4. Paulsen, *German Universities*, p. 62.
5. Roland H. Bainton, *Here I Stand: A Life of Martin Luther* (New York: New American Library, 1950), pp. 1-104.
6. Gerald Strauss, *Luther's House of Learning* (Baltimore: Johns Hopkins University Press, 1978), p. 6; Schwiebert, *Luther*, pp. 676-679.
7. *Luther's Works*, vol. 46 (Philadelphia: Fortress Press, 1967), pp. 348, 354, 355.
8. Strauss, *Luther's House*, pp. 194-195.
9. *Luther's Works*, vol. 46, pp. 242 ff.
10. James W. Richard, *Philip Melanchthon* (New York: The Knickerbocker Press, 1898), pp. 129-136.
11. Roland H. Bainton, "Luther and Education," in *New Dimensions in Lutheran Higher Education* (Washington, D.C.: National Lutheran Education Conference, 1960), p. 13.
12. Ibid., p. 13.
13. *Luther's Works*, vol. 45, pp. 367-368.
14. *Luther's Works*, vol. 46, p. 234; Schwiebert, *Luther*, p. 681.
15. *Luther's Works*, vol. 46, pp. 252-253.
16. Ibid., pp. 243-247.
17. Ibid., p. 215.
18. Preserved Smith and Charles Jacobs, *Luther's Correspondence and Other Contemporary Letters*, 2 vols. (Philadelphia: The Lutheran Publication Society, 1913), 2:176.
19. *Luther's Works*, vol. 45, pp. 368-369.
20. Quoted by Einar O. Johnson, "Soli Deo Gloria: A Study of the Philosophy and Problems of Higher Education among Norwegian Lutherans in the American Environment, 1860–1960 (unpublished Ph.D. dissertation, University of Washington, 1966), p. 52.
21. Ibid., p. 55.
22. *Luther's Works*, vol. 45, pp. 368-370.
23. Johnson, "Soli Deo," p. 56.
24. James E. Russell, *German Higher Schools* (New York: Longmans Green & Co., 1916), pp. 17-45.
25. Michael Rogness, *Philip Melanchthon, Reformer without Honor* (Minneapolis: Augsburg Publishing House, 1969), p. 7; Richard, *Melanchthon*, pp. 137-139.

26. Paulsen, *German Universities*, p. 33; Schwiebert, *Luther*, pp. 603-612.
27. Sydney E. Ahlstrom "What's Lutheran about Higher Education? A Critique," in *Papers and Proceedings*, 1974, Lutheran Educational Conference of North America, pp. 8-12.
28. Russell, *German Higher Schools*, pp. 60-63, and Paulsen, *German Universities*, pp. 44-50.

Chapter 2: Foothold in America (pages 21-31)

1. Samuel Eliot Morison, *The Founding of Harvard College* (Cambridge: Harvard University Press, 1935), p. 432.
2. Allen O. Pfnister, *Survival and Revival: The Transformation of the American Arts College*, Occasional Paper in Higher Education 15 (Sept. 1981, University of Denver), pp. 16-17.
3. Frederick Rudolph, *The American College and University* (New York: Random House, 1962), pp. 7-16.
4. Charles H.. Glatfelter, *Pastors and People: German Lutheran and Reformed Churches in the Pennsylvania Field, 1717–1793*, 2 vols. (Breinigsville, Pa.: The Pennsylvania German Society, 1981), 2:264-265.
5. Conrad Bergendoff, *The Doctrine of the Church in American Lutheranism* (Philadelphia: Board of Publications, United Lutheran Church in America, 1956), p. 21.
6. *Halle Reports*, ed. W. J. Mann, B. M. Schmucker, and W. Germann, trans. by C. W. Schaeffer (Reading: Globe Printing House, 1882), p. 79.
7. Ibid., pp. 81-82; see also Glatfelter, *Pastors and People*, 2:33.
8. Leonard R. Riforgiato, *Missionary of Moderation: Henry Melchior Muhlenberg and the Lutheran Church in English America* (Lewisburg: Bucknell University Press, 1980), pp. 66-71.
9. Sydney E. Ahlstrom, *A Religious History of the American People* (New Haven: Yale University Press, 1972), p. 263.
10. Theodore G. Tappert and John W. Doberstein, *The Journals of Henry Melchior Muhlenberg*, 3 vols. (Philadelphia: Muhlenberg Press, 1942), 1:177.
11. Ibid., pp. 152-154.
12. Theodore G. Tappert, "Was *Ecclesia Plantanda* Muhlenberg's Motto?" *The Lutheran Quarterly* (1953): 308-311.
13. Ahlstrom, *Religious History*, p. 258.
14. W. J. Mann, B. M. Schmucker, and W. Germann, eds., *Nachrichten von den vereinigten Deutschen Evangelisch-Lutherischen Gemeinden in Nord-America, absonderlich in Pennsylvanien*, 2 vols. (Allentown, Pa.: Brobst, Diehl & Co., 1886), 1:342.

Chapter 3: Early Ventures in Lutheran Higher Education (pages 32-46)

1. Abdel Ross Wentz, *Gettysburg Lutheran Theological Seminary*, 2 vols. (Harrisburg: The Evangelical Press, 1965), 1:20-21.
2. Ibid., p. 22.
3. Carl Frederick Haussmann, *Kunze's Seminarium* (Philadelphia: Americana Germanica Press, 1917), pp. 15-16.
4. Wentz, *Gettysburg*, 1:32.
5. Haussmann, *Kunze*, pp. 32-34.

6. Wentz, *Gettysburg,* 1:33.
7. Letter of Henry Melchior Muhlenberg to the Halle fathers, March 30, 1773, quoted in Haussmann, *Kunze,* pp. 25-28.
8. Theodore G. Tappert and John W. Doberstein, trans., *The Journals of Henry Melchior Muhlenberg,* 3 vols. (Philadelphia: Muhlenberg Press, 1945), 2:586-587.
9. Charles H. Glatfelter, *Pastors and People: German Lutheran and Reformed Churches in the Pennsylvania Field, 1717–1793,* 2 vols. (Breinigsville, Pa.: The Pennsylvania German Society, 1981), 2:387-388. The College of Philadelphia was founded by Benjamin Franklin in 1749 as the Philadelphia Academy and received a charter in 1755 as the College, Academy and Charitable School of Philadelphia. Although nonsectarian, from 1754 to 1779 it was headed by an Anglican provost, Dr. William Smith, and was known as the College of Philadelphia.
10. Wentz, *Gettysburg,* 1:38-39.
11. Letter from John C. Kunze to the Halle fathers, May 16, 1773, quoted in Samuel G. Hefelbower, *The History of Gettysburg College* (Gettysburg, Pa.: Gettysburg College, 1932), pp. 8-9.
12. Wentz, *Gettysburg,* 1:39.
13. Ibid., 1:41.
14. Letter from John Frederick Schmidt to the Halle fathers, August 1784, quoted in Wentz, *Gettysburg,* 1:43-44.
15. Frederick Rudolph, *The American College and University* (New York: Random House, 1962), pp. 20-21.
16. Donald G. Tewksbury, *The Founding of American Colleges and Universities before the Civil War* (New York: Columbia University, 1932; reprinted by Anchor Books, 1965), pp. 58-63.
17. Albert J. Beveridge, *The Life of John Marshall,* 4 vols. (Boston: Houghton-Mifflin Co., 1916–1919).
18. Resolution of the Board of Trustees of Dickinson College, addressing the convention of the Ministerium of Pennsylvania at Lancaster, Pa., in April 1784, quoted in Hefelbower, *Gettysburg,* p. 26.
19. Ibid., p. 26.
20. Quoted in Glatfelter, *Pastors and People,* 2:498-499.
21. Ibid., 2:499.
22. The full text of the petition is printed in Joseph Henry Dubbs, *History of Franklin and Marshall College* (Lancaster, Pa.: Franklin and Marshall College Alumni Association, 1903), pp. 18-19.
23. Glatfelter, *Pastors and People,* 2:501.
24. Dubbs, *Franklin and Marshall,* pp. 33-53.
25. Saul Sack, *History of Higher Education in Pennsylvania,* 2 vols. (Harrisburg: Pennsylvania Historical and Museum Commission, 1963), 1:119-120.
26. Henry Hardy Heins, *Throughout All the Years: The Bicentennial Story of Hartwick in America, 1746–1796* (Oneonta, N.Y.: Hartwick College, 1946), pp. 16-17.
27. Ibid., pp. 1-11. Walter R. Kopp, "Johann Christopher Hartwick" (unpublished B.D. thesis, Lutheran Theological Seminary at Gettysburg, 1945).
28. The full text of the "Last Will and Testament of John Christopher Hartwick" is printed in Heins, *Throughout the Years,* pp. 148-157. The original, with many other documents relating to the Hartwick estate, is in the Hartwick College Archives, Oneonta, N.Y.
29. Ibid., pp. 17-28.

30. Sydney E. Ahlstrom, *A Religious History of the American People* (New Haven: Yale University Press, 1942), p. 365.
31. Abdel Ross Wentz, *A Basic History of Lutheranism in America* (Philadelphia: Muhlenberg Press, 1955), p. 229.
32. Henry Eyster Jacobs, *A History of the Evangelical Lutheran Church in the United States* (New York: Charles Scribner's Sons, 1893), pp. 315-316.
33. Ahlstrom, *Religious History*, p. 519.
34. Wentz, *Gettysburg*, pp. 42-58.

Chapter 4: The Road to Gettysburg (pages 47-63)

1. David G. Tewksbury, *The Founding of American Colleges and Universities before the Civil War* (New York: Columbia University, 1932; reprinted by Anchor Books, 1965), p. 16.
2. Ibid., p. 167.
3. Sydney E. Ahlstrom, *A Religious History of the American People* (New Haven: Yale University Press, 1972), pp. 379-380.
4. Ibid., pp. 385ff.
5. Winthrop S. Hudson, *Religion in America*, 3rd ed. (New York: Charles Scribner's Sons, 1981), pp. 136-140.
6. J. H. Patton, *A Popular History of the Presbyterian Church of America* (1900), p. 119, quoted in Tewksbury, *American Colleges*, p. 14.
7. Tewksbury, *American Colleges*, pp. 35-38.
8. Ibid., p. 28.
9. Daniel Boorstin, *The Americans: The National Experience* (New York: Random House, 1965), pp. 152-161. David B. Potts, "Baptist Colleges in the Development of American Society, 1812–1861" (unpublished Ph.D. dissertation, Harvard University, 1967), pp. 135-136.
10. Tewksbury, *American Colleges*, p. 10.
11. John S. Yoder, "An Analysis of Denominational Boards in Church-Related Higher Education" (unpublished Ph.D. dissertation, University of Denver, 1974), pp. 112-122. See also Paul M. Limbert, *Denominational Policies in the Support and Supervision of Higher Education* (New York: Teachers College Press, 1929).
12. David B. Potts, "American Colleges in the 19th Century," *History of American Education Quarterly* 11 (1971): 363-380.
13. Abdel Ross Wentz, *Pioneer in Christian Unity: Samuel Simon Schmucker* (Philadelphia: Fortress Press, 1967), pp. 34-45, 102.
14. Henry Eyster Jacobs, *A History of the Evangelical Lutheran Church in the United States* (New York: Charles Scribner's Sons, 1893), pp. 351-372.
15. Harold A. Dunkelberger, *One Body We: A History of the Central Pennsylvania Synod* (Harrisburg: Central Pennsylvania Synod, 1978), pp. 11-15.
16. Abdel Ross Wentz, *Gettysburg Lutheran Theological Seminary*, 2 vols. (Harrisburg: The Evangelical Press, 1965), 1:89-90.
17. Ibid., pp. 91-92.
18. Ibid., pp. 96-97.
19. Samuel G. Hefelbower, *The History of Gettysburg College 1832–1932* (Gettysburg: Gettysburg College, 1932), pp. 33-43.
20. Samuel Simon Schmucker, "Early History of Pennsylvania College," originally published in 1863 and reprinted in *The College Mercury*, March 1895, p. 6.
21. Charter of Pennsylvania College, printed in Hefelbower, *History*, p. 448.

22. Quoted in Hefelbower, *History,* p. 51.

23. Schmucker, "Early History," p. 5.

24. Hefelbower, *History,* pp. 447-452.

25. Ibid., pp. 54-59.

26. E. S. Breidenbaugh, ed., *The Pennsylvania College Book 1832–1882* (Philadelphia: Lutheran Publication Society, 1882), pp. 146-149.

27. Hartwick Seminary, founded in 1797, is the oldest institution of higher education founded by Lutherans in North America. Its theological program was discontinued in 1941. Hartwick College severed its ties with the Lutheran Church in 1969.

28. The official name of the college, stated in the charter, was Pennsylvania College of Gettysburg. In common usage, however, it was known as Gettysburg College, and in 1921 common usage was recognized by a charter amendment. In the interest of clarity, all subsequent references will use the name Gettysburg College.

29. H. A. Dunkelberger, "Gettysburg College and the Lutheran Connection: An Open-Ended Story of a Proud Relationship," History Series no. 3, *The Gettysburg Bulletin* 66 (1975): 6; Potts, "American Colleges," pp. 363-380; also Potts, "Baptist Colleges," pp. 48-54.

30. S. E. Ochsenford, ed., *Muhlenberg College* (Allentown: Muhlenberg College, 1892), pp. 172-173.

31. Hefelbower, *History,* p. 57.

32. Ahlstrom, *History,* pp. 513-514.

33. Hefelbower, *History,* p. 96.

34. Saul Sack, *History of Higher Education in Pennsylvania,* 2 vols. (Harrisburg: The Pennsylvania Historical and Museum Commission, 1963), 2:389-390.

35. Hefelbower, *History,* pp. 473-476.

36. Sack, *History,* 1:129.

37. Dunkelberger, "Gettysburg College and the Lutheran Connection," p. 8.

38. Statistical data included in this and the following paragraphs are taken from Clyde B. Stover and Charles W. Beacham, eds., *The Alumni Record of Gettysburg College 1832–1932* (Gettysburg: Gettysburg College, 1932), pp. 3-51, 744.

39. Letter of H. L. Baugher to Lutheran clergy, April 23, 1849, quoted in Dunkelberger, "The Lutheran Connection," p. 9.

40. Ibid., "The Lutheran Connection," pp. 10-11.

41. Ochsenford, *Muhlenberg College,* pp. 171-180.

42. Abdel Ross Wentz, *A Basic History of Lutheranism in America* (Philadelphia: Muhlenberg Press, 1955), pp. 137-156.

43. Vergilius Ferm, *The Crisis in American Lutheran Theology* (New York: The Century Co., 1927).

Chapter 5: The Ohio Story (pages 64-76)

1. M. Diehl, *Biography of Ezra Keller, D.D.* (Springfield, Ohio: Ruralist Printing Co., 1859), p. 42.

2. Ohio Synod *Minutes,* 1818, translated from German and quoted by Willard D. Allbeck, *A Century of Lutherans in Ohio* (Yellow Springs, Ohio: The Antioch Press, 1966), pp. 58-59.

3. Allbeck, *Lutherans in Ohio,* p. 59.

4. Herbert William Veler, "A Life of Ezra Keller, D.D." (unpublished S.T.M. thesis, Chicago Lutheran Theological Seminary, 1951; archives of Wittenberg University, Springfield, Ohio), pp. 96-111.

5. Allbeck, *Lutherans in Ohio*, pp. 84-98.
6. The historic German University of Wittenberg was absorbed in 1817 by the University of Halle.
7. Donald L. Huber, "History of Trinity Lutheran Seminary, Columbus, Ohio, 1830–1980" (manuscript, 1983), pp. 8-16.
8. *Minutes of the English Synod of Ohio*, 1841, quoted in Allbeck, *Lutherans in Ohio*, p. 115.
9. Allbeck, *Lutherans in Ohio*, pp. 98-102.
10. Herbert G. Bredemeier, *Concordia College, Fort Wayne, 1839–1957* (Fort Wayne: Fort Wayne Public Library, 1978), pp. 34-50.
11. Huber, "Trinity Seminary," pp. 53-57.
12. Ezra Keller, "The Church in the West," *The Lutheran Observer*, January 3, 1845.
13. Ibid.
14. Ibid., January 24, 1845.
15. Veler, "Ezra Keller," pp. 126-129.
16. Diehl, *Ezra Keller*, pp. 259-263.
17. Harold H. Lentz, *A History of Wittenberg College* (Columbus: The Wittenberg Press, 1946), pp. 30-32.
18. Veler, "Ezra Keller," pp. 130-131.
19. Veler and Dietz give full accounts of Keller's life, with extensive excerpts from Keller's diaries. For an evaluation of Keller, see William A. Kinnison, *Wittenberg: A Concise History* (Springfield, Ohio: Wittenberg Univversity, 1976), pp. 13-25.
20. Keller, "The Church in the West," *The Lutheran Observer*, January 24, 1845.
21. Ibid.
22. Ibid.
23. Ibid., April 4, 1845.
24. Ibid., February 28, 1845.
25. Diehl, *Ezra Keller*, p. 332. See also *Annual Reports, 1847-1855*, Society for the Promotion of Collegiate and Theological Education at the West.
26. Minutes of the Proceedings of the 13th Session of the Ohio Synod, 1830, quoted in David B. Owens, *These Hundred Years: The Centennial History of Capital University* (Columbus: Capital University, 1950), p. 10.
27. Constitution of the German Lutheran Seminary, Article IV, Section 1, p. 39, quoted in Richard O. Bosse, "Origins of Lutheran Higher Education in Ohio" (unpublished Ph.D. dissertation, The Ohio State University, 1969), p. 134.
28. Bosse, "Origins," pp. 145-47.
29. Ibid., pp. 159-62.
30. *Minutes of the Capital University Board of Trustees, 1850–1900*, pp. 1-10, quoted in Bosse, "Origins," pp. 162-165.
31. Owens, *Hundred Years*, p. 168.
32. Bosse, "Origins," p. 168.
33. E. S. Breidenbaugh, ed., *The Pennsylvania College Book* (Philadelphia: Lutheran Publication Society, 1882), pp. 161-162.
34. Allbeck, *Lutherans in Ohio*, p. 100.
35. Owens, *Hundred Years*, pp. 45-47.
36. First Annual Catalog of the Officers and Students in Capital University; quoted in Bosse, "Origins," pp. 185-186.
37. Ibid., p. 185.
38. Owens, *Hundred Years*, pp. 64-65.
39. Huber, "Trinity Seminary," pp. 98-112.

40. Matthias Loy, *Story of My Life,* p. 228, cited in Huber, "Trinity Seminary," pp. 122-123.
41. Owens, *Hundred Years,* p. 71.
42. William A. Kinnison, *An American Seminary: A History of the Hamma School of Theology* (Columbus: Ohio Synod, Lutheran Church in America, 1980), pp. 109-141.

Chapter 6: Particularism in Pennsylvania (pages 77-93)

1. A series of letters written by Benjamin Kurtz, based upon his travel diary and describing his European trip in 1826–1827 to gather funds and books for Gettysburg Seminary, was reprinted after his return in *The Evangelical Lutheran Intelligencer,* Frederick, Maryland, in 1818–1829. An edited collection of the letters was prepared in 1980 by David N. Wiley of Susquehanna University, Selinsgrove, Pa.
2. George H. Genzmer, "Benjamin Kurtz," *Dictionary of American Biography,* ed. Dumas Malone, vol. 5 (1961), p. 514.
3. Ludwig Fuerbringer, ed., "Benjamin Kurtz, 1795–1865," *Concordia Cyclopedia* (St. Louis: Concordia Publishing House, 1927), p. 394.
4. Editorial in *The Lutheran Observer,* January 19, 1855.
5. *The Lutheran Observer,* June 12, 1857.
6. E. Cliifford Nelson, ed., *The Lutherans in North America* (Philadelphia: Fortress Press, 1980), pp. 221-224.
7. Abdel Ross Wentz, *A Brief History of Lutheranism in America* (Philadelphia: Muhlenberg Press, 1955), pp. 142-144.
8. Proceedings of the Board of Managers of the Missionary Institute, Selinsgrove, Pa., Book I, cited in William S. Clark and Arthur H. Wilson, *The Story of Susquehanna University* (Selinsgrove: Susquehanna University Press, 1958), p. 10.
9. Clark and Wilson, *Susquehanna,* p. 11.
10. David N. Wiley, "Benjamin Kurtz and the Founding of the Missionary Institute: The End of an Era or the Dawn of a New Day?" *Susquehanna University Studies* 12 (1983): 12.
11. Letter of David Focht to Benjamin Kurtz, January 7, 1858, cited in Clark and Wilson, *Susquehanna,* p. 19.
12. Letter of Samuel Crist to Benjamin Kurtz, cited in Clark and Wilson, *Susquehanna,* p. 24.
13. Letter of Benjamin Kurtz to Samuel Domer, March 28, 1858, cited in Clark and Wilson, *Susquehanna,* p. 25.
14. Clark and Wilson, *Susquehanna,* p. 29.
15. Ibid., pp. 33-34.
16. J. C. Jensson, ed., "Rev. Prof. H. Ziegler," *American Lutheran Biographies* (Milwaukee, 1890), pp. 881-884.
17. Wiley, "Benjamin Kurtz," p. 14.
18. Ibid., p. 30.
19. Clark and Wilson, *Susquehanna,* p. 41.
20. Ibid., pp. 54-58.
21. Although the Central Pennsylvania Synod of the Lutheran Church in America elects eight members of the board of trustees and provides annual financial support, the control of Susquehanna University is vested solely in its board of trustees.

22. Missionary Institute, Minutes of Managers I, August 31, 1858, cited in Saul Sack, *History of Higher Education in Pennsylvania*, 2 vols. (Harrisburg: The Pennsylvania Historical and Museum Commission, 1963), 2:595.

23. Ibid., p. 595.

24. Clark and Wilson, *Susquehanna*, p. 64.

25. Quoted in Nelson, *Lutherans in North America*, p. 231.

26. Quoted in Wentz, *Brief History*, p. 150.

27. Theodore G. Tappert, *History of the Lutheran Theological Seminary at Philadelphia, 1864–1964* (Philadelphia: Lutheran Theological Seminary, 1964), pp. 28-32.

28. Wentz, *Brief History*, p. 153.

29. S. E. Ochsenford, ed., *Muhlenberg College* (Allentown, Pa.: Muhlenberg College, 1892), pp. 41-42.

30. Ibid., pp. 42-44.

31. Ibid., p. 49.

32. Ibid., p. 50.

33. Report of the College Committee to the Ministerium of Pennsylvania, reprinted in Ochsenford, *Muhlenberg*, pp. 53-54.

34. Excerpts from the inaugural address of Dr. Frederick A. Muhlenberg are printed in Ochsenford, *Muhlenberg*, pp. 65-74.

35. Ibid., p. 65.

36. Ibid., p. 67.

37. Ibid., pp. 70-71.

38. Ibid., p. 71.

39. Ibid., p. 74.

40. Ibid., pp. 79-86. James E. Swain, *A History of Muhlenberg College, 1848–1967* (New York: Appleton-Century-Crofts, 1967), gives a much abbreviated account of the early years of college.

41. Henry Eyster Jacobs, "Frederick A. Muhlenberg," in Ochsenford, *Muhlenberg College*, p. 179.

42. George H. Gerberding, *Life and Letters of William A. Passavant, D.D.* (Greenville, Pa.: The Young Lutheran Co., 1906).

43. Ibid., p. 28; E. S. Breidenbaugh, *The Pennsylvania College Book* (Philadelphia: Lutheran Publication Society, 1886), pp. 145, 158, 160, 169.

44. Robert A. Gahagen, "Background for a College: Early Years of Thiel College" (manuscript in Archives of Thiel College, Greenville, Pa.), pp. 17-23. Ernest G. Heissenbuttel and Roy H. Johnson, *Pittsburgh Synod History: Its Auxiliaries and Institutions, 1845–1962* (Warren, Ohio: Pittsburgh Synod, ULCA, 1963), pp. 56-64.

45. Roy H. Johnson, *The History of Thiel College* (Philadelphia: Dorrance and Co., 1974), p. 5; Gahagen, "Background," pp. 23-26.

46. Gahagen, "Background," pp. 27-32. Johnson, *Thiel*, pp. 7-12.

47. Gahagen, "Background," pp. 34-37.

48. Original draft of letter dated October 16, 1869, from William A. Passavant to the Pittsburgh Synod, offering the buildings and grounds of Thiel Hall in Phillipsburg, Pa., to the synod as a gift from Mr. and Mrs. A. Louis Thiel (Thiel College Archives).

49. Charter of Thiel College, in Katherine Blyley, ed., *Thiel College: An Historical Bulletin, 1866–1931*, pp. 10-11.

50. Johnson, *Thiel,* pp. 13-38.
51. Gerberding, *Passavant,* pp. 509-510.

Chapter 7: Lutheran Higher Education in the South (pages 94-112)

1. William Edward Eisenberg, *The Lutheran Church in Virginia 1717–1962* (Roanoke, Va.: The Virginia Synod, Lutheran Church in America, 1962), p. 81.
2. H. George Anderson, *The North Carolina Synod through 175 Years 1803–1978* Salisbury, N.C.: The North Carolina Synod, Lutheran Church in America, 1978), p. 3. See also G. D. Bernheim and George Cox, *History of the Evangelical Lutheran Synod and Ministerium of North Carolina* (Philadelphia: Lutheran Publication Society, 1902).
3. Anderson, *North Carolina Synod,* pp. 5-6.
4. Robert M. Calhoon, "Lutheranism and Early Southern Culture," *A Truly Efficient School of Theology: The Lutheran Theological Southern Seminary in Historical Context, 1830–1980,* ed. H. George Anderson and Robert M. Calhoon (Columbia, S.C.: Lutheran Theological Southern Seminary, 1981), pp. 1, 11.
5. Raymond M. Bost, "Ministry in an Enlightened Age," in *A Truly Efficient School of Theology,* pp. 37-41. See also Raymond M. Bost, "The Reverend John Bachman and the Development of Southern Lutheranism" (unpublished Ph.D. dissertation, Yale University, 1963).
6. Charles A. Smith, "Biography of Rev. E. L. Hazelius, D.D.," in *Memorial Volume of the Semi-Centennial Anniversary of Hartwick Seminary, August 21, 1866* (Albany: Joel Munsell, 1867), pp. 58-59; Henry Hardy Heins, *Throughout All the Years* (Oneonta, N.Y.: Hartwick College, 1946), pp. 29-31.
7. Paul G. McCullough et al., eds., *A History of the Lutheran Church in South Carolina* (Columbia, S.C.: The South Carolina Synod, Lutheran Church in America, 1971), pp. 229-238. Gordon C. Henry, ed., *A History of Newberry College, 1856–1976* (Newberry, S.C.: Newberry College, 1976) pp. 2-4.
8. Eisenberg, *Virginia,* p. 3338. Charles W. Heathcote, *The Lutheran Church and the Civil War* (Burlington, Ia.: The Lutheran Literary Board, 1919), pp. 124-125.
9. Henry, *Newberry College,* p. 6.
10. Ibid., p. 9.
11. John D. Hicks, George E. Mowry, and Robert E. Burke, *A History of American Democracy,* 3rd ed. (Boston: Houghton Mifflin Co., 1966), p. 344.
12. McCullough, *South Carolina,* pp. 327-328.
13. Much of the material dealing with Roanoke College is based on William E. Eisenberg, *The First Hundred Years: Roanoke College, 1842–1942* (Salem, Va.: Roanoke College, 1942).
14. Eisenberg, *Hundred Years,* p. 72.
15. Ibid., p. 77.
16. Ibid., p. 80.
17. Ibid., p. 84.
18. Ibid., p. 88.
19. Ibid., pp. 96-97. Heathcote, *The Lutheran Church and the Civil War,* pp. 119-122.
20. Eisenberg, *Hundred Years,* p. 108.
21. Ibid., p. 165.
22. Ibid., p. 179.
23. Anderson, *North Carolina Synod,* p. 13.

24. *Charter of North Carolina College and Constitution of the Board of Trustees*, in archives of the Synod of North Carolina, Salisbury, N.C. (Mount Pleasant, N.C.: Southern Lutheran Publishing Co., 1859), p. 1.
25. Quoted in Anderson, *North Carolina Synod*, p. 13.
26. Mary Elizabeth Markley, *Some Chapters on the History of Higher Education for Lutheran Women* (Philadelphia: Board of Education, United Lutheran Church in America, 1923), pp. 40-41.
27. Ibid., pp. 26-32.
28. Thomas W. West, *Marion College* 1873–1967 (Strasburg, Va.: Shenandoah Publishing House, 1970), pp. 1-20.
29. Quoted in McCullough, *South Carolina*, p. 299.
30. Markley, *Some Chapters*, pp. 32-44.
31. Eisenberg, *Hundred Years*, p. 484.
32. Minutes of the Faculty Meetings, North Carolina College, vol. 3, 1893–1902 (handwritten minutes book in Lenoir-Rhyne College Archives, Hickory, N.C.).
33. *The Collegiate Institute*, Annual Catalogue, Alumni Number, 1920 (Charlotte, N.C.: Queen City Printing Co., 1920), contains a brief historical sketch.
34. McCullough, *South Carolina*, pp. 328-340, 366-376.
35. Jeff Norris, "Lenoir College: Its Founding and First Ten Years" (unpublished typescript, 1965, in Lenoir-Rhyne College Library), Part I, pp. 1-4.
36. Ibid., pp. 6-11.
37. Ibid., pp. 15-42.
38. C. O. Smith, "History of the Coming of the Missouri Synod into North Carolina," *Concordia Historical Institute Quarterly* 7 (April, 1934): 14ff.
39. The charter of the college, dated January 4, 1892, is printed in Norris, *Lenoir College*, Part II, pp. 4-7. A handwritten minutes book in the Lenoir-Rhyne College Archives contains the minutes of Lenoir College faculty meetings, 1893–1902.
40. Fundamental Principles of the Trustees and Faculty of Lenoir College, July 4, 1892, printed in Norris, "Lenoir College," Part II, pp. 14-15.
41. The Tennessee Synod's point of view is presented in a pamphlet by R. A. Yoder, *The Situation in North Carolina* (Newton, N.C.: Enterprise Job Office, 1894).
42. Norris, *Lenoir College*, Part II, pp. 95-102.
43. Gaston College in Dallas, N.C., operated as a degree-granting college under the direction of the Reverend M. L. Little, a Lutheran pastor, from 1885 until his death in a railroad accident in 1891. Descriptive material on Gaston College may be found in the Lenoir-Rhyne College Archives.
44. Elizabeth College for Women was established in 1897 as a degree-granting college in Charlotte, N.C., by Dr. Charles B. King, a Lutheran pastor. After graduating nearly 200 young women, it merged with Roanoke Women's College in Salem, Va., in 1915, still retaining the name of Elizabeth College. Following a disastrous fire in 1921, it was forced to close. See J. William McCauley, "Elizabeth College and Related Lutheran Schools," June 24, 1901, in archives of the North Carolina Synod, LCA.
45. Anderson, *North Carolina Synod*, pp. 25-26.

Chapter 8: The Second German Migration (pages 113-137)

1. Marcus L. Hansen, *The Immigrants in American History* (Cambridge: Harvard University Press, 1940), p. 3.
2. Ibid., p. 11.

NOTES   363

3. Marcus Hansen, *The Atlantic Migration 1607–1860* (New York: Harper and Row, 1961), pp. 123, 231-253.
4. Carl S. Meyer, *Log Cabin to Luther Tower* (St. Louis: Concordia Publishing House, 1965), p. 8.
5. Walter O. Forster, *Zion on The Mississippi* (St. Louis: Concordia Publishing House, 1953), contains a full account of the Saxon migration to Missouri.
6. English translation in Forster, *Zion,* p. 502.
7. A. W. Stellhorn, "What Was the Perry County College?" *Concordia Historical Institute Quarterly* 18 (January 1946): 101-103.
8. Diary of G. H. Loeber, Dec. 9, 1839, quoted in Forster, *Zion,* p. 503.
9. John Philipp Koehler, *The History of the Wisconsin Synod,* ed. Leigh D. Jordahl (Sauk Rapids, Minn.: The Protestant Conference, 1981), pp. 25-26.
10. M. Heinrich, *A History of the First Evangelical Lutheran Synod of Texas* (Dubuque: Wartburg Publishing House, 1927), pp. 1-26.
11. Walter A. Baepler, *A Century of Grace* (St. Louis: Concordia Publishing House, 1947), pp. 83-95.
12. Gerhard Ottersberg, *Wartburg College 1852–1952* (Waverly, Iowa: Waverly Publishing Co., 1952), pp. 9-16.
13. Herman F. Zehnder, *Teach My People the Truth: The Story of Frankenmuth, Michigan* (Bay City, Mich.: privately published 1970), pp. 103-105.
14. Gerhard Ottersberg, "Wartburg College and the Iowa Synod" (unpublished resource paper prepared for the LECNA History Project, 1983), pp. 6-8.
15. Zehnder, *Teach My People,* pp. 219-220.
16. Ottersberg, *Wartburg College,* pp. 20-25.
17. Ibid., pp. 29-41.
18. Ibid., p. 41.
19. Ibid., pp. 60-61.
20. Ibid., pp. 65-66.
21. William A. Flachmeier, *Lutherans of Texas in Confluence* (Austin, Tex.: Southern District, American Lutheran Church, 1972), p. 61.
22. Heinrich, *Synod of Texas* (Dubuque: Wartburg Publishing House, 1927), pp. 1-26.
23. Alfred D. Klages, "A History of Texas Lutheran College 1851–1951" (unpublished M.A. thesis, University of Texas, 1951), pp. 17-24.
24. A. G. Wiederaenders, *Coming of Age: A History of Texas Lutheran College* (San Antonio: Paul Anderson Co., 1978), pp. 11-31.
25. H. C. Alden, "The Evangelical Lutheran Trinity College of Round Rock, Texas" (unpublished M.A. thesis, University of Texas, 1929).
26. Dorothy Ann Brown, *We Sing to Thee: A Story about Clifton College* (Waco: Texian Press, 1974), p. 7.
27. Koehler, *Wisconsin Synod,* p. 84.
28. Ibid.
29. Ibid., p. 90.
30. Arthur Hoermann, *Our Northwestern College,* trans. Hans Houssa (Watertown, Wis.: Wisconsin Synod, 1915), p. 11.
31. Watertown *Democrat,* August 31, 1865; quoted in Hoermann, *Northwestern,* p. 13.
32. Erwin Ernst Kowalke, *Centennial Story: Northwestern College, 1865–1965* (Watertown, Wis.: Northwestern College, 1965), p. 33.
33. Quoted in Hoermann, *Northwestern,* p. 14.

34. Ibid., p. 18.
35. Kowalke, *Centennial Story*, pp. 171-176.
36. Hoermann, *Northwestern*, p. 23.
37. Morton A. Schroeder, *A Time to Remember: An Informal History of Dr. Martin Luther College* (New Ulm, Minn.: Dr. Martin Luther College, 1984).
38. George H. Gerberding, *Life and Letters of William A. Passavant* (Greenville, Pa.: The Young Lutheran Co., 1906), pp. 142-143.
39. Carl R. Cronmiller, *A History of the Lutheran Church in Canada* (Canada: Evangelical Lutheran Synod of Canada, 1901), pp. 131-135.
40. Theodore G. Tappert, *History of the Lutheran Theological Seminary at Philadelphia, 1864–1964* (Philadelphia: Lutheran Theological Seminary, 1964), pp. 64-65.
41. Walter Freitag, "Lutheran College and Seminary of Saskatoon" (unpublished manuscript provided by Dr. Freitag, Lutheran Theological Seminary at Saskatoon, 1984).
42. Norman J. Threinen, *Fifty Years of Lutheran Convergence: The Canadian Case Study* (Dubuque: Lutheran Historical Conference, 1983), p. 216, n. 7.
43. George Evenson, *Adventuring for Christ: The Story of the Evangelical Lutheran Church of Canada* (Calgary: Foothills Lutheran Press, 1974), pp. 75-77, 102-103. Also personal recollections of R. E. Sonnenfeld, Business Manager, Luther College, Regina, Saskatchewan, May 10, 1983.

Chapter 9: The Missouri System (pages 139-158)

1. Data provided by the Board for Professional Education Services, Lutheran Church–Missouri Synod, 1985.
2. Carl S. Meyer, ed., *Moving Frontiers: Readings in the History of the Lutheran Church–Missouri Synod* (St. Louis: Concordia Publishing House, 1964), pp. 164-166.
3. English translation in *Concordia Historical Institute Quarterly* 16 (April 1943): 2-18.
4. Carl S. Meyer, *Log Cabin to Luther Tower* (St. Louis: Concordia Publishing House, 1965), pp. 7-9.
5. Meyer, *Log Cabin*, pp. 11.
6. Ibid., pp. 11-13.
7. Ibid., pp. 17-19.
8. Ibid., pp. 33-34.
9. A. C. Stellhorn, "Lutheran Secondary Education in St. Louis," *Lutheran Education* 84 (October 1948): 103.
10. Ibid., 104.
11. C. F. W. Walther, *Der Lutheraner* 9, p. 29, quoted in Thomas Coates, "The Making of a Minister" (unpublished S.T.D. dissertation, Chicago Lutheran Theological Seminary, 1950), p. 99 (note).
12. Carl S. Meyer, *Pioneers Find Friends* (Decorah, Iowa: Luther College Press, 1962), p. 25.
13. Stellhorn, "Lutheran Secondary Education," *Lutheran Education* 84 (March 1949): 408-414.

14. C. F. W. Walther, *Der Lutheraner* 15 (July 26, 1859), p. 193, reprinted in full in Stellhorn, "Lutheran Secondary Education," *Lutheran Education* 84 (March 1949): 415-419.

15. Ibid., p. 417.

16. Meyer, *Log Cabin*, pp. 54-61.

17. Meyer, *Pioneers*, pp. 14-17.

18. Letter from C. F. W. Walther to J. C. W. Lindemann, April 27, 1861, cited in Meyer, *Log Cabin*, p. 40.

19. Ibid., p. 44.

20. Stellhorn, "Lutheran Secondary Education," *Lutheran Education* 84 (October 1948): 95-96.

21. Approved curricula of 1856 and 1882, in Coates, "Making of a Minister," pp. 24-25.

22. E. G. Sihler, "College and Seminary Life in the Old Days," *Ebenezer*, pp. 250-251, quoted in Herbert G. Bredemeier, *Concordia College, Fort Wayne, Indiana, 1839–1957* (Fort Wayne: Fort Wayne Public Library, 1978), p. 291.

23. Coates, "Making of a Minister," p. 23.

24. Meyer, *Moving Frontiers*, p. 297.

25. Alfred J. Freitag, *College with a Cause* (River Forest, Ill.: Concordia Teachers College, 1964), pp. 20-24.

26. Ibid., pp. 27-30.

27. Ibid., pp. 40-41.

28. Ibid., p. 54.

29. Translation of an original copy in Concordia Teachers College Archives, River Forest, Ill.; quoted in Freitag, *College with a Cause*, p. 65.

30. Ibid., p. 66.

31. Henry W. Biermann Jr., "The History of Concordia College, New Orleans," *Concordia Historical Institute Quarterly* 36 (October, 1963): 65-89. A college association in the Southern District of the Missouri Synod established another Concordia in New Orleans in 1904, but it was closed for lack of students in 1917.

32. Alan G. Steinberg, *We Will Remember* (Bronxville, N.Y.: Concordia College, 1981), pp. 1-6.

33. Ibid., pp. 7-22.

34. Ibid., p. 22.

35. Oswald B. Overn, *History of Concordia College* (St. Paul: Concordia College, 1967), p. 4.

36. September 13, 1893, quoted in Overn, *Concordia*, p. 6.

37. Martin P. Simon, "College on the Cornfield" (unpublished Ed.D. thesis, University of Oregon, 1953), p. 41.

38. Ibid., pp. 1-89.

39. Allen H. Nauss, "Concordia Academy, Portland Oregon," *CHIQ* 25 (January 1953): 175-178.

40. Norman J. Threinen, *A Sower Went Out* (Regina: Manitoba and Saskatchewan District, LCMS, 1981), pp. 59-61; Albert H. Schwermann, "Recollections of a President Emeritus," in *1965 Yearbook of Concordia College, Edmonton, Alberta.*

41. H. J. Stoeppelwerth, "History of St. John's College, Winfield, Kansas," *Concordia Historical Institute Quarterly* 5 (January 1933), *Concordia Historical Institute Quarterly* 6 (April 1934), reprinted in *Johnnie Heritage, 1893–1976* (Winfield, Kan.; Alumnni Association of St. John's College, 1976), pp. 43-60.

Chapter 10: Illinois: Threshold to the Great Plains (pages 159-176)

1. *Journal of the Fifth Annual Session of the Evangelical Lutheran Synod of the West,* October 7, 1839, p. 21.
2. *Minutes of the English Synod of Ohio,* 1841, p. 15, and 1842, p. 9, cited in Willard D. Allbeck, *A Century of Lutherans in Ohio* (Yellow Springs, Ohio: The Antioch Press, 1966), p. 127.
3. M. Diehl, *Biography of Ezra Keller* (Springfield, Ohio: Ruralist Publishing Co., 1859), pp. 259-261.
4. *Minutes of the Twelfth Convention of the Evangelical Lutheran Synod of the West,* June 1846, pp. 7-8, 17-18.
5. *Minutes of the First Session of the Evangelical Lutheran Synod of Illinois,* October 1846, pp. 15-16.
6. J. C. Jensson, ed., "John J. Lehmanowsky," *American Lutheran Biographies* (Milwaukee: 1890), pp. 463-465.
7. *Proceedings of the 8th Annual Convention of the Evangelical Lutheran Synod of Illinois,* September 15, 1853, pp. 29-30.
8. Quoted in Henry O. Evjen, "Illinois State University" (unpublished M. A. thesis, The Ohio State University, 1938), p. 21.
9. Ibid., p. 23.
10. *Proceedings of the Thirteenth Annual Convention of the Evangelical Lutheran Synod of Illinois,* September 1858, p. 16. *Minutes of the Board of Trustees, Illinois State University,* July 1, 1858 (handwritten record book in Carthage College Archives, Kenosha, Wis.).
11. Samuel Eliot Morison and Henry Steele Commager, *The Growth of the American Republic,* 2 vols., 5th ed. (New York: Oxford University Press, 1962), 1:647-648.
12. Evjen, "Illinois State University," pp. 66-68.
13. From the Norelius Collection, Augustana College Library, Rock Island, Ill., cited in Emil Erpestad, "A History of Augustana College" (unpublished Ph.D. dissertation, Yale University, 1955), p. 19.
14. Cited in George M. Stephenson, *Religious Aspects of Swedish Migration* (Minneapolis: University of Minnesota Press, 1932), p. 190.
15. G. Everett Arden, *Augustana Heritage: A History of the Augustana Lutheran Church* (Rock Island, Ill.: Augustana Press, 1963), pp. 75-88.
16. *Proceedings of the Second Annual Convention of the Synod of Central Illinois,* June 1868, pp. 7-8; *Proceedings of the Third Annual Convention of the Synod of Central Illinois,* June 1869, p. 8.
17. *Minutes of the Northern Illinois Synod,* 1868, p. 33.
18. Ibid.
19. *Minutes of the 3rd Annual Convention of the Synod of Central Illinois,* June 1869, pp. 16-17.
20. *Proceedings of an Educational Convention,* August 31, 1869, p. 2 (handwritten minutes book in Carthage College Archives, Kenosha, Wis.).
21. Ibid., pp. 5-6.
22. Ibid., p. 15.
23. Evjen, "Illinois State University," pp. 89-92.
24. *Minutes of the Board of Commissioners,* December 29, 1869, pp. 10-11 (handwritten minutes book in Carthage College Archives, Kenosha, Wis.).
25. Ibid., pp. 16-18.
26. Harold H. Lentz, *The Miracle of Carthage: History of Carthage College, 1847–1974* (Kenosha, Wis.: Carthage College, 1975), p. 58.

27. Ibid., pp. 142-144.
28. William C. Spielman, *The Diamond Jubilee History of Carthage College 1870–1945* (Carthage, Ill.: Carthage College Historical Society, 1945), p. 54.
29. Lentz, *Miracle of Carthage*, pp. 89-96.
30. Ibid., pp. 125-128.
31. George Whittecar, "The Story of Midland College through Fifty Years," published serially in the *Fremont Tribune,* 1937, Chap. 1.
32. *Proceedings of the Twelfth Annual Convention of the Nebraska Synod, 1894,* quoted in Lillian W. Hickman, "The History of Midland College" (unpublished M.A. thesis, University of Oregon, 1949), pp. 14-15.
33. Hickman, "Midland College," p. 25.
34. H. A. Ott, *A History of the Evangelical Lutheran Synod of Kansas* (Topeka: Kansas Synod, 1907), pp. 230-231.
35. Quoted in Hickman, "Midland College," p. 24.
36. Ibid., pp. 48-49.
37. "Brief History of Western Theological Seminary" (unpublished typescript in Midland College Archives, Fremont, Neb.), pp. 1-9.
38. Minutes of the Midland Board of Trustees, June 3, 1918, quoted in Hickman, "Midland College," p. 141.
39. John Strietelmeier, *Valparaiso's First Century* (Valparaiso, Ind.: Valparaiso University, 1959), pp. 48-49.
40. Ann L. Wilhite, "A College for All Seasons: Fremont College, 1884–1919" (a paper presented to the Douglas County Historical Society, October 17, 1971; in Midland College Archives), pp. 1-12.
41. Whittecar, "Midland College," Chap. 5.
42. Wilhite, "College for All Seasons," p. 7.

Chapter 11: The Swedish Dimension (pages 177-204)

1. Maldwyn A. Jones, *American Immigration* (Chicago: University of Chicago Press, 1960), pp. 69, 114.
2. George M. Stephenson, *Religious Aspects of Swedish Immigration* (Minneapolis: University of Minnesota Press, 1932), pp. 1-23.
3. Ibid., pp. 1-23
4. *Kyrkohistorisk Aarskrift* (Uppsala, 1946), p. 242
5. G. Everett Arden, *Augustana Heritage: A History of the Augustana Lutheran Church* (Rock Island, Ill.: Augustana Press, 1963), pp. 30-32.
6. Sam Rönnegaard, *Prairie Shepherd: A Life of Lars Paul Esbjörn,* trans. G. Everett Arden (Rock Island, Ill.: Augustana Book Concern, 1952), pp. 96-111.
7. George H. Gerberding, *The Life and Letters of William A. Passavant* (Greenville, Pa.: The Young Lutheran Co., 1906), p. 207.
8. Rönnegaard, *Prairie Shepherd,* p. 149.
9. Arden, *Augustana Heritage,* pp. 70-73.
10. Ibid., pp. 83-87.
11. Letter from L. P. Esbjörn to Jonas Swensson, January 30, 1860, quoted in Rönnegaard, *Prairie Shepherd,* p. 277.
12. Conrad Bergendoff, *Augustana: A Profession of Faith* (Rock Island, Ill.: Augustana College Library, 1969), pp. 24-25.
13. Letter from Esbjörn to Eric Norelius, quoted in Rönnegaard, *Prairie Shepherd,* pp. 279-280.
14. Bergendoff, *Augustana,* pp. 38-42.

15. Ibid., pp. 42-43.
16. Arden, *Augustana Heritage*, pp. 349-350.
17. Bergendoff, *Augustana*, p. 81
18. Ibid., p. 108.
19. Louis Almen, "Some Contributions of Augustana Church Colleges to American Higher Education" (unpublished essay prepared for the LECNA History Project), p. 12.
20. Eric Norelius, *De svenska luterska församlingarmas och svenskarnes historia i Amerika* (Rock Island, Ill.: 1890), 1:848; Cited in G. Everett Arden, *Augustana Heritage*, p. 81.
21. Letter from C. A. Hedengran to Eric Norelius, July 14, 1862.
22. Quoted in Doniver A. Lund, *Gustavus Adolphus College: A Centennial History* (St. Peter, Minn.: Gustavus Adolphus College Press, 1963), p. 13.
23. Ibid., p. 15.
24. Ibid., pp. 21-22.
25. Ibid., pp. 25-31.
26. Quoted in Arden, *Augustana Heritage*, p. 102.
27. *St. Peter Tribune*, May 20, 1874, quoted in Lund, *Centennial History*, p. 37.
28. Ibid., p. 40.
29. Doniver A. Lund, "Educational Experience in America: Immigrant and Native-born," in *Swedish Pioneer Historical Quarterly* (January 1967): 13-31.
30. Catalogue of Gustavus Adolphus College, 1883-84.
31. Quoted in Lund, *Centennial History*, p. 72.
32. Emory K. Lindquist, *Smoky Valley People* (Rock Island, Ill.: Augustana Book Concern, 1953), pp. 9-13.
33. Ibid., p. 86.
34. Emory K. Lindquist, *Bethany in Kansas* (Lindsborg, Kan.: Bethany College, 1975), p. 9.
35. Lindquist, *Smoky Valley*, p. 90.
36. Ibid., pp. 104-105.
37. Lindquist, *Bethany in Kansas*, p. 38.
38. Lindquist, *Smoky Valley*, p. 93.
39. Lindquist, *Bethany in Kansas*, pp. 23-40.
40. Ibid., p. 42.
41. James I. Dowie, *Prairie Grass Dividing* (Rock Island, Ill.: Augustana Historical Society, 1959), pp. 87-105.
42. Stephenson, *Religious Aspects*, p. 335.
43. Paul M. Lindberg, "The Academies and Colleges of the Augustana Synod in Minnesota" (unpublished Ph.D. dissertation, University of Nebraska, 1946); Emeroy Johnson, "Swedish Academies in Minnesota," *The Swedish Pioneer* (January 1981), pp. 21-38.
44. Swedish academies established and closed before 1900 were Hope Academy, Moorhead, Minnesota (1888–1896); Martin Luther Academy, Chicago (1883–1895); Emanuel Academy (1888–1893) and Lund Academy, Christine Lake, Minnesota (1897–1899). Four others developed into collegiate institutions: St. Ansgar's (Gustavus Adolphus), Bethany, Luther (Wahoo), Upsala. A second group of six academies was established between 1901 and 1908: Northwestern (Fergus Falls, Minnesota); Minnesota College (Minneapolis); Trinity (Round Rock, Texas); Mamrelund (Iowa); Coeur d'Alene (Idaho); North Star (Warren, Minnesota). All eventually closed, mostly during the Great Depression.

45. Alvin R. Calman, *Upsala College: The Early Years* (New York: Vantage Press, 1983), pp. 1-27.
46. Ibid., pp. 27-57.
47. Conrad Bergendoff, "The Role of Augustana in the Transplanting of Culture Across the Atlantic," in J. Iverne Dowie and J. Thomas Tredway, eds., *The Immigration of Ideas: Studies in the North Atlantic Community* (Rock Island, Ill.: Augustana Historical Society, 1968), pp. 67-83.

Chapter 12: Early Norwegian Colleges (pages 205-224)

1. Odd S. Lovoll, *The Promise of America* (Minneapolis: University of Minnesota Press, 1984), pp. 10-11.
2. Ingrid Semmingsen, *Norway to America: A History of the Migration*, trans. Einar Haugen (Minneapolis: University of Minnesota Press, 1978), pp. 10-19.
3. Theodore C. Blegen, *Norwegian Migration to America, 1825–1860* (Northfield, Minn.: Norwegian-American Historical Association, 1931), pp. 66-67.
4. George T. Flom, *A History of Norwegian Immigration to the United States from the Earliest Beginning Down to the Year 1848* (Iowa City: privately published, 1909), p. 386.
5. Carlton C. Qualey, *Norwegian Settlement in the United States* (Northfield, Minn.: Norwegian-American Historical Association, 1938), p. 213.
6. E. Clifford Nelson and Eugene L. Fevold, *The Lutheran Church among Norwegian-Americans*, 2 vols. (Minneapolis: Augsburg Publishing House, 1960), 1:3-12.
7. Ibid., pp. 71-81.
8. Ibid., pp. 82-95.
9. J. Magnus Rohne, *Norwegian American Lutheranism up to 1872* (New York: Macmillan Co., 1926), p. 69.
10. Ibid., pp. 134-135.
11. Nelson and Fevold, *The Lutheran Church*, 1:127-134.
12. *Minutes of the First Session of the Synod of Northern Illinois*, September 19-22, 1851, p. 2.
13. Henry O. Evjen, "Illinois State University" (unpublished M. A. thesis, The Ohio State University, 1938), pp. 89-92; Conrad Bergendoff, *The Augustana Ministerium* (Rock Island, Ill.: Augustana Historical Society, 1980), pp. 14-16.
14. A more complete account of Illinois State University is found in Chap. 10.
15. Emil Erpestad, "A History of Augustana College" (unpublished Ph.D. dissertation, Yale University, 1955), pp. 41-48.
16. *Billed Magazin*, August 21, 1869, p. 301, trans. H. M. Blegen, in archives of Augustana College, Sioux Falls, S.D.
17. Nelson and Fevold, *The Lutheran Church*, 1:201-208. The archives of Augustana College, Sioux Falls, S.D., contain an account of the division of the Scandinavian Augustana Synod into the Norwegian-Danish and the Swedish Augustana synods on June 15-17, 1870. Translations based on the annual reports of the Scandinavian Augustana Synod were made by H. M. Blegen.
18. Carl Chrislock, *From Fjord to Freeway* (Minneapolis: Augsburg College, 1969), pp. 5-6.
19. Rohne, *Lutheranism to 1872*, pp. 186-190.
20. Nelson and Fevold, *The Lutheran Church*, 1:138-142.
21. Rohne, *Lutheranism to 1872*, p. 186-190.

22. Chrislock, *Fjord to Freeway*, p. 11.
23. Ibid., p. 12.
24. James S. Hamre, "Georg Sverdrup and the Augsburg Plan of Education," *Norwegian American Studies* (Northfield, Minn.: Norwegian-American Historical Association, 1974), XXVI, 168.
25. Quoted in Chrislock, *From Fjord*, p. 23.
26. Ibid., pp. 21-22.
27. Hamre, "Georg Sverdrup," pp. 166-172.
28. Quoted in Chrislock, *From Fjord*, p. 33.
29. Ibid., p. 45.
30. "Report of the Convention of the Norwegian-Danish Augustana Synod," October 5-12, 1870, trans. H. M. Blegen, in archives of Augustana College, Sioux Falls, S.D.
31. *Lutherske Kirketidende* (December 1876): 183-185, trans. H. M. Blegen, in archives of Augustana College, Sioux Falls, S.D.
32. "Constitution of Salem Seminary" approved by the Norwegian-Danish Augustana Synod, June 1877, trans. H. M. Blegen, in archives of Augustana College, Sioux Falls, S.D.
33. James M. Wahl, "How Augustana College Moved from Marshall, Wisconsin, to Beloit, Iowa," *Sioux Falls Posten*, January 21 to February 25, 1915, trans. H. M. Blegen, in archives of Augustana College, Sioux Falls, S.D.
34. *Lutherske Kirketidende* (July 25, 1882): 1-3, trans. H. M. Blegen, in archives of Augustana College, Sioux Falls, S.D.
35. Erpestad, *Augustana College*, pp. 83-84.
36. Ibid., p. 91.
37. A personal account of the experience of the wife of a leading pastor of the Norwegian Synod in making the transition to America is David T. Nelson, ed., *The Diary of Elizabeth Koren, 1953–1855* (Decorah, Iowa: Norwegian-American Historical Association, 1955).
38. David T. Nelson, *Luther College 1861–1961* (Decorah, Iowa: Luther College Press, 1961), p. 40.
39. Ibid., pp. 25-30.
40. Ibid., p. 31.
41. Ibid., p. 32.
42. Karen Larsen, *Laur. Larsen: Pioneer College President* (Northfield, Minn.: NAHA, 1936), pp. 97-98.
43. Ibid., pp. 116-125.
44. Ibid., p. 129.
45. Theodore C. Blegen, *Norwegian Migration to America: The American Transition* (Northfield, Minn.: Norwegian-American Historical Association, 1940), pp. 418-428.
46. Nelson, *Luther College*, pp. 45-53.
47. Larsen, *Laur. Larsen*, pp. 180-182.
48. Gisle Bothne, *Den Norske Luther College, 1861–1897* (Decorah: Forfatterens Forlag, 1897), pp. 170-172.
49. Larsen, *Laur. Larsen*, p. 239.
50. Ibid., pp. 186-188.
51. Ibid., p. 251.
52. Ibid., pp. 249-250.
53. Ibid., p. 250.

Chapter 13: Later Norwegian Colleges (pages 225-248)

1. Quoted in Theodore C. Blegen, *Norwegian Migration to America: The American Tradition* (Northfield, Minn.: Norwegian-American Historical Association, 1940), p. 241.

2. James S. Hamre, "Norwegian Immigrants Respond to the Common School: A Case Study of American Values and the Lutheran Tradition," *Church History* 50 (September 1981): 304.

3. Quoted in Blegen, *Norwegian Migration to America*, p. 259.

4. Ibid., p. 262.

5. Preus's address to the Madison meeting on March 5, 1869, was printed in *Kirkelig Maanedstidende* 7 (April 1, 1869): 113-126; see also James S. Hamre, "Three Spokesmen for Norwegian Lutheran Academies: Schools for Church, Heritage, Society" (unpublished manuscript provided by courtesy of author), pp. 9-10.

6. Bert H. Narveson, "The Norwegian Lutheran Academies," *Norwegian-American Studies and Records* (Northfield, Minn.: Norwegian-American Historical Association, 1944), XIV, 217-221. Narveson provides a complete list of these schools, their locations, and dates of operation.

7. *Luther's Works*, vol. 46 (Philadelphia: Fortress Press, 1967), p. 215.

8. Blegen, *American Transition*, p. 265.

9. Joseph Shaw, *History of St. Olaf College* (Northfield, Minn.: St. Olaf College Press, 1974), pp. 36-38.

10. *Rice County Journal* (October 21, 1874), cited in Joseph Shaw, pp. 40-41.

11. *Minutes of Board of Trustees Meetings*, Book No. 1, pp. 5-6, quoted in Shaw, *St. Olaf*, p. 42.

12. William C. Benson, *High on Manitou* (Northfield, Minn.: St. Olaf College Press, 1949), pp. 27-28.

13. Georgina Dieson Hegland, *As It Was in the Beginning* (Northfield, Minn.: St. Olaf College Press, 1950), pp. 28-30.

14. For a treatment of the election controversy, see E. Clifford Nelson, ed., *The Lutherans in North America* (Philadelphia: Fortress Press, 1980), pp. 313-325.

15. Shaw, *St. Olaf*, pp. 71-74.

16. E. Clifford Nelson and Eugene L. Fevold, *The Lutheran Church among Norwegian-Americans*, 2 vols. (Minneapolis: Augsburg Publishing House, 1960), 2:23-37.

17. James S. Hamre, "Georg Sverdrup and the Augsburg Plan of Education," *Norwegian-American Studies* (Northfield, Minn.: Norwegian-American Historical Association, 1974), 26:173-176.

18. Quoted in Carl Chrislock, *From Fjord to Freeway* (Minneapolis: Augsburg College, 1969), pp. 51, 56.

19. Ibid., pp. 65-68.

20. Ibid., pp. 73-74.

21. Eugene L. Fevold, *The Lutheran Free Church* (Minneapolis: Augsburg Publishing House, 1969), pp. 94-98.

22. Chrislock, *Fjord to Freeway*, pp. 79-80.

23. Quoted in Shaw, *St. Olaf*, p. 98.

24. Benson, *Manitou*, pp. 90-91.

25. *St. Olaf Catalog*, 1899–1900, pp. 26-27.

26. Shaw, *St. Olaf*, p. 134.

27. Ibid., pp. 123-124.

28. Ibid., pp. 227-247.

29. Emil Erpestad, "History of Augustana College" (unpublished Ph.D. dissertation, Yale University, 1955), pp. 91-99.
30. *Report of the Sixth Annual Convention of the United Norwegian Lutheran Church*, June 12-20, 1895, trans. H. M. Blegen (Sioux Falls, S.D.: Augustana College Archives), p. 77.
31. "Report of the Augustana College Association," *Report of Sixth Annual Convention, United Norwegian Lutheran Church*, trans. H. M. Blegen.
32. Erpestad, "History of Augustana," pp. 115-120.
33. *Annual Report of the Norwegian Lutheran Church of America*, 1918, p. 98, quoted in Erpestad, "History of Augustana," p. 187.
34. *Annual Report of the NLCA*, 1919, p. 236. quoted in Erpestad, "History of Augustana," p. 197.
35. Erpestad, "History of Augustana," pp. 210-216.
36. Ibid., pp. 219-224.
37. O. M. Norlie, *History of the Norwegian People in America* (Minneapolis, Augsburg Publishing House, 1925), p. 360.
38. Narveson, "Norwegian Academies," pp. 219-221.
39. Continuing to operate as academies are Oak Grove High School, Fargo, N.D., Lutheran Collegiate Bible School, Outlook, Sask. (formerly Outlook College), and the high school of the Lutheran Brethren, Fergus Falls, Minn.
40. Erling N. Rolfsrud, *Cobber Chronicle*, 2nd ed. (Moorhead, Minn.: Concordia College, 1976), pp. 11-12.
41. Ibid, pp. 15-18.
42. George H. Gerberding, *Reminiscent Reflections of a Youthful Octogenarian* (Minneapolis: Augsburg Publishing House, 1928), p. 150.
43. Rolfsrud, *Cobber Chronicle*, pp. 60-71.
44. Ibid., pp. 41-43.
45. Rasmus Bogstad, *The Early History of Concordia College, 1891–1910* (Moorhead, Minn.: privately printed, 1941), pp. 82-85.
46. Rolfsrud, *Cobber Chronicle*, pp. 60-71.
47. Ibid., pp. 72-79
48. Richard A. Oppedahl, "Waldorf College: First Fifty Years" (unpublished M.A. thesis, University of South Dakota, 1956), pp. 1-5.
49. Norlie, *The Norwegian People*, pp. 324-326.
50. George O. Evenson, *Adventuring for Christ: The Story of the Evangelical Lutheran Church of Canada* (Calgary: Foothills Lutheran Press, 1974), pp. 73-75.
51. Chester A. Ronning, "A Study of an Alberta Protestant Private School: The Camrose Lutheran College" (unpublished M.A. thesis, College of Education, University of Alberta, 1942).
52. Walter C. Schnackenberg, *The Lamp and the Cross* (Tacoma: Pacific Lutheran University Press, 1965), p. 10.
53. Ibid., pp. 10-30.
54. Bjug Harstad, "A Trip Into the Yukon Region," letters and articles published in the *Pacific Herold*, 1898 and 1899, translated from Norwegian by Oliver Harstad, 1955. Mimeographed collection in Pacific Lutheran University Archives, Tacoma.
55. Schnackenberg, *Lamp and Cross*, pp. 61-70.
56. *The Spokane College Bulletin* (July 1913), 7:56-63.
57. Walter C. Schnackenberg, "The Development of Norwegian Lutheran Schools in the Pacific Northwest from 1890 to 1920" (unpublished Ph.D. thesis, The State College of Washington, 1950), pp. 244-269.

58. Letter of H. G. Stub to N. J. Hong, August 15, 1917, reproduced in Schnackenberg, "Norwegian Lutheran Schools," p. 276.
59. Schnackenberg, *Lamp and Cross*, pp. 79-87.
60. P. O. Holland and J. G. Norby, "Report to the Board of Trustees and the Board of Education of the Norwegian Lutheran Church of America," November 8, 1934 (archives of The American Lutheran Church, Dubuque, Iowa).
61. Schnackenberg, *Lamp and Cross*, pp. 104-108.
62. Ibid., pp. 115-119.
63. Ibid., pp. 133-137.

Chapter 14: Colleges of the Danes and Finns (pages 249-263)

1. U. S. Census reports, 1860.
2. Kristian Hvidt, *Flight to America* (New York: Academic Press, 1975), pp. 127-128.
3. Enok Mortensen, *The Danish Lutheran Church in America* (Philadelphia: Board of Publication, Lutheran Church in America, 1967), p. 39.
4. For biographies of Grundtvig, see Johannes Knudsen, *Danish Rebel* (Philadelphia: Muhlenberg Press, 1955) and Ernest D. Nielsen, *N. F. S. Grundtvig: An American Study* (Rock Island, Ill.: Augustana Press, 1955).
5. Holger Begtrup, *Det danske Folks Historie i det 19 Aarhundrede*, 2nd ed. (Copenhagen, 1916), pp. 312-13, quoted in translation in Mortensen, *Danish Lutheran Church*, p. 11.
6. Mortensen, *Danish Lutheran Church*, p. 34.
7. *Kirkelig Samler* (October 1872), quoted in translation in Thorvald Hansen, *We Laid Foundation Here: The Early History of Grand View College* (Des Moines: Grand View College, 1972), pp. 12-13.
8. Article by Adam Dan, quoted in Paul C. Nyholm, *The Americanization of the Danish Lutheran Churches in America* (Copenhagen: Institute for Danish Church History, 1963), pp. 91-92.
9. Hansen, *Foundation*, p. 14.
10. John M. Jensen, *The United Evangelical Lutheran Church: An Interpretation* (Minneapolis: Augsburg Publishing House, 1964).
11. E. Clifford Nelson, ed., *The Lutherans in North America* (Philadelphia: Fortress Press, 1980), pp. 267-272.
12. Enok Mortensen, *Schools for Life: The Grundtvigian Folk Schools in America* (Junction City, Ore.: Danish-American Heritage Society, 1947), pp. 10-12; Thorvald Hansen, *Foundations*, pp. 15-16.
13. Mortensen, *Danish Lutheran Church*, gives a full account of these developments, pp. 97-121.
14. "Om et Dansk Universitet i Amerika" (Des Moines: Danish Church, 1898), p. 5, quoted in translation in Hansen, *Foundations*, p. 34.
15. Hansen, *Foundations*, pp. 56-57.
16. *Dannevirke*, February 10, 1906, quoted in translation in Mortensen, *Danish Lutheran Church*, p. 152.
17. *Kirkelig Samler*, 1907, quoted in translation in Mortensen, *Foundations*, p. 152.
18. William E. Christensen, *Saga of the Tower* (Blair, Neb.: Lutheran Publishing House, 1959), p. 3-12.
19. Ibid., pp. 17-18.
20. Ibid., pp. 21-32.

21. Peter L. Peterson, *A Place Called Dana* (Blair, Neb.: Dana College, 1984), pp. 31-36.
22. Christensen, *Saga*, p. 63.
23. Peterson, *Dana*, p. 44.
24. Christensen, *Saga*, pp. 85-87.
25. Peterson, *Dana*, p. 193.
26. Ibid., p. 44.
27. Armas K. Holmio, "The Beginnings of Finnish Church Life in America," in *The Faith of the Finns*, ed. Ralph J. Jalkanen (East Lansing: Michigan State University Press, 1972), pp. 122-123.
28. John Wargelin, *The Americanization of the Finns* (Hancock, Mich.: The Finnish Lutheran Book Concern, 1924), pp. 56-58, 61.
29. Arthur E. Puotinen, *Finnish Radicals and Religion in Midwestern Mining Towns, 1865–1914* (New York: Arno Press, 1979), pp. 66-78.
30. Holmio, "Finnish Church Life," p. 127.
31. Ibid., p. 129. The church was named Trinity in recognition of the three nationalities represented among the founders of the church in 1867: Finns, Swedes, and Norwegians!
32. Douglas J. Ollila, "The Suomi Synod: 1890–1920," in *Faith of the Finns*, ed. Jalkanen, p. 166.
33. Arnold Stadius, "Suomi College and Seminary," in *The Finns in North America: A Social Symposium*, ed. Ralph J. Jalkanen (East Lansing: Michigan State University Press, 1969), pp. 93-95.
34. Ibid., p. 108.
35. Ralph J. Jalkanen, "Suomi College: A Brief Review of Its History and Culture," *The Cresset* (April 1976): 12-13.

Chapter 15: Emerging Patterns. . ., 1865–1914 (pages 264-283)

1. U.S. Department of Justice, Immigration and Naturalization Service, *Annual Reports*.
2. Samuel G. Hefelbower, *History of Gettysburg College* (Gettysburg, Pa.: Gettysburg College, 1932), p. 258.
3. Emory Lindquist, *Bethany in Kansas* (Lindsborg, Kan.: Bethany College, 1975), pp. 23, 42.
4. Karen Larsen, *Laur. Larsen: Pioneer College President* (Northfield, Minn.: NAHA, 1936), p. 251.
5. Michael C. D. McDaniel, "Evolution in American Thought, 1860–1925" (unpublished Ph.D. dissertation, University of Chicago, 1978).
6. Lawrence R. Veysey, *The Emergence of the American University* (Chicago: The University of Chicago Press, 1965), pp. 400-407.
7. Quoted in William Edward Eisenberg, *The First Hundred Years: Roanoke College 1842–1942* (Salem, Va.: Roanoke College, 1942), p. 286.
8. Veysey, *The American University*, p. 33.
9. Herbert G. Bredemeier, *Concordia College, Fort Wayne, Indiana, 1839–1957* (Fort Wayne: Fort Wayne Public Library, 1978), pp. 174-176.
10. Alfred J. Freitag, *College with a Cause* (River Forest, Ill.: Concordia Teachers College, 1964), p. 102.
11. Lamar McCarrell, "A Historical Review of the College Band Movement from

1875 to 1969'' (unpublished Ph.D. dissertation, Florida State University, 1971), pp. 22-24.

12. Leola Nelson Bergman, *Music Master of the Middle West* (Minneapolis: University of Minnesota Press, 1944), pp. 93-95, 116-117.

13. Bredemeier, *Concordia College*, p. 201.

14. David T. Nelson, *Luther College, 1861–1961* (Decorah, Iowa: Luther College Press, 1961), p. 93.

15. Frederick Rudolph, *The American College and University* (New York: Random House, 1962), p. 374.

16. Robert Bloom, "Intercollegiate Athletics at Gettysburg College, 1879–1919," *The Gettysburg Bulletin*, 67 (December 1976): 3. See also Bloom, "Intercollegiate Athletics on Lutheran College Campuses" (unpublished resource paper prepared for LECNA History Project, 1984).

17. William S. Clark, "The Beginnings of Football at Susquehanna University, 1890–1900," in *Susquehanna University Studies*. May 1956, p. 268.

18. William A. Kinnison, "History of Athletics at Wittenberg, 1845–1950" (unpublished paper provided by courtesy of the author, 1983), p. 16.

19. Quoted in Doniver A. Lund, *Gustavus Adolphus College: A Centennial History, 1862–1962* (St. Peter, Minn.: Gustavus Adolphus College Press, 1963), p. 93.

20. Rudolph, *The American College*, p. 322.

21. Saul Sack, *History of Higher Education in Pennsylvania*, 2 vols. (Harrisburg: The Pennsylvania Historical and Museum Commission, 1963), 2:568.

22. Ibid., p. 574.

23. Robert A. Gahagen, "Background for a College: Early Years of Thiel College" (unpublished manuscript in Thiel College Archives, n.d.) pp. 30, 81.

24. Erwin Ernst Kowalke, *Centennial Story: Northwestern College 1865–1965* (Watertown, Wis.: Northwestern College, 1965), pp. 111-112.

25. Conrad Bergendoff, *Augustana: A Profession of Faith* (Rock Island, Ill.: Augustana College Library, 1969), p. 103.

26. Anna Mae Hayden, "Glimpses of the History of Women in Twelve Institutions of Higher Learning Related to Selected Lutheran Churches in the United States, 1860–1984" (unpublished resource paper prepared for LECNA History Project, 1984), pp. 78-80.

27. Donald Huber, "History of Trinity Seminary" (manuscript in preparation for publication, provided through courtesy of author, 1984), Chap. 4.

28. "The Lutheran Status of Pennsylvania College" (Gettysburg: The Board of Trustees of Pennsylvania College, 1892), pp. 4-5.

29. *Annual Report for 1906*, Carnegie Foundation, pp. 7-27.

30. William A. Kinnison, *An American Seminary: A History of Hamma School of Theology 1845–1978* (Columbus: Ohio Synod, LCA, 1980), pp. 112-114.

31. David Potts, "American Colleges in the Nineteenth Century," *History of American Education Quarterly* 11 (1971): 363-380.

32. F. V. N. Painter, "Our Educational Institutions," in *The First General Conference of Lutherans in America, Held in Philadelphia, December 27-29, 1898, Proceedings, Essays, and Debates* (Philadelphia: Lutheran Publication Society and the General Council Publication Board, 1899), pp. 95ff.

33. J. M. Ruthrauff, "Our Home Mission Fields—West," in *The Second General Conference of Lutherans in America, Held in Philadelphia, April 1-3, 1902*

(Philadelphia: Lutheran Publication Society and General Council Publication Board, 1902), pp. 178ff.

34. *Minutes*, General Council of the Evangelical Lutheran Church, 1901.

35. *Minutes of the Lutheran Educational Conference*, Harrisburg Pa., June 23-24, 1910 (Archives of Cooperative Lutheranism, Lutheran Council in the U.S.A., New York, N.Y.). William Kinnison, "The Past as Prologue in Lutheran Higher Education: The Pursuit of Opportunity," Presidential Address at the 75th anniversary of the Lutheran Educational Conference of North America, Washington, D.C., January 29, 1985, provides a brief interpretive history of LECNA (*Papers and Proceedings*, LECNA, 1985, pp. 7-20).

36. *Second Annual Report of the Council of Church Boards of Education in the U.S.A., 1912-13*, pp. 3-5.

Chapter 16: The Maturing of Lutheran Higher Education, 1914–1940 (pages 285-302)

1. *Springfield Daily News*, May 29, 1918, quoted in Harold H. Lentz, *History of Wittenberg College 1845–1945* (Springfield, Ohio: The Wittenberg Press, 1946), pp. 227-229.

2. Lentz, *Wittenberg College*, p. 264.

3. "Christian Education Through Twenty Years," in *Annual Report, Board of Education, Norwegian Lutheran Church of America, 1937*, p. 50.

4. *Biennial Report of Board of Education, ULCA*, October 1932, p. 23.

5. William A. Kinnison, *An American Seminary: A History of the Hamma School of Theology 1845–1978* (Columbus: Ohio Synod, LCA, 1980), p. 122.

6. Edward A. Krug, *Salient Dates in American Education, 1635 to 1964* (New York: Harper & Row, 1966), pp. 106-109.

7. Carl S. Meyer, "Past Administrative Policies and Practices in the Schools of the Missouri Synod," in *Yearbook of the Lutheran Educational Association, 1949* (River Forest, Ill., 1949), p. 110. Alfred Freitag, *College with a Cause* (River Forest, Ill.: Concordia Teachers College, 1964), p. 120. Gerhard Ottersberg, "The Board of Education of the Iowa Synod" (unpublished resource paper prepared for LECNA History Project, 1984), pp. 12-15.

8. O. H. Pannkoke, *A Great Church Finds Itself* (Quitman, Ga.: privately published, 1966), pp. 108-177.

9. R. J. Leonard, E. S. Evenden, and F. B. O'Rear, *Survey of Higher Education for the United Lutheran Church in America*, 3 vols. (New York: Teachers College, Columbia University, 1929), 2:1-4.

10. Ibid., 1:23.

11. Gould Wickey, "Documentary Review of Board of Higher Education, ULCA, 1918–1959" (typescript in LCA Archives, Lutheran School of Theology, Chicago, Illinois).

12. "Christian Education Through Twenty Years," pp. 50-51.

13. E. Clifford Nelson, ed., *The Lutherans in North America* (Philadelphia: Fortress Press, 1980), pp. 446-449. The American Lutheran Church (ALC) formed by the merger of 1930 became part of a larger church body in 1960 that adopted a similar name.

14. Constitution of the Board of Christian Higher Education, American Lutheran Church, Article IV.

15. Gerhard Ottersberg, "The Board of Christian Higher Education of the American Lutheran Church: Policies and Actions, 1930–1960" (unpublished resource paper prepared for the LECNA History Project), pp. 10-11.
16. Ibid., pp. 15-19.
17. Ibid., pp. 20, 29.
18. Ibid., pp. 34-38.
19. Ibid., pp. 20-22.
20. Missouri Synod, *Proceedings*, 1920, pp. 14-16.
21. Thomas Coates, "Making of a Minister" (unpublished S.T.D. dissertation, Chicago Lutheran Theological Seminary, 1950), p. 81.
22. Carl S. Meyer, ed., *Moving Frontiers: Readings in the History of the Lutheran Church–Missouri Synod* (St. Louis: Concordia Publishing House, 1965), p. 389.
23. Freitag, *College with a Cause*, p. 120.
24. Carl S. Meyer, "Past Administrative Practices," pp. 69-119.
25. *College Administrative Bulletin*, no. 3 (October 1929), quoted in Coates, "Making of a Minister," p. 84.
26. *Statistical Yearbook, 1931*, Lutheran Church–Missouri Synod.
27. Norman A. Threinen, *A Sower Went Out: A History of the Manitoba-Saskatchewan District of the Lutheran Church–Canada* (Regina: Manitoba and Saskatchewan District, 1982), pp. 59-60.
28. Henry Studtmann and Ray Martens, *Concordia of Texas* (Austin, Tex.: Concordia Lutheran College, 1977), p. 26.
29. Theodore A. Aaberg, *A City Set on a Hill* (Mankato, Minn.: Board of Publication, Evangelical Lutheran Synod, 1968), pp. 95-104. Peter T. Harstad, ed., *Sigurd Christian Ylvisaker, 1884–1959* (Mankato, Minn.: Bethany Lutheran College, 1984), pp. 93-134.
30. *Statistical Yearbook, 1941*, Lutheran Church–Missouri Synod.
31. John Strietelmeier, *Valparaiso's First Century* (Valparaiso: Valparaiso University, 1959), contains a complete and engaging account of the early years of the university and its transition to Lutheran ownership.
32. Inaugural Address of President O. P. Kretzmann, October 6, 1940.
33. Henry Hardy Heins, *Throughout All the Years* (Oneonta, N.Y.: Hartwick College, 1946), pp. 65-66.
34. Ibid., pp. 88-107.
35. The New York Ministerium, the second-oldest Lutheran synod in the United States, was founded in 1796. By 1807 it was so thoroughly Americanized that it adopted English as its official language. However, under the impact of later German immigration, which reached a peak in 1882, the Ministerium was almost completely "Germanized." In 1882, with only three exceptions, every church in the New York Ministerium conducted services in German.
36. Walter T. Schoen, "The Founding of Wagner College and the Early Years of Its Development" (unpublished B.A. thesis, Wagner College, 1957), pp. 19-21; Alfred Beck, "An Historical Account of the Lutheran Pro-Seminary of Rochester, New York" (unpublished manuscript in Wagner College Archives), p. 1.
37. Frederic Sutter, "Wagner College—Fifty Years on Staten Island," as told to Brian Morris (New York: Wagner College, 1968).
38. Based on a composite of economic, educational, religious, and demographic factors, the survey of ULCA colleges conducted in 1926 by Columbia University judged Wagner College to be the most favorably located of the 15 ULCA colleges

surveyed. In number of Lutherans residing within a 50-mile radius, Wagner was exceeded only by Muhlenberg, Gettysburg, and Susquehanna.

39. Carl R. Cronmiller, *A History of the Lutheran Church in Canada* (Canada: Evangelical Lutheran Synod of Canada, 1961), pp. 219-221; D. C. Masters, *Protestant Church Colleges in Canada* (Toronto: University of Toronto Press, 1966), pp. 189-192. Robin S. Harris, *A History of Higher Education in Canada, 1663-1960* (Toronto: University of Toronto Press, 1976), pp. 224, 351-352, 361-363.

40. *Los Angeles Times*, March 11, 1928.

41. Gould Wickey, "Documentary Review."

42. *News Bulletin*, National Lutheran Educational Conference, February 17, 1933.

43. "Minutes, Informal Meeting of Representatives of Various Lutheran Synods and Lutheran Educational Institutions," March 14, 1928, Chicago (Papers of the Lutheran Educational Conference of North America, Archives of Cooperative Lutheranism, New York).

44. *Studies in Lutheran Higher Education*, vol. 1, no. 1 (Minneapolis: Augsburg Publishing House, 1933).

45. Ibid., vol. 1, no. 2 (1935).

Chapter 17: Higher Education's New Age, 1941–1960 (pages 303-317)

1. Roy H. Johnson, *History of Thiel College* (Philadelphia: Dorrance & Co., 1974), p. 114.

2. Personal recollection of the author.

3. Henry Hardy Heins, *Throughout All the Years* (Oneonta, N.Y.: Hartwick College, 1946), pp. 109, 115.

4. Emil Erpestad, "History of Augustana College" (unpublished Ph.D. dissertation, Yale University, 1955), pp. 287, 292.

5. Joseph Shaw, *History of St. Olaf College* (Northfield, Minn.: St. Olaf College Press, 1974), p. 355.

6. Harold H. Lentz, *History of Wittenberg College* (Springfield: The Wittenberg Press, 1946), pp. 302-303.

7. James E. Swain, *A History of Muhlenberg College* (New York: Appleton-Century-Crofts, 1967), p. 77.

8. Gould Wickey, "Documentary Review, ULCA Board of Education" (unpublished typescript in archives of the LCA, Chicago).

9. Gerhard Ottersberg, "The Board of Christian Higher Education of the American Lutheran Church" (unpublished resource paper prepared for the LECNA History Project, 1984), p. 39.

10. Johnson, *Thiel College*, p. 191. The grant in 1970 was made by the Western Pennsylvania-West Virginia Synod, successor of the Pittsburgh Synod after the formation of the LCA in 1962.

11. Henry M. M. Richards, "The Ministerium of Pennsylvania and Its Institutions of Higher Education, 1916–1962" (unpublished monograph in archives of Muhlenberg College, Allentown, Pa.), pp. 145-147, 165.

12. *News Bulletin*, National Lutheran Educational Conference, December 1955, p. 16.

13. *A. P. Smith Manufacturing Co. vs. Barlow*, 346 United States 861.

14. *New York Times*, November 14, 1957.

15. Report on Conference on New Federal Education Programs, under auspices of American Council on Education, December 13, 1965.

16. Carl T. Solberg, *Riding High: America in the Cold War* (New York: Mason & Lipscomb, 1973), pp. 58-59.

17. Philip E. Jacob, *Changing Values in College* (New York: Harper & Bros., 1957), p. 4.

18. Harold Ditmanson, ed., *Christian Faith and the Liberal Arts* (Minneapolis: Augsburg Publishing House, 1960).

19. Howard Hong, ed., *Integration in the Christian Liberal Arts College* (Northfield, Minn.: St. Olaf College Press, 1956).

20. Orville Dahl, *A Concept of a University* (privately published, 1955).

21. *Studies in Lutheran Higher Education*, vol. 1, no. 1 (Minneapolis: Augsburg Publishing House, 1933), pp. 72-73.

22. "Report on the Proposed Plan for the Establishment of a Lutheran University," prepared by an ad hoc committee of the St. Olaf College faculty, June 2, 1955.

23. Gould Wickey "Historical Sketches of the National Lutheran Educational Conference," in *New Dimensions in Lutheran Higher Education*, papers presented at the Golden Anniversary Convention of the NLEC, Boston, January 10-12, 1960, p. 23.

24. Harold Lentz, *The Miracle of Carthage* (Kenosha, Wis.: Carthage College, 1975), pp. 274ff.

25. Three previous attempts at founding a Lutheran college in California had failed. In 1887 Leland Stanford offered a tract of land adjoining the campus of the newly established Leland Stanford Junior University to the Pacific Conference of the Augustana Synod. When the conference responded positively, but added a request for financial assistance as well, the offer was withdrawn. See *Referat öfwer förhandlingarna wid Westkustens Missionsdistrikts aarsmöte i Swenska luth. kyrkan i Takoma, Wash. Terr. den 5-9 April 1888* (Rock Island: Augustana Book Concern, 1888). See also *Protocol of the Proceedings of the Pacific Conference*, Augustana Synod, June 11, 1889, p. 47.

In September 1888, the San Diego College of Letters opened under the presidency of 83-year-old Dr. Samuel Sprecher, former president of Wittenberg College, with 52 students and 13 faculty members, including three Wittenberg alumni. The college closed after two years. See Viola Greenstaff, "Harr Wagner—California Educational Publicist" (unpublished Ed.D. thesis, University of California, Los Angeles, 1956), pp. 103-120.

A third attempt was made in 1928 by a group of Lutherans who were given a tract of land in Santa Monica to establish Los Angeles University. A widely publicized public dedication of the site was held on March 25, 1928, but the project failed for lack of financial backing. See the *Los Angeles Times*, March 26, 1928.

26. Mary Hekhuis, *The First Quarter Century* (Thousand Oaks, Calif.: California Lutheran College, 1985), pp. 12-25; also, oral history interview with Carl W. Segerhammar, conducted by Dr. Jerry Miller, July 5, 1983, in California Lutheran College Archives.

27. *Statistical Yearbook, 1951, 1961*, Lutheran Church–Missouri Synod.

28. Thomas Coates, "Making of a Minister" (unpublished S.T.D. dissertation, Chicago Lutheran Theological Seminary, 1950), p. 85; Carl S. Meyer, ed., *Moving Frontiers* (St. Louis: Concordia Publishing House, 1964), p. 402.

29. Quoted in Coates, "Making of a Minister," p. 88.

30. *Reports and Memorials*, 26th Delegate Synod, LCMS, 1950, pp. 177-178.

31. *Report of the Board for Higher Education*, Lutheran Church–Missouri Synod, 1950, p. 190.
32. Robert T. Handy, *A History of the Churches in the United States and Canada* (New York: Oxford University Press, 1977), p. 396.
33. E. Clifford Nelson, ed., *The Lutherans in North America* (Philadelphia: Fortress Press, 1980), p. 482.
34. Johannes Knudsen, *The Formation of the Lutheran Church in America* (Philadelphia: Fortress Press, 1978), pp. 73-77.
35. *Minutes of the NLEC*, January 1958, p. 4. See also Gould Wickey, *Lutheran Cooperation through Higher Education: A Documentary History of the National Lutheran Educational Conference, 1910-1967* (Washington, D.C.: LECNA, 1967), and Gould Wickey, *The Lutheran Venture in Higher Education* (Philadelphia: Board of Publication of the ULCA, 1962).

Chapter 18: The Sixties: Decade of Testing (pages 318-333)

1. Edmund J. Gleazer, "Developments in Junior and Community Colleges," in *Papers and Proceedings, NLEC*, 1963, pp. 22-23.
2. Report of the Executive Director, NLEC, *Papers and Proceedings, NLEC*, 1967, p. 75.
3. Edgar M. Carlson, *Church Sponsored Higher Education and the Lutheran Church in America* (New York: Lutheran Church in America, 1967), p. 18.
4. Ibid., p. 17.
5. Francis C. Gamelin, "Toward a Master Plan," in *Resources for the Future: Papers and Proceedings of the NLEC*, 1971, p. 51.
6. Carlson, *Church Sponsored Higher Education*, p. 16.
7. *Statistical Yearbook, 1963*, Lutheran Church–Missouri Synod, p. 216; *1970*, p. 61.
8. Gamelin, "Master Plan," p. 52. By 1983–1984 LCA and ALC colleges provided $42,000,000 from college resources for student aid. The total aid distributed by the 29 colleges from all sources was about $150,000,000.
9. Ibid., p. 46.
10. Ibid., p. 43.
11. James W. Albers, *From Centennial to Golden Anniversary: The History of Valparaiso University from 1959–1975* (Valparaiso, Ind.: Valparaiso University, 1976), pp. 28-29.
12. Joseph Shaw, *History of St. Olaf College* (Northfield, Minn.: St. Olaf College Press, 1974), pp. 539-544.
13. Interview with Dr. Sidney A. Rand, president of St. Olaf College, 1963–1979, December 15, 1982.
14. William E. Eisenberg, *The First Hundred Years: Roanoke College 1842–1942* (Salem, Va.: Roanoke College, 1942), pp. 218-219.
15. Ruth C. Wick, unpublished resource paper prepared for LECNA History Project. See also "New Interest in Internationalism: Through International Exchange Programs," *Papers Presented at NLEC*, 1960, pp. 68-73.
16. Gould Wickey, "Lutheran Higher Education and World Understanding," in *Papers and Proceedings, NLEC*, 1964, p. 32; also Educational Statistics, LCA and ALC, 1979-80.
17. The survey was conducted by Jack Landsverk. The data are in the files of the Lutheran Student Association of America, Record Group 14, Archives of Cooperative

Lutheranism, Lutheran Council in the U.S.A., New York. A summary and interpretation of the survey are found in a resource paper prepared for the LECNA History Project by Dr. Milton C. Sernett, "Afro-Americans and Lutheran Higher Education," 1984, pp. 26-30. The author is indebted to Dr. Sernett's research for much
of the material used in the discussion of blacks in Lutheran higher education.

18. Michael Lee Cobbler, "What Price Inclusion?" in *The Mount Airy Parish Practice
Notebook* (Philadelphia: Lutheran Theological Seminary, 1982), pp. 4-5. James K.
Echols, "Inclusiveness and Catholicity: Black Lutherans in the LCA," *LCA Part-
ners* 6 (April/May 1984): 11-14.

19. Sernett, "Afro-Americans," pp. 9-12.

20. Ibid., p. 11; "Higher Education for Negroes," *The Vanguard* 6 (February/March
1959): 11-14.

21. Sernett, "Afro-Americans," pp. 13-14.

22. *Proceedings, 1956*, LCMS, p. 759.

23. Alf M. Kraabel, "Racial and Cultural Practices in Lutheran Educational Institu-
tions in the United States and Canada," December 28, 1956 (manuscript copy in
National Lutheran Council Records, Archives of Cooperative Lutheranism, New
York).

24. Albers, *From Centennial*, p. 45; Shaw, *St. Olaf*, pp. 564-565.

25. Louis W. Bone, "Educational Opportunity Study," July 5, 1968 (typescript, Record Group 2, Board of College Education and Church Vocations, LCA Archives,
Chicago).

26. William L. O'Neill, *Coming Apart* (Chicago: Quadrangle Books, 1971), pp.
173-175.

27. *The Lutheran*, May 20, 1970.

28. Response of Upsala College to a survey on blacks in Lutheran colleges conducted
by Dr. Milton C. Sernett, February 2, 1984. Results of survey are in the files of Dr.
Sernett, Department of Afro-American Studies, Syracuse University, Syracuse,
New York.

29. Sernett, "Afro-Americans," pp. 40-41.

30. *The Lutheran*, January 1, 1969, p. 38.

31. *Minutes*, Board for College and University Services, ALC, April 20-22, 1980, p.
18.

32. Sernett survey, April 1984.

33. Statistical reports for 1984–1985 compiled by the offices of higher education of the
three major Lutheran bodies indicate 647 blacks in attendance at schools of the
LCMS; 352 at ALC colleges; and 1,248 at LCA colleges.

34. Statistical Report, Department for Higher Education, Division for Mission in North
America, LCA, January 1985, Exhibit A.8.2-3.

35. Robert E. Karsten, "A Classification of Interpretations of the Causes and Mean-
ings of Campus Disturbance" (unpublished Ph.D. dissertation, University of
Denver, 1972), pp. 76-78; Alexander W. Astin et al., *The Power of Protest* (San
Francisco: Jossey-Bass Publisher, 1975), pp. 20-22.

36. Alan O. Pfnister, *Trends in Higher Education* (Washington, D.C.: LECNA,
1975), pp. 99-110.

37. Astin, *Power of Protest*, p. 40.

38. Shaw, *St. Olaf*, p. 467.

39. Roy H. Johnson, *History of Thiel College* (Philadelphia: Dorrance and Co., 1974),
pp. 177-181.

40. Arthur M. Schlesinger, *Robert Kennedy and His Times* (Boston: Houghton Mifflin Co., 1978), p. 877.

41. Astin, *Power of Protest*, p. 36.

42. Shaw, *St. Olaf*, pp. 577-580.

43. *Report of the President's Commission on Campus Unrest* (Scranton Commission) (Washington, D.C.: Government Printing Office, 1970).

44. Albers, *From Centennial*, pp. 56-60.

45. *Minutes of the Board of Trustees*, Hartwick College, October 4, 1968.

46. Minutes of the meeting of the Joint Committee on Disassociation of Hartwick College with the New York Synods and the Lutheran Church in America, October 31, 1968; "Memorandum to Members of the Board of Trustees of Hartwick College, Dr. Wallace R. Klinger and Dr. Frederick M. Binder," from Edward K. Perry, dated June 18, 1968; letter from Edward K. Perry to John G. Flack, January 11, 1969 (in files of Upper New York Synod, Syracuse, N.Y.).

47. Letters from Erich R. W. Schultz to Richard W. Solberg, January 5 and February 10, 1984. See also D. C. Masters, *Protestant Church Colleges in Canada* (Toronto: University of Toronto Press, 1966), pp. 189-192.

48. "Special Report of the Chairman of the Board of Governors, Waterloo Lutheran University," *Minutes*, 1982, pp. 103-105.

49. "Summary of Board of Governors Actions regarding University Status" (document containing excerpts from Minutes of Board of Governors of Waterloo Lutheran University from March 1967, to January 1973, 27 pages).

50. Gamelin, "Master Plan," p. 38; Arthur L. Olsen, ed., *Cooperation for the Future* (Washington, D.C.: LECNA, 1976), p. 79; *News Bulletin*, NLEC, November/December, 1960, p. 4.

51. Personal interview with Dr. Harris Kaasa, Luther College, November 3, 1983.

Chapter 19: The Quest for New Directions, 1970–1980 (pages 335-348)

1. *Priorities for Action: Final Report of the Carnegie Commission on Higher Education* (New York: McGraw-Hill Book Co., 1973), pp. 7-9.

2. Alexander Astin, *The Power of Protest* (San Francisco: Jossey-Bass Publishers, 1975), p. 35.

3. Francis Gamelin, "Toward a Master Plan," in *Resources for the Future: Papers and Proceedings of LECNA*, 1971, p. 58.

4. Quoted in Allan O. Pfnister, *Trends in Higher Education* (Washington, D.C. LECNA, 1975), p. 293. See also William W. Jellema, *The Red and the Black* (Washington, D.C.: Association of American Colleges, 1971).

5. Annual Trend Analyses, Department for Higher Education, LCA.

6. Charles Andersen, ed., *1981–82 Fact Book for Academic Administrators* (Washington, D.C.: American Council on Education), p. 59.

7. Edgar M. Carlson, *Public Policy and Church Related Higher Education* (Minneapolis and New York: ALC and LCA, 1972), Introduction.

8. Annual Trend Analyses, Department for Higher Education, LCA.

9. Edgar M. Carlson, "How Private Are Church-Related Colleges?" in *Uncommon Means for the Common Task: Papers and Proceedings, LECNA*, 1972, pp. 10-25.

10. Gamelin, "Master Plan," p. 40; Annual Higher Education Statistical Reports, 1982–1983, LCA and ALC.

11. Kent M. Weeks, "Lutheran Colleges: The Constitutional and Legal Environment" (resource paper prepared for LECNA History Project).

12. Pfnister, *Trends*, pp. 26-28.

13. E. Clifford Nelson, ed., *The Lutherans in North America*, rev. ed. (Philadelphia: Fortress Press, 1980), pp. 528-535, 559-560.

14. Edgar M. Carlson, *Church Sponsored Higher Education and the Lutheran Church in America* (New York: Lutheran Church in America, 1969); Minutes of the Annual Meeting of LCA College Presidents, Chicago, November 20-21, 1966; Minutes of the Board of College Education and Church Vocations, LCA, January 4-5, 1968, pp. 304.

15. *The Mission of LCA Colleges and Universities* (New York: Lutheran Church in America, 1969).

16. Merton P. Strommen, *Research Report to the Joint Commission of the Division for Mission in North America and the Council of LCA Colleges on A Survey of Images and Expectations of LCA Colleges* (Minneapolis: Youth Research Center, 1976). A valuable bibliographic essay dealing with constituency relationships of church colleges was prepared as background for the Strommen survey. Charles R. Bruning, *Relationships Between Church-Related Colleges and Their Constituencies* (New York: Lutheran Church in America, 1975).

17. Richard W. Solberg and Merton P. Strommen, *How Church-Related Are Church-Related Colleges?* (Philadelphia: Board of Publication, Lutheran Church in America, 1980).

18. "Life in Relationship: The College and the Church" (Minneapolis: Division of College and University Services, ALC, 1980). The strong reaffirmation of church-related higher education among virtually all major denominations during the 1970s was reflected in a publication based upon a 1977 symposium sponsored by the National Council of Churches: Robert Rue Parsonage, ed., *Church-Related Higher Education: Perceptions and Perspectives* (Valley Forge: Judson Press, 1978). A National Congress on Church-Related Colleges and Universities, representing 23 denominations, met in June 1979, at Notre Dame University and in February 1980 in Washington, D.C. Its papers and proceedings were published in four volumes: John D. Mosely, ed., *Church and College: A Vital Partnership*, 4 vols. (Sherman, Tex.: The National Congress on Church-Related Colleges and Universities, 1980).

19. *Proceedings*, 1975 Convention, LCMS.

20. Report of Board for Higher Education, *Proceedings*, 1977 Convention, LCMS.

21. *Proceedings*, 1979 Convention, LCMS, p. 165. Arthur M. Ahlschwede, "Backward Glance," *Lutheran Education 115* (November/December 1979): 77-79.

22. *Proceedings*, 1979 Convention, LCMS, p. 139.

23. *Proceedings*, 1983 Convention, LCMS, pp. 90-91.

24. *Resources for the Future: Papers and Proceedings* LECNA, 1971, pp. 1-5.

25. Ibid., pp. 9-10.

26. Arthur L. Olsen, ed., *Cooperation for the Future*, A Report of the Commission on the Future to LECNA, 1976, pp. 6-12.

27. Pfnister, *Trends in Higher Education*.

28. Francis C. Gamelin, *Church-Related Identity of Lutheran Colleges*, A Report to the Commission on the Future, LECNA, 1975.

29. Olsen, *Cooperation for the Future*. A series of essays examining the effects of rapid social change on church-related colleges in the 1970s was made by the Association of Lutheran College Faculties. Richard Baepler, et al., *The Quest for a Viable Sage* (Valparaiso: Association of Lutheran College Faculties, 1977). See also

Edgar Carlson, *The Future of Church-Related Higher Education* (Minneapolis: Augsburg Publishing House, 1977).

30. Thomas H. Langevin, *LECNA Curriculum Consultation Project Report* (Washington, D.C.: LECNA, 1983).

31. Norman D. Fintel, "Attitudes of Lutherans toward Church Colleges," in *The Church, the Student, and the Future: Papers and Proceedings*, LECNA, 1973, pp. 9-28; Merton P. Strommen, "Images and Expectations of LCA Colleges," in *Church Relatedness of Lutheran Colleges: Papers and Proceedings*, LECNA, 1977, pp. 8-19.

32. *The Historical Context and Dynamic Future of Lutheran Higher Education: Papers and Proceedings:* LECNA, 1976.

33. David W. Lotz, "Education for Two Kingdoms: Reflections on the Theological Foundations of Lutheran Higher Education," in *Papers and Proceedings*, LECNA, 1979, 7-19.

34. Arthur L. Olsen, "Unpacking Luther's Heritage for Higher Education," in *Institutional Mission and Identity: Papers and Proceedings*, LECNA, 1979, pp. 25-29.

SELECTED BIBLIOGRAPHY OF LUTHERAN COLLEGE HISTORIES

Alden, H. C. "The Evangelical Lutheran Trinity College of Round Rock, Texas." Unpublished M.A. thesis, University of Texas, 1929.

Albers, James W. *From Centennial to Golden Anniversary: The History of Valparaiso University from 1959–1975.* Valparaiso, Ind.: Valparaiso University, 1976.

Baepler, Frederick A. *Praise for the Past—Faith for the Future. A History of St. Paul's College.* Concordia, Mo.: St. Paul's College Historical Society, 1984.

Beck, Alfred. "An Historical Account of the Lutheran Pro-Seminary of Rochester, New York." Unpublished manuscript in Wagner College Archives.

Benson, William C. *High on Manitou.* Northfield, Minn.: St. Olaf College Press, 1949.

Bergendoff, Conrad. *Augustana: A Profession of Faith.* Rock Island, Ill.: Augustana College Library, 1969.

Bogstad, Rasmus. *The Early History of Concordia College 1891–1910.* Moorhead, Minn.: privately printed, 1941.

Bothne, Gisle. *Den Norske Luther College, 1861–1897.* Decorah, Iowa, 1897.

Brandhorst, C. T. C. *A Short Story of Concordia Teachers College, Seward, Nebraska.* Seward, Neb.: Concordia Teachers College, n.d.

Bredemeier, Herbert G. *Concordia College, Fort Wayne, 1839–1957.* Fort Wayne, Ind.: Fort Wayne Public Library, 1978.

Brown, Dorothy Ann. *We Sing to Thee: A Story about Clifton College.* Waco, Tex.: Texian Press, 1974.

Calman, Alvin R. *Upsala College: The Early Years.* New York: Vantage Press, 1938.

Chrislock, Carl. *From Fjord to Freeway.* Minneapolis: Augsburg College, 1969.

Christensen, William E. *Saga of the Tower.* Blair, Neb.: Dana College, 1959.

Clark, William S. and Wilson, Arthur H. *The Story of Susquehanna University.* Selinsgrove, Pa.: Susquehanna University Press, 1958.

Collegiate Institute, Annual Catalog, 1920. Charlotte, N.C.: Queen City Printing Co., 1920.

Dowie, James Iverne, *Prairie Grass Dividing.* Rock Island: Augustana Historical Society, 1959. (Luther College, Wahoo, Nebraska.)

Dubbs, Joseph Henry. *History of Franklin and Marshall College.* Lancaster, Pa.: Franklin and Marshall College Alumni Association, 1903.

Dunkelberger, Harold A. "Gettysburg College and the Lutheran Connection: An Open-Ended Story of a Proud Relationship." History Series No. 3, *The Gettysburg Bulletin* 66 (December 1975).

Eisenberg, William Edward. *The First Hundred Years: Roanoke College, 1842–1942.* Salem, Va.: Roanoke College, 1942.

Erpestad, Emil. "A History of Augustana College." Unpublished Ph.D. dissertation, Yale University, 1955.

Evjen, Henry O. "Illinois State University." Unpublished M.A. thesis, University of Illinois.

Freitag, Alfred J. *College with a Cause: A History of Concordia Teachers College.* River Forest, Ill.: Concordia Teachers College, 1964.

Freitag, Walter. "Lutheran College and Seminary of Saskatoon." Unpublished manuscript provided by the author.

Gahagen, Robert H. "Background for a College: Early History of Thiel College." Unpublished typescript in Thiel College Archives.

Gienapp, Henry, ed. *The Concordia College Centennial Jubilee, 1881–1981.* Mequon, Wis.: Concordia College Wisconsin, 1981.

Grose, Ingebrikt F. *Fifty Memorable Years at St. Olaf.* Northfield, Minn.: St. Olaf College, 1925.

Hansen, Thorvald. *We Laid Foundation Here: The Early History of Grand View College.* Des Moines: Grand View College, 1972.

Hefelbower, Samuel G. *The History of Gettysburg College, 1832–1932.* Gettysburg, Pa.: Gettysburg College, 1932.

Heins, Henry Hardy. *Throughout All the Years: The Bicentennial Story of Hartwick in America, 1746–1796.* Oneonta, N.Y.: Hartwick College, 1946.

Hekhuis, Mary. *The First Quarter Century.* Thousand Oaks, Calif.: California Lutheran College, 1985.

Henry, Gordon C., ed. *Newberry College, 1856–1976.* Newberry, S.C.: Newberry College, 1976.

Hickman, Lillian. "The History of Midland College." Unpublished M.A. thesis, University of Oregon, 1949.

Hoermann, Arthur. *Our Northwestern College.* Translated by Hans Moussa. Watertown, Wis.: Wisconsin Synod, 1915.

Horn, Robert C. "Muhlenberg College: History of One Hundred Years, 1848–1948." Unpublished manuscript in Muhlenberg College Library, 1948.

Jalkanen, Ralph J. "Suomi College: A Brief Review of Its History and Culture." *The Cresset*, April 1976.

Johnson, Roy H. *The History of Thiel College.* Philadelphia: Dorrance and Co., 1974.

Jordahl, Sivert A. *Memorial History: Lutheran Normal School, Sioux Falls, S.D.* Sioux Falls: Brown and Saenger, 1953.

Kinnison, William A. *Wittenberg: A Concise History.* Springfield, Ohio: Wittenberg University, 1976.

Klages, Alfred D. "A History of Texas Lutheran College 1851–1951." Unpublished M.A. thesis, University of Texas, 1951.

Kowalke, Erwin Ernst. *Centennial Story: Northwestern College, 1865–1965.* Watertown, Wis.: Northwestern College, 1965.

Krause, H. "A History of Texas Lutheran College." Unpublished manuscript in Texas Lutheran College Library, 1930.

Lentz, Harold H. *The Miracle of Carthage: History of Carthage College, 1847–1974.* Kenosha, Wis.: Carthage College, 1975.

——————. *A History of Wittenberg College.* Columbus: The Wittenberg Press, 1946.

Lindquist, Emory. *Bethany in Kansas.* Lindsborg, Kan.: Bethany College, 1975.

Lund, Doniver A. *Gustavus Adolphus College: A Centennial History.* St. Peter, Minn.: Gustavus Adolphus College Press, 1963.

McCauley, J. William. "Elizabeth College and Related Lutheran Schools." Pamphlet published June 24, 1901; Archives of North Carolina Synod, Lutheran Church in America.

Melby, Carl A. *St. Olaf College through Fifty Years 1874–1924.* Northfield, Minn.: St. Olaf College, 1925.

Nauss, Allen H. "Concordia College, Portland, Oregon." *Concordia Historical Institute Quarterly* 25 (January 1953): 175-178; 26 (April, July, October 1953, January 1954): 17-35, 77-94, 119-130, 169-184; 27 (April 1954): 34-40.

Nelson, David T. *Luther College, 1861–1961.* Decorah, Iowa.: Luther College Press, 1961.

Niermann, Henry W. Jr. "The History of Concordia College, New Orleans." *Concordia Historical Institute Quarterly* 36 (October 1963): 65–89.

Norlie, O. M. et al., eds. *Luther College through Sixty Years, 1861–1921.* Minneapolis: Augsburg Publishing House, 1922.

Norris, Jeff. "Lenoir College: Its Founding and First Ten Years." Unpublished typescript in Lenoir-Rhyne College Library.

Ochsenford, S. E., ed. *Muhlenberg College.* Allentown, Pa.: Muhlenberg College, 1892.

Oppedahl, Richard A. "Waldorf College: First Fifty Years." Unpublished M.A. thesis, University of South Dakota, 1956.

Ottersberg, Gerhard. *Wartburg College, 1852–1952.* Waverly, Iowa: Waverly Publishing Co., 1952.

——————. *Wartburg College, 1952-1977.* Waverly, Iowa: Wartburg College, 1977.

——————. "Wartburg College and the Iowa Synod." Unpublished resource paper prepared for LECNA History Project, 1983, 78 pp.

Overn, Oswald B. *History of Concordia College.* St. Paul: Concordia College, 1967.

Owens, David B. *These Hundred Years: The Centennial History of Capital University.* Columbus: Capital University, 1950.

Peterson, Conrad. *A History of Eighty Years 1862–1942.* St. Peter, Minn.: Gustavus Adolphus College, 1942.

Peterson, Peter L. *A Place Called Dana.* Blair, Neb.: Dana College, 1984.

Rolfsrud, Erling N. *Cobber Chronicle,* 2nd ed. Moorhead, Minn.: Concordia College, 1976.

Ronning, Chester A. "A Study of an Alberta Protestant Private School: The Camrose Lutheran College." Unpublished M.A. thesis, College of Education, University of Alberta, 1942.

Quarter-Centennial Souvenir of St. Olaf College, 1874–1899. Northfield, Minn.: St. Olaf College, 1900.

Schnackenberg, Walter C. "The Development of Norwegian Lutheran Schools in the Pacific Northwest from 1890 to 1920." Unpublished Ph.D. dissertation, The State College of Washington, 1950.

——————— . *The Lamp and the Cross.* Tacoma: Pacific Lutheran University Press, 1965.

Schoen, Walter T. "The Founding of Wagner College and the Early Years of Its Development." Unpublished B.A. thesis, Wagner College, 1957.

Schroeder, Morton A. *A Time to Remember: An Informal History of Dr. Martin Luther College.* New Ulm, Minn.: Dr. Martin Luther College, 1984.

Shaw, Joseph. *History of St. Olaf College.* Northfield, Minn.: St. Olaf College Press, 1974.

Simon, Martin P. *College on the Cornfield.* Unpublished Ed. D. dissertation, University of Oregon, 1953.

Sneen, Donald. *Through Trials and Triumphs: The History of Augustana College.* Sioux Falls, S.D.: Center for Western Studies, 1985.

Spielman, William C. *The Diamond Jubilee History of Carthage College, 1870–1945.* Carthage, Ill.: Carthage College Historical Society, 1945.

Stadius, Arnold. "Suomi College and Seminary," in *The Finns in North America: A Social Symposium.* Edited by Ralph J. Jalkanen. East Lansing, Mich.: Michigan State University Press, 1969, pp. 91-123.

Steinberg, Alan G. *We Will Remember: Concordia College: The First Century.* Bronxville, N.Y.: Concordia College, 1981.

Strietelmeier, John. *Valparaiso's First Century.* Valparaiso, Ind.: Valparaiso University, 1959.

Stoeppelwerth, H. J. *Concordia Historical Institute Quarterly* 5 (January 1933): 131-137; 6 (April, July, October 1933 and January 1934): 25-32, 33-41, 74-95; 7 (April 1934): 24-32. Reprinted in *The Johnnie Heritage.* Winfield, Kan.: St. John's Alumni Association, 1947.

Studtmann, Henry T. *Concordia of Texas from the Beginning.* Edited by Ray F. Martens. Austin, Tex.: Concordia College, 1977.

Sutter, Frederic. "Wagner College—Fifty Years on Staten Island." New York: Wagner College, 1968.

Swain, James E. *A History of Muhlenberg College, 1848–1967.* New York: Appleton-Century-Crofts, 1967.

Walle, Oscar T. *Lest We Forget: A History of Concordia Senior College, 1955–1977.* Springfield, Ill.: Privately published, 1978.

West, Thomas W. *Marion College, 1873–1967.* Strasburg, Va.: Shenandoah Publishing House, 1970.

Wiederaenders, A. G. *Coming of Age: A History of Texas Lutheran College.* San Antonio: Paul Anderson Co., 1978.

Wilhite, Ann G. "A College for All Seasons: Fremont College, 1884–1919." Unpublished paper presented to Douglas County, Nebraska, Historical Society, October 17, 1971. Midland Lutheran College Archives.

Whittecar, George. "The Story of Midland College through Fifty Years." Published serially in the *Fremont Tribune,* 1937.

Zimmerman, Paul A. *Concordia 10.* Ann Arbor, Mich.: Concordia College, 1973.

INDEX

389